Anglophone Jewish Literature

Anglophone Jewish literature is not traditionally numbered among the new literatures in English. Rather, Jewish literary production in English has conventionally been classified as 'hyphenated' and has therefore not yet been subjected as such to the scrutiny of scholars of literary or cultural history.

This collection of essays addresses this lack and initiates the scholarly exploration of transnational and transcultural Anglophone Jewish literature as one of the New English Literatures. Without attempting to impose what would seem to be a misguided conceptual unity on the many-faceted field of Anglophone Jewish literature, the book is based on a plurality of theoretical frameworks. Alert to the productive friction between these discourses, which it aims to elicit, it confronts Jewish literary studies with postcolonial studies, cultural studies and other contemporary theoretical frameworks.

Featuring contributions from among the best-known scholars in the fields of British and American Jewish literature, including Bryan Cheyette and Emily Miller Budick, this collection transcends borders of both nations and academic disciplines and takes into account cultural and historical affinities and differences of the Anglophone diaspora which have contributed to the formation and development of the English-language segment of Jewish literature.

Axel Stähler is Lecturer in Comparative Literary Studies in the School of European Culture and Languages at the University of Kent, Canterbury, UK.

Routledge Studies in Twentieth-Century Literature

1 **Testimony from the Nazi Camps**
French women's voices
Margaret-Anne Hutton

2 **Modern Confessional Writing**
New critical essays
Edited by Jo Gill

3 **Cold War Literature**
Writing the global conflict
Andrew Hammond

4 **Modernism and the Crisis of Sovereignty**
Andrew John Miller

5 **Cartographic Strategies of Postmodernity**
The figure of the map in contemporary theory and fiction
Peta Mitchell

6 **Anglophone Jewish Literature**
Axel Stähler

Anglophone Jewish Literature

Edited by
Axel Stähler

Routledge
Taylor & Francis Group
LONDON AND NEW YORK

First published 2007
by Routledge
2 Park Square, Milton Park, Abingdon, Oxfordshire OX14 4RN

Simultaneously published in the USA and Canada
by Routledge
711 Third Avenue, New York, NY 10017

First issued in paperback 2014

Routledge is an imprint of the Taylor & Francis Group, an informa business

Typeset in Times New Roman by
Newgen Imaging Systems (P) Ltd, Chennai, India

British Library Cataloguing in Publication Data
A catalogue record for this book is available
from the British Library

Library of Congress Cataloging in Publication Data
A catalog record for this book has been requested

ISBN13: 978–0–415–41464–7 (hbk)
ISBN13: 978-1-138-01055-0 (pbk)

Contents

Notes on contributors

Karen Alkalay-Gut teaches at Tel Aviv University, and has been Chair of the Israel Association of Writers in English as well as the Vice Chair of the Federation of Writers Unions in Israel for many years. More than twenty books of her poetry have appeared in English as well as Hebrew translation. She has published extensively on poetry. Her articles on the subject of this essay have appeared in *American Book Review* (1984), *Kerem* (1994), *Modern Poetry in Translation* (1993–94) and in *Judaism* (2002).

David Brauner is Director of American Studies at the University of Reading and a member of the English department. His research and publishing interests are in twentieth-century US fiction (with a particular specialism in the work of Saul Bellow, Philip Roth and Joseph Heller). His book-length study on *Post-War Jewish Fiction: Ambivalence, Self-Explanation and Transatlantic Connections* was published by Palgrave in 2001.

Emily Miller Budick is a Professor in American Studies at The Hebrew University of Jerusalem. She has published widely on American and Jewish-American literature. Among her many publications are her monographs on *Blacks and Jews in Literary Conversation* (1998) and on *Acknowledging the Holocaust in the Fiction of Aharon Appelfeld* (2004) as well as edited collections on *Modern Hebrew Fiction, by Gershon Shaked* (2000) and *Ideology and Jewish Identity in Israeli and American Literature* (2001).

Bryan Cheyette holds the Chair in Modern Literature and is Director of Research in the School of English and American Literature at the University of Reading. His research interests include late nineteenth-, twentieth- and twenty-first-century English literature, British-Jewish literature, 'new' literatures in English, theories of 'race' and modernity and Holocaust literature. His many publications include his monograph on *Constructions of 'the Jew' in English Literature and Society: Racial Representations 1875–1945* (1993) and six edited and co-edited collections, among them *Between 'Race' and Culture: Representations of 'the Jew' in English and American Literature* (1996), *Contemporary Jewish Writing in Britain and Ireland: An Anthology* (1998) and, with Laura Marcus, *Modernity, Culture and 'the Jew'* (1998). He is currently completing a critical history of British-Jewish writing in the twentieth century to be published as *Diasporas of the Mind: Literature and 'Race' after the Holocaust* by Yale University Press.

Pascal Fischer is Assistant Professor of English at the University of Würzburg. His study on *Yidishkeyt und Jewishness. Identität in jüdisch-amerikanischer Literatur unter besonderer Berücksichtigung der Sprache* appeared in 2003.

Albert-Reiner Glaap, OBE, is Professor Emeritus of English at the University of Düsseldorf. His special research interests are modern English and Canadian literature, contemporary drama and theatre in England, Canada and New Zealand, the teaching of English literature at secondary school and university level, and theory and practice of literary translation. Among his many publications are *Onstage and Offstage. English Canadian Drama in Discourse* (1996) and *A French Window onto the Old World* (1999). He is the author of numerous articles in different scholarly journals, theatre programmes and reference works.

Oliver Groß studied English, Law and Journalism at the Universities of Bonn, Cardiff and Mainz. He is currently working at the Centre for British Studies at the University of Bamberg on his doctoral thesis on second-generation authors in British fictions of migration.

Karen Grumberg is Assistant Professor of Modern Hebrew Literature at the University of Texas at Austin. Her special research interests are contemporary Hebrew literature, American Jewish literature, comparative Jewish literatures, Mizrahi writing and women's writing in Israel. Her monograph on *The Poetics of Place: Unraveling Home and Exile in Jewish Literature from Israel and the United States* awaits publication.

Catherine Hezser teaches at the School of Oriental and African Studies at the University of London. She is an expert in the social history of Jews in Roman Palestine in late antiquity. In her many publications she examines ancient Judaism within the context of Graeco-Roman and early Christian society. She is also interested in issues of modern Jewish identity and its literary expressions in Europe, America and Israel.

Peter Lawson teaches at the English Department of the University of Tampere. He has published widely on Anglo-Jewish poetry. Among his most recent publications are *Singers of the Diaspora: Anglo-Jewish Poetry from Isaac Rosenberg to Elaine Feinstein* (2005) and the anthology *Passionate Renewal: Jewish Poetry in Britain Since 1945* (2001).

Margaret Lenta taught and researched at the University of Natal, Durban from 1973 until 1999. She is now an Emeritus Professor and an Honorary Research Fellow at the same institution, renamed since 2004 the University of KwaZulu-Natal. Her special research interests include eighteenth-century literature, South African literature and Jewish literature in South Africa.

Sigrun Meinig teaches at the English Department of the University of Dresden. Her particular research interests are postcolonial literatures and theory, literary theory, the body and literature, Victorian literature, Modernism and empathy and literature. Her book-length study on *Witnessing the Past: History and Post-Colonialism in Australian Historical Novels* was published in 2004.

Elisa Morera de la Vall teaches at the English Department of the University of Barcelona. Currently, she is Public Relations Officer for the Australian Studies Centre at the University of Barcelona. Her main interest of research is in Australian Jewish writers. From 1996 to 1998, she was co-editor of *Barcelona University Australian Studies.* She is also co-editor of *Changing Geographies: Essays on Australia* (2001) and *Australia: Aboriginal Land, Land of Exile, Land of Promise* (2002). In 2006 she was guest editor of a special issue of *Eucalypt* on Jewish writers in Australia. Her monograph *A Contribution to the Study of Jewish Writing in Australia* awaits publication.

Ranen Omer-Sherman teaches English and Jewish Studies at the University of Miami. His special research interests are in modernism and Jewish identity, representations of the Arab in modern Hebrew literature and film, and the relation between Jewish writers and the desert, both as metaphor and place. His study on *Diaspora and Zionism in Jewish American Literature* was published in 2002. He has edited *Jewish Diasporism: The Aesthetics of Ambivalence* (1998) and, most recently, *Jewish Orientalism* (2006).

Jamie S. Scott is Professor at the Division of Humanities at York University, Toronto. His current publications include interdisciplinary research on representations of Christian missions in colonial and postcolonial literatures, Christian missions and Canadian cultural identities, Christian missions and material and popular cultures, religion and geography, and literature and geography. Previous publications and professional contributions include interdisciplinary work in religious and political pluralism, the religious dimensions of Western secular literature, autobiography and confessional literature, and Dietrich Bonhoeffer as a post-modern figure. Among his many publications are, co-edited with Gareth Griffiths, *Mixed Messages: Materiality, Textuality, Missions* (2005) and, co-edited with Paul Simpson-Housley, *Mapping the Sacred: Religion, Geography and Post-Colonial Literatures* (2001).

Miriam Sivan emigrated to Israel from the USA in 1995. She teaches English literature at Haifa University and writes fiction. She has widely published on Cynthia Ozick and her book-length study on *The Seeker and the Sought: Cynthia Ozick's Fiction in Motion* awaits publication. Her fiction has appeared in *Wasafiri*, *Arts and Letters*, and *Lilith*. She has also translated Hebrew poetry of Leah Goldberg and from the Middle Ages into English.

Axel Stähler is lecturer in Comparative Literary Studies in the School of European Culture and Languages at the University of Kent, Canterbury, UK. He has published widely on Jewish authors from the Anglophone and German-speaking diasporas and from Israel as well as on early Modern festival culture. His book-length study on Anglophone Jewish writing and Jewish postcoloniality, *Zion's Fiction: Postcolonial Fictions of Jewish Identity*, awaits publication.

Jonathan Wilson is the author of two novels, *A Palestine Affair* (2003), a finalist for the National Jewish Book Award, and *The Hiding Room* (1995), two collections of stories, *Schoom* (1995) and *An Ambulance Is on the Way: Stories of Men in Trouble* (2005), two critical works on the fiction of Saul Bellow and a biography of Marc Chagall published by Schocken Books (2007). His work has appeared in *The New Yorker*, *The New York Times Magazine*, *Best American Short Stories* and *Ploughshares*, among other publications, and he has received a Guggenheim Fellowship in Fiction. He is Fletcher Professor of Rhetoric and Debate, Professor of English and Director of Creative Writing in the English Department at Tufts University.

Foreword

Jonathan Wilson

I have spent my writing life in three countries, England, Israel and the United States, and in each one I have hung around with other writers, plenty of them Jewish, plenty not. Perhaps this puts me in a better position than most to offer a few words on 'Anglophone Jewish Writing' although I have to admit that the endless debates over who and what constitutes a 'Jewish' writer, or a 'Jewish story' or a 'Jewish novel' have never interested me nearly as much as the stories and novels themselves. Sometimes, I think, writers whose work isn't all that compelling are drawn to jack up readers' fascination in their biographies, as if the life one has lived is a credential that will guarantee a good read. It used to be like this in the 1930s when proletarian affiliation was all the rage. 'Dave works in a paper plate factory' ran the contributor's note that once appeared under a poem in the radical journal *The New Masses*. Nowadays, ethnic, rather than political, identifications are hot, although in Western Europe and America, the Jewish square has mysteriously been cut out of the multicultural quilt – but I'll come back to that. On second thoughts let's get to it right now.

The Jewish square has been cut out of the multicultural quilt because Jews are perceived either as white and comfortably off or as linked to Israel and its supposed 'colonialist' agenda. In those circles of the intellectual left, where cultural taxonomies occur, these are not sexy perceptions. Lots of Jews are white and middle class, and lots are poor, black, brown and so on. The Jews were certainly one of the last groups in the twentieth century to have their nationalist aspirations realized, and for this reason their achievement of statehood has often appeared anachronistic and invited all kinds of challenges. The Palestinians, even more belated, have equally compelling nationalistic aspirations that are yet to be realized, as do, for example, the Kurds. But if you are perceived as a 'colonialist' nation rather than as a victim of colonization, you cannot be a bona fide member of the multicultural community. There is, of course, not another 'colonizer' in the world that has dug up its own history in the 'colonized' place.

And this brings me to 'Anglophone Jewish Writing'. What most Jewish writers have in common, whether Anglophone, Francophone or simply on the cell phone, is the past. We all come from the same place, and, by the measure of humankind's time on earth, not all that long ago. 'We are the children of kings and queens, a holy nation and a kingdom of priests' the playwright David Mamet wrote in his recent, controversial book, *The Wicked Son* echoing, perhaps intentionally, the title of the intensely moving documentary *When We Were Kings* which charts Muhammad Ali's return to Africa to fight George Foreman in the 'Rumble in the Jungle'. 'We are the children of a mystery that has not abandoned us and that has come for us', Mamet goes on, 'it is both described and contained in the Torah'. This poignant reminder to 'choose dignity' as Schlossberg, Saul Bellow's wise old journalist, says in *The Victim* ('Choose dignity. Nobody knows enough to turn it down.') also prompts us to remember that the Hebrew Bible is the urtext for Jewish writers – as, of course, it is for many of the world's other writers. Most Anglophone Jewish writers can read Hebrew without being able to understand, except in the vaguest way, what they are reading. This is largely the result of bad education in Hebrew School up until the age of 13. Nevertheless, stories from the Hebrew Bible permeate Jewish writing in all kinds of ways: think only of the titles *The Book of Daniel* by E.L. Doctorow, *Joy Comes in the Morning* (from the book of Psalms) by Jonathan Rosen, *Out of Egypt* by Andre Aciman, or the plethora of poems by Anglophone Jewish poets in which the poet takes on the persona of a character from the Hebrew Bible. If we leap a couple of thousand years into the present we discover that Jewish writers around the globe tend to nominate, decade by decade, the same Jewish antecedents as major influences upon their work: Freud (perhaps the greatest fiction writer of us all), Babel, Kafka, Singer, Bellow, Malamud, Roth, Ozick, Paley and so on. And then there is the dark bond of recent history. I don't know a Jewish writer whose family wasn't touched in some way by the Holocaust.

But what about the 'Anglophone' stuff? If I ask myself whether I have more in common as a writer with the South African Jewish novelist Nadine Gordimer, or with the English Jewish novelist Will Self, who, like his Jewish-American counterpart Norman Mailer, never writes about Jews, than with say, Nick Hornby, who is English but not Jewish, I would have to say that I feel a closer affinity with Hornby (even though he is an Arsenal fan, *aka* a Gooner). In that case my Englishness trumps my Jewishness, at other times it doesn't. In England, when I lived there, I frequently felt more Jewish than English, in Israel more English than Jewish and in America more of an English Jew than I ever did in England. I don't think that this kind of slippery identity is uncommon. When I sit down to write, however, whether in London, or Jerusalem or Boston, I do not sense myself as belonging to any group at all. I am in the business of turning sentences around in the best way that I can and there is nothing 'Jewish' or 'English' or 'American' about that activity. We write *out of* who we are, and that always works better than writing *about* who we are.

Nevertheless each writer must find his or her own place in which to be comfortable writing, for some it is a hotel room or a coffee shop, for others a particular city or a country retreat, some writers like to be around others, some don't. For whatever reason I have felt most comfortable on the East coast of the United States where there is a large Jewish population. I don't envy my Anglophone writer friends in Israel. English, while still widely used, is in decline in that country. It was never an official language, like Hebrew and Arabic, and the recent influx of over a million Russians has created a seismic cultural shift. To write in English in Israel you have to strain your ear in order to stay tuned to the vernacular: cable TV helps of course, and movies and trips abroad, but to hear the ever morphing, endlessly inventive language of the street you have to be on the street. Neither would I want to write as a Jew in England, where, it seems to me, a graceless anti-Semitism is pervasive even, or perhaps especially, in intellectual circles. But who knows? I may have got it all wrong and I'm sure that plenty of Anglophone Jewish writers would want to correct me. Great art has been, and continues to be, produced in the direst and oddest circumstances, and, *pace* Wordsworth, emotional comfort is not necessarily a catalyst for creative expression.

In his diaries Kafka famously wrote, 'What do I have in common with the Jews? I do not even have anything in common with myself'. He was talking about his writing life, of course, and the disassociation that all writers experience when they are, as Yeats described, 'caught in the cold snows of a dream'. In his social life (not as oxymoronic a concept as his fiction would suggest) he spent a great deal of his time hanging out with other Jews, especially the Jewish writers Oskar Baum, Felix Weltsch and Max Brod. Perhaps the notion of a viscerally attached group of 'Anglophone Jewish writers' should be expanded worldwide to include all Jewish writers, whatever their language of choice. But that is for the critics to figure out, and undoubtedly, like the contributors to this essential book, they will do so as elegantly as possible.

Jonathan Wilson
Newton, MA
2006

Part I

Introduction

1 Introduction – Jewish literature(s) in English?

Anglophone Jewish writing and the 'loquation'[1] of culture

Axel Stähler

Anglophone Jewish literature is not traditionally numbered among the emergent, or new, literatures in English. Rather, Jewish literary production in English has conventionally been classified as hyphenated, as American-, Anglo-, Australian-, Canadian-, Irish- or South African-Jewish, etc., and in the minds of some it has simply been equated with Jewish-American literature.[2] Of course, the definition of what 'Jewish literature' is proves to be notoriously difficult (see, for example, Wirth-Nesher 1994a,b: 3; Siegel 1997: 17–22; Budick 2001: 2–3), and to enquire into the nature of a 'Jewish literature in English' initially may seem of secondary importance. Yet, English is nowadays spoken by the majority of Jews living outside Israel (Rubinstein 1996: 2–5) and is the language also of a number of 'returnee' writers in Israel. Next to Hebrew and the ever-retreating Yiddish, English has thus become the major language of contemporary Jewish literary production; it has even been suggested that Israeli authors writing in Hebrew 'have the [translated] English version in mind from the start, because there lie international fame and hefty advances' (Green 2001: 95).[3]

But is there really anything like a transnational Jewish literature in English? Or, in view of different production contexts, should we speak rather of Anglophone Jewish literature-*s*, or, in deference to tradition and convention, of 'hyphenated' Jewish literatures, after all? Or, is the question posed in the title of this introduction rendered purely academic by an (allegedly) 'vanishing diaspora' (Wasserstein 1996) and 'vanishing Jews' (Dershowitz 1996)?

To anticipate the suggestion advanced by this collection: It appears that the earlier assessment should indeed be revised and that the Anglophone segment of Jewish literature constitutes, to some extent, a discrete, if widely diverse, body of literary achievement. One reason for this assumption is, quite obviously, the use of English as a common vernacular and as a language of literary expression in the Anglophone diaspora. This is compounded, with regard to its manifold and often divergent constructions which are admittedly vague, by the notion of 'Jewishness'. A third reason is that there are a number of cultural affinities not only between the English-speaking countries but also between the Jewish communities living in these countries.

Recent research by the historian W.D. Rubinstein suggests that despite 'considerable differences in both the Jewish communities of each of the

English-speaking countries and, still more, in the national histories and institutions of each country', the similarities are 'more significant still' (1996: 7). As the most important common features, Rubinstein notes the comparatively late establishment of Jewish communities in the English-speaking world since the latter half of the seventeenth century and the fact that these communities for centuries remained very small; that in the wake of the Reformation religious intolerance was focused on dissenting Christian beliefs rather than on the Jewish creed; that the Anglophone world has a tradition of philo-Semitism and of liberalism, pluralism and democracy; and that neither the countries of the Anglophone diaspora nor their Jewish communities experienced any significant breaks with the past (7–13). From this, Rubinstein concludes that, contrary to the widely held view of the paradigmatic quality of the Jewish experience in pre-Holocaust Germany, the English-speaking world provides an 'appropriate matrix for Jewish history' (1). In Rubinstein's argument, the role of English as a language is accorded particular significance (19–21). 'These facts', he suggests, 'have clearly enhanced the nexus between Jewry and English as a vernacular, increasing both the importance of English-speaking Jewry *per se* and the centrality of English to Jewish communications, as with the communications among all other groups' (21). Yet 'the implications of this linguistic transformation', Rubinstein continues, 'remain only partly explored, if at all' (5).

Indeed, as pointed out above, Anglophone Jewish writing has not yet been considered as a coherent system of literary utterance and has, as such, not yet been subjected to the scrutiny of scholars of literary or cultural history. It is the purpose of this collection to address this lack and to initiate the scholarly exploration of transnational and transcultural Anglophone Jewish literature as one of the new English literatures. A suggestion concomitant with this is that Anglophone Jewish literature, itself variously situated within cultural contact zones of a 'postcolonial' character, reveals some analogies to postcolonial literature, and that the two not only engage productively in processes of mutual stimulation but that this also indicates the useful interchangeability of the respective tools of critical enquiry.[4]

The importance of writing in English: Cynthia Ozick and the 'New Yiddish'

'Imaginative writers', said Cynthia Ozick in an address to an Israeli audience at the Weizmann Institute in Rehovoth in 1970, 'are compelled to swim in the medium of culture; literature is an instrument of a culture, not a summary of it. Consequently', she continued, 'there are no major works of Jewish imaginative genius written in any Gentile language, sprung out of any Gentile culture' (1970; 1983: 167–8).[5] A bold statement, one may think, and one that seems uncomfortably close, perhaps, to bygone anti-Semitic claims of the lack of Jewish creative genius. In 1903 Adolf Bartels, of infamous memory and notorious for his attempts to write an anti-Semitic history of German literature, declared: 'The greater a Jewish poet is, the more obvious is, of course, his Jewishness; mediocre talents and indistinct personalities may hide their Jewishness the longest.' (105)[6]

Bartels was interested in the identification of 'Jewishness' primarily with a view to eradicating it from German literature because he considered it to be a distorting and detrimental influence. Yet, although he felt confident that his racial theory as such was reliable enough for this purpose, he deemed himself hampered because, as he put it, 'the Jewish poet and writer is husbanding, of course, with our German elements of poesy' (104). In her lecture, first published as 'America: Toward Yavneh' (1970), Ozick seems to turn the same argument on its head, when she suggests that American culture, especially what she calls the religion of Art, deflects the Jewish fiction writer from his Jewishness. For, 'if the religion of Art', she says, 'is to dominate imaginative literature entirely, and I believe it will in America for a very long time, can he [the Jewish fiction writer] stay out of American literature?' Her answer is simple: 'If he wants to stay Jewish, I think he will have to. Even as a writer, especially as a writer, he will have to acknowledge exile' (1970; 1983: 165). That is, Jewish writers will have to acknowledge their otherness and shape their literature accordingly.

In 1970, Ozick suggested as a solution to this problem the creation of a new liturgical or aggadic literature in New Yiddish.[7] The New Yiddish was to be English, because in 1970 about 50 per cent of all Jews had English as their mother tongue (170) – surveys confirm this number for the 1990s.[8] Ozick envisaged English as a New Yiddish to become a 'vessel' of the 'Jewish vision', a language, as she said, 'for our need, our possibility, our overwhelming *idea*' (176). Of the new Jewish literature which was to find expression in the medium of the New Yiddish, Ozick demanded that it was to be 'centrally Jewish', by which she meant that it was to touch on the liturgical. 'Obviously', as she went on to explain,

> this does not refer only to prayer. It refers to a type of literature and to a type of perception. There is a critical difference between liturgy and a poem. Liturgy is in command of the reciprocal moral imagination rather than of the isolated lyrical imagination. [...] Liturgy is also a poem, but it is meant not to have only a private voice. Liturgy has a choral voice, a communal voice: the echo of the voice of the Lord of History. Poetry shuns judgment and memory and seizes the moment. In all of history the literature that has lasted for Jews has been liturgical. The secular Jew is a figment; when a Jew becomes a secular person he is no longer a Jew.
>
> (169)

As a literary mode on which to model the new liturgical, and 'centrally Jewish', literature Ozick suggests the Aggadah, which, as she explains, 'comprises the storytelling, imaginative elements in Talmud' (173). The Talmud, of course, is, somewhat simplified, an extensive rabbinical commentary to the Mishna, the teachings of the oral Torah, which in conjunction with the written Torah to a large degree defines Jewishness in a religious sense.

Thus, although she set out in 'dispraise of Diaspora' (156),[9] motivated by her revulsion against 'Western Civilization' (156) and its encroachment on 'Jewishness', Ozick perceives the creation of a new Jewish literature in the New Yiddish to give meaning to Jewish diaspora existence and even to act a necessary part in Jewish reconstruction after the Shoah:

> [F]or the moment our two parts, Diaspora Israel and Jerusalem Israel, have between us the responsibility of a double reconstruction – the healers, the health-bringers, the safekeepers in Jerusalem; the Aggadists, the makers of literature, just now gathering strength in America.
>
> (173)

Although she hastens to add that 'this is not to deny culture-making to the Land of Israel' (173), it is the Anglophone diaspora, and more specifically America, she looks to for progress towards a metaphorical Yavneh. Yavneh was the little town in ancient Palestine, where a rabbinical academy was established after the destruction of the Second Temple and where parts of the Talmud were compiled. And thus she concludes:

> We can give ourselves over entirely to Gentile culture and be lost to history, becoming a vestige nation without a literature; or we can do what we have never before dared to do in a Diaspora language: make it our own, our own necessary instrument, understanding ourselves in it while being understood by everyone who cares to listen or read. [...] From being envious apes we can become masters of our own civilization – and let those who want to call this 're-ghettoization', or similar pejoratives, look to their own destiny.
>
> (177)

Of course, Ozick's proposal has found its detractors (see, for example, Wisse 1976), and by the time she included her essay under its new title 'Toward a New Yiddish' in her collection *Art & Ardor* in 1983, Ozick herself said that she no longer believed 'that the project of fashioning a Diaspora literary culture, in the broadest *belles-lettres* sense, can be answered by any theory of an indispensable language – i.e. the Judaization of a single language used by large populations of Jews' (152).[10]

Jewish literary production in non-Jewish languages

And yet, Ozick was not, of course, the first to pose the question of the language of Jewish literary production in exile, nor was, or is, the Anglophone diaspora the only 'contact zone' in which it became pertinent. For Ozick, the Shoah and the havoc it wrought are significant factors in the phrasing of her proposal, compounded by the fact that the Ingathering of the Exiles has largely passed by America. Yet, before the ascendancy of the Anglophone Jewish diaspora and before the Shoah, in the German-speaking countries a similar issue had been negotiated. Indeed, it seems to me that Rubinstein's claim that the Anglophone diaspora provides an adequate matrix for the Jewish experience needs to be qualified to some extent because, at least in some respects, the German precedent in turn may be seen as a matrix for the matrix, and I would argue that the debate about German as a language of Jewish literary production, engaged in (at times) quite fiercely by both German and Jewish intellectuals for several decades, is of some interest in the context of this volume.

For one, the arguments put forward then are echoed in the more recent debate about the 'New Yiddish'. Furthermore, they seem to be pertinent even now, with regard to questions of Jewish 'postcoloniality' no less than in view of the question posed in the title of this collection – despite the obvious differences in the cultural contexts of the here and now and the there and then, when Yiddish and (the emerging) Ivrit were contenders for a Jewish national language. A comparative exposition, I suggest, may well enhance our sensibility for the question whether there are Jewish literature(s) in English, and it may contribute to an approximation of the phenomenon discussed in the individual chapters of this book.

Earlier, I quoted from Adolf Bartels, whose essay on the alleged Jewish 'infiltration' of German literature appeared in 1903. His was only one of a number of texts addressing the question of Jewish cultural production in the German-speaking countries around the turn of the century. And it was not only from the outside that the nature and the properties of Jewish cultural production in the exilic contact zones were discussed but also from within. Especially in Zionist discourse attempts were being made to define Jewishness and the 'loquation' of Jewish cultural production.

In an early attempt to sketch a Zionist poetics, published in 1898, the German Jewish author Robert Jaffé claims Zionism to be a power which restitutes to the Jewish writer the joy of being alive and which, by restoring his[11] pride of being Jewish, enables him to achieve 'authenticity' (1898: 14). For corroboration of his theory, Jaffé quotes extensively from *Rembrandt als Erzieher. Von einem Deutschen* [Rembrandt as an Educator. By a German]. Published anonymously by Julius Langbehn in 1890, this pamphlet, in which Rembrandt is styled an artist of the Nordic race, later became the basis of National Socialist artistic theory. In it Langbehn prophecies the advent of a 'secret emperor' and he says, as quoted by Jaffé:

> [W]hoever is a true Israelite without guile, as it is told in the Bible, will certainly be welcome to this future judge and leader; welcome as an honest and perhaps also sage stranger. [But] for the 'fake' Jews, who at the same time want to be Germans, this will not hold good. For honest and honourable is only he who remains faithful to himself. With genuine Jews genuine Germans can well strike a friendship; also with such [Jews] who, like Spinoza, Rahel, Börne, have retained a noble and abstract Jewishness, but against all false Jews all genuine Germans will always stand by each other. (15)[12]

That Jaffé quotes for Jewish self-definition from an overtly anti-Semitic text is an example of the uncanny convergence of the Zionist and anti-Semitic discourses around the turn of the nineteenth to the twentieth century in the German-speaking countries as it had been denounced most scathingly perhaps by the Viennese critic and satirist Karl Kraus in his *Eine Krone für Zion* [A Crown for Zion] in the very same year 1898. Intriguingly, the use of German by Jewish authors was never challenged by Jaffé and when, with the title of his essay he apostrophizes 'Our Poetry', what he refers to is, primarily, Jewish literature in German.

Its first climax was reached by this discussion about Jewish cultural production in Germany (which, in one way or another, was to continue for the next two decades) in 1912 when an essay by a Jewish journalist initiated what, with reference to the journal in which most of it was enacted, became known as the *Kunstwart* debate.[13] In his 'Deutsch-Jüdischer Parnaß' [German-Jewish Parnassus], Moritz Goldstein points out that in contemporary cultural production 'Jewishness' was considered to be a reproach even by Jews and advances the theory that, according to the principle of nationalities, whatever is 'centrally Jewish' (in Ozick's words) should rather be considered the very best in any Jew (1912: 281–94). Indeed, Jewish national characteristics were to be enhanced and 'Jewishness' to be made a virtue until it gathered a special creative force. Yet, to achieve this, Goldstein considers it prerequisite that the Jewish people be given a national home and that Jewish art should draw on the renaissance of Hebrew and of Hebrew poesy. For his own generation, the 'happy-hapless heirs to Western European culture' (290), he envisages only renunciation and resignation.

Here, of course, Ozick differs emphatically. By according to the language of the Anglophone diaspora the status of a New Yiddish, and by entrusting to it the creation of a liturgical or aggadic literature that is centrally Jewish, she enhances its standing, if always with reference to the State of Israel. Why, then, mention at all the German precedent (if such it is) in the introduction to a collection of essays on Jewish literature(s) in English? Because I think that it shows not only that the very question of the languages of Jewish literary production is inherently trans-cultural but that the question itself and some of the answers – by Goldstein and Jaffé, and yes, also by Bartels and Langbehn – are transported transculturally.

Considering that the way of thinking developed by Bartels or Langbehn and their followers contributed to the formation of an ideological mindset which was to make possible the cataclysm of the Shoah, it may easily be understood that, as the historian Michael Brenner points out, 'the mere comparison between Jewish culture in Weimar Germany and contemporary America still seems shocking to most observers' (2002: 14). Yet Brenner himself makes a convincing case for the comparison of the Jewish experience in Weimar Germany (1918–33) to that of American Jews since the late 1960s and, more particularly, the last two decades of the twentieth century. Though he is very much aware of the obvious differences (13), Brenner concludes: 'While the answers German Jews provided were restricted to the particular conditions of their place and time, the questions they asked were very similar to those posed by American Jews two generations later' (14). However, it seems to me that not all the answers were really that different: Ozick's proposal, idiosyncratic as it may be in the American context and though Brenner sees nothing more in it than 'a desperate cry for a safe identity' (11), is for this very reason reminiscent of the German Jewish writers' concerns. This is acknowledged by Brenner himself when he concedes: 'As much as Ozick, reflect-ing the new ethnicity of many American Jews, wants to write in a different language and thereby be part of the East European tradition, her "New Yiddish" is just another version of American English and thus resembles earlier searches for authenticity among German Jewish writers' (11).

One of the 'answers' German Jews came up with was the promotion of a national revival with the ultimate objective of Zionist emigration to Palestine. This never really was an option for the Jews of *di goldene medine* (the golden land) which, from the very beginning of the Zionist movement and its nineteenth-century precursors was to most Jewish emigrants rather the very often much more promising alternative to the Promised Land, although there is a relatively small segment of emigrants from the USA to Israel. Nor was *aliyah* attractive, in general, for many Jews from other countries of the Anglophone diaspora, with the exception of South Africa whence have emigrated more than 15,000 Jews to Israel since the 1960s, which was mainly due to the difficult political situation in this country. However, in the same period, another 35,000 South African Jews chose the Anglophone countries of the USA or Australia as their destination. But then, emigration to Palestine was not, before 1933 or, even more markedly, 1935 (when the Nuremberg Laws were proclaimed), what most German Jews aspired to. Until it became the last resort for mere survival, the Zionist movement in Germany was marginal (although its influence in the World Zionist Organization was disproportionately high), and many of its supporters never dreamed of making *aliyah* themselves but rather strove to make it possible for the persecuted Jewish masses from Eastern Europe. In this last respect, too, if only up to the beginning of the Shoah, the German Jewish experience resembles that of American Jews who also sought to build up Palestine 'as an asylum for other Jews' (Urofsky 1974; 1986: 217).

Another 'answer' German Jews proffered, and one at the extreme opposite of the scale, was the call for further assimilation as it had been expressed, for instance, by the aggressively anti-Zionist literary critic and scholar Ludwig Geiger in an ardent German-nationalist appeal to German Jewish writers in 1905:

> The German Jew who expresses himself in German literature should recognize, as he has been wont to do for the last one and a half centuries, only Germany as his fatherland, only the German tongue as his mother tongue. He should call only the German people his and only the future of this nation should be, and should remain, that to which he attaches his hopes. Any desire to form a people outside Germany with his co-religionists is, apart from its impracticability and the blatant ingratitude towards the nation in whose midst he lives, a delusion: for the German Jew is according to his national character a German and Zion, for him, is the land of the past, not the future.
>
> (1905: 1)

The desperate desire to belong is tinged here with a slightly hysterical quality which betrays the subliminal but insistent doubt that it might not be fulfilled. This is not so much due to the perceived rejection by the German majority, although since the so-called *Berliner Antisemitismusstreit*, the Berlin anti-Semitism row, of 1879–80 this was no longer to be doubted,[14] but rather to 'separatist' activities by Jewish 'subversives'. Later in the same year, another sign of his mounting hysteria, Geiger would denounce Zionism as dangerous to the German state and demand the passing of an emergency legislation to pursue Zionists as enemies of the state (Heuer 2000: 336–7).

The very different quality of the self-perception of American Jews is expressed, for instance, in the preface to the translation of the Hebrew Bible into English published under the auspices of the Jewish Publication Society in Philadelphia in 1917:

> The greatest change in the life of Israel during the last two generations was his renewed acquaintance with English-speaking civilization. Out of a handful of immigrants from Central Europe and the East who saw the shores of the New World, or even of England and her colonies, we have grown under Providence both in numbers and in importance, so that we constitute now the greatest section of Israel living in a single country outside of Russia. We are only following in the footsteps of our great predecessors when, with the growth of our numbers, we have applied ourselves to the sacred task of preparing a new translation of the Bible into the English language, which, unless all signs fail, is to become the current speech of the majority of the children of Israel.
>
> (Bible JPS 1917: iv)

This statement is remarkable for a variety of reasons. For one, it already envisages a transnational community of Anglophone Jews in what then still was the British Empire and the USA, while emphasizing the particular national context of the latter country as a contact zone. At the same time, making explicit reference to the relatively recent establishment (or, more properly speaking, increase) of the transnational community of English-speaking Jews, this is envisioned to become, as indeed it did, the worldwide largest linguistically determined Jewish community. That the translation itself was into a language that many of those it was intended for still had to learn, among them future Jewish immigrants from Eastern Europe speaking Yiddish and familiar with Hebrew for ritual purposes, is another indication of the project's orientation towards the Jewish future in the Anglophone diaspora.

Accordingly, another remarkable characteristic of the 1917 preface is that it makes no reference whatsoever to Palestine. In contrast, in the preface to a bilingual German-Hebrew prayer book, edited by the eminent reform rabbi Abraham Geiger (the aforementioned Ludwig's father) first, in 1854, for the Jewish congregation of Breslau and in its second edition of 1891 for the congregation of Frankfurt, it was explicitly stated that all pretence to the Jewish land of origin was to be renounced (1854; 2nd edn 1891: x).[15] Similarly, on occasion of the laying of the foundation stone in 1855 and, in 1860, of the opening of the new main synagogue (Hauptsynagoge) of Frankfurt, Rabbi Leopold Stein repeatedly stressed Jewish loyalty to the German nation (Hammer-Schenk 1981, 1: 299–300). Indeed, a commemorative text in both Hebrew and German had been placed in the foundation stone in 1855

> to bear witness that once there shall resound the holy tongue of the Scriptures here, the inspired tongue of our past and, affectionately twinned with it, our

> mother tongue, the dear and familiar, the tongue of our present and our future. On the foundation of both tongues shall rise the shrine which we want to build on the very basis of the past into the future
>
> (cit. Hammer-Schenk 1981, 1: 300; my translation).

The exterior of the new synagogue, built by Johann Georg Kayser, combined both Moorish (Oriental) and Gothic elements to show the remembrance of, and the attachment to, the old religion and to demonstrate the affiliation to the German nation (300). By 1905, when Ludwig Geiger phrased his appeal to German Jewish writers, the optimism expressed in the immured commemorative text, which, after all, was not so different from that informing the 1917 preface, had become strained. In 1938, the Frankfurt Hauptsynagoge, like so many others, was destroyed and its congregation brutally disabused of the myth of the German Jewish symbiosis.

This, of course, is where all similarities end. Not even remotely comparable threat has endangered Jews in the Anglophone diaspora since their readmittance to England in the seventeenth century. There is, however, some fear that assimilation may prove as lethal. In America, one Israeli settler's argument in Philip Roth's *The Counterlife* (1987) runs, assimilation and intermarriage

> are bringing about a second Holocaust – truly, a spiritual Holocaust is taking place there, and it is as deadly as any threat posed by the Arabs to the State of Israel. What Hitler couldn't achieve with Auschwitz, American Jews are doing to themselves in the bedroom.
>
> (1987: 103)

In the novel, it takes England, with its snobbish anti-Semitism, with its 'closed doors', much like Sartre proposed in his *Réflexions sur la question juive* [*Anti-Semite and Jew*] (1943), to 'make' a Jew of the narrator:

> I find myself in a situation that has reactivated the strong sense of difference that had all but atrophied in New York, and, what's more that has drained the domestic idyll of its few remaining drops of fantasy. Circumcision confirms that there is an us, and an us that isn't solely him and me. England's made a Jew of me in only eight weeks, which, on reflection, might be the least painful method.
>
> (Roth 1987: 324)

The very situation which 'makes' the British Jew (or, in Roth's novel, the Jew in Britain) appears at the same time to bar Jews in Britain from participating in the English, or even British, national project – in contrast to America. This divergence is expressed quite succinctly by Linda Grant in her prize-winning novel, *When I Lived in Modern Times* (2000), when she has her protagonist remember her childhood in Britain in the following terms: 'I was a Jewish child in a country where, unlike America, there was no contribution I could make to the forging of the national identity. It was fixed already, centuries ago' (12). Although later revealed to be a fallacy, in Grant's novel, the one place where her protagonist seems to be able to actively contribute to the forging of her own as well as a Jewish national identity is Palestine immediately before the foundation of the Jewish state. She recalls: 'I had come to the place where there was, mercifully, no past and in which it was the duty and destiny of everyone to make the future, each for himself and for his country' (74).

Turning inward or outward or somewhere else

The differences between the Jewish experience in America and in Britain upon which the fictional texts of both Roth and Grant reflect from different perspectives appear to be indicative of what amounts almost to a binary opposition with regard to the production and reception contexts of Anglophone Jewish writing: America seems to provide an open and liberal environment, conducive to cultural production; Britain, in contrast, appears to be exclusive and suffocating. Exploring these differences, Bryan Cheyette observes that 'American Jews can constantly reinvent themselves using prevalent American mythologies' (1996: 22). In fact, resisting facile attempts at 'Americanizing' cis-Atlantic diaspora Jewish culture(s) and insisting on their distinctive character, Cheyette argues that it is this very quality of the writing of American Jewish authors which distinguishes it in particular from the literary endeavours of their British Jewish counterparts whom he perceives, in contrast, to be confronted not only with 'an enforced cultural amnesia' but also with 'an alternative Englishness, rooted in the past, that they are meant to absorb uncritically' (21). However, as Cheyette points out, British Jewish literature found it hard to assimilate a monolithic and 'exclusive' Englishness, or to be assimilated to it, because English national culture rests on homogenous and intransigent constructions of the past. Cheyette concludes: 'The very impossibility of absorbing the Jewish past into a territorial Englishness – or even Britishness – has led precisely to the continuation of a culture of Jewish extraterritoriality' (22). The extraterritoriality of British Jewish literature, a key concept for Cheyette, manifests itself in Jewish writers turning to non-English territories in their fiction, especially to the diaspora and Israel, where it is possible for them to sidestep the hegemony of English or British constructions of the past. Once again, Grant's *When I Lived in Modern Times* appears to be paradigmatic in this respect, although her choice of British Mandate Palestine as the main setting of her novel engages colonial, and therefore rather essentialist, constructions of British identity and the British past in a space that is 'extraterritorial' from a British perspective, too. Historically, as well as in her novel, Mandate Palestine is the space of a colonial confrontation in which British and Jewish history converge and, indeed, clash rather violently. Yet in Grant's novel the colonial encounter in faraway Palestine is really a metonymy for the larger colonial encounter between the British and the Jews that is located also in contemporary Britain. In her novel, as well as in other recent British Jewish fiction dealing with the Mandate, Jonathan Wilson's *The Hiding Room* (1995) and his *A Palestine Affair* (2003),[16] or Bernice Rubens' *The Sergeants' Tale* (2003), Jewish extraterritoriality is thus being 'trans-territorialized'.[17]

The nature of British Jewish 'extraterritoriality', it seems, may be undergoing a change. In addition, Victoria Aarons' recent study (2005) on reinventions of the covenant in American Jewish fiction may suggest the necessity of a reassessment, or at least a readjustment, of Cheyette's conceptions of the way in which 'American Jewish writers are able constantly to reimagine or remythologize their relationship to a European past' (1996: 22) and, even more pertinently, to an American past and present. The very openness of Jewish American constructions of the past seems to be exposed in recent fictional texts of Jewish American authors as deceptive because in effect it proves to be no less repressive for Jewish constructions of the past than a normative Englishness. Thus, Aarons argues that Allegra Goodman represents recent American history in her novel *Kaaterskill Falls* (1998) not only as 'the direct antithesis of a Jewish past, but also as its antagonist, as arresting and redefining all other histories' (2005: 119). The subtle hegemony of American pop culture appears to be an integral element of this process of negation and redefinition, and Aarons suggests that '[t]he embrace of popular culture in modern and contemporary American Jewish fiction might thus be seen as a rejection if not repudiation of Jewish history, disinheritance, a disavowal of the past' (121). In Goodman's novel, like in her earlier collection of loosely connected stories published as *The Family Markowitz* (1996), the surprising turn of some of her characters towards Jewish orthodoxy is then to be seen as a move to counter this phenomenon which is obviously experienced as a crisis. Another reaction to the repudiation of Jewish history, which indirectly confirms Cheyette's reading, is Henry Markowitz' attempt, in Goodman's collection of stories, to assume an unambiguously defined and normative Englishness. Henry 'literally runs from contemporary American life toward the sanctuary of a borrowed past and a gentile wife', as Aarons explains. 'He substitutes one culture, a diluted, stricken one, for another, appropriated to fill in the emptiness he so acutely feels' (2005: 125). Yet for Henry Markowitz, too, the assimilation of Englishness signifies the surrender of his Jewish identity (125).

The 'surrender' of Jewish identity to constructions of Englishness or Britishness initially resulted in the markedly apologetic character of British Jewish literature. 'The originating moment of British-Jewish writing indicates', as Cheyette has it, 'the continual struggle within Anglo-Jewry in the face of the enormous authority of the idea of England in the age of empire. The seductive power of a superior Englishness meant that Jews were extremely anxious to win acceptance in their adopted country' (1998: xv). Thus,

> [w]hat the literary history of Anglo-Jewry reveals, above all, is the dual pressure on British-Jewish writers to universalize their Jewishness out of the public sphere (which takes the extreme form of conversionism) or to particularize it in preconceived images. This reductive 'either/or' has, until recently, deformed much of the literary output of Anglo-Jewry into tame satire or crude apologetics.
>
> (xxxiv)

Yet most contemporary British Jewish writers 'are not merely unapologetic in their Jewishness but can be characterized as Jews "with attitude" who disrupt all conventions' (lxiv). Thus, in analogy with postcolonial literature, Cheyette sees recent British Jewish literature characterized as a counter literature: 'It exposes a radically different sense of the past and rewrites an alternative Englishness from the margins' (lxii). Once again, Grant's novel seems the perfect example. However, the same tendency, to transcend the dominant culture and to rewrite both its past and its present, is perceived by Cheyette also in much of contemporary British fiction (liii). British Jewish literature thus appears not only to assert its particular 'identity', but at the same time, in a manner, to overcome its marginalization.[18]

While British Jewish writers have been turning towards extraterritoriality, in Jewish American literature what has been called an inward turn has been noticeable in recent years (Brenner 2002: 10). An 'interest in intensely Jewish subject matter' (10) appears to have surfaced in much of contemporary Jewish American writing, although there may be a number of Jewish American writers whose Jewishness seems to be 'lost' in the way Ozick feared it would be, among them possibly Norman Mailer, Arthur Miller or Nathanael West, and, as Bryan Cheyette argues in his contribution to this book, maybe even Philip Roth in whose recent works Cheyette sees a 'narrowing or Americanization of his concerns which sadly limits his previous extraterritorial reach'.

Diaspora(s) and multiculturalism(s)

The inward turn, the establishment of a minority literature among other such literatures, it appears, may be seen in some measure as connected to the rise of multiculturalism and the ethnic diversity it celebrates. Given the assertion of Jewishness also by British Jewish writers, and the concomitant 'mainstreaming', superficially it may seem as if a similar process was unfolding in Britain, the extraterritoriality of British Jewish writers and the inward turn of Jewish American writers being simply the obverse sides of the same coin.

However, the concerns of Jewish writers in Britain and in America seem to be at variance, and although a strengthening of the 'Jewish' component in Anglophone Jewish literature seems to be ensuing in both cultural contexts (and perhaps also in other cultural contexts of the Anglophone diaspora), the question rather must be which elements of Jewishness are coming to the fore in each case, and we best remind ourselves that they need not, and perhaps cannot, be the same. The similarities of Jewish communities in the Anglophone world evoked by Rubinstein notwithstanding, the situation of Jewish writers in any of these cultural contexts is certainly distinct, as is their individual and collective positioning towards the majority and towards other minorities.

For the American context, David Biale has argued that as a result of the ongoing multicultural debates Jews find themselves 'doubly marginalized' in that to the majority culture they appear to be outsiders while to other minorities they appear to be insiders (1998: 27). While this evaluation seems plausible enough in view of the power politics informing the American multiculturalism debates, the characterization of what is Jewish American by 'the received discourses of religion, roots, tradition and victimhood' (Cheyette 2003: 52) implicit in this understanding is not easily transferable to other cultural contexts. Thus, Cheyette points out that 'ethnicity in Britain is founded neither in the hierarchy of victimhood nor in the institutional power of a particular ethnic grouping' (52). Repudiating the tendency to universalize the American context, Cheyette therefore emphasizes the 'unprogrammatic nature of Jewish writing in Britain – neither wholly multicultural, nor ethnic, nor postcolonial – that resists delimitation within the received discourses that make up American multiculturalism' (52). He stresses the 'cosmopolitanism of many Jewish writers in Britain who represent the diaspora as a place without a beginning or end, a place that is always doubled and contested' and insists that this is a 'radically different construction of diaspora from that current within American-Jewish discourse, which stresses Jewish tradition and rootedness in Eastern Europe, an autochthonous "homeland" of Israel, and the universalization of diaspora Jewishness in the USA' (78).

Of course, it would not do simply to substitute the universalization of American diaspora Jewishness with that of British diaspora Jewishness, not in the context of the Anglophone diaspora and certainly not in the context of *the* Jewish diaspora. In fact, considering the rise of Anglophone Sephardic literature in America, connected as yet mainly with the name of Ruth Knafo Setton (and possibly Jordan Elgrably), or the fact that even some Mizrahim in Israel, like Moshe Benarroch or Osama Massarwa, adopt English as a language of artistic expression, the cultural diversity within the Anglophone diaspora and the linguistic diversity in Israel bespeak the increasing complexity and cross-fertilization of Anglophone Jewish literature. Still, it seems to me that Jewish writers from the Anglophone diaspora as a whole find their 'loquation' somewhere in-between extraterritoriality and the inward turn. In Australia, Canada, Ireland and South Africa, Jewish writers, if they feel to be such, will have a sense of diaspora, of the past, of belonging and of difference, and this means that they, either of their own accord or else from the outside, will be compelled to position themselves not only 'territorially' and 'inwardly' but also linguistically and culturally as well as towards the respective majorities and other minorities – if to varying degrees and in different ways.

English as a transnational and transcultural 'Jewish' language

The near-infinite linguistic variety of a people dispersed among the nations of the world is, of course, only to be expected. Despoiled of its centre and consigned mainly to its periphery, it may rather seem an oddity that the Jewish people for two thousand years retained Hebrew as the holy tongue (*leshon ha-kodesh*) and that among the exiles its ritual use continued to contribute to the creation of cultural coherence. George Steiner's attempt to explain this oddity by designating 'the text' as the Jewish homeland has become famous (1996).[19] With the re-establishment of a Jewish 'centre', the rebirth of the holy tongue as a 'modern' language and the steady decline of Yiddish and Ladino on the one hand, as well as the ascendancy of the Anglophone diaspora since the late nineteenth century on the other, the model of a circular periphery with its one centre seems no longer to be tenable and an elliptoid model of a periphery with two focal points (an image first suggested by the philosopher Simon Rawidowicz, see Zeller 2003: 8) appears to approximate the interrelations of Jewish collectives all over the world more closely. This is not to say that a 'near-infinite' variety of languages spoken by Jews does not still exist but that in terms of power relations as well as in terms of cultural production, of representation and perception by the self and the other, a polarization of English and Hebrew as the most prominent among those languages appears to be manifest.

For a very long time, as has been suggested, the second of these focal points has been equated more or less with the Jewish presence in America. Thus, in an attempt to identify 'Some Patterns of Exile in Jewish Writing of the Commonwealth', the Canadian Jewish critic Carole Gerson in 1982 maintained that 'Jewish writers face the [...] dilemma of writing from a colony within a colony, looking backward to continental Europe, forward to Israel, and sideways at the United States, the current homeland of English-language Jewish culture' (104). While mentioning the 'sideways' look at America may reflect as much on Gerson's Canadian background as it does on the Jewish writer, Cynthia Ozick's earlier vision of America evolving into another Yavneh is an acknowledgment of the same relationship from an inside perspective. However, in the intervening twenty-odd years the validity of Gerson's assessment has become ever more doubtful. Ozick's 'retraction' of 1983 already gives an indication of this. In 1999, Jerome A. Chanes, then Associate Director of the National Foundation for Jewish Culture, argued more succinctly that 'the relationship of Israel to American Jews – the term of art has long been "Israel-Diaspora relations" [...] – may very well have been itself nudged over to the margins by the larger, transcendent question of the emergence of a trans-national Jewish culture' (387–8).[20]

The conception of Jewish culture as transnational is not, of course, entirely new. The transnational quality of Jewish literature, for instance, had been emphasized much earlier. Thus, in 1918, the Yiddish literary critic Israel Isidor Elyashev, better known under his pen-name Ba'al Makhshoves, took issue with the *kulturkampf* between Yiddish and Hebrew that was being enacted during the first decades of the twentieth century: 'We have two languages and a dozen echoes from other foreign languages, but [...] we have only one literature', Ba'al Makhshoves contended. 'And therefore', he continued,

> the reader who seeks to become acquainted with the currents of Jewish life, to comprehend the spirit of the Jewish individual and multitude and how they find expression in Jewish literature, that reader dares not separate Hebrew writers from Yiddish ones, [...] all are representatives of our literature, all embody a piece of Jewish life in their writing; all of them are Jewish artists.
>
> (1918; 1994: 74)

The parameters of Ba'al Makhshoves' equation may have changed, inasmuch as English has, as a matter of fact and as suggested by Ozick, more or less replaced Yiddish – even though there may be the first stirrings of a revival of *Yiddishkayt* and though, as Hana Wirth-Nesher recently emphasized, and explored, there is also the 'multilingual dimension of Jewish American writing' (2006: xii) to be considered. But is there really only one transnational Jewish literature? And what role plays language in the formation of Jewish literatures, if there are more than just one?

Comparing the Jewish and Caribbean experiences of displacement in the Anglophone diaspora, Sophia Lehmann recently claimed that 'because of the centrality of language to both Jewish and Caribbean cultures, creating a mother tongue which incorporates both history and contemporary culture and experience is tantamount to creating a home within the diaspora' (1998: 115). Of interest in the present context is not only the explicit analogy of Jewish and Caribbean literatures in English argued for by Lehmann, which suggests a whole dimension of transcultural interrelations awaiting to be explored. Of particular interest is the integrative function ascribed to English as a diasporic language. For it appears to be a language which encompasses the past and the present and envisages, at least tacitly, a temporal dimension neglected by Lehmann but insisted on quite explicitly by the authors of the 1917 preface – the future of Jewish communities in the Anglophone diaspora.[21] It is thus a tool of identity formation, community building and the creation of culture in this linguistically defined space.[22] Yet it is also a shared language and an archive of the memory and culture of several 'Others'; and as a shared language it makes Jewish history and contemporary culture and experience accessible to those very Others, a point made already by Ozick and referred to by Rubinstein. A medium, and, indeed, a product, of 'border-crossings' between the particular (or 'tribal') and the 'universal' (Lehmann 1998: 106, 111–12), English thus facilitates the negotiation, and hybridization, of cultures and cultural production.

Lehmann introduced her argument with the observation that 'disparate diasporic communities are now faced with the shared struggle of articulating a cultural identity in which history and home reside in language, rather than nation, and in which language itself must be recreated so as to bespeak the specificity of cultural experience' (101). Paradoxically, in the case of Anglophone Jewish writers in Israel, their language seems to answer the same need. Karen Alkalay-Gut, herself a poet writing in English, a professor of English at Tel Aviv University and Chair of the Israel Association of Writers in English (IAWE), estimates that there are about '500 professional and semi-professional writers of literature in English in Israel, in addition to at least a thousand people who make writing their hobby' (2002: 459). This number may seem surprisingly high and one of the reasons for this, pointed out also by Alkalay-Gut, may be that there is hardly a forum for those writers in Israel. Rather, they suffer severe problems of integration into the culture of their, usually freely, chosen homeland whose language, at least for artistic purposes, they cannot or do not want to adopt: 'For many of these writers', Alkalay-Gut observes, 'there is a degree of "Diaspora" in their work, a sense of a cultural, literary and personal center elsewhere, that is concurrent with a varying but steady commitment to Israel as the homeland.' This phenomenon, 'of being physically Home in the Holy Land, but native and/or loyal to another language', has been labelled by Alkalay-Gut a 'double diaspora' and qualified as 'almost unique to the Zionist experience' (458–9).[23] 'Most Anglos', she concludes, 'remained loyal to English, and either deserted writing or Israel, or fell silent' (459).

If, as Lehmann argues, to create 'a mother tongue which incorporates both history and contemporary culture and experience is tantamount to creating a home within the diaspora' (1998: 115), then the very tenacity with which Jewish writers from the Anglophone diaspora adhere to their English 'mother tongue' even in Israel may not only prove Lehmann's point. But the same token, it also seems to me that the phenomenon of the 'double diaspora' of Anglophone Jewish writers in Israel may, in turn, sustain the claim that it is, indeed, reasonable to make the distinction of a Jewish literature in English, precisely because it links those authors with their cultural rather than with their chosen national homeland – bridging the 'divide' discerned by Emily Miller Budick between the secular, intellectual Jewish communities in Israel and America (2001: 2) and, by extrapolation, in other Anglophone countries – and because the cultural affinities of the countries of the Anglophone diaspora are sustained in the Israeli setting by their work and by their interrelation.

The vexing question of definition

So far, after its initial mention in the introductory paragraphs, I have evaded the first pitfall any enterprise of this sort is confronted with, that of definition. But, of course, in a collection of essays purporting to enquire into Anglophone Jewish writing this is not an issue to be avoided indefinitely and it is grappled with also in several of its individual contributions: What is 'Jewish'? And who is a 'Jewish writer'? The problematic inherent in questions of this sort has been articulated quite succinctly by the Jewish Australian writer Serge Liberman:

> This is one of those topics which regularly appear in different guises – 'Is there a Jewish literature?' 'What is a Jewish writer?' 'What is a Jewish book?' – reminds me of Humpty Dumpty in Lewis Carroll's *Through the Looking-Glass* – 'When I use a word, it means just what I choose it to mean – neither more nor less.'
>
> (1998: 6)

While the prerogative of arbitrary designation claimed by Humpty Dumpty may be entirely satisfactory to the individual it can hardly be considered adequate in a scholarly context. Yet if Humpty Dumpty's prerogative is not exerted, conceptions of Jewishness with respect to literature and the writer will always retain, if not a plurality, then at least a vagueness of meaning. Yet it seems to me that this is a vagueness to be cherished as it beckons to explore new ground, and as any comparison of phenomena which share even vague similarities is illuminating precisely because they exhibit not only sameness but also difference, throwing each other into sharp relief. For this reason, neither this introduction nor the chapters it introduces aim to narrow down the plurality, or vagueness, of conceptions of Jewishness but rather attempt to explore some of its aspects, possibly even adding to the confusion in the process.

The sometimes perhaps annoying vagueness of conceptions of Jewish literature which was acknowledged also by Hana Wirth-Nesher in her thoughtful introduction to her classic collection of essays on *What Is Jewish Literature?* is largely due to Jewish writers' stubborn resistance to being categorized (1994b:3–5);[24] the same stubborn resistance has been documented more recently also in the collection of Jewish American writers' statements edited by Derek Rubin under the title of *Who We Are. On Being (and Not Being) a Jewish American Writer* (2005). A simple biological determinism of the sort practiced by Adolf Bartels is problematical for obvious reasons. The application of Jewish religious law, the halachical definition, according to which Jewish identity is determined matrilineally differs not much from this with respect to the differentiating criteria, if with the one essential difference that it is an ascription not from the outside but from (a segment of) the inside. Liberman, the editor of the authoritative bibliography of Australian Judaica (1987; 1991), and confronted in this capacity with the question of definition quite directly, accepts the halachical definition for purely pragmatic reasons, not least because it does not admit grey areas and is, in fact, the only 'legal' definition of Jewish identity that is currently valid (1998: 6). Yet at the same time, Liberman acknowledges nuances of the still vague conception of Jewishness and therefore favours a 'dual' definition:

> Jewish literature is that which is written by all writers who are halachically Jews. However, the extent to which the literature and its authors (as reflected through their works) may be deemed Jewish, ranging from the totally traditional across a broad field of acclimatizing, adaptive, integrated and acculturated writers to a total absence of any Jewishness at all, is determined by the permutations of interaction or amount of overlap (if any) of the works' characters, the ambience in which their dramas are played out, their subject matter or thematic concerns, the place and language in which they are written, and their recourse to Jewish sources.
>
> (7)

Of course, this definition, too, is not without its problems. Not least because it does not take into account the *befindlichkeit*, in Heidegger's sense,[25] of Jewish writers in search of their 'writing identity' which, to Efraim Sicher, is the distinctive feature of Jewish writers. Pragmatically passing by the vexing question of definition, Sicher argues: 'The Jewishness of writing in non-Jewish languages which does not directly draw on Jewish literary traditions poses a problem not of definition but description.' Accordingly, he states: 'Jewishness, as distinct from Judaism, is a question not so much of biographies as of the writers' search for a writing identity and for a language, in the sense of a moral as well as a cultural code' (1985: xiv).

Franz Kafka's touching image for the linguistic predicament of German Jewish writers, echoing the desperation of the metamorphosing Gregor Samsa, is well known: '[W]ith their posterior legs', he wrote to Max Brod in June 1921, 'they were still glued to their father's Jewishness and with their waving anterior legs they found no new ground' (Kafka 1977: 289). In the same letter he further elaborated: 'They existed among three impossibilities [. . .]: The impossibility of not writing, the impossibility of writing German, the impossibility of writing differently. One might also add a fourth impossibility, the impossibility of writing' (289). Ironically, with regard to Anglophone Jewish literature, nowadays the fourth impossibility appears to be suffered by a number of writers in Israel, as has been pointed out by Karen Alkalay-Gut. Yet in turn, as Karen Grumberg argues in her contribution to this volume (American) English lashes back at Hebrew by insinuating itself in many ways into the Jewish language of the Jewish land.

Kafka's fourth impossibility is disregarded by Robert Alter when, referring to America, he acknowledges that the 'quandary of a possible Jewish culture in this country is felt most acutely as a linguistic problem, though it is certainly not exhausted by considerations of language', and points out that '[s]ome American Jewish writers have been locked into just this three-sided dilemma' (1982; 1986: 269). Yet, Alter emphasizes 'that for a good many others the dilemma has rather easily dissolved' (269), and continues to say that he considers the latter alternative 'more feasible in America than it could have been in Kafka's German-speaking world because in this country the wide-open gates of assimilation do not have a hidden trip-wire inside' (270). That things may not be quite as simple is suggested by British-born Jonathan Wilson's American experience. 'A Jew can never be English', the writer asserts, 'but is it also possible, despite my insistence on the democratic openness of the world of American letters, that an English Jew can never be quite an American?' (2005: 157). As Wilson states, this has precisely been his experience. Conversely, it may well be that in America, as has been suggested above, the 'trip-wire' is in fact that easy assimilationism which, as indicated by the recent 'inward turn' of many Jewish American writers, some authors feel the need to avoid. Allegra Goodman, for instance, believes that 'Jewish American writers must recapture the spiritual and the religious dimension of Judaism' (1997; 2005: 274), as she herself, in her fiction, has done and as writers as Nessa Rapoport or Dara Horn have done. In voicing her belief, Goodman not only harks back to Ted Solotaroff's dark prophecy that '[o]nly those writers steeped in Judaism will survive' (cit. Goodman 1997; 2005: 275), but also to Cynthia Ozick's bid for a 'centrally Jewish' literature which, once again, brings us back to the question not only of what is centrally Jewish but also of which language might be the proper 'vessel', as Ozick calls it, for this Jewish literature.

Postcoloniality, bilingualism and hybridity

Kafka's deeply felt resignation with regard to the four impossibilities of the German Jewish writer was also quoted by the Tunisian-born, Francophone Jewish sociologist Albert Memmi (1966: 163) in his discussion of Jewish *befindlichkeit*.

For Memmi, who quite explicitly elaborates on the analogy of the Jewish experience with the colonial paradigm, language is a central element of the colonial confrontation. The double language of the Jews, referred to by Ba'al Makhshoves (1918; 1994: 74) and, more widely known, by Shmuel Niger (1941),[26] Memmi argues in his 1966 study *La libération du Juif* [*The Liberation of the Jew*], is one of the signs of their oppression (164). In his *Portrait du colonisé précédé de portrait du colonisateur* [*The Colonizer and the Colonized*], first published in 1957, in the year after Tunisia had gained its independence, Memmi states that the liberation and restitution of its language had to be the most pressing concern of any (de)colonized collective (1957; 1985: 129). In the person of the colonized writer (*écrivain colonisé*), Memmi sees the *befindlichkeit* of the colonized embodied in concentrated form, with all its ambiguities and impossibilities (126). It is therefore imperative, for Memmi, that colonized writers attempt to write in their mother tongue, so as to reconcile their destiny with themselves (129).

Jewish bilingualism, which he compares to that of the colonized, Memmi considers to be dangerous because of its inherent potential for psychological conflict (1966: 162). The absence of a unique and stable language is equivalent, for Memmi, to the absence of any language at all (160), and the bilingualism of the colonized is thus interpreted by him as the symptom of a fragmentation which originates in their suppression and which has a marked effect on their cultural production (168).

Obviously, from a transcultural or transnational perspective, bi- or even multilingualism are still categories which apply to the Jewish collective. As to the relevance of conceptions of bilingualism for individual contemporary Anglophone Jewish writers, it may be argued that for many of them it has become a thing of the past. Yet, as Hana Wirth-Nesher posits,

> for many Jewish American writers, subsequent to the immigrant generation, Hebrew and Yiddish are sources of self-expression and identity even if the authors cannot 'remember' them in the sense of ever having possessed them as a means of communication. Their understanding of what these languages signify is always the result, borrowing from Werner Sollors, of both descent, a continuous cultural legacy, and consent, an embrace of American English that also structures their sense of those Jewish languages and accents. Their remembering, therefore, is not the result of an essential Jewishness that hearkens back to some racial memory but the result of socialization where practices, expectations, and assumptions about the entanglement of language and identity linger in their consciousness.
>
> (2006: 5)

The residual bilingualism described by Wirth-Nesher is firmly situated by her in the Jewish American experience and, bearing in mind Cheyette's well justified admonition not to universalize the Jewish American diaspora, it may be doubtful whether the same kind of hidden bilingualism exists also in other cultural contexts of the Anglophone diaspora. Yet it seems to me that what Wirth-Nesher and, as referred to by her, Werner Sollors describe is really a form of 'biculturalism'. This, as a superordinate category, is certainly something that applies to all Jewish writing, even in Israel where, as Alkalay-Gut has shown, Anglophone Jewish writers are in the position of a 'double diaspora' and where, as is argued by Karen Grumberg in her contribution to this book, the use of English in modern Hebrew fiction is revealed to challenge the success of Hebrew as a language of national homogenization as which it has been promoted in accordance with the anti-colonial ambitions of the Zionist project.

When, in 1966, Memmi invoked *La libération du Juif*, he stated that what might properly be called a Jewish literature, that is the literature of 'liberated' Jewry, was still in the offing (156). The reason for this he saw not only in Jewish bilingualism but also in the ambiguity of the definition of Jewish literature. His own characterization of Jewish literature was comprised of two central aspects. On the one hand, he ascribed to it the function of a medium of collective self-reflection, as a platform for finding adequate answers to the questions posed by Jewish destiny (148). On the other hand, he perceived there to be an apologetic dimension to Jewish literature and that it was incumbent on the Jewish writer to explain the Jewish condition to the other as well as to the self so as to make it acceptable (152).

In *Portrait du colonisé*, Memmi had considered two alternatives towards the solution of the quandary of bilingualism: first, to continue to write in the language of the colonizer until the natural alternation of generations would lead to its substitution by the colonized's own, newly recovered language (*langue retrouvée*); or, to succumb to the temptation to fuse completely with the metropolitan literature (*littérature métropolitaine*). But this was to him equal to the suicide of the colonized literature. In any case, however, Memmi concluded that any colonized literature in a European language was doomed to an early demise (1957; 1985: 130).

With respect to Anglophone Jewish literature Memmi's diagnosis certainly proved to be wrong. For Anglophone Jewish literature – perhaps as a result also of the rise of what is now referred to as the New English Literatures – has never before been as productive and as varied. In fact, in the larger context of overall Jewish cultural production it may even be considered, to some extent, to be hegemonic. At the same time it may be said to be a product of the hybridity which Homi Bhabha described itself as the effect of the colonial confrontation and whose recognition entails 'an important change of perspective' (1994: 112), in that it challenges essentialisms of all kinds. In a 'post-essentialist' age it seems necessary to relativize Memmi's literary essentialism and to recognize in their very hybridity the aesthetic, social and political potential of all literatures which emerge from the cultural contact zones of the colonial confrontation – among them also Anglophone Jewish literature.

Approaching Anglophone Jewish literature: the chapters of this book

The chapters of this book are arranged in three thematic clusters: 'The Jewish imaginary in non-Jewish Anglophone literature(s)', 'Changing centres, changing peripheries, and spaces in-between – Jewish writing from the Anglophone diaspora(s)', and 'The "loquation" of Jewish culture'; in addition, two chapters are gathered under the heading of 'Introduction': the present introduction and another introductory chapter in which Bryan Cheyette approaches the subject from the perspective of, and on, the 'Jewish' critic.

To invoke the notion of Anglophone Jewish literature entails questions of inclusion and exclusion, and whenever such questions are being asked there is a danger to think in categories of purity and impurity. With a view to the scope of this book and the literature it deals with, the concept of purity has already summarily been rejected. In 'On being a Jewish critic' (chapter 2), Bryan Cheyette, aiming to locate the impurity of Jewish culture in relation to received definitions of Western culture and the Anglo-American literary canon, argues in more detail for what he calls cosmopolitan impurity. Taking issue with recent attempts at writing a canon of Jewish literature, Cheyette argues against exclusive canonization and against relegating literature to being merely explanatory of history and thus yoking it to narratives of national redemption. With reference to Matthew Arnold and Lionel Trilling, he discusses conceptions of cultural purity and impurity and claims that the literary history of cosmopolitanism did not end with the Shoah, as has been alleged. Rather, Cheyette sees cosmopolitan impurity alive in British Jewish literature, in contrast to Jewish American literature which he perceives to be bounded by the language of identity politics: religion, roots, tradition and victimhood.

In the first cluster of chapters, 'The Jewish imaginary in non-Jewish Anglophone literature(s)', approximations and appropriations of Jewishness, or constructions of the 'Jewish imaginary', by non-Jewish writers in English are discussed to provide a foil against which the analyses of Jewish Anglophone writing of the second and third clusters may usefully be read.

In 'Postcolonial cultures and the Jewish imaginary' (chapter 3), Jamie S. Scott argues that Jewish history has been written in terms of four pivotal signs, 'Exodus', 'Exile', 'Diaspora' and 'Holocaust', and that in recent years these signs have appeared in literary and cultural contexts that, on the surface at least, have nothing to do with Jewish historical experience, most notably under the rubric of the postcolonial. Exploring the interface between postcolonial writing and the Jewish imaginary, Scott examines various instances of exodus, exile, diaspora and holocaust in writers and writings as diverse as Ngugi wa Thiong'o's *The River Between* (1965), David Malouf's *Remembering Babylon* (1993) and Basil Johnston's *Indian School Days* (1988). More suggestive than conclusive, the chapter closes with some reflections on the implications of this tropical exchange for a variety of postcolonial issues, from indigenous land claims to historical and cultural debates about immigrant identity.

The 'availability' of conceptions of Jewishness for appropriation by 'others' is further pursued by Sigrun Meinig who, focusing on Zadie Smith's *The Autograph Man* (2002), enquires into ' "What's more important than a gesture?" The cultural performativity of Jewishness' (chapter 4). She argues that, in this novel, Jewish culture, its traditions and the performativity of its rituals become the 'solution' to the conundrums of cultural difference which Smith already engaged with in her best-selling 'multicultural' first novel, *White Teeth* (2000). But in *The Autograph Man*, as Meinig points out, Jewish culture is also one of the resources for a trendy, 'spiritual' lifestyle which incorporates the Kabbalah as well as Zen Buddhism, smoking weed and trading the autographs of the novel's title. Meinig examines in which ways *The Autograph Man* negotiates such representational extremes and what the effects for the cultural positioning of Jewishness are. She argues that Smith's novel reveals a general conundrum of a globalized postcolonial culture, where cultural stereotypes are scorned, but where recognizable identity markers are required by the ubiquity of the media and the necessity of 'identity building'.

The second and central cluster, 'Changing centres, changing peripheries and spaces in-between – Jewish writing from the Anglophone diaspora(s)', is subdivided according to the three geopolitical and cultural spheres perceived to be pertinent to conceptions of the Anglophone diaspora: 'America', 'Britain' and 'Postcolonia'. In this cluster the diversity of Jewish writing in English, its common ground, its 'otherness' and its affinities with its various production contexts, are probed. Although the emphasis of the collection is on transcending borders, the traditional geopolitical and cultural boundaries have been reproduced in its structure for the very reason to reveal where they are permeable and where transnational and transcultural border-crossings occur.

America, usually rather prominently represented in expositions of non-Hebrew Jewish literature, is considered here in three chapters. In the first of these, 'Literary symptomology and Jewish fiction: envy; or, the New Yiddish in America' (chapter 5), Emily Miller Budick posits that literary fictions are symptoms in the fully complex, already linguistically mediated sense of the word as it is employed by Slavoj Žižek and Jacques Lacan. Accordingly, Budick reads Cynthia Ozick's long short story 'Envy; or Yiddish in America' (1969) as a highly personal expression of what it means to be both Jewish and American (and also that hybrid phenomenon known as Jewish American). At the same time, she considers Ozick's story as partaking as well of the larger traumatic condition of Jewish history outside the United States, often expressed in languages other than English. She argues that the psychic phenomenon known as inherited trauma, a transgenerational phantom, in which the secrets of others enjoy encrypted existence within the self, is a relevant category in this context and that Ozick's story marks out a distinct territory both of symptomology and inherited trauma.

Exploring aspects of America as a contact zone in which Jewish literary production in English is situated, in 'Jewish/queer: thresholds of vulnerable identities in Tony Kushner's *Angels in America*' (chapter 6), Ranen Omer-Sherman discusses Kushner's two-part drama as a cultural production that is informed by its production history, audience reception and particularly by what Judaism in America has made of homosexuals, and the bearing of the play's many political and religious trajectories on contemporary Jewish identity. Omer-Sherman argues that *Angels in America* (1993) evokes an imaginatively porous America of open-mindedness and open-endedness gracefully allowing the audience (Jews, homosexuals and others) to exit through a door of hope in which loneliness, betrayal and banishment are supplanted by increasing prospects for cultural and individual stamina, reconciliation and reconstruction of America's lost promise.

Another threshold, the borderlines of what may be considered Jewish and non-Jewish literature, is probed by David Brauner in 'Fifty ways to see your lover: vision and revision in the fiction of Amy Bloom' (chapter 7). Arguing against the dominant critical discourse on Jewish American writing and the received classifiers of religion, roots, tradition and victimhood also pointed out by Cheyette, Brauner maintains that Bloom's work resists essentialist identity politics fashionable in contemporary multiculturalism and disappoints the 'moral/religious agenda' of the Jewish American critical establishment. Through a discussion of the variety of representations of vision and revision in Bloom's fiction with particular focus on the eye as a metaphor for the constantly shifting, perpetually metamorphosing self that she prefers to a historically, religiously or culturally determined, fixed entity, Brauner argues that the writer's heterogeneous and unorthodox fiction demands a revision of the Jewish American canon and a redefinition of Jewish textuality hinging on a more inclusive, pluralistic vision of what Jewish literature might be and do.

Britain is the focus of the second section of this part. 'Otherness and affiliation in Anglo-Jewish poetry' (chapter 8) are the subjects of Peter Lawson's exploration of the twentieth-century Anglo-Jewish poetic tradition. Lawson demonstrates that Anglo-Jewish poetry reveals a continuity of concerns which implies much about the Jewish diasporic condition and examines commonly expressed tensions between otherness and affiliation. Otherness, as Lawson suggests, relates to what the First World War poet Isaac Rosenberg identified as the 'ungraspable' nature of poetry itself, and a prevalent sense of secular Jewish identity as similarly uncategorizable. According to Lawson, countering such otherness is a common Anglo-Jewish affiliation with the diasporic narrative of exile and deferred return to a textually-imagined homeland. He argues that Anglo-Jewish poetry tends to follow a Romantic tradition and often evinces a struggle for Romantic transcendence of quotidian circumstances in order to be free of tensions in the English diaspora. Lawson further suggests that, because Modernism continued the Romantic tradition of speaking for those marginalized by English literature and society, Anglo-Jewish poets who consider themselves exilic, such as John Rodker and Elaine Feinstein, self-consciously affiliate with Modernism. In addition, he explores the exilic, Anglo-American Modernism with which several poets, such as Isaac Rosenberg and Jon Silkin, engage and reflects on the differing ways in which Anglo-Jewish poets, like Rosenberg and Siegfried Sassoon, look to Palestine and Israel.

The diasporic experience and the negotiation of Jewish identities in recent works of second- (or third-) generation Jewish writers in Britain are investigated by Oliver Groß in 'Diasporic voices? Second-generation Jewish authors in Britain' (chapter 9). Focusing particularly on Jeremy Gavron's *The Book of Israel* (2002), Linda Grant's *Remind Me Who I Am Again* (1998), Elena Lappin's *The Nose* (2001) and shorter fiction by Jonathan Treitel, Groß demonstrates in which ways representations of family histories, community formation, migration, the loss and recovery of personal memories, and the tribulations of minority politics are aspects pertinent to the transcultural and/or diasporic literature written by the younger generation of British authors with Jewish cultural-religious backgrounds. He argues that affiliation with and assimilation to either the host country or Jewish minority culture in that country are not essential concerns of second-generation Jewish writers in Britain and that their nuanced versions of liminal lives in the interstices between dominant and marginal cultures transcend received notions of diaspora as they are promulgated especially by Jewish American writing.

For want of a better word, the third section of this part has been called 'Postcolonia'. Yet the perhaps somewhat clumsy designation serves a purpose in that it pinpoints the underlying similarities of the cultural contexts of the Anglophone Jewish diaspora and its literature(s) and emphasizes their argued-for postcolonial status while highlighting, at the same time, the position of Jewish collectives as insider–outsiders. The ambiguities of this position, to some extent, seem to apply also to the Jewish presence in the land of Israel. In Mandate Palestine Jews experienced 'colonization' at the hands of the British while being, arguably, colonizers themselves. With the foundation of the 'Jewish state' begins what may be considered a postcolonial history. Finally, as has been suggested particularly in the ongoing post-Zionism debates (Silberstein 1999), the State of Israel itself may be held to be a colonial power.

The post-Zionism debates as well as notions of Jewish postcoloniality and Israeli colonialism are surveyed by Catherine Hezser in the first chapter of this section, 'Postcolonialism and the Irish Jewish experience' (chapter 10), as the background on which she develops her argument that Anglophone Jewish literature, because it shares the topics of home(lessness), assimilation, displacement and identity with postcolonial literatures, may be considered to be postcolonial too. In her analysis of three Irish Jewish novels, *To Next Year in Jerusalem* (1954) and in *A Land Not Theirs* (1986) by David Marcus, and Ronit Lentin's *Songs on the Death of Children* (1996), she demonstrates that their authors construe an analogy between the Irish and Jewish experiences of colonialism and postcoloniality and thematize the practices and consequences of colonialism for both Jews and the Irish. In Marcus's novels, as Hezser shows, the Zionist struggle for national independence and a Jewish homeland in the period of the British Mandate in Palestine is presented as an anti-colonial movement analogous to the Irish fight for freedom from the British; in Lentin's novel Israeli politics towards the Palestinians are likened to the colonialism of the British in Northern Ireland. Hezser concludes that in their novels both authors, if for different reasons, reject cultural hybridity, that they do not envisage its positive connotations, as emphasized by Homi Bhabha, and the cross-cultural possibilities it provides.

The postcolonial situation in South Africa seems to suggest to Jewish writers in this country a very different approach towards hybridity. Since the fall of apartheid in 1990 and the first democratic election in South Africa in 1994, the need for people of European ancestry to define themselves as 'white Africans', of which Nadine Gordimer has been writing for many years, has become apparent to almost all. In 'Jewish writers and postcolonial choices in South Africa' (chapter 11), Margaret Lenta enquires into the complicated position of Jewish writers in post-apartheid South Africa. The choices which confront all South African whites are those of emigrating, or of identifying with the preoccupations and problems of a predominantly black country undergoing reconstruction. The collapse of apartheid, as Lenta points out, marked the end of a period in which difference was strongly maintained in South Africa. In the ensuing period of national reconstruction, Lenta suggests, the constituent groups are likely to downplay their cultural differences even if this means losing a part of their inheritance and in this phase of the process of hybridization, South African literature, especially the literature of particular ethnic groups, is likely to change its character. Focusing first on the work of Nadine Gordimer and that of some Jewish writers (Joe Slovo, Ronnie Kasrils and Albie Sachs) who were exiled or silenced before 1990, Lenta then discusses the work also of the younger generation of Jewish writers (Karen Press and Damon Galgut) and suggests that Jewishness, in the sense which it might have had in the early decades of the twentieth century, is ceasing to matter in postcolonial South Africa. She argues that the special pressures of an immediately postcolonial state and of national reconstruction are as strongly felt by these younger writers as were the pressures of life in the African National Congress (ANC) in exile by an earlier generation.

The concerns of Jewish writers in Australia, examined by Elisa Morera de la Vall in 'Jewish literature in Australia' (chapter 12), once again, seem to be different. Despite its postcolonial 'history' this country is a stable political entity in which the creative imagination of writers of diverse ethnic backgrounds revolves around questions of integration and assimilation. Jewish writing in Australia, Morera suggests, is not transgressive in the sense of engaging in resistance to the host culture. Jewish writers in Australia, she posits, want to be heard not as coming from the margins but as part of a multicultural national culture. Focusing on eight writers, Morera provides a survey of the increasing variety and complexity of Australian Jewish writing in English which she traces back to its bilingual beginnings by examining the work of Pinchas Goldhar and Herz Bergner and the influence these writers had on the subsequent generation of Jewish writers in English. Proposing that Australian Jewish literature in English is at a crossroads, Morera points out that one of its central concerns has been the Holocaust which, she suggests, will recede, in time, from its prominent position, the literary imagination being kindled by other aspects of Jewishness.

To Australia large numbers of Jewish immigrants were admitted in the aftermath of the Second World War and the Shoah. This may be one reason for the Holocaust exercising the imagination of many Jewish writers in this country which differs, however, as Morera argues, from the Jewish American preoccupation with the Holocaust. While in Britain, Ireland or South Africa, the Shoah did not achieve the same prominence in Jewish writing, which focused rather on different aspects of Jewishness, in Canadian Jewish literature, perhaps because the dominion, like Australia, had admitted larger numbers of refugees after the Second World War, the Holocaust appears to be a recurring concern.

Focusing on 'Contemporary Jewish plays on the Canadian stage' (chapter 13), Albert-Reiner Glaap demonstrates that contemporary Jewish playwrights frequently turn to the Holocaust, but that most of these plays are more than merely dramatized documents of the Holocaust. As Glaap shows, they are reflections and assessments written with the benefit of hindsight by mostly young authors with different personal experiences of life and with challenging commitments to human values. As these works are contributions from different angles, be it that of survivors of the Holocaust, outsiders looking in or critical observers living in our day and age, Glaap investigates in how far they provide insight into the making of different Jewish identities and how these are shaped by transculturality. In stylistic and dramaturgical respect, Glaap shows most of these plays to reveal innovative concepts, unhampered by conventional approaches to drama and concludes that, generally speaking, Jewish plays are increasingly becoming a major asset to the 'polyphony' of Canadian drama.

The contribution of Anglophone Jewish authors to the 'polyphony' of Israeli literature is oftentimes neglected. In 'The Anglo-Israeli writer: double identities in troubled times' (chapter 14), Karen Alkalay-Gut argues that English writers in Israel, although in no way integrated into the culture of Israel, are nevertheless a part of the cultural life of Israel, and that their literature reflects and dialogues with this culture. Sketching the Anglo-Israeli writers' quandary that the specificity of these references closes off the possibility of their communicating with the non-Israeli world, while the Israeli reader and Israeli society are generally not exposed to these writings, Alkalay-Gut examines in this chapter the references to Israeli culture in the literature of Anglo-Israelis and the critical responses to this literature in order to determine the concept of self-identity and its accessibility to a potential readership.

In the third cluster, 'The "loquation" of culture', particular attention is given to the use of English as a language of Jewish literary production and to the Jewish writers' situation and self-positioning between languages and cultures.

The role of language in novels of Jewish-American writers in the twentieth century is explored by Pascal Fischer in 'Voices of identity: language in Jewish-American literature' (chapter 15). Based on the assumption that Jewish identity is very closely tied to language, Fischer argues that a thorough analysis of the ways in which Jewish authors deal with languages in their fiction provides deep insights into many facets of Jewish existence. Discussing the works of a wide variety of writers, among them Abraham Cahan, Anzia Yezierska, Henry Roth, Ludwig Lewisohn, Bernard Malamud, Saul Bellow, Cynthia Ozick and Philip Roth, Fischer shows that social and political developments and momentous events, even if they are not explicitly mentioned, are reflected in the novels by the use of languages: the ever deepening immersion of the Jews into the mainstream of American society, the annihilation of European Jewry and the establishment of the state of Israel all influenced the way Yiddish, German or Hebrew were perceived.

Already the main focus of Budick's contribution to this volume and discussed also by Fischer, Cynthia Ozick's story about the Yiddish poet Edelshtein in search of a translator is also Miriam Sivan's concern in 'The words to say it: the loss of language and power in Cynthia Ozick's 'Envy; or Yiddish in America' (chapter 16).

Sivan understands Ozick's story to be an exploration of the nature of language as one of the key elements of cultural identification and autonomy. Her particular interest is in the status of subcultures (i.e. Jewish culture or civilization) which live alongside, in varying degrees of subordination and reconciliation, a dominant culture. She argues that the Jews and the hybrid languages they developed in relation to the majority cultures (Yiddish in medieval Germany, Ladino in Spain) represent the tensions and overlaps between postcolonialism and globalization, for these very same indigenous languages became a way for Jews from different parts of the globe to communicate. In Sivan's reading of the story, Edelshtein, the narrator, comes to interpret his inability to secure an audience as a deliberate silencing and disempowerment; he begins to see it as part of a historical conspiracy against the Jews. In 'Envy; or Yiddish in America,' Sivan maintains, it is possible to see the convergence of political and literary forces attempting to strip an individual of his voice, his language and thus of his identity as well: Without a Yiddish audience, Edelshtein is a poet only to himself; without the power of translation, he is twice robbed.

This cluster, and indeed this book, is brought to a close with another reference to Israel. In 'Ricki Lake in Tel-Aviv: the alternative of Orly Castel-Bloom's Hebrew-English' (chapter 17), Karen Grumberg investigates the use of English in the Hebrew works of Orly Castel-Bloom. In the writer's novels English permeates Israeli Hebrew in different ways, not only on the level of the plot, but also on the level of the text itself. Castel-Bloom's use of untranslated English, transcribed in Latin characters, and her use of Americanized Hebrew have become trademarks of her style. In this chapter, Grumberg examines why an author such as Castel-Bloom, who is widely regarded in Israel as one of the most renowned younger writers of Hebrew, interjects specifically American English in her writing. She maintains that Castel-Bloom uses American English in her works in the context of *presence* rather than past-ness. Her stories and novels portray an Israel which, though not entirely de-historicized, is highly apathetic to its Jewish history. The shallow superficiality that is one of the consequences of this apathy has much in common with the widespread political and historical apathy in the United States, particularly as it is represented in Hollywood. English, for Castel-Bloom, is not a language that has anything to do with Jewishness or Jewish history. It is the language of movies and of television – not of the Bible, not of Eastern Europe or the Holocaust, not of the ancient Canaanites, and certainly not of her Egyptian parents. Ultimately, as Grumberg demonstrates, Castel-Bloom's use of English deflates the belief in the Hebrew language as the crowning jewel of Zionist-Israeli culture, the supposed unifying force of a diverse nation: It is precisely because English is so unattached and, therefore, meaningless, that she uses it.

Instead of a conclusion

This collection is quite deliberately not conceived as encyclopaedic. It rather focuses on individual case studies, producing a mosaic effect, contextualized and commented by the introduction. However, to document the scope of Anglophone

Jewish writing and to stimulate further academic interest in the subject, the volume is rounded off with an admittedly eclectic list of 'Anglophone Jewish writers' as an invitation to further research and study, and a 'Bibliography' including suggestions for further reading, reference works and research aids. There is no conclusion in this volume because it has been conceived as a beginning, and its individual contributions are meant to initiate, not to foreclose, the dialogue on Anglophone Jewish literature.

Finally, it should be said that I am feeling very ambiguously about this book being party to denying Anglophone Jewish writers their mere 'humanity'. In *The Counterlife*, Philip Roth echoes Jean-Paul Sartre's question whether Jews, if they existed at all, were to be considered foremost as Jews or as human beings. He has his narrator ask: 'Why can't Jews with their Jewish problems be human beings with their human problems?' (1987: 228). There may be many answers to this question or, perhaps, none. Yet, I am sure, that some approximations are to be found in that rich and varied body of Jewish literature on which this collection offers a few glimpses.

Notes

1 A contraction of 'location' and the Latin 'loquor' ('to talk, to speak'; cf. 'locution'), this self-fashioned 'neologism' alludes to Homi Bhabha's *The Location of Culture* (1994). It will subsequently be used to signify the inseparable connection of language and culture and to refer to the Jewish writers' situation and self-positioning between languages and cultures.

2 See, for example, Bryan Cheyette's (2003: 51–2) criticism of the 'Americanization' of the Jewish diaspora.

3 Green discusses this allegation, made by Israeli critics, with regard to his potential 'complicity' as a translator of Hebrew works into English.

4 The postcoloniality of Jewish literature has recently been discussed, for example, by Boyarin (2000), or in Cheyette and Marcus (1998). See also my forthcoming study on *Zion's Fiction. Postcolonial Fictions of Jewish Identity*.

5 John Hollander (1988; 1994: 46), although only with reference to a 'Jewish literary culture in English', expresses a similar sentiment. Intriguingly, V.S. Naipaul (1962; 1969: 29) made a similar, and much contested, statement in his *The Middle Passage* where he claimed that 'history is built around achievement and creation; and nothing was created in the West Indies and nothing will ever be created'. For a discussion of similarities between Caribbean and Jewish literatures in English, see, for example, Lehmann (1998: 101–19).

6 Unless otherwise indicated all translations from German are my own.

7 Yiddish, a common vernacular (*la'az*) of mainly Eastern European Jews (*Ashkenazim*) and based largely on medieval German and on Hebrew, was spoken up to the Shoah by the large majority of Jews; in the 1890s by about 75 per cent, see Rubinstein (1996: 3). Zionism and its promotion of Hebrew as an internal cultural language further diminished Yiddish, although in the so-called 'Jewish language war' enacted during the first decades of the twentieth century a strong case was made for the Eastern European Jewish vernacular. Today Yiddish is spoken mostly in Jewish Orthodox communities. For a history of Yiddish see Weinreich (1980).

8 According to Rubinstein (1996: 3), in the 1990s c. 48 per cent of the world's Jewish population were English speakers, c. 30 per cent were Hebrew and c. 3.5 per cent Yiddish speakers.

9 Ozick's phrase is probably intended to echo A.M. Klein's 'In Praise of the Diaspora (An Undelivered Memorial Address)' (1953). Klein, in his 'eulogy' emphatically opposes the final negation of the diaspora (*shlilat ha-galut*) put forward by the 'new' Israeli Jews and their claims to the exclusive authenticity of their 'Jewish' identity. Instead, Klein understands the diaspora to have been, and to continue to be, a necessary formative experience and inspiration of Jewish life, even after the cataclysm of the Shoah. For a more detailed discussion of Klein's text, see Stähler (2003: 190–2).

10 The author followed this up in another essay in which she suggests as 'the new alternative' the 'fusion of the offerings of the Enlightenment' with 'Jewish primacy', Ozick (1983; 1991: 236–7). To Ozick, the English language remained her 'everything', as she maintained in the Preface to her *Bloodshed and Other Novellas*; yet it is also, to her, a 'Christian language. When I write in English', she states resignedly, 'I live in Christendom', Ozick (1976: 9). For a discussion of Ozick's embrace of English in the larger context of Jewish American literature, see Wirth-Nesher (1998: 215).

11 Jaffé's use of the masculine pronoun is, of course, common in his time; however, in the light of Daniel Boyarin's (2000) research in the discourse of masculinity in early Zionism, the gendering of the Jewish author as male, in contrast to anything that may be construed as effeminate, seems to be significant and is therefore reproduced here.

12 Jaffé quotes almost verbatim from Langbehn (1890: 41–2).

13 For the *Kunstwart* debate, see Schoeps et al. (2002).

14 Heinrich von Treitschke, editor of the *Preußische Jahrbücher*, and the liberal historian Theodor Mommsen were the main protagonists of the *Berliner Antisemitismusstreit*. It had been sparked off by von Treitschke's anti-Semitic reaction to the eleventh volume of the monumental *Geschichte der Juden von den ältesten Zeiten bis zur Gegenwart* (1853–75) by the German Jewish historian Heinrich Graetz. Von Treitschke's assault was instrumental in first preparing the stage for a widespread anti-Semitism in circles of German academia and the bourgeoisie. For a comprehensive documentation, see Krieger (2003).

15 The first prayer book to eliminate or alter references to the return to Zion was that of the New Israelite Temple Society of Hamburg, published in Hebrew and German in 1819 by S.I. Fränkel and I.M. Bresslau.

16 Wilson himself prefers the designation 'British-born American' (2005: 157), but I would argue that his preoccupation with the British colonial mentality and its encounter with conceptions of Jewishness in Palestine make at least both of his novels works of British Jewish fiction.

17 For a further development of this argument see my forthcoming study on *Zion's Fiction. Postcolonial Fictions of Jewish Identity*.

18 See also Sicher (1985) and the title of his study: *Beyond Marginality*.

19 For a discussion of Steiner's argument see, for example, Ezrahi (2000a: 11).

20 Indeed, Chanes (1999: 388) claims that 'the polarized model of "Israel and the Diaspora" – regnant for almost fifty years – is no longer appropriate (if it ever was [...])', because it 'is too oppositional for the late 1990s, and reflects the political and social dynamics of previous decades'.

21 With the establishment of Jewish statehood the conception of *galut*, the enforced exile, became obsolete because exile, now understood as diaspora or *golah*, ultimately appears to be 'self-inflicted'. Although the wish for a return to the home country has been identified in recent critical opinion as a constitutive element of 'diaspora', and has, of course, been highly significant in the Jewish context, it appears for many Jews living in the Anglophone diaspora, as Avtar Brah observes in a more general context, that ' "home" is a mythic space of desire in the diasporic imagination' and 'a place of no-return even if it is possible to visit the geographical territory that is seen as the place of "origin" ' (1997: 192). For a discussion of Jewish non-return with a particular view on the American context, see Galchinsky (1998: 199–200). For definitions

of 'diaspora', including the desire for an eventual return to the homeland, see, for example, Safran (1991: 83–99) and Cohen (1997: 23–6).

22 According to Jörn Rüsen (2001: 10), language, as a medium of historical narrative, appears to be instrumental in community building, the formation of identity and the construction of meaning through interpretive patterns specific to different temporal contexts, which Rüsen identifies as the most important functions of historical consciousness.

23 Usually, the term 'double diaspora' is understood 'quantitatively' rather than 'qualitatively' and alludes to consecutive displacements within the diaspora, see, for example, Lehmann (1998: 101, 111) and the discussion of 'double or even triple diasporization' in Fludernik (2003: xxvi).

24 Wirth-Nesher falls back on the contextualization of Jewish literature as the most important feature for any definition: 'Its characterization as Jewish will depend upon the reader and all of the circumstances of its reception [. . .], we simply cannot read outside a framework of expectations dictated by familiar categories. While the categories themselves may be unstable and problematic, they are an inherent part of the reading process' (1994b: 5). She concludes her introduction with the declaration of intent 'to undermine any one essentialist view of Jewish culture, while at the same time tracing the distinctive features of the act of self-definition in recent Jewish literary history. Each of these definitions is an invention that answers specific needs of time and place. What *is* Jewish literature? Why do you want to know? Who said such a thing exists anyway? And why not ask?' (12).

25 Heidegger's term (1956: §§28–30) is usually translated as 'state of mind' (Macquarrie and Robinson), 'attunement' (Stambaugh) or 'affectedness' (Dreyfus).

26 For a more detailed discussion, see Wirth Nesher (2006: 5–7).

2 On being a Jewish critic[1]

Bryan Cheyette

Three images have haunted me during the writing of this chapter. The first is taken from Isaac Rosenberg's 'Break of Day in the Trenches', which he wrote in 1916 as a private soldier in the British Army during the First World War. In this poem, Rosenberg gives the reader an ironic self-image of someone who is between cultures and who is unable to assimilate, even in wartime, into any one nation:

> Droll rat, they would shoot you if they knew
> Your cosmopolitan sympathies.
> Now you have touched this English hand
> You will do the same to the German –
> Soon, no doubt, if it be your pleasure
> To cross the sleeping green between.

Rosenberg's poetry is full of such subversive mergings across seemingly incongruous domains. His self-fashioning as a droll, cosmopolitan rat is an act of extraordinary imaginative poise in the most extreme circumstances.[2]

The second image is taken from Kafka's 'Metamorphosis' (1915), when the metamorphosed Gregor – a giant insect – inadvertently begins to cross the boundary from his bedroom into the living room as he becomes transfixed by his sister playing the violin. 'Was he an animal, that music had such an effect on him?', Gregor wonders. In a letter to Max Brod, Kafka famously described his generation of Germanized Jews as four-legged animals: '[T]heir hind legs were still mired in their father's Jewishness and their thrashing forelegs found no new ground. The ensuing despair became their inspiration' (cit. Bauman 1991: 86).[3] Kafka understood only too well the empty spaces in which his characters were suspended.

The final image is taken from Primo Levi's *The Periodic Table* (1975), a book about impurity with a knowing impure form. In the Zinc chapter, at the beginning of the book, Levi is a young student performing his first experiments and is drawn into broader areas of speculation by the resistance of Zinc to chemical breakdown:

> One could draw from [this experiment] two philosophical conclusions: the praise of purity, which protects from evil like a coat of mail; the praise

> of impurity, which gives rise to changes, in other words, to life. I discarded the first, disgustingly moralistic, and I lingered to consider the second, which I found more congenial. In order for the wheel to turn, for life to be lived, impurities are needed. [...] Dissension, diversity, the grain of salt and mustard are needed: Fascism does not want them, forbids them, and that's why you're not a Fascist; it wants everybody to be the same.
>
> (34)

Culture as purity, culture as impurity. It is these two clashing versions of culture that I will examine throughout this chapter. Its title, 'On being a Jewish critic', is meant to be a provocation rather than assert identity. The one thing that we can say with any certainty about Jewish identity is that it is always in dispute and open to redefinition and reinterpretation (whether religiously, ethnically, culturally, nationally). Being a Jewish critic does not mean that I claim a spurious personal authenticity, nor do I assert the primacy of an individual identity. It is in these terms that 'On being a Jewish critic' is provocative. If I am regarded as a Jewish critic, then it is what I do with that regard which is the subject of this chapter.

David Hollinger, in a valuable book called *Postethnic America* (1995), quotes Ishmael Reed on Alex Haley's best-selling genealogy *Roots* (1976). Reed argues that, 'if Alex Haley had traced his father's bloodline, he would have travelled 12 generations back to, not Gambia, but Ireland' (Hollinger 1995: 19). This Hollinger refers to as 'Haley's Choice'. Haley chose not to trace his father's ancestry back to Ireland but took the matrilineal route to Gambia. I was struck by Reed's comments because I, too, could trace the Irish ancestry on my mother's side, for at least three generations, and then, I suppose, I could travel to Spain for a few more branches on one of the family trees (to spice up the Eastern European stetlekh on my father's side), but this would have been patently ridiculous. The point is that all public identities are constructed and partial choices, which, though this is 'known' in theory in the academy, still does not prevent a rather too fashionable and all-pervasive identity politics. For this reason, Gillian Rose began her invaluable *Judaism and Modernity* (1993) by refusing to participate in the current academic fashion of declaring one's personal identity.

As an undergraduate looking for a possible doctoral research topic, I was advised to write a thesis (in the words of my adviser) 'from the heart'. This was 1980, and the chances of getting a job in 'Thatcher's Britain' at the end were, to say the least, rather slim. I have thought about this moment a great deal when writing this essay – when I was thrown back on my own resources by the institution (when 'my heart' was asked to take the load, as it were) as it seems to coincide with the growth of a university-based identity politics. (What could be a more authentic version of the self than that which is 'written from the heart'?) There is nothing more individualistic than 'Haley's Choice' – which is, after all, a personal and very deliberate act of will.

How can I speak on the subject of Jewish literature when, as soon as it is named, it is reduced to the banalities of cultural conformity? At its worst, this conformity speaks in the name of closed cultures, roots and traditions.

Hana Wirth-Nesher, in her standard collection *What is Jewish Literature?* (1994), entitles her introductory essay 'Defining the Indefinable' and proceeds to offer indefinable definitions of Jewish literature based on nation, race, language, ethnicity, religion, motif and thematics, all of which fail in their task of encompassing the Jewish writers and critics in her anthology. But this defining uncertainty seems to me to be the point and helps us to understand the impurity of culture.

There are, of course, many Jewish thinkers who speak with a misguided certainty about the purity of Jewish culture. Norman Podhoretz, for instance, dismissed the generation of American-Jewish critics and writers who published immediately after the war with the following typically combative words:

> They praised Maimonides and Sholem Aleichem [. . .] in terms of St Thomas, Wordsworth, Blake and Chekhov. In other words, before they would permit themselves the luxury of investigating their own origins, they had to be persuaded that these origins were objects of general interest. They had, as it were, to get the smell of garlic out of the breath of Jewish culture.
>
> (Cit. Brauner 2001: 12–13)

Podhoretz is speaking about a range of critics – Irving Howe, Alfred Kazin, Leslie Fiedler, and Lionel Trilling – all of whom I value highly. What troubles me about Podhoretz's blunt dismissal is that it was done in the name of roots and origins and the purity and self-sufficiency of Jewish particularity. It is not surprising that, shortly after this statement was made (in the mid-1970s), Podhoretz became a cheerleader for Reaganite America and Beginite Israel.

Ruth Wisse's recent *The Modern Jewish Canon* (2000) is written from the same perspective as Podhoretz's piece. Wisse speaks with certainty about what she calls the 'Jewish experience' (14) or a 'centrally Jewish perspective' (19), and she firmly believes that her canon helps us to understand the main historical events affecting Jews. This facile relationship between literature and history becomes the clarion call of her book. As she says in the introduction: 'Modern Jewish literature is the repository of modern Jewish experience. It is the most complete way of knowing the inner life of the Jews' (4). Literature is important, therefore, insofar as it sheds light on history. What is most depressing about this reading of literature is not just the circular loop between literature and history but the implied reduction of Jewish history to the question of a single national culture. She believes that 'language [is] synonymous with national identity' (7), and, to this end, she argues that 'Hebrew has begun to dominate Jewish literature, just as Israel now largely determines the future of the Jewish people' (29).

And so the argument goes: literature helps us to understand the great events of Jewish history that are, in the end, reduced to the creation of the Jewish state. Here the many different kinds of cultural histories that make up diasporic Jewry (what Podhoretz objected to) are replaced with the certainties of national history, and the mixture and plurality of diasporic Jewry is reduced to a single story of national redemption. Although this particular story of redemption becomes something of a master narrative, other kinds of redemption are ruled out of court. We are told unsurprisingly that the Christianized Proust must remain outside Wisse's Jewish canon, whereas Kafka is allowed a walk-on role via his Hebrew teacher. To show how seriously she defends the borders and purity of her Jewish canon, Wisse refuses to include Bernard Malamud's fiction because he 'imagines the Jew as the ideal Christian' and therefore 'nudges his novel towards Christianity' (16). (She is thinking in particular of the suffering Yakov Bok in *The Fixer* [1966].)

Zygmunt Bauman, in his *Legislators and Interpreters* (1987), distinguishes between two kinds of modern cultural critics. If Wisse is par excellence a legislator – certain of her cultural power in relation to the boundaries of the nation-state, subduing everything that is ambiguous and impure – then the alternative critical position is that of the interpreter, who is not confined to a single interpretative community but straddles many possible communities. Whereas Wisse's story of exile and return has a beginning, a middle and an end, the interpreter refuses a single, redemptive ending. This legislative act of closure, according to Sidra DeKoven Ezrahi, threatens the very storytelling enterprise itself: 'an enterprise that remains alive [. . .] by suspending endings'. Here, then, we have two radically different versions of the Jewish critic. The first stresses the national territory – and the purity of the Jewish language and homeland; the other embraces a 'meandering', 'never-ending' story. The choice can be said to be between those who value the 'rites of reading and interpretation' over the 'rites of pilgrimage or return to a territory' (2000a: 10–11).

In her *Booking Passage* (2000), an exemplary account of Jewish literature in plural and unbounded terms, Ezrahi is most concerned with those Jewish writers who go beyond the dialectic of ends and beginnings. This story without an end or beginning reminds me of Israel Zangwill's *Dreamers of the Ghetto* (1898), a fictionalized history made up of a group of heterodox Jews – Uriel Acosta, Benjamin Disraeli, Heinrich Heine, the biblical Joseph, Ferdinand Lassalle, Spinoza, Sabbatai Sevi – converts, revolutionaries or false messiahs. These figures represent what Zangwill called 'the middle path', somewhere between Judaism and Christianity, not unlike my own imagined canon of disruptive and unplaceable writers, poets and song-makers.[4]

My aim is to locate the impurity of Jewish culture in relation to received definitions of Western culture and the Anglo-American literary canon. The two figures who will help me in my task are Matthew Arnold and Lionel Trilling, a non-Jew who Judaized himself and a Jew who de-Judaized himself, both in the name of cosmopolitanism. These figures are still considered to be the most influential literary and cultural critics of their respective periods (Arnold in the late nineteenth century, Trilling in the mid-twentieth century). It is with reference to these two individuals that I will think again about the uneasy relationship between Jewishness, culture and impurity that, as we have seen, haunted the imaginations of my representative diasporic writers of the twentieth century: Rosenberg, Kafka and Levi.

The importance of being Arnold

I return to the nineteenth-century cultural critic, poet and schools inspector, Matthew Arnold (who opened my first book), because he is both a legislator – quite literally, as a schools inspector – and an interpreter. His scrupulous generalizations have meant that 'critics of the future' (in his words) could interpret Arnold in the most various ways possible. In recent years, for example, we have had Geoffrey Hartman's midrashic Arnold; Robert Young's multicultural or ethnic Arnold; Jonathan Freedman's cosmopolitan Arnold; and Michael Ragussis's Disraelian Arnold.

Arnold's best known work, *Culture and Anarchy* (1869), remains a book that is endlessly interpreted and reinterpreted and can be read in a variety of ways but always against itself. At its heart is the tension between Hebraism and Hellenism that Arnold argued was the essential creative dialectic of Western culture. His call for the ideal balance of Hebraism and Hellenism (or Judaism and Christianity, Greek and Jew, Aryan and Semite) is couched in surprisingly indeterminate terms. As he states in a well known quotation:

> Hebraism and Hellenism – between these two points of influence moves our world. At one time it feels more powerfully the attraction of one of them, at another time of the other; and it ought to be, though it never is, evenly and happily balanced between them.
>
> (Arnold 1869; 1965: 163–4)

In the last chapters of the book, Arnold attempted to put an end to this uncertainty by holding up the liberal nation-state as the ideal vehicle for institutionalizing culture.

The cosmopolitan Arnold, as we will see, thought of culture as existing outside the institutions of the state, influencing all classes equally. Culture would ultimately replace Christianity as the means of creating a coherent society. The nation-centred Arnold, however, thought of culture as existing within the institutions and boundaries of the state, with Jews (here thought of racially as Semites) outside the pantheon of culture. (Arnold especially feared London's East End immigrant population in this regard.) Whereas the former Arnold valued free-thinking across all boundaries, the latter Arnold stressed harmony and order within certain fixed borders and institutions.

The problem for Arnold was that he never quite knows whether to become a Hebraic legislator or a Hellenic interpreter, whether 'spontaneity' or 'strictness of consciousness' was needed to achieve his ideal of culture. If culture is associated with home, order, cohesion and stability, which are policed by the nation-state (and limited by Arnold's frequent use of a racial discourse), then the opposite of culture becomes a state of homelessness, where anarchy will persist and disrupt a sense of tradition and the supposed coherence of the state. The mistake, however, is to assume that there was only one Arnold writing his cultural criticism. After all, Arnold called his book (once he had collected together its individual chapters) *Culture 'and' Anarchy* not *Culture 'or' Anarchy*. What I want to show is that both of these versions of culture, embracing home and homelessness, power and powerlessness, purity and impurity, are part of Arnold's legacy. I'll give just two examples to show what I mean.

Many critics who followed Arnold interpreted *Culture and Anarchy* in the narrowest possible way, making culture static and fixed within certain boundaries. One example of such narrow interpretations (to me a low point) can be found in 1949, when the Fellows of the Library of Congress in the United States unashamedly awarded Ezra Pound the first Bollingen Prize for poetry with the following justification:

> To permit other considerations than that of poetic achievement to sway the decision [to award Pound the Bollingen Prize] would destroy the significance of the award and would in principle deny the validity of that objective perception of value on which civilized society must rest.
>
> (Library of Congress 1949)

Here we have 'an objective perception of [poetic] value', with the legislative critic deciding what is valuable and what is not. The pure and transcendent realm of culture has nothing to do with Pound's fascist politics of only a few years earlier. Pound, for most of the 1940s, had been a willing propagandist for the Nazis in Mussolini's Italy, so it is hard to find a more extreme version of the asocial or purifying definition of culture that is deemed to be beyond the purview of society or politics.

A radically different response to Arnold can be found in the work of C.L.R. James, the teacher, political activist, critic and journalist (in the Caribbean, Britain and the United States) who was born in Trinidad in 1901. In one of his best-known books, *Beyond a Boundary* (1963), he recalls the influence of Thomas and Matthew Arnold in the Caribbean in the 1930s and 1940s (in other words the same time as the Bollingen Prize was being awarded) (20, 28, 121, 161–70). James's work is preoccupied with what he regards as the processes of creolization and hybridization in the Caribbean, and he specifically employed Thomas Arnold (while acknowledging the influence of *Culture and Anarchy*) in this process. In *Beyond a Boundary*, Caribbean cricket emerges as a field of play (both literally and metaphorically) where Western culture undergoes many strange and wonderful permutations (Dash 1996: 53–4). Others have noted that Matthew Arnold's Hellenic ideal of the 'free play' of the mind is not dissimilar to Jacques Derrida's own deconstructive 'free play', but what James offers is a specifically Caribbean version of 'free play' using the resonant metaphor of a boundary-less colonized cricket team.

These are, I believe, the two versions of culture that clash in Arnold's work. First, culture as purity, an asocial essence within the nation-state that somehow extends seamlessly into the colonies and back again to the metropolitan centre. Second, culture as impurity, which James promoted from his cosmopolitan and heterogeneous perspective.

The Arnold that interests me is the Arnold who refigured himself as an 'alien', as culturally impure, who, as an insider-outsider, stood at the heart of English national culture and also promoted his version of culture from an 'alien' perspective. To illustrate this, I will look at the well known ending of Arnold's essay, 'The Function of Criticism at the Present Time', written in 1864 and published a year later. It was the horrified response to this essay in his *Essays in Criticism* (1865), when Arnold was lambasted for being unpatriotic and un-English, that resulted in *Culture and Anarchy* – in part a response to the charge of being un-English. Arnold famously concludes 'The Function of Criticism' with not uncharacteristic despair at the possibility of 'genuine [literary] creation' in contemporary English culture:

> The epochs of Aeschylus and Shakespeare make us feel their pre-eminence. In an epoch like those [there] is, no doubt, the true life of literature; there is the promised land, towards which criticism can only beckon. That promised land [. . .] will not be ours to enter, and we shall die in the wilderness; but to have desired to enter it, to have saluted from afar, is already, perhaps, the best distinction among contemporaries; it will certainly be the best title to esteem with posterity.
>
> (1993: 51)

Thus, as Jonathan Freedman has so ably shown in *The Temple of Culture* (2000), we have Arnold's self-fashioning as a second Moses who cannot enter the 'promised land' of culture but can only, as an alienated critic, salute the cultural 'promised land' from the wilderness of contemporary English philistinism. One should not underestimate just how radical a statement this was in the 1860s. At a time when Britain was at the height of its imperial powers, Arnold was making a forceful case for the parochiality and irrelevance of English culture. To quote from 'The Function of Criticism' again:

> By the nature of things, as England is not all the world, much of the best that is known and thought in the world cannot be of English growth, must be foreign. [. . .] The English critic of literature, therefore must dwell much on foreign thought.
>
> (1993: 49)

Instead of the civilizing mission of colonial England, which assumes that England, or at least the English language, might just be 'all the world', Arnold identifies with unbounded cosmopolitans such as Heine, Spinoza, Ernest Renan and the actress Rachel. In a poem written to the Jewish actress at about the same time as 'The Function of Criticism', Arnold eulogizes the 'contending powers' within Rachel:

> Germany, France, Christ, Moses, Athens, Rome.
> The strife, the mixture in her soul, are ours;
> Her genius and her glory are her own.

This cosmopolitan perspective, an alternative to the British Empire, meant that Arnold in *Culture and Anarchy* describes the purveyors of culture (including himself) as 'aliens': 'persons who are mainly led, not by their class spirit, but by a general humane spirit, by the love of human perfection' (Arnold 1865; 1962: 334–5). And, in these terms, he also emphasizes his own racial hybridity and that of the English in general: 'And we, then, what are we? what is England [...] why, my very name expresses that peculiar Semitico-Saxon mixture which makes the typical Englishman' (Arnold 1896; 1965: 146).

My point is that Arnold, by writing as an insider-outsider, from a cosmopolitan perspective, made it impossible to locate his ideal of culture within the nation-state – which has indeed made him, arguably, a 'critic of the future'. The figure of the cosmopolitan at the heart of a supposedly pure and homogenous English culture took many forms after the death of Arnold, not least as part of the history of modernism. During his lifetime, the tension between the nation and cosmopolitanism structured George Eliot's *Daniel Deronda* (1876), an extraordinarily divided story (based as it is around competing national and cosmopolitan versions of Jewishness) that is the first and best reinterpretation of *Culture and Anarchy*.

Two decades after Arnold's death, his biographer G.W.E. Russell confirms that the 'famous conjunction' of Hebraism and Hellenism was, by 1904, 'closely associated with [Arnold's] memory', even to the extent that the Arnold family was itself thought to be of 'Jewish extraction'. Arnold's 'remote ancestors', Russell tells us, had 'emigrated from Germany to Lowestoft' and might well have belonged to 'the ancient Race' (162–3). George Meredith, in a letter to Lucien Wolf, described the Arnolds as descending from what he called (after Disraeli) 'the Arab Jew' (1970, 3: 1339). Hilaire Belloc, 20 years later, also Judaized what he called the 'Arnold Families' (1922: 47) – but then again Belloc tended to Judaize virtually everyone he disagreed with. However, the Judaizing of Arnold is, after all, not unlike the plot of *Daniel Deronda*, where the harmonious 'contending forces' of Victorian England come together in its hero. As Lionel Trilling was to argue, *Daniel Deronda* was proof positive of the efficacy of race over culture:

> The English public had a conclusive demonstration of how race might work when Daniel Deronda, reared as an English aristocrat and believing himself to be of Spanish 'blood,' began in maturity to exhibit specific Jewish qualities – chiefly a Prophetic morality – and found himself, despite his complete ignorance of a common ancestry, irresistibly drawn to the Jews.
>
> (1939: 233)

Here at the heart of a supposedly pure English national culture was the figure of the cosmopolitan Jew.

Five decades after *Daniel Deronda*, James Joyce published *Ulysses* (1922), which once again scandalized its readers by placing the ultimate cosmopolitan, Leopold Bloom, at the heart of European culture. Joyce took to its logical extreme the Judaized rewriting of Greek mythology or Hellenism by making his Odysseus an unplaceable Jew. When confronted by the Citizen in Barney Kiernan's pub and forced to define his nationality (on pain of a beating), Bloom imagines himself in a long line of cosmopolitan non-Jewish Jews like himself – Moses Mendelssohn, Karl Marx, Spinoza and 'the Saviour' – all, he says, are Jews 'like me'. Here we have another version of Arnold's cultured aliens or Zangwill's heterodox Jews. Bloom is, after all, described by Joyce as a 'cultured, allaround-man' in *Ulysses*, which is not a million miles from Arnold's cultured Jews (Joyce 1984, 1: 505; 1984, 2: 735).

But whereas Joyce embraced Jewish cosmopolitanism and placed it at the heart of his impure version of culture, others saw the same cosmopolitanism as threatening the purity of English culture. This can be seen in an extraordinary outburst by C.S. Lewis in the 1920s, who rewrites T.S. Eliot and the modernist avant-garde as a group of cosmopolitan aliens:

> Assuredly [Eliot] is one of the enemy: and all the more dangerous because he is sometimes disguised as a friend. And this offence is exaggerated by attendant circumstances, such as his arrogance. And (you will further forgive me) it is further aggravated for an Englishman by the recollection that Eliot stole upon us, a foreigner and a neutral, while we were at war – obtained, I have my wonders how, a job in the Bank of England [sic] – and became (am I wrong) the advance guard of the invasion since carried out by his natural friends and allies, the Steins and Pounds [...] the Parisian riff-raff of denationalized Irishmen and Americans who have perhaps given Western Europe her death wound.
>
> (Cit. Ricks 1988: 197–8)

Here Eliot, like 'the Jew', is a 'disguised' enemy who wheedles his way into key financial institutions and, with a few alien co-conspirators, helps to bring about the collapse of European civilization. But this is a story of endless projection and displacement. Lewis, himself a 'denationalized Irishman' (as Christopher Ricks points out), projects his own sense of foreignness on to the son of a Hebraized Unitarian (T.S. Eliot), who in turn projects his own sense of alien cosmopolitanism onto what he calls 'free-thinking Jews' and even onto the Judaized Matthew Arnold, whom he could never forgive (in essay after essay) for replacing Christianity with culture. It is these projections and displacements that I will now explore in postwar America.

Matthew Arnold in the United States

One way of thinking of the cultural and literary history of cosmopolitanism, which I have outlined, is that it came to an end after the murder of the vast majority of Diaspora Jews. Geoffrey Hartman has summarized this post-Holocaust perspective in an essay on cultural relativism:

> The fact is that cosmopolitanism [...] has not succeeded as a creed. The attractive notion of a 'citizen of the world' failed to overcome the suspicion

> that this type masks a self-deceiving Luftmensch. The worst of nationalisms arose in Germany, where the cosmopolitan ideal of Bildung (or cultural growth) was strongest; and that fortifies our sense of its failure.
>
> (1995: 72)

Here we have the dismissal of the cosmopolitan creed at its starkest, with the Arnoldian ideal of culture or *Bildung* especially failing. Nationalism, its polar opposite, has triumphed. The title of Hartman's *Criticism in the Wilderness* (1980) is taken from Arnold's 'The Function of Criticism', but Hartman speculates that 'the wilderness' might actually be 'the promised land' for the contemporary critic (14–15). In the wilderness that is our post-culture (to borrow George Steiner's phrase), all we are left with are a few individuals such as Steiner or Hartman, each a kind of survivor (Hartman coming to England from Germany on the Kindertransport in 1938; Steiner leaving Paris for the United States with his parents in 1940). Both are self-conscious cultural couriers shuttling between the lost worlds of central European humanism (Prague, Vienna, Paris and Berlin) and Anglo-American culture. Steiner's *Language and Silence* (1967) reads Matthew Arnold after the war with typical bombast:

> The ultimate of political barbarism grew from the core of Europe. [. . .] This is of obvious and appalling relevance to the study or teaching of literature. It compels us to ask whether knowledge of the best that has been thought and said does, as Matthew Arnold asserted, broaden and refine the resources of the human spirit.
>
> (Steiner 1967; 1979: 23)

Hartman, in his *Criticism in the Wilderness*, notes with his usual modest authority: 'When we set Arnold beside Nietzsche, or set I.A. Richards and F.R. Leavis, beside George Lukacs and Walter Benjamin, the differences cannot be overlooked' (1980: 5). There is a clear contrast between the cultural pessimism of the Frankfurt School – of Adorno, Benjamin and Horkheimer (which Steiner echoes) – and Arnold's optimistic belief that culture would renew itself in a new epoch and subsequently redeem the critic in the wilderness. If we place this Arnoldian sense of cultural renewal next to Benjamin's oft-quoted dictum – 'there is no document of civilization which is not *at the same time* a document of barbarism' – we have a sense of the gulf that separates Arnold and Benjamin. It is certainly Benjamin who has been taken as speaking for our age – our postcolonial, post-Holocaust age – who understands only too well the complicity of culture, in all of its forms, with barbarism.

But I would like to contrast this post-Holocaust dismissal of the cosmopolitan tradition with the considerable figure of Lionel Trilling, easily the most influential American literary critic of the postwar generation until his death in 1975, who single-handedly adopted and redeemed Arnold in the United States. The story of Trilling's tenure has become the stuff of legend. Trilling, as is well known, was the first Jewish tenured professor of English at Columbia (or just about any other major university) in the 1940s, after being told that as a 'Jew, Marxist and a Freudian' – the archetypal cosmopolitan – he would never be 'happy' in an English department and that he would therefore not be offered tenure.[5]

After this rebuff, the frantic lobbying that Trilling engaged in to gain his position at Columbia was astonishing (given his later reticence and patrician detachment). He sent the published version of his doctoral thesis on Arnold to the president of Columbia University who, not knowing that he was a Jew, could not understand why the author of such a definitive 400-page study was not being offered a job. Trilling later commented that if his name had been the same as his grandfather's, Israel Cohen, the Columbia president would have acted quite differently. Matthew Arnold was, literally, Trilling's ticket into the pantheon of culture as represented by the Ivy League English departments in the United States. Such departments were made up of the kind of individuals who awarded Ezra Pound a prestigious poetry prize in the late 1940s but, in exactly the same period, refused to employ any Jewish academics in their universities. No wonder Trilling's professorship was regarded as a victory. As Susanne Klingenstein states: 'It marked the happy ending of a painful conquest, the fall of the WASP bastille' (1991: 198).

The difficulties that Trilling had in writing his account of Arnold are also quite legendary. As Mark Krupnick has noted, in 'successive revisions [of his manuscript on Arnold], Trilling found himself renouncing Marx's idea of the dialectic and interpreting Arnold positively in Arnold's own terms. But the concept of the dialectic remained' (1986: 51). Trilling's mother, who moved to New York at the age of 16, was born in the East End of London, close to where Israel Zangwill's family lived, and intended that her son should gain an Oxford doctorate. She also described Queen Victoria eccentrically as her 'little English mother'. Trilling retained his mother's English accent and became known as 'the Matthew Arnold of Morningside Heights'. The last section of his doctoral book details Arnold's 1886 lecture tour in the United States and presents us literally with an American Arnold (the birth of his granddaughter during the lecture tour). But the lack of interest in Arnold's work in the United States is recounted quite movingly by Trilling (who felt the same about his own book on Arnold). There are also many amusing anecdotes about the cultural wilderness that Arnold felt during his unhappy lecture tours; we learn that he even breakfasted on hashed veal and mince pies, to his disgust, in Andover (1939: 396).

As Krupnick notes, Trilling's best-known work, *The Liberal Imagination* (1948), is, not unlike *Culture and Anarchy*, a critique of liberal culture from the viewpoint of an idealized liberalism. Both Trilling and Arnold write with dialectical poise (both learned from Hegel in this regard); both engage in fastidious generalizations; both regarded themselves as failed creative writers (Trilling was an unsuccessful novelist, Arnold disdained his own poetry); and both were deeply uncomfortable in their roles as critics. Trilling even writes in his notebook: '[M]y being a professor [...] even [an] admired one is a great hoax' (cit. Klingenstein 1991: 184).[6] Both figures were, above all, divided against themselves, and this self-division became the subject of much of Trilling's literary and cultural criticism.

According to Mark Shechner, Trilling was that 'rarest of creatures, an academic celebrity' who 'even though he spoke for no one but himself [...] was looked upon as a spokesman for the culture' (1990: 134). In this he also resembled Arnold, whom he appropriated wholesale, especially Arnold's self-image as an alienated cosmopolitan. As Jonathan Freedman has noted:

> Trilling crafts for himself throughout his work – his tone, his range of reference, his enactment of the free play of supple consciousness for which he argues – [...] that of the sympathetic but distanced figure invoking a more capacious sense of consciousness and a cosmopolitan perspective to critique the lacunae of the American scene.
>
> (2000: 198)

Edward Said, who is thought to have initially occupied Trilling's room at Columbia, also went on to fashion himself in relation to Trilling's cosmopolitan construction of 'modern literature'. Said comments in *The World, the Text and the Critic* (1983) that Trilling was:

> Arnold's best critic [...] whose work in the United States had most assuredly placed English studies centrally on the literary agenda [...] [that he] spoke of a modern literature that included Diderot, Mann, Freud, Gide and Kafka was a significant announcement of how international and dialectical English-speaking criticism had become.
>
> (142)

The comparison with Said is worth pursuing because Trilling, in his book on Arnold, offered the first and still the best account of Arnold's use of a racial discourse in *Culture and Anarchy*. Trilling's chapter on Arnold's racism was quoted approvingly by Said in his *Orientalism* (1978), published three years after Trilling's death, and the link between Trilling, Arnold and Renan (who was a major influence on Arnold and a central figure in *Orientalism*) was reinforced throughout Said's book.

Trilling and Said were two key figures in my early work, although, until now, it has not occurred to me to bring them together. Said's argument that an Orientalist discourse – which divides the world into east and west, civilized and barbaric – saturated liberal culture (with Arnold as a prime example of this saturation) is central to *Orientalism*. This contention is also prefigured in Trilling's account of Arnold where he notes that in Arnold's day 'racial theory [...] was almost undisputed' (1939: 234), which Said also quotes. Trilling goes on to list some of the many examples of those who were 'to foster and elaborate the notion of a racial constant' in the nineteenth century: 'Stendhal, Meredith [...], Carlyle, J.A. Froude, Kingsley, J.R. Green, Taine, Renan' (1939: 234–5). Similar lists appear throughout *Orientalism*, and Trilling in fact concludes that his 'list could be made to include nearly every writer of the time who generalized about human affairs' (235) and this is also the main conclusion of my own work. But Trilling then goes on to make quite an astonishing claim:

> And if some used [a 'racial hypothesis'] for liberalizing purposes, as Arnold himself did, still, by their very assent to an unfounded assumption, they cannot wholly be dissociated from the [. . .] whole of official German thought in the present day.
>
> (235)

It is worth remembering that Trilling's book was first published in 1939 and written initially as a doctoral thesis in the mid-1930s. Nonetheless, this is quite an extraordinary quotation as it argues that, however liberalized Arnold's racial discourse was, there was a direct line from his racial distinctions between 'Semite' and 'Aryan' to the rise of Nazi Germany. It goes without saying that no one in 1939 knew that such liberalized race-thinking would lead to genocide. (I am at pains in my own work to move away from this teleological view of European anti-Semitism and racism that makes a discussion of liberal culture impossible.) What must Trilling have been thinking in 1939 (and throughout most of the 1930s) as he worked on a figure whom he associated with the rise of Nazism?

Here, again, the link with Said is a fruitful one. Before *Orientalism* Said, much like Trilling, was a cosmopolitan critic of the left and the representative outsider-figure in Columbia's English and Comparative Literature department, with Trilling (rather like Said) eventually becoming something of an orthodoxy. But by the time of *Orientalism*, Said is at pains to make the connection between an Orientalist discourse and his own personal history as a displaced Palestinian living in America; he tells us that: 'my own experiences of these matters are in part what made me write this book' (1978: 27). Both figures make diametrically opposed choices – Haley's Choices, one might say – in relation to their national or ethnic particularities; one in the direction of identity politics (however qualified), the other in the direction of Arnoldian disinterestedness. Whereas Said's work has had a marked autobiographical turn (in stark contrast to his residual and Trilling-inspired cosmopolitanism), the increasingly forlorn Trilling had barely started his autographical memoir before his death (although he had long professed his intention to complete it). Writing in 1944, Trilling made it quite clear what he had to do to become a cosmopolitan critic – and that was to jettison his Jewishness:

> As the Jewish community now exists it can give no sustenance to the American artist or intellectual who is born a Jew. And so far as I am aware, it has not done so in the past. I know of writers who have used their Jewish experience as the subject of excellent work; I know of no writer in English who has added a micromillimetre to his stature by 'realizing his Jewishness', although I know of some who have curtailed their promise by trying to heighten their Jewish consciousness.
>
> (Cit. Shechner 1990: 136)

After this statement, as is well known, Trilling went on to refuse an editorial role in the founding of *Commentary*. While writing for the *Menorah Journal* in the 1930s, he published a series of articles with titles such as 'The Jewish Problem Novel' and 'The Changing Myth of the Jew', and was centrally involved with left-wing Jewish cultural life in New York, becoming a leading New York intellectual in part due to his essays in Philip Rahv's *Partisan Review*. As his wife, Diana Trilling, notes in her posthumous collection of *Menorah* pieces (among much else):

> I wanted very much to get down at least the dim outline of a personal narrative: Lionel's failed search for 'a Jewish identity' in his early writing for *The Menorah Journal*; his failed search in Marxism for an answer to the social and economic questions raised in the wake of the stock market crash of 1929.
>
> (1980b: viii)

Quite typically, Trilling's search for identity can only be described in terms of negatives. This is the Trilling limited by a liberalism that, as he puts it in the preface to *The Liberal Imagination*, 'unconsciously tends to develop theories and principles [. . .] that justifies its limitations' (1950: xiii).

An example of the limitations of liberal tolerance can be found in Trilling's essay on 'The Changing Myth of the Jew', which he wrote around 1930 for *The Menorah Journal*, though it was not published until 1978. This essay was extremely important for me when I was researching my own account of 'the Jew' in English literature because Trilling, in his Marxist phase, stresses the malleability or protean nature of his subject and, especially, what he called the 'political or social motive [. . .] of each myth of the Jew' (1980a: 52). As he tells us at the beginning of the essay, 'the Jew in English fiction took many shapes', and so we have the 'mutations of the Jewish myth in English literature' (from Chaucer to George Eliot), which 'almost always serves some purpose of explanation [. . .] for its makers' (52). There is a key quotation at the end of the essay when Trilling assesses the 'importance' of the 'myth of the Jew' for the contemporary novelist not unlike himself (he was writing fiction at the time) and concludes with the following:

> When the Jew [. . .] entered into the life of the Western world, he found the myths awaiting him. Sometimes he fought them, sometimes he accepted them to his own advantage, often he went off and contemplated them in great confusion of mind. When he came to write of himself he was not able to free himself from them. Some one of them had become a Doppelgänger of his, moving by the side of the real person we supposed he must be. And the task that every Jewish novel presents to the critical reader – and the serious writer – is that of disentangling what is mythical from what is actual. And that task is difficult, for in the mythical there is usually, of course, a little of what is true.
>
> (76)

As Adam Phillips has shown, being a Jew for Trilling meant primarily not 'submitting to the myths of the Jew' and finding instead a 'legitimate decadence', in such figures as E.M. Forster, the younger decadent Arnold and Freud, which his objective and detached mind, devoid of the 'confusion' caused by 'the Jew', could clarify. Phillips characterizes Trilling's critical project as the 'avoidance of victimhood' (for obvious reasons, given his initial experience at Columbia), and in these terms 'dignity must be privileged' and the 'childish' and 'anarchic' must be kept at bay or displaced onto the writers of fiction – most of the figures in Roth and Bellow can be described as 'childish or anarchic' as Phillips notes (2002: 156–68). Whereas Said decided to confront and challenge the myths that surrounded him, Trilling instead writes criticism that is characterized by the doubling and splitting of the self, and he therefore constructs a largely deracinated and free-floating Freud to help in this task. What is more, as the disturbing last lines of his essay suggests, he is not quite sure what is 'mythical' and what is 'true' when it comes to Jews.

Philip Roth has articulated most thoroughly the ambivalent and all-consuming impact of Trilling's version of Arnoldian high culture on his generation of university graduates 'from the semiliterate and semi-assimilated reaches of urban Jewish society'. He argues that, as his 1950s generation of American-born Jews 'went off to universities and infiltrated the departments of English [. . .] [a]ll manner of cultural defection, conversion, confusion, enlightenment, miscegenation, parasitism, transformation and combat ensued' (1975: 83). The language used in Roth's response to the Jewish-American 'infiltration' of English departments encompasses the widest possible range of emotions from acculturation to cultural conflict. On the one hand, 'enlightenment', 'conversion' and 'transformation', which suggest the power of culture to shape and assimilate. On the other, 'defection', 'miscegenation' and 'parasitism', which refuse any notion of cultural purity and instead articulate Jewishness as a form of unassimilable and troublesome impurity. It was these two versions of culture that shaped Roth's own dialectical imagination. And yet, the cosmopolitan Roth of *The Counterlife* (1987) and *Zuckerman Bound* (1989), influenced by his editorship of the *Writers from the Other Europe* series, has been replaced by an Americanized Roth of recent years who is finally writing the 'great American novel'. But I believe that his thematic history of postwar America, on a par with John Dos Passos's *USA* (1936), represents a narrowing or Americanization of his concerns which sadly limits his previous extraterritorial reach.[7]

Writing on British-Jewish imaginative literature over the past two decades, my promised land of culture, which is also my wilderness, has been a great privilege, and I have been most fortunate that there has been a creative as well as a social context for my work. A sense of marginality and in-betweenness has led to an extraordinary growth in the inventiveness and originality of British-Jewish literature since the 1980s, and this is beginning to be recognized generally beyond the realms of academe. I firmly believe that being outside the dominant modes of contemporary English and Jewish history and culture has been a great fillip to the British-Jewish diasporic writers whom I value, such as Elaine Feinstein,

Linda Grant, Alan Isler, Dan Jacobson, Howard Jacobson, Gabriel Josipovici, Simon Louvish, Clive Sinclair, Muriel Spark, Jonathan Treitel (aka 'Jonathan Tel') and Jonathan Wilson. The work of these writers contrasts tellingly with recent American-Jewish literature, which is characterized by the language of identity politics – religion, roots, tradition and victimhood. (The shortened reach of the later Roth is symptomatic in this regard.[8]) It is my role as a Jewish critic, I firmly believe, to celebrate such cosmopolitan impurity wherever it may flourish.

Notes

1 This essay was first given as an Inaugural Lecture in November 2002, at the University of Southampton, UK, to mark the appointment of Bryan Cheyette to a Chair in Twentieth Century Literature. It has previously been published in *Jewish Social Studies*, 11 (2004): 32–51 and is reprinted here with permission of Indiana University Press.
2 The best recent account of Isaac Rosenberg in these terms is Phillips (1994).
3 For an influential discussion of Kafka in this context see also Bauman (1991: 179–84).
4 For a longer version of this argument, see my *Diasporas of the Mind* (forthcoming).
5 For a recent account of this story see Rose (1996: 133–48).
6 See also Krupnick (1986: 51–5).
7 For the comparison between Roth and Dos Passos see Marcus (2000). See also Cheyette, *Diasporas of the Mind* (forthcoming), chapter six for a longer version of this argument.
8 For an elaboration of this argument see Cheyette (1998).

Part II

The Jewish imaginary in non-Jewish Anglophone literature(s)

3 Postcolonial discourse and the Jewish imaginary

Jamie S. Scott

Israelite-Jewish self-understanding has developed a particular *modus operandi*. In particular, the terms 'exodus', 'exile', 'diaspora' and 'holocaust' serve as key markers of what I am calling 'the Jewish imaginary'. Here, following Vijay Mishra, I am using the term 'imaginary' in Slovenian philosopher Slavoj Žižek's sense of 'identification with the image in which we appear likeable to ourselves, with the image representing "what we would like to be"' (Mishra 1996: 421; Žižek 1989: 105). Today, however, exodus, exile, diaspora and holocaust have made their way, separately or in sequence, into the historical self-expression, and hence cultural and social identity, of numerous other groups: Armenians, South Asian labourers indentured to plantations as mutually distant as Fiji and Guyana, Cambodians, Rwandans and so forth. Without offending the role and status of these markers as fundamental constituents of Jewish identity, I want to invoke their appearance in texts often gathered, in the wake of the British colonial and imperial project, under some such rubric as 'Postcolonial Literatures', 'New Literatures in English', 'Third World Literatures' or 'International Literatures'.[1] More suggestive than conclusive, a 'Theological Epilogue' offers some reflections upon the implications for the Jewish sense of historical and theological chosenness arising from this tropical exchange with postcolonial writers and writings, specifically the possibility of a post-holocaust theology so imagined that Jews might 'appear likeable' to themselves.

Exodus

Classically, Jews look to the exodus narratives in the Hebrew scriptures as the founding myths of the Jewish nation. After the creation of the cosmos comes the creation of Israel, after the book of *Genesis*, the book of *Exodus*.[2] But I am not concerned here with the historical circumstances of the ancient Israelite invasions of Canaan; it may well be, for example, as Nahum N. Sarna has claimed, that 'the land of Canaan was in an advanced state of decay' when the Israelite armies began to reduce Canaanite cities to ashes, likely in the mid-thirteenth century BCE (1986: 13). Rather, looking beyond the Hebrew scriptures, we find that these narratives have inspired a host of other writers and writings. A thorough investigation of postcolonial reworkings of the exodus narratives would range across a number of contemporary literatures in a number of languages, often making odd literary bedfellows.[3] Here, let me simply cite a couple of instances from the postcolonial writings of southern Africa.

In such novels as Peter Abrahams's *Wild Conquest* (1950) or Jack Cope's *The Fair House* (1955), we find the Dutch colonial Boers invoking the exodus narratives to claim a sacred right to the lands of the Transvaal and the Orange Free State. A sense of divine dispensation animates the Great Trek of the Afrikaners, as they move eastwards across southern Africa in the 1830s to escape the encroaching presence of British colonists in the Cape Province. Here, the Boers are the Israelites, the British the Egyptians, though little mention is made of indigenous Africans, who are presumably the Canaanites. Oddly enough, though, Kenyan novelist, Ngugi wa Thiong'o, finds structurally analogous, but historically quite variant meanings in the exodus narratives. In *The River Between* (1965), for example, Ngugi interlaces Jewish biblical and Gikuyu tribal traditions. Independence leader, Jomo Kenyatta, becomes a 'black Moses', leading his people into freedom in the 1950s, and the Kameno tribal deity, Mrungu, echoes Yahweh's gift of Canaan to the Israelites: 'This land I give you, O man and woman. It is yours to till, you and your posterity' (148). In this case, the Gikuyu are the Israelites, and the British are the Egyptians and the Canaanites rolled into one, at once enslavers of the Gikuyu and wrongfully in possession of the land of Kenya. As Ngugi explains elsewhere, the Kenya Land and Freedom Army – the British terrorist Mau Mau – echo the righteous claims of the Israelites to the land of Canaan (1981: 27). For Ngugi, the very name 'Kenya Land and Freedom Army' embodies the interwoven notions of 'actual political, visible material freedom and struggle for land' which lie at the heart of the exodus narratives (27).

Today, it is sometimes tempting to read the biblical exodus narratives in radically oppositional ways. Edward Said (1986), for example, criticizes Michael Walzer's *Exodus and Revolution* (1985) for its liberationist appropriation of these accounts. Instead, Said's more nuanced 'Canaanite reading' finds a narrative of conquest and colonization entwined with the Jewish story of freedom and self-determination. The biblical encounters did not exist in a historical vacuum, Said argues, and we need always to ask ourselves about the Canaanites who already inhabited the land so graciously bestowed upon his chosen people, the Israelites, by their god, Yahweh. I do not wish to engage in the barbed politics of the Israeli-Arab face-off in today's Middle East. Rather, as Jonathan Boyarin has noted of the debate between Walzer and Said, I want to stress '[t]he ways in which poets and politicians have *interacted* with the Old Testament narrative of the Israelites', and how the variety of these interactions should awaken us to the dangers of 'simplistic dichotomies' (1992b: 533; emphasis in the original). As my southern African examples reveal, contemporary postcolonial interpellations elaborate the complexities of the exodus narratives. Moses, Mount Sinai, the Ten Commandments, the wilderness and the promised land are exodus terms, but so are pharoah, Egypt and Canaan, and exactly who is who, what is what and where is where may or may not remain consistent, as you move from one retelling to another.

Exile

Jonathan Boyarin has noted that the ritual perhaps most definitive of Jewish identity, 'the Passover Haggadah, the retelling of the Exodus, culminates in the hopeful shout of "next year in Jerusalem"' (1992b: 540). Less shrouded in the mists of myth than exodus, exile refers to the conquest of Judah in 586 BCE by the Babylonian king, Nebuchadnezzar, and the destruction of the first temple, constructed by Solomon in Jerusalem. The Hebrew word *hurban* describes this evisceration of the centre of Israelite ritual life, and the consequent deportation of large numbers of Jews to Babylon.[4] Whereas the exodus narratives have to do with the shedding of servitude, and an absolutely new beginning for the ancient Israelites, the biblical literature of exile – literally, 'leaping out' – speaks of an enforced expulsion from home, laments the difficulties of making a new home in a foreign land, and looks forward to the time of return.

As with exodus, however, so with exile, simple oppositions tend to dominate interpretations of the narrative, especially the opposition of home and away, with their concomitant associations of nostalgia and anticipation. On the one hand, for instance, the psalmist famously laments, 'How shall we sing Yahweh's song / in a foreign land' (Psa 137:4). The Hebrew word *galut*, literally meaning 'exposed', which in turn may be parsed as 'placed away from', captures this mixture of loss and longing (Schreiber 1998: 276). On the other hand, for Deutero-Isaiah, the exile rewrites the ancient covenant between Yahweh and his chosen people; the Jews will become 'a light to the nations, that [Yahweh's] salvation may reach the end of the earth' (Isa 49:9). The conquest of Babylon by Cyrus, in 539 BCE, enables this sort of reversal. Although the Persian king's edict, celebrated in Hebrew scriptures by Ezra, allows the exiles to return to Jerusalem, restores their sacred objects, and encourages the rebuilding of the temple, return seems not to have been an attractive option for all exiles (Ezr 1:2–4 and 6:3–5). The Jewish communities prospered in Babylon, which became, 'until the early eleventh century, the single most important centre of Jewish learning in the world' (Seltzer 1980: 260). Indeed, the Babylonian Talmud cites Rabbi Hoshaya: 'God did Israel a favour in scattering them among the nations' (*Pesahim* 87b; cit. de Lange 2000: 42).

Here, I do not wish to pursue what this notion of carrying divine salvation to the ends of the earth might mean; rather, once again, I simply want to focus on the interplay between postcolonial discourse and the mixed meanings of exile as a marker of Jewish historical and theological identity. As with exodus, a thorough exploration of the biblical theme of exile in postcolonial contexts would engage with a variety of contemporary writers and writings in various languages. In many instances, we find quite explicit rehearsals of the biblical themes. Take, for example, what Arnold Itwaru, the Guyanese Canadian writer, has to say in and about exile:

> We are *here*, not *there*, in the region of our birth. [. . .] For to be in exile is considerably more than being in another country. It is to live with myself knowing my estrangement. [. . .] But this estrangement goes further. It touches upon the very notion of home, the lands and places of our birth.

> For that land, there, that region, lives in us as a memory and dream, as nostalgia, romance of reflection, that which defines us as different, that to which we *think* we belong but no longer do. It is thus that many of us repeatedly invent scenarios of our return but never realize them. It is thus also that those of us who do visit *there* return *here* to find that after the painful winters of our struggles a deep sense of uneasiness prevails.
>
> (1989: 202–3)

In tone and topos, these lines might easily be read as a contemporary gloss on the lament of the psalmist. But Itwaru lingers among the mixed meanings of 'here' and 'there' at play in the discourse of exile and return. Neither Guyana nor Canada seems home, partly because, in *both* cases, someone else's definition of 'here' dominates, always already forestalling the exile's ease. For Itwaru, the exile is a perpetual visitor, at home neither in his place of birth nor in his adopted land. In Said's words, 'what is true of all exile is not that home and love of home are lost, but that loss is inherent in the very existence of both' (1984: 171).

Whether of his own or of another's making, feelings of unease define exile for Itwaru. Other postcolonial explorations of the tensions of mixed belonging are less plaintive, more expectant. Here, let me simply refer to *Remembering Babylon* (1993), by the Lebanese Australian writer, David Malouf. The story of Gemmy Fairley, the mysterious orphan around whom Malouf weaves his narrative, epitomizes the theme of exile. Transported to the penal colonies, shipwrecked on the shore of North Queensland and raised by Aboriginal Australians, several years later this waif from Dickensian London finds his way back to a remote farming settlement, where he is adopted by the kindly Beattie family. Gemmy attempts to reacculturate, only to be rejected as Aboriginal by the farming community. He disappears into the outback.

If Itwaru laments the doubled displacement of exile, *Remembering Babylon* meditates upon the ambiguities and ironies involved in making a home. Time among the Aboriginals has taught Gemmy that '[t]here was no way of existing in this land, or of making your way through it, unless you took unto yourself, discovered on your breath, the sounds that linked up all the various parts of it and made them one' (Malouf 1993: 65). There are no short-cuts here; the exile's utopian quest for comfort in a foreign land all too easily lapses into dystopia. Janet Beattie, for example, reflects how once she thought of 'the many-sided, one-minded swarm' of the beehive 'as an angel', but now, after the atrocities of Australia's involvement in Europe's Great War, it seemed more like 'a machine, which was a change but not a difference' (192). The oppositional stance of home *versus* exile does not apply, for in some sense, the place of exile for Malouf's characters is home, or will become so.

The Reverend Frazer, a botanizing cleric for whom Gemmy shows some affinity, eloquently captures this sentiment:

> This is what is intended by our coming here: to make this place too part of the world's garden, but by changing ourselves rather than it and adding thus

> to the richness and variety of things. Our poor friend Gemmy is a forerunner. He is no longer a white man, or a European, whatever his birth, but a true child of the place as it will one day be, a crude one certainly, unaware of what he has achieved – and that too perhaps is part of His intention: that the exemplum should be of the simplest and most obvious sort, deeply moving to those who are willing to look, and to see, without prejudice, that in allowing himself to be at home here, he has crossed the boundaries of his given nature. (132)

Frazer here articulates Gemmy's role, at once existential and symbolic, as the future hope of an Australia in which the exile *is* at home. It may well be, as Said writes, that '[t]he exile knows that in a secular and contingent world, homes are always provisional' (1984: 170). Equally, though, as the Blakean epigraph to *Remembering Babylon* advises us, 'Whether this is Jerusalem or Babylon, we know not'. In other words, postcolonial writers and writings further expose the ambiguities of exile. Like exodus, this second biblical marker of Jewish self-understanding fractures and fragments into a number of signifiers, some having to do with the loss of home and the longing for return, others with the exile's unanticipated opportunity for transcending 'the boundaries of his given nature'.

Diaspora

In Jewish tradition, there is discursive overlap between exile and diaspora. First, a number of Jewish writers have used the Hebrew words *hurban* and *galut* to refer to the exposure of Jewish social and cultural identity attendant upon the destruction of both the first and second temples. Second, according to Nicholas de Lange, diaspora and exile are 'virtually synonymous' in Hebrew, 'where the same word *galut* is used to describe either condition', so that diaspora 'can be traced back at least as far as the first *hurban* in 586 BCE' (de Lange 2000: 27; Schreiber 1998: 276). But these historical catastrophes do differ in one key respect: '[I]n the aftermath of the Roman destruction it was probably assumed that there would be a return and rebuilding after a generation or two, just as had happened the first time' (de Lange 2000: 27). This expectation, of course, proved false.

In modern times, as Erich S. Gruen points out in an essay titled 'Diaspora and Homeland', Jewish responses to this condition have tended to polarize. On the one hand, dominating, we have the view that 'diaspora dissolves into *galut*, exile, a bitter and doleful image, offering a bleak vision that leads either to despair or to a remote reverie of restoration' (2002: 232). In this view, '[r]ealization of the people's destiny rests in achieving the "Return", the acquisition of a real or mythical homeland' (232). On the other hand, '[t]he alternative approach', writes Gruen, 'takes a very different route' (232):

> Jews require no territorial sanctuary or legitimation. They are 'the people of the book.' Their homeland resides in the text – not just the canonical scriptures but an array of Jewish writings that help to define the nation and give

> voice to its sense of identity. Their 'portable temple' serves the purpose. A geographic restoration is therefore superfluous, even subversive. To aspire to it deflects the focus from what really counts: the embrace of the text, its ongoing commentary, and its continuous reinterpretation. Diaspora, in short, is no burden, indeed a virtue in the spread of the word. This justifies a primary attachment to the land of one's residence, rather than the home of the fathers.
>
> (232)

But Jewish thinkers have not always posited diaspora's options in terms of such a radical opposition. Indeed, Gruen's painstakingly researched account of Jewish life amidst the Greeks and Romans in the four hundred years between Alexander the Great and Nero leads him to conclude that 'the self-perception of Second Temple Jews' did not compel them 'to choose between restoration to Eretz Israel and recourse to the Word as their "portable homeland"' (247). On the contrary, '[c]ommitment to the [gentile] community and devotion to Jerusalem were entirely compatible' (244).

As various observers have pointed out, contemporary understandings of diaspora are rooted in the Jewish experience. In the inaugural issue of the scholarly journal *Diaspora*, for example, William Safran draws specifically upon this experience to formulate a model of diaspora in terms of six key features: dispersion to at least two 'peripheral' locations; collective 'memory, vision or myth about their original homeland'; a sense of homelessness in diaspora; belief in the sacrality of the ancestral homeland; expectation of return to this homeland; defining identity in terms of individual and collective relationship with this homeland (1991: 83–4). But other postcolonial commentators focus not only on what diaspora leaves behind, but also on where it might lead. The cultural anthropologist, James Clifford, talks about the possibilities of articulating contemporary diasporas as 'real, if incomplete, ruptures with past structures of domination, sites of current struggle and imagined futures' (1994: 328). For Clifford, 'the diaspora discourse and history currently in the air would be about recovering non-Western, or not-only-Western, models for cosmopolitan life, nonaligned transnationalities struggling within and against nation-states, global technologies, and markets – resources for a fraught coexistence' (328).

Numerous studies of specific postcolonial diasporas bear out such suggestions. Vijay Mishra, for example, contrasts what he calls 'exclusivist' notions of first-generation South Asian diaspora, associated with 'relatively self-contained "Little Indias" in the colonies', with '[t]he new Indian diaspora [. . .] mediated in the works of Salman Rushdie, Hanif Kureishi, Meera Nair, Rohinton Mistry, M.S. Vassanji, Gurunder Chadha, Meera Syal and others' (1996: 422). For Mishra, 'the overriding characteristic [of this new Indian diaspora] is one of mobility' – 'the immense social mobility of culture-specific food', for example (422, 430). 'The cultural logic of the new Indian diaspora', Mishra concludes, 'has to be located in the idea of the hyphen itself, in what may be called the epistemology of borders' (432). Similarly, in her studies of the Chinese diaspora communities in Southeast Asia and Australia, cultural theorist, Ien Ang, identifies 'much more radical, complicated, and chequered routes of diasporic dispersal', in which 'the very category of Chineseness is in question [...] to the extent that any residual attachment to the centre tends to fade' (1998: 236). In *1492: The Poetics of Diaspora*, the Jewish Australian scholar, John Docker, defines 'diaspora' as 'a sense of belonging to more than one history, to more than one time and place, more than one past and future' (2001: vii). For Docker, the Judeo-Islamic world of medieval Spain exemplifies this understanding of a diasporic world marked by 'a circulation of cultures, ideas, discourses, languages, where cities were linked with cities, Baghdad with Beirut with Damascus with Jerusalem with Cairo' (50). Interestingly, though, Docker makes his argument, in part at least, in and through Salman Rushdie's imaginary representation of that world in *The Moor's Last Sigh* (1995). For all their differences in matter and method, what unites such analyses seems to be, to quote a recent essay by David Chariandy (2006), the conviction that ' "the postcolonial diasporas" might best be understood not as self-evident sociocultural phenomena, but as "figures" which may help us to better read and animate the cultural politics of specific racialized collectivities within the modern West'.

In recent years, other Jewish scholars have travelled similar hermeneutical roads. Introducing a collection of essays analysing visual representations of Jews and Africans in a variety of diasporic situations, Nicholas Mirzoeff identifies a tension at the heart of diaspora: 'the diasporists', he writes, 'are the sign that modern aspirations to a fully authentic national culture can never be realized' (2000: 10). Here, in my view, Mirzoeff does not intend to idealize diaspora as somehow the only way of being truly authentic in today's simultaneously fractured and increasingly globalized societies. Rather, as Daniel and Jonathan Boyarin put it, '[d]iaspora can teach us that it is possible for a people to maintain its distinctive culture, its difference, without controlling land, a fortiori without controlling other people or developing a need to dispossess them of their lands' (1993: 723). Literally, diaspora means 'scattered apart', often in the sense in which the sower scatters seeds. As Maeera Y. Schreiber has noted, the Hebrew *tefusa*, which is often used 'to speak of the diasporic condition, carries the same duality as the Greek word' (1998: 284 n. 3). For Schreiber, this duality of meaning 'trouble[s] the opposition between exile and home' lying at the heart of diaspora. She writes of the 'diasporic poetics' of Jewish identity in terms of 'a renegotiated sense of community, however fragile [...] of replanting, rerooting, and subsequent growth' (275). As we have seen, postcolonial writers and writings also bear varied and frequent testimony to the inadequacies of reducing our understanding of diaspora to naïve antimonies.

Holocaust

With 'Holocaust', needless to say, I arrive at a marker far less simply susceptible to the sort of interpretive nuance I have been trying to tease out of exodus, exile and diaspora.[5] But let me try. A few years ago, in the 'Opinion' section of *The*

Sunday Age, a Melbourne, Australia, newspaper, we were faced with a piece headlined, 'Montenegro, the Next Holocaust?' by William Shawcross (1999). Reprinted from *The Guardian*, the celebrated – or notorious, of course, depending on where you plant your pole – leftist-leaning organ once published in Manchester, England, now in London, the piece presumed an international recognition for the message these words were designed to convey. Involving other times and places under the interrogative, 'Who Owns the Holocaust?', Canada's *Globe and Mail*, a right-of-centre daily, ran a feature on an exhibition called *Mirroring Evil: Nazi Imagery/Recent Art*, at New York's Jewish Museum (Houpt 2002: R1). The author, Simon Houpt, quotes Rabbi Brad Hirschfield, Vice-President of the National Jewish Centre for Learning and Leadership, who argues that '[t]he memory does not belong only to the generation that lived through the Holocaust', and warns that '[a]ny time an event is owned by one community, the memories of it will die with that generation' (R1).

What do these headlines signify? What do we understand by them? How do they come to mean what they mean? And why? More specifically, have we not been brought up to believe in only a single holocaust, the Shoah associated with the German Nazi campaign in the Second World War literally to extinguish the Jewish race through incineration? Do we not always see the word 'Holocaust' written with an upper case 'H', designated by the definite article, 'the', not the relative article, 'a'? How, then, may we interpret the qualification of the-one-and-only, capital 'H' Holocaust with the relativizing, temporal signifier, 'next'? How many generations may own the capital 'H' Holocaust, and how many communities may stake a claim to the meaning of 'holocaust'? Is 'The Holocaust' one in a series, after all? Does 'holocaust' have a history? And if so, what are the implications of this discovery not only for Jews, but for those who have chosen to interpret their histories in terms of this, until recently, most unutterable, let alone interpretable of terms for Jews?

Many Jewish thinkers have expressed profound uneasiness about the possibility of interpreting the holocaust in historical terms. Saul Friedländer, for example, asks: 'Does an event like the "Final Solution" allow for *any kind* of narrative, or does it foreclose certain narrative altogether?' (1991: 32). Despite the fact that the relativizing, hence historicizing little comparative 'like' seems logically to entail otherwise, Friedländer concludes that no conventional narrative of the holocaust is possible. 'No one of sound mind would wish to interpret the events from Hitler's standpoint', for example, and more broadly, 'this past teaches us nothing commensurable with the very enormity of the event; it does not help us to understand the present-day world or the future of the human condition' (31–2). By contrast, however, in *Reading the Holocaust*, Inga Clendinnen expresses the view that Friedländer's position 'is grim news indeed [...] given that inhuman policies persist in our world, and given our need to achieve some analytic understanding of them if we are to resist them effectively' (1999: 88). So Clendinnen votes for the narrativity of the holocaust. Just as Egypt and the Canaanites are part of the exodus narratives, Nebuchadnezzar and Cyrus part of the exile narratives, and the worlds of ancient Rome and medieval Spain parts of key moments in Jewish diaspora experience, Adolf Hitler, the National Socialist Party and the whole fabric and weave of events constituting what, in one of those deeply subconscious acts of undisputed global branding, very quickly came to be known as the Second World War, are part of the holocaust narrative.

Certainly, some Jewish scholars seem to be moving in this more nuanced and ambiguous direction. While refusing to trivialize the holocaust 'as one more atrocity', for example, Alan Rosenberg argues that 'the various processes, techniques and methods of destruction' characterizing the uniqueness of the holocaust 'help us to understand not merely why the Holocaust is unique but also how it was possible that such an event could occur in our history and in the context of our age' (1987; 2000: 157, 156). We find analogous arguments among recent commentators on holocaust literature. In *Foregone Conclusions: Against Apocalyptic History* (1994), for example, Michel André Bernstein discusses the holocaust and narrative strategies of historical plotting in and through analyses of the work of Marcel Proust, Aharon Appelfeld and Robert Musil. Novelists and literary critics who write the holocaust as an apocalyptic, tragic end to history, Bernstein argues, forget all too conveniently that history is open, contingent, to be valued in and for the moment. 'The task for us both as storydwellers and as storytellers, that is, as individuals who learn to understand ourselves and our world through the stories we tell and are told', Bernstein concludes, 'is how to construct the leanings we require in our personal and collective narratives without hypostatizing those narratives as absolute and inevitable' (1994: 124–5). Similarly, Daniel R. Schwarz (1999) has argued that, among other things, autobiographical texts like Elie Wiesel's *Night* (1958) and Primo Levi's *Survival at Auschwitz* (1947), realistic novels like Tadeusz Borowski's *This Way for the Gas, Ladies and Gentlemen* (1948) and Jerzy Kosinski's *The Painted Bird* (1965), more imaginatively adventurous fiction like André Schwarz-Bart's *The Last of the Just* (1959) and William Styron's *Sophie's Choice* (1976), as well as such works as Claude Lanzmann's *Shoah* (1985) and Stephen Spielberg's adaptation of Thomas Keneally's *Schindler's Ark* (1993), all taken together, demonstrate that the further we move from the holocaust in history, the more varied the narrative representations of it.

Such approaches to the narrativizing of holocaust speak to the situation confronting many postcolonial writers, too. As Vivian M. Patraka has noted, 'however proprietary the claims on the use of this term have been in some [Jewish] quarters, the evocative power of the term *Holocaust* has begun to extend its use tropologically to contemporary considerations of the destruction of groups other than Jews' (1997: 54). Clearly, a full investigation of this process would have to take account of the way in which those who would memorialize the horrors of postcolonial killing fields from the mountains of Armenia to the forests of Rwanda have adopted and adapted the language of holocaust in their attempts to recover a sense of individual and collective hope. Here, let me simply refer to the struggles of Native Canadians to come to terms with their experiences of American colonialism, most notably in a system of educational institutions known as 'residential schools'.

The first efforts of Native Canadian writers to narrativize the threat to identity posed by these schools quickly turns to the language of incarceration. Jane Willis, for example, describes 'those years in Indian boarding-schools' as 'ten and a half years of boot camp' (1973: 195). Similarly, words like 'committal' and phrases like 'served their term' pepper Ojibwa Basil Johnston's account of life at St Peter Claver's Roman Catholic School, in Spanish, Ontario, from which the boys constantly express hopes of 'release' or being 'sprung loose' (1988: 78). Elsewhere, though, Jeanette Armstrong and Freda McDonald take this discourse of the carceral to its logical limits. Using terms like 'totalitarianism' and 'indoctrination camps', Armstrong signifies her conviction that an unofficial policy of cultural genocide was in force throughout the government-funded, church-run system (1998: 239). Under this policy, Armstrong writes, 'our language, our religions, our customs, our values and our societal structures almost disappeared' (239). Similarly, McDonald talks of '[t]he holocaust of the boarding school and its far-reaching, genocidal attempt at erasing a people' (1998: 72), and concludes: 'We are still living with the aftermath of this holocaust today' (73). Invoking the apocalyptic overtones of 'holocaust' in this way makes us sit up and pay attention, partly, I suspect, because we are used to being called to outrage when the term appears, and partly perhaps because here it appears in an unfamiliar context. At the same time, though, Armstrong's barely noticeable qualifier 'almost' and McDonald's ability as survivor to speak in terms of 'attempt' and 'still living [. . .] today' represent glimmers of hope and the determination to fuel it into reality.

As we have seen, exodus, exile and diaspora have directly or indirectly offered means of articulating and understanding other histories in and through their interpellation into postcolonial discourse. An often unqualifiable and uninterpretable marker of Jewish identity, holocaust generates for Native Canadians the potential for articulating and understanding the experience of prolonged persecution and the threat of social and cultural annihilation. In so doing, like exodus, exile and diaspora, holocaust serves as a historical marker in the Native Canadian community's efforts to recover radically threatened identity and in so doing, to prepare the ground, at least, for a meaningful collective future. Is it possible that what at first might seem like an offence to Jews and Judaism – the deployment of holocaust in and through other histories – may turn out as an avenue for at once admitting the uniqueness of *the* holocaust – its Jewishness – yet also a way of articulating its radical historicity? At once unique, because Jewish, yet not so, but historically relative, like exodus, exile and diaspora in postcolonial discourse, holocaust becomes less a matter of exclusivity beyond history, and more a matter of the exemplary limits of the historical, at once a threat and a lure to our continued humanity, a marker of horror, absolutely, but also of hope.

A theological epilogue

Some years ago, Jonathan Boyarin asserted that the crucial difference between exodus and other key markers of Jewish identity lies in the idea of absolute beginning associated with the former *versus* the notion of return common to exile and diaspora, albeit in historically and theologically diverse ways (1992: 541). Thus my explorations confront a paradox: Jewish identity in dialogue with postcolonial discourse suggests *both* the inimitable uniqueness of Jewish history *and* the historical relativity of this history in its paradigmatic discursive reference for the equally inimitable histories of other groups. The discursive interplay between postcolonial writing and the Jewish tropes exodus, exile and diaspora suggests at once the right of return and the responsibility, even desirability, of always making new beginnings. True, when we come to holocaust, things get more complicated. But Nicholas de Lange and other Jewish scholars have established some sort of interpretive continuity between exile, diaspora and this seemingly unspeakable sign, too; they point out that the Hebrew term *hurban*, always associated with the destruction of the first and second temples, 'is sometimes applied to the Nazi destruction of Jewish life in Europe' (de Lange 2000: 230). Indeed, for de Lange, Reeve Robert Brenner's analyses of faith and doubt amongst holocaust survivors reveal, on the existential level, at least, 'not only that many had come through with their faith in God unimpaired, but that for some their faith was strengthened, while a significant minority who had previously been atheists found God in the camps' (160). That said, de Lange agrees that with 'holocaust' Jewish thinkers seem more often to admit an impasse, even an absolute ending to the absolute beginning of exodus. In de Lange's words,

> [s]o far no radical new theology has emerged from the Shoah to compare in its daring and its impact to the ideas of the biblical prophets that followed the catastrophe of the Babylonian exile, or those of the Rabbis following the Roman destruction, or those of the Lurianic Kabbalah that followed the reconquest of Spain.
>
> (185)

Perhaps Docker's *1492: The Poetics of Diaspora* suggests a way beyond this impasse. The book closes with a 'Concluding Mosaic' – a *mélange* of afterthoughts and asides. Among these remarks, Docker writes: 'Contemporary cultural theory is too determinedly secular. To accompany, converse with, the poetics of diaspora we need a theological poetics' (2001: 260). In my view, the interplay between postcolonial discourse and the Jewish imaginary that I have tried to outline here carries this sort of theological significance. I do not want to enter the hermeneutical thickets of confessional rabbinics here; rather, let me appropriate Hannah Arendt's non-apologetic reading of Jewish theology. In *The Origins of Totalitarianism*, Arendt identifies 'the two basic elements of Jewish piety – the Messianic hope and the faith in Israel's chosenness' (1951; 1973: 74). She goes on to analyze the effects of secularization upon Jewish piety:

> Without the Messianic hope, the idea of chosenness meant eternal segregation; without faith in chosenness, which charged one specific people with the redemption of the world, Messianic hope evaporated into the dim cloud of

> general philanthropy and universalism which became so characteristic of specifically Jewish political enthusiasm.
>
> (74)

This failure to maintain a theological perspective on chosenness produces paradoxical and perilous consequences, as the notion of chosenness transmutes into something akin to 'modern race ideologies' (73):

> The most fateful element in Jewish secularization was that the concept of chosenness was being separated from the Messianic hope, whereas in Jewish religion these two elements were two aspects of God's redemptive plan for mankind. Out of Messianic hope grew that inclination toward final solutions of political problems which aimed at nothing less than establishing a paradise on earth. Out of the belief in chosenness by God grew that fantastic delusion, shared by unbelieving Jews and non-Jews alike, that Jews are by nature more intelligent, better, healthier, more fit for survival – the motor of history and the salt of the earth. [...] Secularization, therefore, finally produced that paradox, so decisive for the psychology of modern Jews [...] the old religious concept of chosenness was no longer the essence of Judaism; it became instead the essence of Jewishness.
>
> (74)

If, as Arendt argues, the ancient simplicities of conventional Jewish piety – 'a specific religion, a specific nationality, the sharing of specific memories and specific hopes' (73) – are no longer sufficient or even possible conditions for representing the Jewish imaginary, in Žižek's sense, I am suggesting that the working presence of the markers exodus, exile, diaspora and holocaust in post-colonial discourse offers an alternative reading. Moreover, construed along the lines of Docker's missing theological poetics, such a reading possesses likely implications for a wide range of social and cultural issues, both Jewish and non-Jewish, from nationalistic claims to territory to political debates about immigration and identity.

In *Why Should Jews Survive? Looking Past the Holocaust toward a Jewish Future* (1995), Michael Goldberg argued that the 'Holocaust Cult' of shrines like the Holocaust Museum in Washington, DC, of high priests like Elie Wiesel, of rites like United Jewish Association death camp pilgrimages may ironically further the aims of the Nazis in destroying Jewish identity. For Goldberg, this holocaust 'master story' interprets the chosennness of the Jewish people in terms of the unique victimization of those who have managed to survive despite God's complicity in their persecution. Goldberg prefers to read chosenness in terms of the exodus narratives, which he sees as the master story of God's leading a people out of servitude and making an eternal covenant with them, and in so doing, providing them with a unique place in the universal divine plan. Other Jewish scholars take this sort of reading of exodus as election a step further. In *Exodus to Berlin: The Return of the Jews to Germany* (2003), Peter Laufer invokes the trope as a vehicle for restoring Jews to the very centre of the Nazi onslaught not only upon Jewish life, but upon European, even global civilization. Here, Jews and Jewish recovery once more become the lynchpin in the divine redemption of the whole world.

For Docker, however, the exodus narratives are themselves subject to the sort of interpretation Goldberg abhors. 'Exodus', writes Docker, 'creates a representation of history which authorizes the pathos and desirability for individuals, nations and peoples to regard themselves as victims and to be regarded as victims' (2001: 146). By contrast, postcolonial writers and writings provide another, more challenging reading of the discursive trajectory from exodus, through exile and diaspora to holocaust, a reading couched in terms of transnational community and intercultural identity. The awfulness of holocaust victimhood resides not in its status as the end of history, even of Jewish history, but in its transparency as the signifier of ultimate horror and total displacement in the historical line exodus, exile and diaspora. In the 'radical particularity' of *the* Holocaust lies a disruption of a particular history so radical that it shatters 'virtually all of our assumptions about humanity and the Divine' (Shapiro 1984: 5).

As George Steiner once rather sardonically commented, when interviewed by Eleanor Wachtel on Canadian radio:

> I've got the following theory now [...] God has decided to make Jews of everybody. By that I mean very simply He's going to teach everybody else what it's like to have to wander, what it's like not to have safety and protection. [...] I mean it as a shorthand: refugees, hunted people, people who have to learn languages to survive, people who have to relearn jobs, ways of life. Well, it's pretty awful, but it's a lot of fun too.
>
> (Wachtel 1992: 842)[6]

Perhaps Steiner had in mind Jacques Derrida here, for whom Jewish experience epitomized 'tradition as adventure' (1978: 74). Either way, if retelling Arendt's essential elements of messiahship and chosenness poses the main challenge to Jewish post-holocaust identity – the challenge of the sort of theological poetics which Docker invites – perhaps the conversation between postcolonial writing and the key markers of the Jewish imaginary constitutes an important element in this retelling. In other contexts, Boyarin explores links between Jewish traditions of historical and theological self-understanding and what he calls 'the postmodern ideal of Diaspora', a position he elaborates into 'a search for models of interpretation which are translatable across cultural boundaries' (Boyarin 1992a: 124; 1992b: 546). Maybe in postcolonial writers and their writings, I am suggesting, albeit all too partially, we have useful models of and models for this sort of 'intercultural and contentious dialogue' (Boyarin 1992b: 547). At any rate, we may certainly take inspiration in this regard from that godfather of things postcolonial, Frantz Fanon, who, in 'The Fact of Blackness', recalls how his 'philosophy professor' once counselled him: 'Whenever you hear anyone abuse the Jews, pay attention, because he is talking about you' (1952; 1967: 122). Here, surely, we find the possibility of a post-holocaust sense of historical and theological chosenness so imagined that Jews might 'appear likeable' to themselves.

Notes

1 The imperial British, too, were somewhat preoccupied with Jewish history and experience, of course. For the origins of this preoccupation in colonial and imperial life and letters, see Rhodes (1995).

2 All references to and citations of Hebrew scripture use the *New Oxford Annotated Bible with the Apocrypha* (1977). Literally 'way out', exodus captures the emigration of the ancient Hebrews from Egypt, though this title from the Greek Septuagint does not exactly translate the Hebrew name for these narratives, *Sefer Sh'mot*, which simply refers to the first words of the book's first chapter, 'These are the names of the sons of Israel' (Exo 1:1). Still, the Hebrew scriptures recapitulate the exodus narratives around 120 times (N.N. Sarna 1986: 2–3).

3 See, for example, Miller (1985), Redkay (1969) and Tepper (1980).

4 Solomon's father, David, conquered and established Jerusalem as capital of an Israelite empire-in-the-making in the tenth century BCE. Some accounts reckon Nebuchadnezzar's victory dropped the city's population from c. 250,000 to c. 20,000, though scholars generally agree that 'Babylonia killed or captured the wealthy, the landowners, the temple officials, the military leaders, and the political governmental elite, but not the majority of the people' (Berquist 1995: 15).

5 Here, I do not wish in any way to introduce into my discussion anything even remotely resonant of the sort of forced ambiguity revisionist historians and holocaust deniers like David Irving attempt. Rather, I wish simply to gesture towards the possibility of holocaust becoming interpretable in and through the conversational trajectory I have tried to trace between postcolonial discourse and the key markers of Israelite–Jewish identity – exodus, exile and diaspora.

6 I would like to thank Jenny Kerber, a doctoral student in the Faculty of Environmental Studies, York University, for bringing this interview with Steiner to my attention.

4 'What's more important than a gesture?'

Jewishness and cultural performativity

Sigrun Meinig

Cultural and religious identity is the site of often painful individual and communal struggle or even strife. In recent years, it has also increasingly become subject to marketing and to media hype, raising the question what the relationship between the struggle for identity and the hype about certain cultural traits or ethnic features is. The VJs on television music channels such as MTV make diversity 'cool' with their host of cultural and ethnic backgrounds, just as the Benetton advertisements that adorn streets and magazines do. Certain cultural elements and ethnic traits even acquire cult status. In the rap and hip-hop scene, for example, black culture is emulated with regard to linguistic features, gestures and sports clothes because of the fascination it exerts on fans also of other ethnicities and cultures. Film stars like Richard Gere, who famously is a friend of the Dalai Lama, have helped to bring Buddhism into the headlines and to make it trendy and desirable. With her very name and the crosses she wore in her early career Madonna played with the symbols – and the taboos – of Roman Catholicism. Madonna, however, has recently undergone a name-change and now wishes to be called Esther. She now adheres, together with other celebrities such as actress Demi Moore or fellow singer Britney Spears, to Kabbalah. Madonna/Esther does not only attract attention by attending the Jewish New Year's celebrations in Israel and by visiting the graves of Kabbalist sages for meditation and prayer, but by also using the iconography connected with the Kabbalah for the promotion of her CD and tour (cf. McGreal 2004; Doward 2004). Especially in the latter case, fans and commentators remain unsure whether Madonna/Esther's recent penchant for Judaism is strategic 'product' placement – and, as the singer's critics say, a harmful distortion of Jewish faith – or whether other explanations must be found.

The prism of literature and more specifically that of Zadie Smith's second novel *The Autograph Man* (2002) arranges such questions so as to illuminate the nature and the logic of contemporary multi-ethnic and 'multi-faith' identity building, especially in popular culture with its cult of the celebrity. It moreover allows this chapter to pursue within this force field the role of Jewishness and Judaism that Madonna's conversion highlights so strikingly. Jewishness has become more visible as a marketable identity option in the cultural arena in recent years, for example in the rise of recognisable Jewish characters in television series (Zurawik 2003: 9–10). In the course of this development, Jewishness has acquired a mainstream trendiness that earlier explicitly Jewish stars such as Barbra Streisand never possessed. Zadie Smith's second novel, *The Autograph Man*, engages with the contemporary hipness of Jewishness and certain strands of Judaism when it precedes its story of the professional autograph dealer Alex-Li Tandem with a visual image of a sefirot tree called 'Kabbalah of Alex-Li Tandem' and with a passage from the sketch *Jewish & Goyish* by the Jewish-American comedian Lenny Bruce: an 'in and out' list of music, food and ethnicities that attributes the terms 'Goyish' and 'Jewish' to the items on the list. This list identifies being Jewish with being 'cool'. Since the protagonist continues to develop his vision of the sefirot and a list of the attributions 'Jewish' and 'Goyish' throughout the novel, Jewishness constitutes a seminal point of reference for the evolvement of *The Autograph Man*. Jewish culture eventually also provides the finale of the novel with a communal speaking of the Kaddish. This trajectory from Kabbalah to Kaddish is embedded in the multicultural setting which one has come to expect from the author of British-Jamaican descent who is herself a celebrity. Zadie Smith has been referred to as the 'Tiger Woods of Literature' (Cowley 2001) after the success of her first novel *White Teeth* (2000), which was read as the epitome of the post-colonial condition and as the exemplary case of such theoretical concepts as Homi Bhabha's notions of difference or hybridity. By being the work of a celebrity author whose writing is occasionally suspected of emptying the multi-ethnic, post-colonial experience of its emotions and complications and of turning it into marketable 'gimmickery' and slapstick,[1] and by moreover exploring the role of celebrities amidst the cultural intersections of contemporary life, *The Autograph Man* highlights the double-edge that is the central field of investigation in this chapter: the depth of the search for identity and the surface of the drive for an image and identity marketing.

This ambiguity is particularly pronounced with respect to the Jewish cultural and religious elements, which are so prominent in Smith's novel. Indeed, the novel was awarded the *Jewish Quarterly* Wingate Literary Prize in 2003 for being 'an original look at contemporary forms of Jewishness, and at Jewishness as a template of today's hybrid identities and multicultural societies' (Anonymous 2003). I will accordingly conduct my exploration of multi-ethnic identity building in terms of an inquiry into the image of Jewishness and its possible role as a model in the contemporary multi-ethnic world and especially the post-colonial realm. Jewishness is often regarded as different in comparison with other ethnicities. Either being Jewish is considered as being already part of the mainstream, in particular in the American context (Brauner 2001: 22), in a way that neither being black or being Asian are. Or, because of the centuries of persecution and its culmination in the Shoah, Jewishness is regarded as the exemplary case of being at the receiving end of the disastrous and deadly persecution that destroys those who are different. The experience of exile and diaspora is, after all, seminal for Jewish culture.[2] Jewishness thus throws a special light on multicultural life and the post-colonial condition and its pressing dilemmas, such as the question of agency.

To trace this unique perspective, I will begin by analysing the representation of the 'identity market' and the various 'identity options' that the media culture in

The Autograph Man involves. Concentrating on the novel's representation of the Kabbalah, I will explore the ways in which this central part of Jewish mysticism connects with the requirements of the 'identity market'. After discussing the seemingly free-floating quotability this market involves, I will approach the conspicuous consumption in the cultural and ethnic arena from a different angle and move on to the representation of the Kaddish in *The Autograph Man*. I will trace the significance of the performativity and the communality that is epitomized by the Kaddish. Eventually, the performative, embodied dimension of Jewish culture, together with its humour, will prove to be those cultural strategies that determine the role of Jewishness in the spectrum of cultures, religions and ethnicities.

From the first, Jewishness constitutes a bond in Zadie Smith's *The Autograph Man*, since the novel's central characters do not only share a past in the same London suburb which is ironically named Mountjoy, but as boys they also used to attend *cheder* together. Nevertheless, the Chinese, African–American and German origins of Alex, Adam and Joseph make that bond recede to the background as the colour, the mix and the speed of London and later of New York City claim attention. Thus, for large portions of the novel, Jewishness seems to be just one more lifestyle option in a rich array of possible choices. The citizens of the global community just select and mix as it pleases them. Within this array, Alex-Li's book draft *Jewishness and Goyishness* sets out to collect evidence that Jewishness is cool. The book is a synopsis of what is cool and what is uncool in the manner of Lenny Bruce's sketch that serves as an epigraph for the novel. By now Alex has written

> three hundred pages and [. . .] what amounted to a two-sided list. Jewish books (often not written by Jews), Goyish books (often not written by Goys); Jewish office items (the stapler, the pen holder), Goyish office items (the paper clip, the mouse pad); Jewish trees (sycamore, poplar, beech), Goyish trees (oak, Sitka, horse chestnut); Jewish smells of the seventeenth century (rose oil, sesame, orange zest), Goyish smells of the seventeenth century (sandalwood, walnut, wet forest floor).
>
> (Smith 2002: 77)

Alex's book project attributes 'Jewish' and 'Goyish' randomly to individual cultural traits and elements, independently of their history and background. Alex's selection thus blunts even that usually very sharp and dangerous weapon, binary opposition, because the usual hierarchies are ignored. It also means that he can make elements from different cultures his own in any terms he chooses. Alex thus broadens the effect that Lawrence Epstein identifies with regard to Lenny Bruce's original sketch. According to Epstein, Bruce's work helped to loosen Jewish culture from its religious background and thus fostered its development towards becoming a secular cultural choice (2001: 171).

This looseness from the religious background also characterizes *The Autograph Man*'s engagement with the structuring principle of its first book, the Kabbalah. The novel's two books are called 'The Kabbalah of Alex-Li Tandem' and

'The Zen of Alex-Li Tandem'. Both books are organized according to their titles; the chapter headings in book one follow the ten sefirot, those of book two each follow the wisdom of a Koan. Be it Buddhism or the mystical variety of Judaism, in Zadie Smith's novel as in contemporary pop culture the hipsters just adopt what suits their lifestyle and their search for meaning. Thus, when Alex and his friend Adam get together to discuss religion or – especially in the case of religious Adam – to aim for a spiritual experience when contemplating the twenty-two foundation letters of the Hebrew alphabet that Adam has painted on the wall, they smoke weed, a practice that Esther, who is Adam's sister and Alex-Li's girlfriend, strongly disapproves of. She says it distorts the spiritual experience. Both Alex and his friend Adam have created their own kabbalistic tree diagrams on their walls. They identify film stars such as Bette Davis, writers like Virginia Woolf and celebrities such as Muhammad Ali with the ten emanations of God by blu-tacking them on the wall in the respective spots. The friends' engagement with the Kabbalah is a mixture of youthful nerddom and fandom and an (at least in Alex's case) half-hearted search for spiritual enlightenment. The mystic nature of the Kabbalah and the Zohar lend itself to such highly individualized appropriations within the frame of popular culture because mysticism relies on intense individual experience and requires individual interpretation processes (Holm 1990: 57–61).[3] The frame employed for the second book in *The Autograph Man*, Buddhism, also makes the individual the central authority, especially because there is no anthropomorphic figure of a God. As Damien Keown explains, this constitutes Buddhism's popularity and produces its affinity to the secularized, modern Western world where it is often perceived as not really being a religion. Buddhism's undogmatic, rationalist approach which does not follow firm rules but instead posits certain maxims which are meant to lead to the good fortune of everyone appeals to Western ideals of tolerance and liberalism (2001: 145–8). As a consequence, the Kabbalah and Buddhism share the New Age appeal with Feng Shui or Yoga when extracted from their traditional backgrounds: they hold the promise of wholeness and relaxation for the stressed Western soul and body without the snares of religious commitment. Indeed, in the case of the popular, New Age readings of the Kabbalah, the traditional features of Judaism – ritual and rules, discipline, communality – remain hidden from view. It is this obscuring of traditions which turns cultural and religious elements into free-floating signifiers and commodities, a practice that Madonna/Esther is also criticized for with regard to her conspicuous consumption of Kabbalah.

Conspicuous consumption and the hyped life of stars, their images, their paraphernalia and the money that can be made out of all this are of course the central focus of the novel since the protagonist is the autograph man of the title. He specializes in trading autographs by film stars of the 1950s and the 1960s and has a particular penchant for the 1952 film *The Girl from Peking*, starring the rather obscure actress Kitty Alexander whom he hunts down in New York City in the novel's main plot. Intriguingly, while the novel exploits Alex's dabbling with lifestyles and his pseudo-spiritual and pseudo-philosophical questing mainly for comic effects and gets much of its slapstick out of it, the tone sharpens noticeably with regard to the role of the media. Alex-Li can only earn a living as an autograph man because the world he lives in is dominated by the media, creating the hype that gives the identities he tries on and, more significantly, the signatures he buys and sells their market-value. The recognizability that is essential for successful mass marketing has also led Alex's generation to communicate with the help of slogans (Smith 2002: 15). Quoting is thus in every respect a ubiquitous phenomenon and any recombination of elements and contexts is possible. *The Autograph Man* criticizes this repeatedly and very emphatically with regard to the role of the media. The narrative observes Alex-Li's reaction bitterly when Kitty Alexander tells him of her mother's early death: 'Alex prepared to exchange one of those TV consolations that everyone of his generation learns by heart' (261). We also find statements such as: 'It's impossible these days to follow a man or quit a job without an encyclopedia of cinematic gestures crowding you out' (225). Alex's generation thus finds in the media an overwhelming array of possible gestures and sayings – and identity options, a whole spectrum of religious and cultural elements. But the novel alerts us to the problem that they remain empty semiotic signals because they do not allow for adequate individual expression.

The novel's criticism is particularly powerful because the commodity Alex deals with, the signature, evokes an epitome of postmodernism, Jacques Derrida's discussion of the impossibility of a stable identity, a fixed origin or a clear-cut context in 'Signature, Event, Context' (1977). Not least Derrida's own signature at the very end of his essay[4] demonstrates graphically that the intention of the individual has no hold over what he or she produces and that equally the context can never fully determine the meaning of any sign. In what is a groundbreaking discussion of performativity and a response to J.L. Austin's speech act theory, Derrida emphasizes the linguistic side of the performative. Linguistic signs have a history that exceeds any individual usage and, moreover, in every individual usage linguistic expression is subject to a complex, unfixable process of signification which Derrida describes in terms of his concepts of *différance*, the trace and the supplement. For Derrida the performative is thus not only, as for Austin, found in certain speech acts, such as the marriage vows whose performative success – their power 'to do things with words' as Austin's famous book holds – is granted by the context, by convention and by the law. In contrast, Derrida sees the performative happening in the general process of repetition and citation that each linguistic expression is subject to (Butler 1997: 148–51). Even if Derrida does not advocate complete arbitrariness, since for him meaning is inextricably linked with the historicity of cultural and linguistic expression, it is his seemingly boundless description of performativity that also governs the exchange of famous signatures in *The Autograph* Man: they can be exchanged, bought and sold in the general flow of cultural signifiers that people seem to be able to adopt and adapt at will.

True to the criticism of the novel of empty gestures and signs, however, the protagonist does not really cut their umbilical cord to the individual. Instead, that very cord constitutes his professional passion for autographs. Autographs have value because they originate from a (famous) person. Following this logic,

Alex has been writing letters to the actress he most admires, Kitty Alexander, for years and in the course of the novel he even begins to search for her in New York City. Thus, the very fact that the most significant free-floating elements in the novel are autographs – seemingly the epitome of 'empty' signatures – allows *The Autograph Man* to specify its criticism of the media world. Alex states that he can only watch films made before 1969 because the actors then 'played essences of themselves' (Smith 2002: 115) and managed to convey the Benjaminian aura that contemporary method actors do not possess. The protagonist specializes in the autographs of that period to get hold of this greatness which stems from the 'false religion' of Hollywood (115). We realize at this point that the free flow of signs and cultural and religious traits leaves something to be desired, an 'essence' in Alex's term, but also a sense of unity and oneness if one thinks of the promise that Buddhism and Kabbalah – the latter after all means 'tradition' – hold for Alex.

This lack is interrelated with the cult of the individual that the celebrities embody. Indeed, the novel complements its criticism of the role of the media with that of an over-developed self-consciousness and possessive individualism.[5] Thus one celebrity whom Alex meets in New York City hates her stardom and at the same time confesses that she loses her sense of herself without it: 'You asked, I'm telling you. Fuzzy. Like I can't sense myself' (218). But Alex, too, is guilty of making his 'favourite noise, the first-person pronoun' (328). By his friends, and by the novel, he is accused of selfishness and heartlessness towards others, especially where his girlfriend Esther is concerned, since he leaves for New York City although she has an operation to have her pacemaker replaced. Alex's immature sense of himself becomes most apparent in the contrast to the happiness his spiritual and religious friend Adam possesses. Like undecided Alex, Adam, too, significantly had to test several identities first:

> [Adam used to lurch] from one ill-fitting identity to another every summer, going through hippiedom, grunge, gangsta lite, various roots-isms (Ebonics, Repatriation, Rastafarianism), Anglophilia, Americanization, Afros, straightened, corn-rowed, shaved, baggy jeans, tight jeans, white girls, black girls, Jew girls, goy girls, conservatism, socialism, anarchism, partying, drugging, hermiting, schizing, rehabbing – how did he get from there to *this*? How did he get so *happy*?
>
> (109)

Alex embarks on the way from 'there' to 'this' when he broadens the gap between the autographs and life even further with an artificial success. In his development we recognize a way out of a hectic search for identity within a marketplace of free-floating, emptied options.

Alex makes a fortune at the end of the novel from selling Kitty Alexander's autographs since their prices explode in 'the Autograph Scoop of the Century' (289) after the media mistakenly announce her death and Alex does nothing to correct them, although she lives in his house. His private life turns chaotic, since both Adam and his sister Esther, the two most positive, emotional and spiritual characters in the novel, who interestingly are black, criticize him for his selfishness even more strongly than before. Esther almost turns away from him. When, during this phase, he enters a room where Esther and Kitty Alexander sleep at night he thinks in a state of great confusion that they are dead. He experiences this shock – 'the death punch, the infinite slap' (325) – viscerally. This is a novelty: 'He hadn't taken it personally, not for years. He took it cinematically, or televisually – if he took it at all' (324). This realization of death is a return of the repressed for Alex whose father, in the prologue to the novel, dies suddenly of a brain tumour, when he takes his son and his friends to a televised boxing match. After all those years Alex instinctively responds to this return of his lost mourning for his father by speaking the Kaddish, although he had earlier been extremely reluctant to participate in the *yahrzeit* for his father.[6]

Alex's physical reaction in this situation – he weeps, he is breathless, he needs to release emotional pressure in the speaking of the Kaddish – reveals the lack within contemporary culture as transmitted by the media which *The Autograph Man* condemns. As we know, for example, from Judith Butler, discourse, speech and language – cultural expressions – are seminally determined by their embodiment (Butler 1997: 10–11, 141–2; Krämer 2001: 247–8). Speech is literally enacted because the body acts and is active when we speak. With recourse to Shoshana Felman, Butler refers to this relationship as 'scandalous': '[T]he relation between speech and the body is a scandalous one, "a relation consisting at once of incongruity and inseparability [. . .] the scandal consists in the fact that the act cannot know what it is doing" ' (1997: 10).[7] In view of Butler's emphasis on the role of the body and the 'excess of speech' (152) it brings, we find that *The Autograph Man* complements Derrida's view of performativity in the way that Butler does when she contrasts Derrida's linguistic position with Pierre Bourdieu's emphasis on convention and habitus and eventually mediates between the two, taking recourse to the body and the 'scandal' it brings. As Butler points out, the embodied view of performativity alerts us to the agency and the opportunity for subversive acts that result from our embodied speaking. The body doubles what we say when we use expressions which are saturated with social and historical meaning and thus opens up a realm beyond those already established expressions. Thus, new meaning and also self-determination become possible. It is this inherent opportunity for enactment and even self-conscious theatricality which Butler refers to as performativity (Krämer 2001: 253–5). In this sense, what we say can never 'just be TV' as Alex so often fears. It is just that we forget about such possibilities, or else that the bodily doubleness of speech and expression is suppressed in order to maintain structures of power. In a novel in which embodiment is very important, especially because of its significant instances of illness (Alex's father dies of a brain tumour; Esther has a pacemaker; at the end of the novel, visiting a friend in hospital contributes to Alex's increasing awareness of himself and others), Alex learns more about this when he deals with the Kaddish a second time, this time in a communal situation. In the Kaddish the representation of the mix and match of individual identities thus intersects again with Jewishness, which is no longer merely a reservoir for lifestyle options. As a ritual that has remained unchanged over the centuries, the Kaddish is instead 'a signifier of the "essence" of Judaism or Jewishness, a ritual untouched by the processes of assimilation and accommodation' (Wirth-Nesher 2001: 122). Jewish culture and its religious rituals offer a significant contrast to a world determined by mass media offering one hip identity op after another. In this representation of Jewishness, *The Autograph Man* also reveals what the status and role of Jewish culture in the multi-ethnic whirl and the post-colonial context is. It is, however, not the safety of a fixed position with a secure faith.

Alex's friends want him to attend the *yahrzeit* for his father because they believe the communal speaking of the Kaddish will help him in his mourning. He is unwilling before his repressed emotions about his father's death return in the scene where he believes the two sleeping women to be dead. He remains reluctant even after this scene which occasions his spontaneous speaking of the Kaddish. Positive Adam makes Alex see the Rabbi about the *yahrzeit* anyway and Rabbi Burston explains why the Kaddish he spoke on his own did not help: 'Come *on*. Do you play football by yourself? Hockey? You watch a play by yourself? Do the tango by yourself? You make love by yourself? Actually, don't answer that' (Smith 2002: 337). So Alex learns about the communality that is central to the Kaddish and to Jewish culture in general. He thus also encounters a different model to the one he is familiar with, the excessive individualism and self-consciousness that juggles with identity snippets, fuelled by a ubiquitous media culture. Although Alex remains doubtful, at the end of the novel he participates in the communal speaking of the Kaddish for his father.

To Emmanuel Lévinas, who works from the basis of Jewish culture and religion, communality, mutuality and the structure of response, as we find it for example in the Kaddish, are typical features of the powerful ethical perspective inherent in Jewish culture. The responses in the Kaddish point us to the responsibility that Lévinas envisages for humanity. In his vision the other is more important than the self. The other is even the defining point for the self and thus the foundation of an inevitably ethical attitude.[8] Lévinas adds another layer to the notion of performativity when he emphasizes that speaking necessarily means speaking to an other. He defines speaking as an act that is free of violence, with the address of the other and the reciprocal exchange necessarily creating the equality of the other (1992: 17). The emphasis on embodiment and on bodily acting that the Kaddish brought in the first instance when Alex felt compelled to speak it in a moment of being emotionally overwhelmed thus does not represent a return of the powerful individual who makes his intentions work. Instead, as the second speaking of the Kaddish in the required group of (at least) ten shows, it rather epitomizes an emphasis on communal responsibility in connection with the bodily enactment of performativity. The latter element is emphasized in Judaism as a whole since it possesses a very practical side in the sense that its customs and rituals shape the days of its followers (Lévinas 1992: 30–1).

When Alex remains doubtful that the communal occasion for mourning that the prayer offers will be successful, since it is for him only a gesture, his spiritual friend Adam answers: 'What is more important than a gesture?' (Smith 2002: 326). While this corresponds to much current thinking on religion in general,[9] it is significantly mirrored in Lévinas's insight that in Judaism the adventures of the spirit happen on earth and among human beings (1992: 40). It also transpires in Friedrich Nietzsche's words cited repeatedly by Judith Butler in her tracing of performativity: 'there is no "being" behind doing, effecting, becoming [...] – the deed is everything' (1997: 45). Alex remains unconvinced of this until the end of the novel, but the novel's epilogue, which gives the words spoken and thought by those present at the *yahrzeit* for Alex's father, does its best to convince the sceptical protagonist of whom the text says twice at its very end: 'And Alex wonders what this meant' (Smith 2002: 347). This happens each time the bodily dimension is emphasized, with the lines from the prayer given in English framing it: 'Eleanor Loscher held her small Belly with both hands (And Alex wondered what this meant) *Make peace upon us and all Israel* Jonathan Verne yawned shamelessly (and Alex wondered what this meant) *And All Say Amen!*' (347).

As the last words of the novel, this largely unspoken, in parts almost corporeal interchange demonstrates aptly that the novel's main instrument for not idealizing Jewishness is its protagonist who will not be swayed easily, even by his great friend Adam, the advocate of the Jewish ritual, although Alex eventually gives up on one seminal instance of fiddling with identity snippets and stops working on his list of things Jewish and Goyish because he 'has grown tired of filing' (182, see also 275). Since Adam's portrayal verges on the idealizing, the contrast to the sceptical protagonist allows *The Autograph Man* to hold the balance very convincingly between not asking us to see salvation in the cultural strategies of Jewishness and at the same time presenting them as a feasible and probably successful path for the conundrums of identity building in the contemporary multiple world. Jewishness presents itself as a viable path according to the novel especially because of the dynamic embodiment of performativity, which receives its specific aptness by Lévinas's move of putting the other first and the ensuing ethical dimension. The alternative to the empty gestures and signatures of the complex world dominated by the media which *The Autograph Man* criticizes so vividly thus cannot be found in the security of a firm religious faith or the authentic membership in a community: 'The value in belonging to a community, or signifying a sense of collective solidarity, does not lie in cultivating some deep structure of cultural authenticity conserved in the homogenous empty time of tradition' (Bhabha 1998: xix). Homi Bhabha, one of the key figures of post-colonial criticism, gives this verdict in the introduction to a volume edited by Bryan Cheyette and Laura Marcus on the cultural position of 'the Jew'. In Bhabha's discussion of the possibilities of cultural belonging in the post-colonial world which takes Jewish humour as its example, we find the strategies mentioned again that characterize the performativity of Jewish culture: the enacting of cultural belonging, communality, the Lévinasian 'relentless drive towards the "third person"' (Bhabha 1998: xx): 'the uncertainty or indeterminacy of modern knowledge becomes an *act* of cultural survival and historical renewal. To take the hearer into account is to share *in* the making of a 'collective person' – nation, community, group' (xx; emphasis in original). Bhabha finds in Jewish culture crucial strategies for countering the aftermath of that 'lethal modernity' (xv) that colonized cultures have also encountered. And it is here that we realize why Jewish culture can serve as a model not only for the contemporary, hectic, medialized multi-ethnic world but centrally also for the conundrums of the post-colonial condition. As Bhabha points out, the necessary awareness of one's own position as a 'working basis' in the multiplicity of contemporary life, an awareness that results from the workings of performativity, is amplified by the crucial self-displacement that the Jewish joke represents. In the light of Jewish humour an alternative model to the inflation of the individual in the cult of the celebrity becomes apparent. It also undermines the over-estimation, the 'hype' of 'hip' individual cultural and religious features, which can be read as a searching for authenticity – if fragmented and individually put together – that Bhabha declares to be impossible. We realize that the invocation of cultural and religious belonging of Madonna's/Esther's current fervent adherence to Kabbalah is hard to credit because it lacks the irony and concomitant constant reflection of individual positions that characterize also the narrative of *The Autograph Man*. While exploring the features of Jewish culture in terms of performativity, Smith's second novel engages in the 'joke-work' Bhabha describes and makes light of its own journey:

> Accompanied by birdsong, the Zen lady says, 'Knowledge is the reward of action, because it is by doing things that we are transformed. Executing a symbolic gesture, truly living through a role, this is when we come to realize the truth inherent in the role. [. . .]' Alex turns to channel 6 in preparation for watching the popular classic *Casablanca*.
>
> (2002: 185)

Notes

1 John Mullan (2002) writes of *White Teeth*: 'Yet the ethnic and cultural identities of the characters are so various that Smith seems to be taking and enjoying new liberties rather than plotting the consequences of the empire'.

2 For this complex the work of Zygmunt Bauman (1998) is central, especially with his concept of allosemitism.

3 More precisely, mysticism refers to an experience of immediate knowledge of the deity and often a sense of direct communication with the divinity that culminates in a sense of unity and wholeness (*unio mystica*), cf. Scholem (1973: 12).

4 This was originally a paper delivered orally to The Association of the French Speaking Societies of Philosophy, but participants were requested to hand in their presentations in written form in advance and to sign them to authenticate them. Derrida discusses the contextuality of signs in his paper and comments ironically on the notion of an origin or source that is at the bottom of every communication (language is traditionally regarded only as a 'transport' of clear meaning from an 'author'). He does this by paradoxically 'signing' a text that was delivered orally and by pointing us to the text's path through different forms of textuality: it was written first and after its oral delivery we now find it printed in a book. Cf. Derrida (1982: 330).

5 For a discussion of the pronounced individualism in modernity in the context of alienation and alienness see Waldenfels (1999: 49).

6 This is mirrored in the novel in a description of Queen Victoria mourning the loss of her husband which is characterized by a strong theatricality. It was literally 'enacted' in the Royal Albert Hall with a myriad of performances.

7 Later on in her book, Butler summarizes the relationship between body and speech as follows: 'The relationship between speech and the body is that of a chiasmus. Speech is bodily, but the body exceeds the speech it occasions; and speech remains irreducible to the bodily means of its enunciation' (1997: 155–6). Significantly, Butler does not follow Derrida in considering mainly writing.

8 As Lévinas points out, one only gets a sense of one's own responsibility when one is confronted with one's responsibility for the other (Taureck 2002: 55–6).

9 For a discussion of religion being in the world and not being located in a transcendent realm, see Gargani (2001: esp. 154).

Part III

Changing centres, changing peripheries and spaces in-between

Jewish writing from the Anglophone diaspora(s) – America

5 Literary symptomology and Jewish fiction

'Envy; or, The New Yiddish in America'

Emily Miller Budick

> It doesn't matter what you speak, envy sounds the same in all languages.
>
> Ostrover in Ozick (1969; 1971: 83)

At least as early as Freud's 1908 essay 'Creative Writers and Day-Dreaming', critics have spoken of literary texts in terms of an authorial unconscious. 'Psychoanalyzing' texts and/or their authors has become increasingly sophisticated since the 1950s and 1960s when critics read with the aim of discovering within the text one or another Freudian plot or neurosis – whether on the part of the author or of the characters. Contemporary psychoanalytic criticism of literary texts has abandoned this more simplistic, reductive, allegorical reading of literary fiction. Instead, and more profitably, it has increasingly focused on the dynamics of transference within the psychoanalytic setting and the corresponding, analogous intersubjectivity of the writer-reader or text-reader relationship.

What has been lost, perhaps, in this very important move away from a reductive Freudian approach is the relationship between the text and basic psychological processes. These are the processes that structure and provide content to the transferential habits of the human mind that have come to dominate interest of sophisticated psychoanalytic literary critics like Peter Brooks and others. Even if we want quite strenuously to avoid psychoanalysing the writer, nonetheless, it is clear that conflictual elements of the writer's ego dynamics come to bear on the composition of his or her texts (as, for that matter, do such features of the reader's dynamic unconscious in the explication of those texts). This is especially the case, perhaps, in ethnic and other minority literatures, in which the socioeconomic, cultural, and historical contexts and conditions of the text's composition are hardly incidental to both the conscious and unconscious motivations of the writer, not to mention – in at least a good percentage of instances – of the reader as well.

Such literary fictions might profitably be thought of as *symptoms* (personal or collective), to which we, the readers, are being asked by a particular human being, who is a member of one community or another, to attend. This is by no means to foreclose the issue of what might constitute the symptom called a literary fiction. Nor is it to decide what might be an appropriate response to that symptom. Curing the author and/or the text may not at all be the desirable response to a literary symptom, though a certain form of acknowledgement of what the symptom expresses might.

'The symptom', writes Slavoj Žižek, of actual psychological symptoms, 'not only can be interpreted but is, so to speak, already formed in view of its interpretation [...] In other words, there is no symptom without its addressee.' This does not mean, however, that such symptoms are transparent and therefore easy to understand. Nor does the symptom 'dissolve itself' when it is interpreted. Rather, the symptom persists despite treatment and/or interpretation, because of what is called in Lacan's now familiar and famous term *jouissance.* 'The symptom', Žižek explains,

> is not only a ciphered message, it is at the same time a way for the subject to organize his enjoyment. [...] In other words, the symptom is the way we – the subject – 'avoid madness', the way we 'choose something [...] instead of nothing' [...] through the binding of our enjoyment to a certain signifying, symbolic formation which assures a minimum of consistency to our being in the world. [...] [I]n the real of [the] symptom [is] the only support of [an individual's] being.
>
> (1991: 206–8)

The symptom, in other words, is in some ways synonymous with the uniqueness of the self, with the desire that we not be explained away or made transparent by some external definition or, as it were, diagnosis of who we are. Rather than signal a state of psychosis, then, or even high neurosis, the designation of a literary text as a symptom may well enable us to see its utterly irreducible, perhaps even uninterpretable uniqueness and specificity as a text.

At the same time, by importing the language of psychological dis-ease (which isn't synonymous with disease or illness) into the analysis of the text, the idea of the symptom may nonetheless point us to the ways in which literature often hovers on the border between creative reason and desperate madness. Two other ways that literary texts have traditionally been defined is as either fetishistic or as perverse, as erotic or sexual substitutions. Through the writer's '*ars poetica*' ('metaphor, synecdoche, and metonymy'), writes Freud in 'Creative Writers and Day-Dreaming', 'the creative writer [...] like the dreamer and the playing child [...] has found a way of rendering unacceptable desires into shareable form. [...] To be a poet is to be able to make the apparently impossible thing an acceptably pleasurable transgression' (Freud 1985: 12, 7). This *ars poetica* is, for Freud, akin to what he elsewhere describes as sublimation. But this same *ars poetica*, 'where', as Peter Brooks puts it, 'objects, details, metonymies, and synecdoches predominate' may also evidence the text's fetishistic qualities (1994: 30). Fetishism is the worship of a substitute object instead of the true human object of devotion or affection. Literature, Brooks suggests, is not fetishism per se. Rather it 'implies the *possibility* of fetishism, the *interesting threat* of being waylaid by some element along the way to the "proper" end, taking some displaced substitute of simulacrum for the thing itself' (30; emphasis added). Embodying what Brooks calls 'forepleasure' (29), a term he takes from the Freud essay, literature, we might say, is also not strictly speaking a perversion, but rather, as in foreplay itself, the playful threat of one.

Being a symptom, the text, then, is neither a fetish nor a perversion. Yet, it is the threat or possibility of both, which the text somehow resists. The idea of the symptomology of the text preserves this intermediary position, somewhere between the dysfunction and disease of genuine neurosis and the sterility of denial and/or pure normalcy – whatever that might be. The symptom expresses authorial or textual dis-ease.

Insofar as a literary symptomology or the expression of textual dis-ease is not manifested in an individual's personal behaviour but, rather, in a text, which is to say (usually) also in a shared tradition of other people's other words and other texts, it achieves something of the condition of a public as well as a private condition. Maria Torok and Nicholas Abraham describe a psychic phenomenon that their translator Nicholas Rand designates as *inherited trauma*. This is a trans-generational phantom, in which the secrets of others enjoy encrypted existence within the self; 'what haunts', suggest Torok and Abraham, 'are not the dead, but the gaps left within us by the secrets of others', 'the tombs of others'. 'Thus, the phantom cannot even be recognized by the subject' since it is

> the formation of the unconscious that has never been conscious – for good reason. It passes [...] from the parent's unconscious into the child's. [...] The phantom's periodic and compulsive return lies beyond the scope of symptom-formation in the sense of a return of the repressed; it works like a ventriloquist, like a stranger within the subject's own mental topography.
>
> (Torok and Abraham 1994: 171–3)

Often, it is encoded in words, which repeat a symptom that, initially at least, belonged to someone else (Torok and Abraham 1994: 171–3).

The symptomology of literary texts very often expresses such inherited and indeed communal traumas, which are themselves locked – expressed and repressed – in the words of others. What is produced by the literary tradition in the intertextual, intersubjective relation among these texts is something of a collective consciousness or mind, which, like an individual mind, contains both conscious and unconscious components. This collective consciousness, also like the individual mind, wishes to express itself and be understood. It also, however, and simultaneously, desires to keep hidden and out of direct conscious knowledge secrets both contemporary (and pertaining largely, perhaps, to the individual author) and past. And it harbours secrets of which it is itself unaware. The question that may then be put to a particular literary tradition, say, the tradition of Jewish or Jewish American literature, is not only: what does this body of texts intend to say about the Jewish experience, but also, and just as vitally, what would it particularly like *not* to say? and what, in this not saying, is it nonetheless saying, which may *also* be a part of a collective, phantom-like expression of secrets that precisely do not belong to the actual lived experience of the particular writer but to the tradition from which he comes?

Take, for example, a text like Cynthia Ozick's 1969 classic short story, 'Envy; or, Yiddish in America'. This story would seem to have a fairly straightforward if nonetheless highly fraught subject: namely, the condition of Jewish authorship in the United States in the period immediately following the Holocaust. The text would seem, in fact, to be offering a diagnosis of the disease of Jewish authorship and even offering a few remedies. Yet, the text, I want to suggest, exhibits just the symptom it seems to be diagnosing. Envy, I propose, is more than the story's subject. It constitutes its very subject-hood, its subjectivity, the symptom of nothing less than its Jewishness. Consumed by envy, the story perceives the world through envious eyes. It also (somewhat defensively) sets itself up as an object of envy, both of its potential readers and of its own protagonists.

To be sure, and as most readers have taken it, the story is specifically about a group of American Yiddish writers and their envy concerning the one writer among them who, defying all odds, has succeeded in breaking into American, not to mention world, culture (Lowin 1988; Cohen 1994; Kauvar 1993). Yankel Ostrover, the successful Yiddish American author, is a flimsily veiled I.B. Singer, still perceived by many (as recently as 2004, the year of his centenary) as a corruptor of the Yiddish language and the least deserving of *all* the Yiddish writers to have achieved international prominence. Indeed, the story's major protagonist Edelshtein may well be modelled on American Yiddish poet Jacob Glatstein. Glatstein had numerous unflattering things to say about his more successful rival Singer, many of them quoted almost verbatim in Ozick's text (Lowin 1988: 21–4).

Yet written for large segments at a time in a barely literate, Yiddish-inflected English, and proceeding through fits and starts of transliterated and often untranslated, but hardly eloquent or complex Yiddish, might not the story be understood to be expressing its own envy of the Yiddish writers who are the objects of its critique? To pick up a word that the text uses in relation to Edelshtein, to which we will return, the story virtually belches forth its Yiddish. Ozick herself, we know, translated Glatstein into English. She also lamented the loss of Yiddish in the essay she was composing just at the time she was writing 'Envy'. In 'Towards a New Yiddish', which she delivered as a lecture in Israel in 1970 ('Envy; or, Yiddish in America' is initially published in *Commentary* in 1969), Ozick identifies the need for a new Yiddish that might become, as the old Yiddish once was, a vehicle of the preservation of Jewish literature and culture. In many ways, I suggest, Ozick imagines her own story, with its immigrant English and Yiddish-speak, to be a model of what such a New Yiddish might look and sound like. But rather than resolve the text's own envy of the more skilled Yiddish writers, this move on the part of the text only produces one more turn of the screw. For in claiming itself the new vessel of Yiddish in America, the story is also directed towards producing envy both in the reader and, even more startlingly perhaps, in the Yiddish writers whom the story evidences itself as envying. The story's unwillingness to translate many of its Yiddish terms cannot but produce in the assimilated, non-Yiddish-speaking reader of the story (like me) a feeling of his or her lack (and thereby, perhaps, envy – technically envy has everything to do with *lack*) in relation to the language, even in its compromised representation in the story itself.

There is a moderately hostile, aggressive move, here, on the part of the story, to exclude at least some readers, to make them feel the loss of the language and the impoverishment that that loss brings with it. At the same time, however, and just as forcibly, the story also presents itself as the object of envy of its protagonists. 'Envy; or, Yiddish in America' is a specifically American work of fiction such as its major protagonist Edelshtein envies, even more, perhaps, than the success of the translated Ostrover. Ozick modestly, or is it contemptuously?, arrogantly even?, omits her name from the list of 'so-called Jewish novelists' (1969; 1971: 79) whom Edelshtein so abhors: 'Roth Philip/Rosen Norma/Melammed Bernie/ Friedman B.J./Paley Grace/Bellow Saul/Mailer Norman' (52). Yet the native-born English-speaking Ozick, whose story we are at this very moment reading, must certainly be numbered among the most important of these American Jewish writers, the '*Amerikaner-geboren* [as Edelshtein designates them], spawned in America, pogroms a rumour, *mamaloshen* a stranger, history a vacuum' (41), 'picking at their crotches [...] [o]ne [Yiddish] word here, one word there. *Shikseh* on one page, *putz* on the other, and that's the whole vocabulary. And when they give a try at phonetic rendition!' (79). All of this ranting and raving might well apply to the very story by Ozick in which we are now reading these words. Edelshtein, we are told, 'was certain he did not envy' the American Jewish writers, 'but', nonetheless, 'he read them like a sickness' (41). Indeed, insofar as Ozick's story contains many of the elements attributed to Ostrover's fiction – the modernist satire, comedy, irreverence and down-right wickedness, which Edelshtein tells us he so deplores in Ostrover; and, furthermore, insofar as the story actually tells twice-over the same story of the failed Yiddish American author that Ostrover tells (first, by quoting Ostrover's reading of the story at the YMCA and then by retelling the story, in its own voice, as the narrative entitled 'Envy; or, Yiddish in America'), Ozick's story also counts as a translation from the Yiddish, such as Singer-Ostrover himself might have produced. Ozick has written in praise of Singer in, for example, 'I.B. Singer's Book of Creation'. She has also expressed respect and admiration for American Jewish writers such as Roth (to whom she dedicates *The Messiah of Stockholm*), Bellow and Malamud (see, for example, the essays 'Literary Blacks and Jews', 'What Drives Saul Bellow' and 'Saul Bellow's Broadway'). If Ozick's story, then, is *about* envy, it is, itself, both admiring and envious, and, at the same time, it also makes itself an object of envy (and hopefully admiration) as well.

What is envy that it should figure so obsessively in this story? And what might envy have to do, not simply with Yiddish in America, but with Yiddish itself? After all, Ozick goes out of her way to trace the origins of Edelshtein's envy back to his childhood in Russia, long before the Holocaust and the migration to the United States. Yiddish *in America* may only be a specific moment in the much longer and continuous history of Yiddish as such. What might be imagined as the internal relationship between Yiddish and envy and why might this be a fit subject for a text that is itself clearly enamoured of the Jewish *mamaloshen*, indeed, that, like its major protagonist, is in mourning for the murdered language?

Envy, we should keep in mind, is not a specifically Jewish phenomenon, though Ostrover, I think, is not quite accurate when he says 'It doesn't matter what you speak, envy sounds the same in all languages' (83). Ozick's story has everything to do with the specificity of Jewish, Yiddishist envy – hence, the title of the story. Indeed, Ozick's is a great work of Jewish fiction precisely because of the sound that her 'envy' (as subject and subjectivity both) speaks.

Psychoanalytically speaking, envy (like every other feature of the ego) has, of course, everything to do with childhood and the specific, personal origins of who we are, where the personal by necessity also includes, of course, the familial and the communal. These childhood origins of the envying self have to do, not only with the father (as expressed in the classical idea of penis envy, an idea certainly not irrelevant to this story of a group of men vying with each other for authority and dominance). Rather, and usefully for interpreting a story of the *mamaloshen* – the mother tongue – by the writer who might well be designated mother of American Jewish fiction, these origins occur also and even earlier in relation to the mother as well. While jealousy, albeit a derivative of envy, is, to quote Melanie Klein, 'mainly concerned with love that the subject feels is his due and has been taken away, or is in danger of being taken away, from him by his rival' (as in sexual jealousy such as characterizes the relationships of Ostrover, Edelshtein and Baumzweig), envy is 'the angry feeling that another person possesses and enjoys something desirable – the envious impulse being to take it away or to spoil it. Moreover, envy implies the subject's relation to one person only. It goes back to the earliest exclusive relation with the mother' (1957: 6–7).

Understanding what Klein and Freud mean by the term *envy* requires, of course, understanding what psychoanalysis as a discipline means by the terms it uses. Psychoanalytic vocabulary is no more transparent or to be taken for granted than any other professional, or, for that matter, literary vocabulary. This is not the place to undertake a thoroughgoing 'defence' or even explication of Klein and Freud. What is to be recalled, however, is that, whatever forces of competition, conflict and 'envy' these analysts describe, and however they account for them in terms of early childhood development, these features of the human psyche do *not* exist in isolation of the equally powerful force that gets much less emphasized in psychoanalysis (or, at least, its application to literary texts) but that is just important: namely, love, or, in the case of Klein's essay 'Envy and Gratitude', gratitude. Indeed, envy, like other psychological forces, embodies conflict. It exists *because* of internal conflicts, which the individual, for one reason or another, does not and often cannot resolve. Envy and gratitude are an inseparable, conflictual pair.

To speak of Ozick's story entitled 'Envy' in terms of penis-envy or breast-envy is only to take the hint of the fiction's own language. It is to imagine that the story takes seriously its own words, and therefore that it might be as interested in the phenomenon of envy as it is in Yiddish or Yiddish in America. It might even be interested in the relationship between the two, which it seems to be equating in the title. That the story should itself embody or express envy may well evidence the degree to which Ozick's analysis of the relationship between Yiddish and envy (only or also in America) is accurate. It may also, however, evidence the author's own unconscious inheritance of the tradition. This would in no way compromise the deep, paradigmatic centrality of her text within that tradition. Indeed, insofar as tradition is imbibed along with the mother's milk or the *mamaloshen*, one might even go so far as to argue that it is precisely *because* the story inherits the tradition in this way that it is paradigmatic and central.

It is all to the point both of the story's analysis of Edelshtein and its own repetition of the tradition of Jewish envy that Ozick traces the protagonist's problems back into his childhood, where they have as much to do with the situation of the Yiddish-speaking shtetl Jew in post-Enlightenment Europe as with anything else. For Edelshtein (and, I would venture, other of his compatriots as well), all of 'Western Civilization was a sore point. He had never been to Berlin, Vienna, Paris, or even London. He had been to Kiev . . . once, as a young boy', with 'his father, a *melamed*', who had been engaged to teach Hebrew to a little rich Jewish boy named Alexei (1969; 1971; 41–2). Kiev, we discover, is a far sorer point than Berlin and Alexei is even more painful than Kiev itself. 'What had become of Alexei Kirilov?' Edelshtein muses to himself early in the text:

> Edelshtein, a widower in New York, sixty-seven years old, a Yiddishist (so-called) poet, could start at anything at all – a subway car-card, a garbage lid, a streetlight – and cause the return of Alexei Kirilov's face, his bright cheeks, his Ukraine-accented Yiddish, his shelves of mechanical toys from Germany – trucks, cranes, wheelbarrows, little coloured autos with awnings overhead. Avremeleh had a knack of getting things by heart. He was a golden head. . . . Edelshtein remembered every coveted screw of the German toys.
>
> (42)

Edelshtein envies Alexei's wealth, his position, his intellect. He envies his education and the access that it provides into non-Jewish European culture, even beyond the Russian pale. And perhaps above all Edelshtein envies Alexei's relationship to his own (Edelshtein's) father, and perhaps (in the absence of his mother on the scene of the story) to his own (Alexei's) mother and father as well.

Language and literature play a major role here in Edelshtein's growing envy of the child's access to European culture. 'On the afternoons the Latin tutor came', Edelshtein recalls, he (Edelshtein) 'crouched outside the threshold [and] heard *ego, mei, mihi, me, me.* May may. Beautiful foreign nasal chant of riches. Latin! Dirty from the lips of idolators. An apostate family' (81). To the young Edelshtein Latin (like everything else about the Kirilovs) sounds like the language of entitlement: 'may may'. (We might well see it also as the language of narcissism: me me.) His protest, then, against the family's 'filth' and 'apostacy' barely conceals his well-censored desire for all those forbidden pleasures Russian culture seems to him to offer the wealthy assimilated Kirilovs. (Kirilov, we are told, is the family's *Russified* name.)

Like Alexei, Edelshtein would assimilate. 'He wished he had been born a Gentile' (67), the story tells us, in a voice not wholly the narrator's and also not wholly of Edelshtein's conscious mind either. Edelshtein will not readily admit this wish. Nor will he even give himself permission to long for this culture from which he has been excluded, the culture that is *not* Yiddish, but Russian, even perhaps Hebrew. Edelshtein's father, who is lavishing so much affection on the golden Alexei, is teaching the child Hebrew, not Yiddish. Yiddish is not Edelshtein's language of choice but the language to which he is condemned: while his father is permitted to call Alexei by his Russian name, Edelshtein himself, he recalls, is only permitted to call Alexei by his Yiddish name, Avremeleh. Edelshtein is prohibited from learning any of the classical languages, including Hebrew, in all its formal, scholastic purity: '*kal, nifal, piet, upal, hifil, hofal, hispael*' (81).

Yiddish, the text is reminding us here and elsewhere, was considered by many the inferior of the two Jewish languages. (Yiddish, Ozick says in 'Towards a New Yiddish', 'with all its glories [...] is second to Hebrew', 1970; 1983: 173.) In Palestine it lost out in the battle with Hebrew, because, in Ostrover's words, 'in the God-Given State of Israel they had no use for the language of the bad little interval between Canaan and now. Yiddish was inhabited by the past, the New Jews did not want it' (Ozick 1969; 1971: 48). Given his status as an American Yiddishist who is only read in English translation, Ostrover is certainly to be accused of dissimulation when he claims to have 'left Palestine during the 1939 Arab riots, not [...] out of fear, out of integrity rather – it was a country which had turned its face against Yiddish' (48). Neither, in this context, is his defence of Yiddish particularly pure, especially when it becomes the instrument of his seduction of the American public. According to his translator, Ostrover 'woos' this public even more ardently than he does his 'translators', whom he keeps 'in a perpetual frenzy of envy for each other' (55; 'he sleeps with the right translators', says another one of the characters, 48). The licentiousness of Ostrover's use of Yiddish is represented in all of its perverse sordidness in his seduction of Edelshtein's wife Mirileh, whom he also 'woo[s]' (49) by regaling her with stories of 'how rotten it was in Israel for Yiddish and Yiddishists. In Israel the case was even lamer than in New York, thank God!' (48).

The question the text raises, however, is whether Ostrover's somewhat salacious and compromising use of Yiddish (especially in his fiction of the demonic and the perverse) is the exception or the rule. One need only think of some of the classic Yiddish writers, from Mendele Mocher Sefarim to Sholem Aleichem to S. Ansky (author of *The Dybbuk*, to which the story at one point refers) to gain some measure of the 'perversity' of the tradition itself. Furthermore, as Edelshtein himself acknowledges, Yiddish is, by definition, an impure language. '[O]ur treasure-tongue', says Edelshtein, 'is derived from strangers. [...] 90 per cent German roots, 10 per cent Slavic.' Always one to repress Edelshtein tells us that 'this means nothing' (85). He also occludes completely the relationship between Yiddish and that other, loftier language his father teaches, Hebrew. And yet we readers might well ask just how 'irrelevant' (85) this impurity of the *mamaloshen* is.

Edelshtein claims to be as little jealous of Ostrover's and Mirileh's 'toying affair' as he is unenvious of the American Jewish writers, 'but', just as he reads those writers with a sickness, so 'he thought himself obliged to throw a kitchen chair at Ostrover' (48–9). The '*toys*' Edelshtein 'coveted' so long ago in Kiev he covets still, as much in the toying love affair as anywhere else. The coveted 'screws' return. Is Edelshtein's fantasy of the purity of the *mamaloshen* any less self-deceiving? Is it not also only another turn of the screw?

The Yiddish writer assimilated into American culture through translation – whom Edelshtein and Baumzweig refer to as '*der chazer*' – the pig – may, like the assimilated American Jewish writers (including Ozick and her 'new Yiddish'), be no more *treyf* (81) – unkosher – than the *mamaloshen* itself. *Treyf*, especially as represented by the most *treyf* of the *treyf*, *der chazer*, is just the right term to designate what is for Edelshtein a virtually bodily disgust and revulsion of the things which he refuses to admit he desires. That these two terms are left untranslated in the text suggests their utter untranslatability, the ways in which the taboos and prohibitions of the tradition (like the other more explicitly psychosexual inhibitions of any child's socialization) are almost literally imbibed, from birth, along with the mother's milk. Hence, Edelshtein's chronic indigestion, his constant belching forth his disgust.

Says one of Ostrover's translators of herself, carrying forward the text's near obsession with oral and anal imagery – assholes and mouths –, she is 'his pig, his stool (I mean that in both senses, I assure you)' (54; Baumzweig's income is guaranteed, we are told, by a Jewish manufacturer of laxatives, 45). Fated not to dine at the 'long and luminous' 'refreshment tables' of local synagogues, but rather to swallow 'scraps' from them, Edelshtein still hungers for the '*treyf*' denied to him at the Kirilovs' table ('Edelshtein and his father took their coffee and bread, but otherwise lived on boiled eggs; the elder Kirilov one day brought home the *mashgiach* from the Jewish poorhouse to testify to the purity of the servants' kitchen but to Edelshtein's father the whole house was *treyf*', 81). Or, more accurately, Edelshtein hungers to be relieved, or purged (hence those laxatives) of his own wish to thus dine at the tables of those others whom he (envies and) scorns.

Treyf is exactly the right word to define the interplay in an endogamic religion like Judaism between reproductive relations and food. Of 'fundamental importance' in the psychoanalytic understanding of envy, Klein writes, is 'the infant's first object relation – the relation to the mother's breast and to the mother.' 'If this primal object, which is introjected, takes root in the ego with relative security, the basis for a satisfactory development is laid' (1957: 3). And Klein goes on:

> The first object to be envied is the feeding breast, for the infant feels that it possesses everything he desires and that it has an unlimited flow of milk and love which the breast keeps for its own gratification. [...] But [...] it is not only food he desires; he also wants to be freed from destructive impulses and persecutory anxiety. [...] [E]nvy spoils the primal good object [...] The

> breast attacked [...] [loses] its value, it has become bad [...]. [E]nvy spoils the capacity for enjoyment.
>
> (10–16)

Given the condition of 'insecurity' defining Jewish life even preceding the Holocaust, represented in the story, in part, by the absence of Edelshtein's mother on the scene of his childhood, it is not surprising that envy should dominate over love or gratitude as what defines Edelshtein's relationship to the *mamaloshen*; or that fixated on the purity of the mother tongue, which contains everything and is compromised by nothing, that Edelshtein should be incapable of producing offspring of his own.

'He had no children', the text records, immediately following his revery of Alexei on the train (Ozick 1969; 1971: 44). According to his wife, this is due to his 'sperm-count' (48) – one more bodily fluid from one more orifice in this story awash with digestive juices and gases. His biological and literary sterility are not unrelated. Thus, walking home after two of his many unsatisfying temple lectures on his grand subject (the death of Yiddish), the first of them at an affluent synagogue which boasted in '14-karat gold' the inscription 'And thou shalt see My back; but My face shall not be seen', the second in Mt Vernon where a young girl mimicks his accent, Edelshtein falls into the following reverie, which brings together the sexual and culinary taboos:

> [H]e dreamed he was in Kiev, with his father. He looked through the open schoolroom door at the smoking cheeks of Alexei Kirilov, eight years old. 'Avremeleh,' he called, 'Avremeleh, *kum tsu mir, lebst ts' geshtorben*?' He heard himself yelling in English: 'Thou shalt see my asshole!' A belch woke him to hot fear. He was afraid he might be, unknown to himself all his life long, a secret pederast.
>
> (44)

And again, later in the story, after having met the niece of a fellow Yiddishist Vorovsky, a young woman who knows Yiddish and whom Edelshtein sees as a potential translator, Edelshtein once again lapses into dream. Once more, amidst belches, he sees himself 'kissing Alexei's cheeks like ripe peaches [but] it was not Alexei, it was a girl, Vorovksy's niece' (72).

While Ozick's story, as a work of fiction, playing with this or another perverse subject, may well toe the line on this side of perversion, what Edelshtein desires in relation to Alexei and Hannah is perversion itself, pederasty in Edelshtein's own self-diagnosis. Not only is Edelshtein's desire not fully mature sexually, it isn't even fully sexual. What Edelshtein really desires in relation to Alexei is not to engage in sexual intercourse with him, but, actually, 'to be Alexei' (96), to injest, imbibe and become him. 'You remain. You remain', he says in a letter addressed to Alexei Yosifovitch:

> An illumination. More than my own home, nearer than my mother's mouth. Your father slapped my father. You were never told. Because I kissed you on the green

> stairs. The shadow-place on the landing where I once saw the butler scratch his pants. They sent us away shamed. My father and I, into the mud. Again a lie. Never near the child. [...] Only through the doorway, looking, looking.
> (80–2)

The case of Hannah is, if anything, even more disturbing. Sliding seamlessly from Alexei to Hannah in his burp-punctuated sexual fantasy, Edelshtein expresses his desire, not for Hannah herself, but for her 'cheeks', like 'ripe peaches'. He desires her 'mouth', which, in keeping with the culinary imagery that controls Edelshtein's imagination, metamorphoses into 'the little apple of her womb' (95). For Edelshtein Hannah is, as it were, good enough to eat; indeed, insofar as peaches and apples are, in their roundness, reminiscent of breasts (an image reinforced by the idea that it is her cheeks that are peaches), what Edelshtein wishes is to nurse at the font of her abundance. When, like the adolescent girl in the first scene, Hannah later mocks him, he will slap her 'mouth' (97), and, in so doing, he will, for the first time, '[feel] like a father' – perhaps like his own father, Edelshtein now taking revenge for being slapped by Alexei's father, after Edelshtein had kissed Alexei or fantasized kissing him on the mouth (since it is by no means clear that he has). 'Her mouth lay back naked on her face', the scene with Hannah continues: 'He had put a bulge in her lip' (97) – a bulge that might be understood to represent a different kind of swelling that needed to be put elsewhere if it was to produce procreative consequences. Insofar as there is an orifice that Edelshtein would penetrate, it is Hannah's mouth, but he would do so to have her, through that organ, give birth to *him*: 'Breathe in me! Animate me! Without you I'm a clay pot', Edelshtein rails at her; 'Dybbuk! [...] I'll become a golem [...]. Translate me!' (94).

What Edelshtein desires is what the text calls over and over again *translation*. In addition to its ordinary, everyday literary meaning, translation, we might recall, also means to transform (a word which also appears several times in the text). It is to produce one substance out of another – as, perhaps, in defecation itself. It is one of those more frequent theories among children that faeces and babies come into the world in the same way. Certainly the tradition of golems, which Edelshtein here invokes, has something to do with a fantasy of non-genitally, non-sexually reproduced beings, creatures of earth and dirt, which might nonetheless function as nothing less than saviours. '[Y]ou'll be like a Messiah to a whole generation', Edelshtein says to Hannah, which is to say that the 'born poet' whom she would translate, namely himself, would be such a Messiah through her translation or transformation of him.

But translation can mean even more than transformation in some material way. It can mean nothing less than the miracle of immortality, which is certainly what Edelshtein wishes to achieve through the translation of his literary works. This other meaning of the word translation is obliquely hinted at in one of Edelshtein's imaginary letters to Hannah: '[P]lease remember', he advises her,

> that when a goy from Columbus, Ohio, says 'Elijah the Prophet' he's not talking about *Eliohu hanovi*. Eliohu is one of us, a *folksmensh*, running

> around in second-hand clothes. Their's is God knows what. The same biblical figure, with exactly the same history, once he puts on a name from King James, COMES OUT A DIFFERENT PERSON. Life, history, hope, tragedy, they don't come out even. They talk Bible Lands, with us it's *eretz yisroel.*
>
> (82)

Translation, we might be reminded by this reference to Eliohu, can mean, not simply to come out a different person or substance (as in birth or defecation or the manufacturing of golems) but, specifically 'to convey to heaven or to a nontemporal condition without death', as is reported to have been the case with the Old Testament '*Eliohu hanovi*'.

Translation, in other words, is a kind of non-procreative regeneration, a kind of life in spite of and even through death. The escape of noxious gases from Edelshtein's body, literally from his mouth, but, we might feel, given the anal ambience of the text, from his 'asshole' as well, displace the more life-affirming, life-creating ejaculations, the absence of which have rendered Edelshtein literally childless: the low sperm-count, on which Edelshtein's wife blames their childlessness (49), though Edelshtein blames their failure to reproduce on her 'belly', once again confusing digestive and reproductive organs. Edelshtein's *Translate me* is, throughout the story, a plea, not for a procreative relationship with the woman or the language that will bear his offspring but to nurse at breast of the *mamaloshen* and to be thereby transformed and immortalized. 'A man my age', Edelshtein says later, 'do I want a lover or a translator?' (98). Good question. But it raises the question also about the younger Edelshtein earlier on: did he ever desire a lover or did he always only wish for a translator?

'The difference between him and Ostrover', Edelshtein muses at one point in the text, 'was this: Ostrover wanted to save only himself, Edelshtein wanted to save Yiddish. Immediately he felt he lied. [. . .] [H]e lied, lied, lied. [. . .] What did the death of Jews have to do with his own troubles. [. . .] Whoever mourns the dead mourns himself' (56, 75). It is probably safe to say that most writers write out of personal need, not public conviction. Insofar as Ozick's story is an elegy for the dead language, Edelshtein's comment pertains to her and her story as well; indeed, it pertains to the tradition of Yiddish fiction, as, perhaps of all fiction. Hannah refuses to translate Edelshtein's Yiddish because, she says, Yiddish is the language of Jewish suffering (92, 95). Such suffering certainly has to do with the subjects of Jewish fiction: the condition of Jews worldwide and throughout history. But such suffering is also the ambience of Yiddish literature in another way, a way that the young, American-born Hannah herself utterly fails to understand. Like the mother who, in the views of analysts like Klein and Winnicott, suffers the child greedily to envy the breast without denying the child access to that breast, so the *mamaloshen* may be understood to have continuously provided for the needs of the Jewish people over the generations of their want and desire.

It is the tolerance of Ozick's story, its long-suffering affection for and nurture of its protagonists and the Jewish condition of which it is itself a part and a symptom, which makes it a story written in the (new) *mamaloshen*. Envy is one of those most primary of human emotions. It can either tear us apart (as it does Edelshtein and Vorovsky) or it can help guide us to that shared condition of our humanity (perhaps, for those of us who are Jews, the special condition of our shared Jewish humanity), which defines us as human beings. The problem with envy, as Klein notes, is that, unchecked, it 'spoils the primal good object' (i.e., the breast) and, in so doing, 'spoils the capacity for enjoyment' (1957: 15–16). From the start, Edelshtein has demanded from the *mamaloshen* more or less what he is now demanding from Hannah (perhaps this is what all writers childishly demand from language): that it transform him, immortalize him, translate him. Literature is the symptom of this desire and, along with whatever else it expresses, it expresses as well the dissatisfaction and envy that such desire provokes. The question then becomes: how does a tradition sustain desire? How does it turn envy into gratitude? Another way of asking this question would be: can the literary text be produced without the symptom, which, in the case of Ozick's story, is the envy, the other side of which is the desire, which will never be wholly supplied but without which there can be no vitality, no gratitude, no generosity and no love?

Envy is not a Jewish problem. It is a human problem. But it is a problem about which Jews can speak from within a certain kind of knowledge and experience as contained within a particular tradition of texts, written largely, in Ozick's view, in the *mamaloshen* Yiddish. 'Ostrover', Hannah argues in the writer's defence, 'doesn't stink from the ghetto. He is a Freudian, a Jungian, [. . .] [a] contemporary. He speaks for everybody. [He speaks for] Humanity', to which Edelshtein replies, in words that echo (or are echoed in) 'Toward a New Yiddish': 'And to speak for Jews isn't to speak for humanity?' (95). 'A liturgical literature', writes Ozick in that essay,

> has the configuration of the ram's horn: you give your strength to the inch-hole and the splendour spreads wide. A Jewish liturgical literature gives its strength to its peoplehood and the whole human note is heard everywhere, enlarged. [. . .] If we blow into the narrow end of the *shofar*, we will be heard far. But if we choose to be Mankind rather than Jewish and blow into the wider part, we will not be heard at all.
>
> (1970; 1983: 175–7)

To speak for humanity, one must speak as a specific, individual human being, a Jewish human being, if one happens to be one. And to speak as a specific, individual human being one must acknowledge one's origins. We are not born into the world as the fully formed, wholly potent mouthpiece of the nations or even of the specific nation. Rather, we are born as the much smaller, quite literal mouth of the suckling child, who might nonetheless discover, in particular through the mother who suffers the desire, the gratitude and love that exists on the other side of envy and greed. Writes Adam Phillips in relation to the same Freud essay we have already introduced, 'the art of poetry [...] is the art of being happily unacceptable in public, of making known one's otherwise forbidden desires' (2001: 8). We are all, whether we intend to be or not, in this way 'born poets', to allude to Edelshtein's definition of himself. All of us discover ways of enacting our unacceptable desires in acceptable, even if not aesthetically brilliant or even personally satisfying ways. It is in this failure to achieve personal satisfaction and art that the poetry that is Edelshtein's life fails. For the poetry of our lives to succeed, Ozick's story suggests, we need to acknowledge and accept the condition of our humanness, in all its compromising biological and emotional urges. To strike the human note (whether in literature or in life), we need, like Ozick's story, to blow into the narrow of the shofar, and in deriving sustenance from the older traditions that have fed into ours, and in suffering the demands that could not be met then and that will not be met now, we need to continue to express the gratitude and love that are also a part of our unspoken and largely (perhaps) unspeakable inheritance.

6 Jewish/Queer

Thresholds of vulnerable identities in Tony Kushner's *Angels in America*

Ranen Omer-Sherman

> Souls were rising, from the earth far below, souls of the dead, of people who had perished, from famine, from war, from the plague, and they floated up, like skydivers in reverse, limbs all akimbo, wheeling and spinning. And the souls of these departed joined hands, clasped ankles and formed a web, a great net of souls.
>
> Tony Kushner, *Angels in America*

When HBO aired the two parts of Mike Nichols's television adaptation of Tony Kushner's *Millennium Approaches* (1993) and *Perestroika* (1996), in December 2003, what seemed manifestly apparent was that the mammoth work had emerged as one of the great dramatic achievements of the twentieth century. Having opened at the Walter Kerr Theatre a decade earlier, it had clearly stood the test of time.[1] After earning the Pulitzer Prize (1993) and two Tony awards, between the time of its Broadway closing and the star-studded HBO spectacle (which earned five Golden Globes), *Angels in America* was widely performed across America, mostly by not-for-profit theatres and campus theatre departments.

Daniel Mendelsohn's assessment comes close to assessing both the scope and causes of the enormous excitement it generated in the gay community in its early days during a grim time of emergency:

> *Angels in America* came as an enraged, seethingly articulate, intellectually ambitious, high-flown response to that stultifying and smug atmosphere of denial, silence and wilful ignorance. The admiration and, in a way, relief that immediately greeted its premiere [. . .] had to do with the general sense that finally someone was saying something grand, if occasionally grandiose, and important not just about AIDS, but about AIDS as a symptom of a profound rupture in American life. . . . The message – that what the AIDS crisis was revealing wasn't a moral flaw on the part of gay men, as the conservatives running the country would have it, but rather a moral failing in America itself – may not have come as a surprise to many in those first audiences, but it came as a profound relief to many that someone, finally, was delivering it with such fervour.
>
> (2004: 42)

But of course, *Angels* proved to have lasting value beyond the heartbreaking moment of official America's early response to AIDS. And in the new century, it triumphantly re-emerged as an urgent address that might speak to the crisis of any moment (including the numbing catastrophes and miscalculations of the Bush administration). For many, the time was again all too ripe for here it was, somehow the 1980s ad nauseam once again, with a Republican president wreaking havoc on the economy and health care. In making the successful transformation to the small screen (at last available to America's 'heartland', so to speak), the drama's numerous seductive pleasures brought the humanity of gays into the cognizance of popular culture in a way not seen since the appearance of Jonathan Demme's compassionate film *Philadelphia* (1993) a decade earlier.

For those unfamiliar with *Angels*, I should note that it is set during the early years of the AIDS crisis (a five-month period between October 1985 and February 1986), and follows a web of characters, men and women, gay and heterosexual, whose ambivalent relation to those that depend on them are revealed in troubling flights from and journeys towards responsibility and community. Though a work with epic range, featuring weighty and imaginative treatment of such disparate matters as the historical migration of the Mormons, McCarthy hearings, the politics of the Reagan era, historical figures such as Roy Cohn and Ethel Rosenberg, the supernatural presence of ghosts and angels, and even the nature of Heaven, its most fully realized character is Louis Ironson. The son of Jewish leftists who works as a clerk in the Brooklyn Court of Appeals, we first encounter Ironson at his grandmother's funeral where he confesses to his Gentile boyfriend Prior Walter, who is diagnosed with Kaposi's sarcoma, that he hadn't visited her for a decade. But rather than transforming this guilt into responsibility, the admission merely proves prophetic of a further betrayal when Prior's AIDS causes Louis to flee, abandoning his virus-infected lover just as he abandoned his deceased grandmother. Capable of overarching theoretical judgments about history and politics, he is a moral failure when it comes to personal relationships. Louis's responses to those around him become key to the drama's approach to Jewish ethics; the fate of the nation and even the cosmos hinges on the personal here.

For many, it has long seemed apparent that Kushner aspired to forge some vital but unspoken alliance between Judaism and gay struggle. For many, this remains one of the play's most interesting and yet not altogether coherent arguments. Ultimately the central biblical motif of the drama is not really its angelic beings but rather the figure of the prophet Prior, whose drug-induced hallucinations bring portents of apocalypse to the stage and screen with powerful images of burning books, an angel crashing through a ceiling and even the celestial bureaucracy of Heaven. In traditional Judaism, the prophet is not a seer (understood as one who merely predicts the future) but rather an often marginalized outsider who critiques society, sometimes anticipating disastrous consequences if society does not abandon its pursuit of certain practices. In recasting the biblical outsider as AIDS victim, Kushner sought to ameliorate the encoded tribalism of liberation, to ensure that the prophetic message of the sacred texts was restated in the most inclusive terms possible. Just as earlier generations of Jewish comic book writers and illustrators masked ethnic and immigrant difference in the guise of superhuman traits with redemptive capacities for humanity, Prior's affliction transcends its social stigma, proving transformative for society as a whole. As Allen Frantzen observes, 'Prior moves ahead, not in spite of AIDS but rather *because* of AIDS. The "virus of time" has jolted him out of torpor and self-pity and eventually transforms him into the play's strongest character' (1998: 288).

Angels has often been rightly analyzed, and appreciated, as part of a steady stream of 'gay' plays that highlighted the doom of the AIDS crisis as well as the persecution of homosexuals, seen in the 1980s as the most marginal of American identities.[2] Kushner had subtitled *Angels* 'a gay fantasia on national themes' (though this was omitted from the HBO production), and the work highlights the struggles of closeted as well as self-identified gay men under the shadow of the modern plague. Yet it has also been rightly acclaimed by cultural critics for advancing a visionary pastiche of conflicted and multiple identities: 'gay men who are white and black, Jewish and Mormon, conservative and liberal, butch and femme [...] recognizing the differences within identity categories [...] that any individual's identity is potentially contested and riven: sexuality, gender and race do not come together without conflict and contradiction' (Kruger 1997: 153–4). Apparently for Kushner, gays, dwelling in liminality (in transcending racial, biological and cultural lineages) constituted the ideal community to herald in Kushner's visionary multicultural, hybrid, tolerant America. At the same time, the spirit of *Angels in America* owes to the Jewish contributions to the American political theatre of the 1930s and 1940s, during which Jewish dramatists with socialist leanings, such as Arthur Miller and Clifford Odets addressed economic and other forms of oppression in American society. Kushner sees the theatre of the early twentieth century in 'pursuit of truth, a rejection of theatre as being entirely vulgar entertainment [...] art is meant to be difficult. And Jews love difficulty' (Monde 2004: 38).

Even though the AIDS crisis is by no means over (its catastrophic dimensions in North America have shifted to Africa and possibly Europe as of this writing), its afflicted are no longer treated with indifference; perhaps for that reason the play's other concerns are more visible to us now. The time has come to recognize that Kushner's visionary achievement has not been sufficiently examined in relation to its specifically Jewish themes of exile, *mentshlichkeit*, *tikkun olam* and *t'shuva*, or as Sarah Ironson proclaims in the streets of Heaven, '*Azoi toot a Yid*' (it's the Jewish way; Kushner 1996: 135).[3] As the play develops, it exposes the failure of abstract 'ideology' (so that Tocqueville quoting Louis's failure of responsibility is as heinous as Roy Cohn's betrayal of Ethel Rosenberg; he regards her death sentence in the electric chair as his loftiest legal achievement in spite of the manifest illegality of his role in the proceedings). Kushner wants us to recognize in both betrayals disturbing symptoms of the larger culture's inauthentic response to suffering, calling on us to replace indifference with the traditional principle of compassion.[4] Neither liberalism nor conservatism (both ideologies are eloquently voiced throughout the drama) prove redemptive when conduct and conscience fail. Kushner seems to want the audience to recognize Louis and Roy as moral *doppelgangers* for 'Louis lives outside Jewish communal life, whereas Roy is completely accomunal' (Felman 1995: 29). In Prior's stern censure of Louis, he declares: 'There are thousands of gay men in New York City with AIDS and nearly every one of them is being taken care of by [...] a friend or by [...] a lover who has stuck by them [...]. Everyone got that, except me. I got you' (Kushner 1996: 87). What the hauntingly *insistent* name 'Prior' has always suggested to me is a strong hint of the late French Jewish philosopher and Talmudic commentator Emmanuel Lévinas's severe formulation of obligation, 'ethical anteriority of responsibility' or demand of being-for-the-other which has no limits: 'I am thrown back toward what has never been my fault or deed' (1999: 157) – a primordial responsibility that predates my subjectivity and well-being. By this Lévinas conceives an instant burden beyond reciprocity, before ethics.

In this regard, it seems clear that Kushner wants his audience to know that when Louis fails in his personal responsibilities as a gay man or a lover, he should disappoint them as a Jew as well. Moreover, the Jew's role as morally and spiritually sensitive outsider and victim has been supplanted in an inhuman world restless for new categories to persecute and betray. When an interviewer asked him to what degree Jewish identity informed his creative vision, Kushner offered his idiosyncratic vision of Judaism as a 'political tradition' dependent on recasting Jacob's foundational encounter with a mysterious being in *Genesis*:

> It's fuelled by what Walter Benjamin says – hope for future generations and the memory of murdered ancestors. There is a very forward-looking, aspirational [sic] aspect of Jewish thought in the sense that the defining human characteristic is a struggle towards improvement and a struggle towards, even if it's unreachable, perfection. At least a wrestling with perfection, a wrestling with the divine – not a submission to it, but an active engagement with it [...] the Jewish tradition [...] asks that you keep the self alive and actively engaged with trying to know a very difficult-to-know divinity [...] I'm an inheritor of at least a 2,500-year-tradition of oppression and murder and holocaust, and so I know, like all Jews know in a bone-deep way, what political mischief, bigotry, and xenophobia lead to. The only thing that we can actively do to speak to the Holocaust now is to make sure no other holocaust happens, and if we do make sure that no holocaust happens – of course they're happening all the time – but if we struggle against that, every time we're successful, in some way I believe the dead are comforted.
>
> (Marcus 2003: 60)[5]

Invoking Benjamin, the dramatist weaves the latter's imperative about memory and the obligation the past imposes on us into the heart of *Angels*: 'There is a secret agreement between past generations and the present one. Our coming was expected on earth. Like every generation that preceded us, we have been endowed with a *weak* Messianic power, a power to which the past has claim' (Benjamin

1940; 1969: 254). Kushner's post-Holocaust consciousness encompasses the prophetic relationship between Judaism and social change as well as the violent consequences that always follow when the dominant culture fails in its empathy with the Other within. The title of the first part of his drama, *Millennium Approaches*, strongly suggests that, at the beginning of the 1990s, the dramatist was anxious about both the apocalyptic traditions and anxieties that would be unpredictably expressed across a broad spectrum of global and American culture as the year 2000–1 approached. But in another sense, the theme of Judgment Day, which since antiquity has contained both deep pessimism and exuberant optimism, was a perfect vehicle for expressing the condition of America's heart struggling with tumultuous social change. As the epigraph of the drama, drawn from Stanley Kunitz's 'The Testing Tree', nakedly declares:

> In a murderous time
> the heart breaks and breaks
> and lives by breaking.
> (Kushner 1993: 7)

And, insofar as apocalypticism has been intrinsic to the histories and texts of the three monotheistic faiths, this paradigm hints at the kind of inclusive framework that is at the heart of *Angels*' social vision. Jewish and Christian strains of apocalypticism have wielded a considerable influence on the aesthetics of Western culture, engendering not only the soaring visions of strange theological narratives in works such as the Dead Sea scrolls but also the literary and visual art of masterpieces such as Dante's *Divine Comedy* (c. 1308–21), Michelangelo's fresco of *The Last Judgment* (1535–41) and William Blake's *America: A Prophecy* (1794). For societies self-consciously preoccupied with the trauma of change, apocalyptic narratives (that first sprang from the Hebraic imagination) offered a structure of history and thus a sense of divine control over bewildering events. As Bernard McGinn, a leading scholar of apocalyptic texts, explained in an unpublished address (1996), in Hebraic Scripture and subsequently,

> [a]pocalypse originally signified a genre of text containing a mediated unveiling of heavenly secrets dealing either with the description of the celestial realm or with the course of history and the imminent end of the present age. These two poles of the apocalyptic imagination – the vertical one connecting heaven and earth and the horizontal one stretching out through time into the prophetic future – have always coexisted.

In his analysis of the unique characteristics of the 'apocalyptic literature created by Jews' McGinn notes the strategically entwined strands of hope and fear that would 'empower and sustain an all-embracing religious decision.' Intrinsic to the millennial imagination is the way its 'literature of consolation' is a catalyst for both inner and outer apocalypse for, 'to be consoled in a time of persecution by the message that final deliverance is just around the corner is also to be encouraged to deepen one's commitment to the divine power that will bring a deliverance transcending death.' Interestingly, McGinn concludes that, rather than lay stress on the spirit, the most ancient apocalyptic narratives were attentive to the body, the urgent demands of living in the here and now, even including satiating the pleasures of the flesh and the life of the biological body.

Contrary to contemporary expectations perhaps, during an age in which clear demarcations between rabbinic Judaism and orthodox Christianity had not yet emerged, McGinn says that 'apocalyptic expectations emphasized the material pleasures of the messianic kingdom, including an abundance of food and drink and the begetting of thousands of children'. It is not difficult to glean the way Kushner's postmodern drama about suffering bodies draws from this genre's penchant for coercing pessimism about the present into an encouraging view of future history. Ultimately both depend on the Hebrew Bible's fiercely sardonic view of both divine conduct and human ethical conduct. That *Angels* has at its heart a very serious commitment to life, as violent process and painful but necessary transformation, is evident in one of its most memorable speeches. Observing that authentic change seems to have 'something to do with God so it's not very nice', the 'Mormon Mother' relates its visceral attributes:

> God splits the skin with a jagged thumbnail from throat to belly and then plunges a huge filthy hand in, he grabs hold of your bloody tubes and they slip to evade his grasp but he squeezes hard, he *insists*, he pulls and pulls till all your innards are yanked out and the pain! We can't even talk about that. And then he stuffs them back, dirty, tangled and torn. It's up to you to do the stitching.
>
> *Harper:* And then get up. And walk around.
> *Mormon Mother:* Just mangled guts pretending.
> *Harper:* That's how people change.
>
> (Kushner 1996: 77–8)

Certainly in its own blend of consolation (its empathy for 'mangled' lives) and call for more life and compassion *Angels* spoke at once to the apocalyptic dread of the AIDS community whose numbers were so devastated as well as to the anxieties of the larger society. And just as traditional apocalyptic narratives seek to unify the course of history to create meaning, it might be said that *Angels* presses towards its own agenda, in the form of a renewed unification of present day humanity united by a common plight with the angels, dwelling in a cosmos that God has abandoned.[6] In a revealing speech, Prior combines Borscht Belt shtick with the ancient tradition of arguing with God that can be traced back to Abraham pleading for the inhabitants of Sodom and Gomorrah:

> If he ever did come back, if he ever *dared* to show His face . . . if after all this destruction, if after all the terrible days of this terrible century He returned to see . . . how much suffering His abandonment had created, if all He has to

offer is death, you should *sue* the bastard... Sue the bastard for walking out. How dare He.

(130)

But as Kushner takes pains to demonstrate, amidst the AIDS crisis, God is not the only one who abandons his loved ones or who wanders. His play is deeply attuned to the betrayals and vulnerability, as well as creative triumphs of exile and exilic states. There is a great deal of wandering at the heart of *Angels*. Besides references to the epic historical movements of diasporic Jews and migrating Mormons, a troubled woman visits Antarctica in the company of a cosmic 'travel agent' (at least in her drugged hallucination), two lovers leave home, a Mormon mother sets out on a perilous journey to confront her wayward son in the urban jungle of the South Bronx and an AIDS victim is visited by angelic beings and sojourns briefly in Heaven. The greatest value in the play is openness to change and transformation – and the generosity to Others that such adaptiveness affords. As Allen Frantzen argues about the Mormons, Blacks, and (most of the) Jews of the play, denied 'stability and permanence and driven by persecution and need from place to place' these 'migratory and transitional cultures' are 'open to, and indeed dependent on, change' (1998: 280). By the end of the drama each of these characters will have not only experienced, but embraced, startling changes and shifts in identity. Even the structure of *Angels* is organized around the theme of a universe and a human society receptive to the change that brings about redemption; nearly all the flights and abandonments of *Millennium Approaches* are resolved in the unexpected twists and turns of forgiveness and reconciliation in *Perestroika*. Only the morbidly cynical Roy Cohn remains unredeemable; trapped in the stasis of selfishness, he succumbs to mortality by the end of the play.[7]

Unlike virtually every other character who in one form or another embraces some confidence in historical and individual progress, Cohn's fatal indifference to all but his own jungle struggle is signalled by a devastatingly morbid Social Darwinism that infects his vision of eternity: 'I see the universe, Joe, as a kind of sandstorm in outer space with winds of mega-hurricane velocity, but instead of grains of sand it's shards and splinters of glass' (Kushner 1993: 13). He advises his apprentice to learn to 'live in the raw wind, naked, alone' (58). In submitting to this nightmare of the cosmos and indifferent human society, entrenched in his contempt for progress and redemptive social struggle, Cohn, forgiven by Belize and the ghost of Ethel Rosenberg remains obdurately indifferent to the fate of others, is set apart, the drama's sole Cain. Disbarred just before his death, he remains unrepentant in his isolation. In contrast Joe, who initially thinks he will go to hell for succumbing to homoerotic leanings and thinks he must kill off that buried identity, learns to live with the messiness of his once opposed Republican and homosexual selves. In *Angels*, radically disavowing either Self or Other wreak terrible violence on the individual and society.[8]

In the first scene of *Millennium Approaches* (performed by a nearly unrecognizable Meryl Streep in the televised version's playful nod to her audacious versatility), the ancient East European immigrant Rabbi Isidor Chemelwitz presides at a funeral. In this first speech of the play, the audience learns that Sarah Ironson, grandmother of Louis,

> was [...] not a person but a whole kind of person, the ones who crossed the ocean, who brought with us to America the villages of Russia and Lithuania – and how we struggled, and how we fought, for the family, for the Jewish home, so that you would not grow up *here*, in this strange place, in the melting pot where nothing melted. Descendants of this immigrant woman, you do not grow up in America, you and your children and their children with the goyische names. You do not live in America. No such place exists. Your clay is the clay of some Litvak Shtetl, your air the air of the steppes – because she carried the old world on her back across the ocean, in a boat, and she put it down on Grand Concourse Avenue, or in Flatbush, and she worked that earth into your bones, and you pass it to your children, this ancient, ancient culture and home.
>
> (Kushner 1993: 10)

The rabbi's elegy reverberates with allusion here to all of Judaism's displacements and migrations, including its foundational movement in God's command to Abraham: 'Get thee out of thy country, and from thy kindred, and from thy father's house, unto a land that I will show thee' (Gen 12:1). As Jyl Lynn Felman observes, in 'using the plural "we" rather than the singular "she;" the rabbi purposefully includes himself in the historic crossing of Askenazi Jews from the old country to the "new" country' (1995: 27). Moreover, the theatre audience is implicated as well, a sort of extended family of undetermined proportions and untested solidarity. Though Sarah remains unknown to the audience, unknown to the rabbi and apparently even unknown to Louis, the rabbi's eulogy for her manages to affirm continuity. Altogether, it is a fraught and bittersweet speech, juxtaposing the imperative of memory, the inevitability of forgetting and the perils of assimilation.

Addressing the drifting young generation 'with the goyische names', the aged rabbi (stage directions instruct the actor to speak with a 'heavy Eastern European accent') sternly reminds them that '[y]ou can never make that crossing that she made, for such Great Voyages in this world do not any more exist. But every day of your lives the miles that voyage between that place and this one you cross. Every day. You understand me? In you that journey is' (Kushner 1993: 10–11). But it is the play's openly gay and closeted gays who carry forward the once Jewish debates on power vs. powerlessness, memory vs. forgetting. As Prior says: 'I can handle pressure, I am a gay man and I am used to pressure, to trouble, I am tough and strong' (Kushner 1996: 117); whereas Roy asserts: 'Homosexuals are men who know nobody and who nobody knows. Who have zero clout' (Kushner 1993: 45). And perhaps the existence of a monster like Roy Cohn is proof enough that Jews are all too much at home in America. And being-at-home with comfort and clout (while overlooking the plight of those lately assigned the category of 'Other') means failing to grasp the rabbi's message about the 'journey'. Ironically, even Cohn's mask of hyper-aggressiveness and confidence slips away when, in the face of professional and political ruin, he sadly acknowledges: 'The disbarment committee: genteel gentleman Brahmin lawyers, country-club men. I offend them, to these men . . . I'm what, Martin, some sort of filthy little Jewish troll?' (66–7). Signalling his lack of self-knowledge and sense of origins ('the clay of some Litvak shtetl', 10), Cohn will later echo this sentiment (but without true comprehension of its import): 'The immutable heart of what we are that bleeds through whatever we might become' (Kushner 1996: 80).

Through the device of the second-person 'you', the rabbi implicates the alienated Diaspora Jew as well as all others in the audience who might be estranged from the world of values represented by their origins, ethnic or otherwise: 'In *us* that Journey *is*. Even if we want to forget where we came from, we can't. It's impossible. The journey lives in us, in spite of us; not only as cultural, but also as spiritual inheritance' (Felman 1995: 28). In indelible ways, Kushner's entire epic, as it unfolds from this moment, affirms this imperative to remember and to honour the 'journey', for the drama's Jewish and non-Jewish characters alike. Approaching the rabbi immediately after Bubbe Sarah's funeral, Louis seems to seek absolution for both past and future actions:

Louis: Rabbi, what does the Holy Writ say about someone who abandons someone he loves at a time of great need?

Rabbi Isidor Chemelwitz: Why would a person do such a thing?

Louis: Because he has to.

Maybe because this person's sense of the world, that it will change for the better with struggle, maybe a person who has this neo-Hegelian positivist sense of constant historical progress towards happiness or perfection or something, who feels very powerful because he feels connected to these forces, moving uphill all the time . . . maybe that person can't, um, incorporate sickness into his sense of how things are supposed to go. Maybe vomit . . . and sores and disease . . . really frighten him, maybe . . . he isn't so good with death.

(1993: 25)

In the face of Louis's faltering solipsistic and intellectual rationalizations, the rabbi responds with stark sadness: 'The Holy Scriptures have nothing to say about such a person' (25). Because of its emphasis on the individual's obligation (for all its ostensibly liberal politics), the film version even expressed what might seem to many an unforgiving approach to Joe, its just out-of-the-closet gay character when he flees the lie of his marriage:

Hannah: And what are you running away from now? You have a responsibility to your wife, and you cannot wish it away.

Joe: I want to – I don't want any more than I want.
Hannah: What you want what you want. Well, that shifts with the breeze. How can you steer your life by what you want? Hold to what you *believe*.

(Kushner and Nichols 2003: n.p.)

The problem here with this added dialogue, as Mendelsohn points out, is the false moral equivalence which may be one of the drama's weakest moments: 'It's so clearly an attempt to saddle Joe with a moral failure [...] to make it seem as if the reason for his abandonment is a kind of selfish, self-indulgent whim, like the reason for Louis's abandonment of Prior [...] as if the desire to be a fully fledged human being unashamed of his most profound self is nothing more than a between-meal snack' (2004: 46). As this exchange suggests, Louis and Prior's domestic mess is awkwardly paralleled by the faltering marriage of Joe and Harper Pitt. As a protégé of Cohn, Joe shares with the latter a closeted gay identity but after a series of amorous encounters with Louis, he prepares to leave Harper whose sexual dissatisfaction and growing suspicions about her husband's sexual identity lead her into a downward spiral of Valium-induced hallucinations that include blissful escapes to a serene Antarctica. Prior, the other abandoned party, also experiences visions, apocalyptic intimations of books consumed by flames, celestial messengers, nurses suddenly spouting ancient Aramaic.

If, as I have argued, Kushner's emphasis on the trials faced by gay characters never diminishes the play's provocative focus on the diminished spirit of Jewish conscience and identity, it should also be noted there are times when even the Mormon characters seem to channel a Jewish sensibility perhaps because, as Kruger notes, 'both religions [...] originary movement is a conversional one that involves a movement of dis- and relocation' (1997: 156). That underlying consciousness emerges in unexpected moments. For instance, it rings false that Hannah Pitt, the mother of Joe who has left Utah to come to New York to settle the chaos in her son's life says that 'angels are beliefs with wings' for this belies the literal core of the Mormon faith even while it affirms progressive Judaism's more relaxed relationship with metaphor. Even the identity of the angel that visits Prior, and would proclaim him as a biblical prophet, owes to the Jewish tradition. When she visits Prior she admonishes that she has come to liberate the universe from 'the virus of TIME' that God released in humanity (Kushner 1996: 42) which enabled humans to transcend their fixed position in the natural order. The angel complains that God himself began to find time seductive and preferred human life to the stasis of heaven; all of which is consistent with midrashic traditions.[9] As Mendelsohn observes, 'the drama takes the side of churning, complex, ultimately redemptive forces of "life" – suffering, change, emotional evolution, even politics (as distinguished from stultifying ideology)' (2004: 44).

In all times and places, community must be affirmed, but in the Reagen era of abandonment and indifference to the AIDS plague, a special affirmation, an urgent plea had to be expressed and *Angels in America* was that timely utterance. For Kushner, the 'absolute triumph of Reaganite ideology' in our own moment (which he perhaps exaggerates when he says 'the worst, most dangerous moment the human race has ever faced') depends cynically on substituting 'the social human, the communal human, with this little sealed monad of an ego fragment that has no connection, or is at least not willing to admit to any connection, to any other living being' (Marcus 2003: 59). That is why *Angels* emphasizes that, whereas the rabbinical imagination had posited that angels were nostalgic, conservative beings resistant to the change and flux embodied by humanity, it is also true that human society has become fossilized over time, unwilling to acknowledge the humanity of homosexuals and opposed to a more encompassing vision of America. Ultimately, the ethical imperative of community that Kushner expresses in the 'Afterword' to *Perestroika* also derives from Jewish tradition. What is this sentiment if not a midrashic reworking of the law requiring ten men as the minimum required for a *minyan*?[10]

Condemning the terrible losses sustained by Americans 'for maintaining the myth of the Individual', Kushner affirms that 'the smallest indivisible human unit is two people, not one; one is a fiction. From such nets of souls societies, the social world, human life springs' (1996: 149, 155). Though resisting an exclusively ethnocentric triumphalism, seeking out 'community' in the widest possible sense, the life-affirming spirit of the *minyan* seems to inflect Kushner's heartfelt coda to the written text. As Alisa Solomon points out, Kushner's intentions for *Angels* are greatly illuminated by the Talmudic imperative: 'When a man appears before the Throne of Judgment, the first question he will be asked is not "Have you believed in God?" or "Have you prayed and observed the ritual?" – but "Have you dealt honorably with your fellow man?"' (1997: 124).[11] Kushner sees Louis as a modern Jewish Everyman, at least insofar as that identity encompasses the limits of the self-serving Jewish American liberal conscience.

In the play's tense opposition (at times explicit and at others implied), between diasporic and Zionist identities, it is clear that Kushner privileges the expansive, open-ended identity of wandering over the narrowly proscribed politics and monolithic identity that accompanies territorialism. Indeed, to understand the primacy the Jewish dramatist places on paradigm shifts and expanded human consciousness (the true gifts born of movement) it bears mentioning the Jewish tradition's rich and creatively productive relation to exile. One need only return to the *Book of Genesis*, beginning with the pervasive sense of *felix culpa* that accompanies the exile from the Garden, the command given to Abraham, *Lech Lacha* ('Get you gone from your country and from your birthplace and from your father's house'), the expulsion of Ishmael into the desert, the narrative of Ruth the Moabite, all of which offer a richly circuitous terrain, repetitions of wandering that haunt the certainties of the present. Indeed, it is this primordial, sadly neglected essence of Hebrew monotheism (often vilified as the source of global violence), that offers the richest counter-traditions to rebuke those who would root themselves in blood-drenched soil. The radical monotheism that engendered Jewish writers as disparate as Yehudah Halevi, Franz Kafka and Tony Kushner, after all, evolved as a cultural strategy for being-at-home wherever one was – learning the discipline demanded of moving fluidly between disparate worlds.

Kushner's interest in progressive Judaism's interest in *tikkun* or global healing is apparent in his introduction to the printed text of *Perestroika* which, pointedly renouncing sentimental closure to the traumas of the first part ('It shouldn't be easy'), nonetheless restores the audience's confidence in the efficacy of human striving:

> *Perestroika* is essentially a comedy, in that issues are resolved, mostly peaceably, growth takes place and loss is, to a certain degree, countenanced. But it's not a farce; all this happens only through a terrific amount of struggle, and the stakes are high [. . .] There is also a danger in easy sentiment. Eschew sentiment! Particularly in the final act – metaphorical though it may at times be (or maybe not), the problems the characters face are finally among the hardest problems – how to let go of the past, how to change and lose with grace, how to keep going in the face of overwhelming suffering.
>
> (1996: 8)

The second part of *Angels* features some stunning changes and acts of compassion: Belize, the gay, black nurse on the AIDS ward, despises Roy Cohn but gives him crucial advice about how to make the best of his deteriorating condition; Hannah Pitt, who in the first part is repulsed when her son Joe reveals he is gay, tenderly cares for Prior when he is at his lowest ebb; and most spectacularly of all, the ghost of Ethel Rosenberg appears to say Kaddish for Cohn, the metaphoric son who abandoned her just as he betrays his gay brethren 'by always fucking in a locked closet' (Felman 1995: 29). Finally, Louis and Prior are reconciled after Louis shows genuine remorse. Moreover, in spite of Kushner's disavowal of sentiment, the final scene of *Perestroika*'s 'comedy', set in Central Park, with the Bethesda Fountain in the background, seems to drift towards a utopian closure wherein its outcast blacks, Jews, Mormons and gays learn to reconcile the messy reality of human existence. The Mormon mother Hannah intends to celebrate the *new* millennium Prior in the waters that sprang up in Jerusalem when the angel Bethesda appeared amidst Romans and Jews in the previous one, a distant age of strife and upheaval mirroring the present one. Suddenly, Louis interrupts to interject 'Not literally in Jerusalem, I mean we don't want this to have sort of Zionist implications –' to which Belize rejoins:

Belize:	Right on.
Louis:	But on the other hand we *do* recognize the right of the state of Israel to exist.
Belize:	But the West Bank should be a homeland for the Palestinians, and the Golan Heights should . . .
Louis:	Well not both the West Bank and the Golan Heights, I mean no one supports Palestinian rights more than I do but . . .
Belize (*Overlapping*):	Oh yeah right, Louis, like not even the Palestinians are more devoted than . . .

(Kushner 1996: 145–6)

The parodic exposé of Louis's liberalism here is a necessary respite from the grim scenes of death and suffering that precede it. But at the same time, its gentle humour serves as serious rebuke to exclusively tribal narratives of truth and apocalyptic visions of territorial destiny and control. After the grave seriousness of betrayal, madness and disease that hitherto dominate the text, the barbed and catty exchange that ensues between these adversaries, whether on stage or film, is experienced as a gentle respite of comic relief – an acknowledgement of the sheer unresolved messiness of the world that will always defy messianic resolution. Here is where Kushner struggles to reconcile his manifestly Jewish identity with his refusal to spare any tribe from assuming its full responsibility for the disastrous state of the world. For in Jewish America this terse exchange, though revealing that the parties that have wounded one another have moved on, marks the limits of Jewish American liberal pieties in the face of the Israel and Palestine conflict.[12]

'In you that journey is.' Returning to Prior, shouldering his ethical burden, Louis at last realizes the rabbi's admonition to *remember* by acting compassionately. But though Louis is the character that most resembles the identity and politics of Kushner, we have seen that the dramatist remains ruthless in exposing the shallow hypocrisy of the Jewish liberal zeitgeist. If one considers the trajectory from Rabbi Isidor Chemelwitz's opening, elegiac speech to the liberal bickering that culminates in *Perestroika*'s happy conclusion; one gleans the significance of the provocative bookend device that Kushner offered the Jews in his audience. For *Angels* begins and ends with the recitation of the Kaddish, Judaism's ostensible prayer of mourning that is really a reaffirmation of the living's proper orientation to the world. If the first is an aging rabbi's elegiac farewell to a vanished world, the final (recited by a confused and forgetful Louis prompted by Ethel's ghost) is a cautionary nod to the lost values of Jews of the post-assimilation era.

The heart of the matter, for Jews and Gentiles, constituents of the Right and Left, is how a democratic society treats its outsiders – as well as how its individuals contribute to shaping that process. As Steven Kruger puts it, *Angels* conscientiously presents identity 'as social and relational: one is not oneself in isolation but only in contrast to, in solidarity and negotiation with a variety of other selves [...] even a character's fantasies and imaginations are conceived of as not solely his or hers. These gather their full meaning only in relation to, even interpenetration with, one another – just as, in Kushner's stagecraft, the "split scenes" suggest that discrete actions must, if we are to understand them fully, be read together' (1997: 154). As one character comes to understand, 'Freedom is where we bleed into one another... Freedom is the far horizon where lines converge' (Kushner 1996: 73). For it is clear that the self-hatred of both Jews and homosexuals produce some of *Angels*' most powerful examinations of moral failure. Though Felman's reading of the fallen secular world of self-loathing revealed by the first play also seems apt – '*Angels* is about Jewish male self-loathing in the twentieth century held tightly within the ever expanding embrace of Miss Liberty's very tired, porous hands' (1995: 27) – it seems clear that something restorative *has* transpired. Indeed above all else, *Angels* posits an imaginatively porous America of open-mindedness and open-endedness gracefully allowing the audience to exit through a door of hope. Loneliness, betrayal and banishment are supplanted by increasing prospects for cultural and individual stamina, reconciliation and reconstruction of America's lost promise.

Like other self-consciously Jewish writers, Kushner is never free 'intertextually' – he can never invent a new prophetic language out of nothing. Instead, he toils, patching together fragments of the Bible's contradictory and multiple strands to respond to the urgent needs of the present. Hence, in Kushner's sense of the term, 'Zion' seems to delineate a portable text that sustained Judaism as a civilization in diaspora but now must serve humanity in its widest definition. More importantly, in the return from spirit to the mundane world of politics, there is an implicit burden laid by Prior (who here evokes both the theatricality of Shakespeare's Prospero and the Hebraic prophet's moral urgency), on the audience/reader, requiring that when they emerge blinking into the sunlight, they accept the burden of fully living in and engaging with the world in all its messy politics and violent realities: 'The world only spins forward. We will be citizens. The time has come. Bye now. You are fabulous creatures, each and every one. And I bless you: *More Life*. The Great Work Begins' (Kushner 1996: 146).[13]

Notes

1 To be precise, *Millennium Approaches* opened on 4 May 1993 and *Perestroika* on 23 November. Five years later, Britain's National Theatre ranked it among the greatest dramas of the twentieth century, alongside O'Neill's *Long Day's Journey Into Night* (1956) and Beckett's *Waiting for Godot* (1952).

2 *Angels* was actually preceded by Larry Kramer's *The Normal Heart* (1985) which investigated the indifference of the government and gay community alike to respond to the AIDS catastrophe; subsequent productions of note include the critically acclaimed musical *Falsettos* (1990), Moisés Kaufman's interview-based *The Laramie Project* (1999), which portrayed the aftermath of the Matthew Shepard murder, and, more recently, Richard Greenberg's Tony Award winning *Take Me Out* (2003) which interweaves the gay subculture and closeted identity with America's national game of baseball. For a further examination of this trajectory, see McCabe (2003).

3 'Mentshlichkeit' derives from the German *mensch* and the Yiddish *mentsh*, both denoting a human being or person. However, in Yiddish, there is no greater compliment than to say that someone behaves as a *mentsh*, demonstrating personal integrity and moral uprightness. Hence, *mentshlichkeit* is the quality of being a *mentsh*. 'Tikkun Olam' is ethical activity working toward the repair or restoration of the world. 'T'shuva', which means turning in Hebrew, is central to the Jewish conception of human life; the notion of turning to God, or to the right ethical path, derives from the Jewish conception of human redemption and underlies both the intrinsic hopefulness about humankind, and the longing for messianic salvation.

4 Felman notes all the 'prodigal Jewish sons' who betrayed Rosenberg before her execution: 'Irving R. Kaufman, Irving Saypol, Roy Cohn and her own brother David Greenglass' (1995: 30).

5 'Wrestling' – which connotes the struggle between Jacob and the angel, is a key trope that often surfaces in Kushner's interviews. When asked whether he thought that 'wrestling is a Jewish imperative' he responded with the Yiddish words of one of his own characters, Sarah Ironson: ' "*Az er darf ringen mit zain Libm Nomen. Azoi toot a*

Yid. You should struggle with the Almighty. That's the Jewish way". I believe that' (Monde 2004: 39).

6 Accordingly, in a scene omitted from the film, Prior counsels the Angels, in the abysmal wake of His irresponsibility, to 'take Him to court. He walked out on us. He ought to pay' (Kushner 1996: 130); as Solomon observes, this is 'a theology that bears not a trace of Christianity' (1997: 133).

7 Ironically, Kushner seems to associate Cohn's lack of *Yiddishkayt*, or human ethics, with the fate of his 'Jewish nose' in early infancy: 'See this scar on my nose?' asks Roy. 'When I was three months old, there was a bony spur, she made them operate, shave it off. They said I was too young for the surgery, I'd outgrow it but she insisted. I figure she wanted to toughen me up. And it worked' (1996: 81).

8 As Kruger observes, Joe's 'secret self [...] makes itself known not just internally but externally; he develops a "bleeding ulcer" that forces the messiness hidden inside to appear on the surface, with blood coming from his mouth' (1997: 163).

9 Though it is Hannah who wisely explains that mortals must transcend the danger of angelic entrapment if it means succumbing to life-smothering dogma: 'An angel is just a belief, with wings and arms that can carry you. It's naught to be afraid of. If it lets you down, reject it. Seek for something new' (Kushner 1996: 103).

10 *Minyan* (from a Hebrew root meaning to count or to number) translates as prayer quorum. In Judaism, prayer is largely conceived as a group activity rather than an individual activity. Certain prayers and religious activities cannot be performed without a *minyan*. This need for a *minyan* has often helped to keep the Jewish community together in isolated areas. Although it is generally permissible to pray alone, the individual Jew must always make every effort to pray with a group.

11 The Talmudic precept is quoted in Rosten (1972: 279).

12 Kushner has not shied from making his views on Palestinian rights public: 'Like a lot of progressive Jewish Americans, I've been increasingly horrified by what's going on in the Mideast. I believe that Ariel Sharon is an unindicted war criminal and I can't believe that this figure from the absolute margins of Israeli right-wing politics has become this popular prime minister. And that people who formerly would have called themselves liberal or progressive Jews are now standing up in defence of Ariel Sharon' (Marcus 2003: 58). Kushner's outrage later found an outlet when he assembled nearly sixty contributors for his co-edited collection of essays and poetry, see Kushner and Solomon (2003).

13 In declaring that gays 'will be citizens', Prior effectively cements the juxtaposition of Jewish and queer struggle in *Angels*, explicitly echoing the Enlightenment dream of civic belonging that the Jews of eighteenth-century France pursued.

7 Fifty ways to see your lover

Vision and revision in the fiction of Amy Bloom

David Brauner

When the roll call of 'third-generation' Jewish-American writers is taken, Amy Bloom's name does not usually appear. Steve Stern, Melvin Jules Bukiet, Michael Chabon, Rebecca Goldstein, Allegra Goodman and Pearl Abraham, among others, have had their work frequently collected in anthologies of Jewish-American literature and appear regularly in bibliographies of Jewish-American fiction.[1] In spite of having been nominated for two of America's most prestigious literary awards (the National Book Award and the National Book Critics' Circle Award) Bloom, on the other hand, has so far been excluded from the Jewish-American literary canon. True, she has only published four books, but this is one more than Abraham. True, also, that she seems not to be particularly preoccupied with questions of Jewish identity (though many of her characters are Jewish), but then nor was Chabon, until the publication of *The Amazing Adventures of Kavalier and Clay* (2000). Why, then, the critical neglect of Bloom?[2] It may be partly to do with her rather uncomfortable subject matter: her books contain more than their fair share of adultery, incest, miscegenation, paedophilia, transvestism, transsexuality, homosexuality, bisexuality, alcoholism, mental and physical illness and disability, not to mention the odd accidental killing and suicide. You might expect a young (WASP) turk to deal with such controversial material, but when it comes to Jewish-American women it seems that many readers find anything stronger than 'chicken soup for the soul' difficult to stomach.[3] Although Bloom herself dismisses the notion that there is anything extraordinary about her characters (they are, she claims, 'just everyday, reasonably bright people from different kinds of backgrounds') or their circumstances ('I wish they were unusual but they seem to me in fact to be commonplace', Birnbaum 2000: n.p.), it is difficult to accommodate her fiction in any of the established traditions of Jewish-American fiction, or indeed to locate in her work any of the themes conventionally regarded as quintessentially 'Jewish'. As I have argued elsewhere (Brauner 2001: 5–9, 22–9), there are as many definitions of Jewish-American fiction as there are critics of Jewish-American fiction, but most of these definitions are rather conservative, focusing on religion and morality (which are often taken to be synonymous with each other) as the main paradigms of Jewishness.[4]

The extent to which these paradigms pervade criticism of Jewish-American fiction is apparent in two books published at the start of the new millennium by critics who would at first sight seem to differ radically in their understanding of what makes Jewish fiction Jewish. Ruth Wisse, in *The Modern Jewish Canon* (2000), argues that 'Modern Jewish literature is the repository of modern Jewish experience [...] the most complete way of knowing the inner life of the Jews', that it 'attests to the indissolubility of the Jews [...] by illuminating Jewish experience from within' and that 'the Jew who has no access to the heart of the Jewish polity is ever less likely to generate a valuable literature of Jewish experience' (4, 15, 29). In this totalizing, didactic scheme (where 'Jewish experience' is indivisible and Jewish writers become the legislators of, and apologists for, an exclusive idea of Jewish particularity), Bernard Malamud is disqualified from inclusion in the modern Jewish canon because he 'imagines the Jew as the ideal Christian' (16) and Lionel Trilling is vetoed on the grounds that he 'neutered' the protagonist of his novel *The Middle of the Journey* (1947) by making him 'an indeterminate New York Protestant' rather than an ethnically determined Jew (17).[5] Wisse's book, in spite of its title, bases its canonical criteria unashamedly on traditional, rather than modern (let alone postmodern) definitions of Jewishness and so it should come as no surprise that Jewish-American authors do not feature prominently. Although she acknowledges in an aside that '[t]he energy of American Jewish writers was so charged, so buoyant, that for a time they seemed to dominate American fiction' the only Jewish-American writers who merit extended discussion in her view are Henry Roth, Saul Bellow, Philip Roth and Cynthia Ozick.[6]

Andrew Furman, in contrast, is an unequivocal advocate of the importance of Jewish-American fiction and his book, *Contemporary Jewish American Writers and the Multicultural Dilemma* (2000), announces explicitly its aim to 'explore in some depth the work of [a] largely neglected group of contemporary American writers' (15). Though Furman begins with a chapter on Philip Roth, he devotes the rest of the book to a consideration of seven of the third-generation of Jewish-American writers of fiction: Melvin Jules Bukiet, Thane Rosenbaum, Rebecca Goldstein, Robert Cohen, Allegra Goodman, Steve Stern, and Gerald Shapiro. In his introduction, Furman bullishly states that '[t]oday, scholars of Jewish American fiction need not search for distinctively "Jewish" American voices' since they 'abound in unprecedented numbers' (15) and he ends his chapter on Robert Cohen 'with the plea that we broaden rather than narrow our vision concerning what might qualify a given work by a Jewish American writer as a Jewish American work' (120). Yet the terms in which he argues for this extension of the boundaries of the Jewish-American canon (and the criteria that he adduces as the index for measuring the distinctiveness of these Jewish voices) paradoxically reaffirms their limits.

Although Furman in principle 'bristles against the defensiveness of Jewish-American literature scholars who incessantly grope for definitions and redefinitions of the genre' (19) and gestures towards a pluralistic, flexible set of attributes that 'appropriately reflects the manifold possibilities for realizing a Jewish identity' (120), in practice he invariably equates what he calls the 'renaissance' of Jewish-American fiction in recent years with a 'resurgence' of religious sensibility.[7] Indeed, he informs his readers that 'as one who received a fairly lackadaisical Jewish education [...] but who currently studies Talmud with a *chevrusa*, I consider myself very much a part (and proof) of this resurgence' (18). As a *Baal T'shuvah* (a Jew who has returned to the fold, 'come back' to Judaism) himself, Furman tends, even while he is ostensibly arguing for a fluid conception of Jewish identity that is 'not predetermined or fixed, but dynamic' (116), to construct Jewish identity in religious terms. Hence he closes his chapter on Robert Cohen by observing that his fiction 'challenges us, above all, to recognize that even the most secular Jewish American may possess an irrepressible and ever emergent Jewish soul' (120). Furman argues that to consider 'works that manifest not the slightest concern with Judaism, Jewish culture or other issues relevant to Jewish identity [as] Jewish American fiction would be to descend into a shabby multiculturalism of bloodlines' (20). However, as Stephen Whitfield points out in his book, *In Search of American Jewish Culture* (1999), 'to expel from consideration whatever omits Jewish subject matter' begs many questions, such as: 'How much Jewish content would count? And how overt or emphatic should Jewish themes be to merit inclusion?' (19). Furthermore, who is to decide whether the content of a story is 'Jewish' or not? Furman claims that 'what makes the essays in [his] book cohere [...] is [their] pervasive concern with the Jewish content of the work' (Furman 2000: 20), but his definition of 'Jewish content', as the subtitle of his book (*The Return of the Exiled*) makes clear, is predicated on assumptions that are likely to exclude a writer like Amy Bloom. It comes as no great surprise, then, that in spite of the inclusion of a final chapter purporting to survey the field of 'Emergent Voices' in contemporary Jewish-American fiction, there is no mention anywhere in the book of Bloom's work.

Hana Wirth-Nesher's powerful condemnation of the 'moral imperialism' and 'intellectual shabbiness' of the idea that 'theme determines Jewishness' notwithstanding (1994b: 4, 3), what these books by Wisse and Furman seem to confirm is that 'Jewish content' remains the arbitrary yardstick by which most critics judge the claims of any work to be included in the canon of Jewish-American literature. Bonnie Lyons' decision, in her essay on 'American-Jewish Fiction Since 1945' (included in the *Handbook of American-Jewish Literature*, [Fried 1988], still a standard reference book for students and scholars of the field), to produce a checklist of quintessentially Jewish themes accurately reflected the prevailing tendencies in Jewish-American criticism at the time. Moreover, her emphasis on what she calls the 'humanistic assumptions' of post-war Jewish-American fiction and its 'vision of the individual as embedded in history and the family' is arguably still representative of the dominant critical discourse on Jewish-American literature. It is a discourse, however, based on premises that are inimical to the work of Amy Bloom (Lyons 1988: 84, 85).

In this article I shall argue that Bloom's fiction is humane but not humanistic, sensitive to ethnicity but deeply skeptical about ethnic (or other) types of classification and that her focus on individual misfits and dysfunctional families is the result of a vision of the individual as a self-created, mutable construct, rather than a historically, religiously or culturally determined, fixed entity. Bloom's favourite metaphor for this constantly shifting, perpetually metamorphosing self is the eye (with its implied pun on 'I') and through a discussion of the variety of representations of vision and revision in her fiction I will argue that she resists both the essentialist identity politics so fashionable in contemporary multiculturalism and the moral/religious agenda of the Jewish-American critical establishment. To do justice to her work it should be read in its own terms, and should be included in (though not bound by) any canon of Jewish-American fiction.

Towards the end of 'Love Is Not a Pie', the opening story of her first book, *Come to Me* (1993), the fiancé of the narrator, Ellen, offers his commiserations on the day of her mother's funeral: 'I'm so sorry [...] You must be very upset. What a difficult day for you' (Bloom 1993; 1995: 21). Ellen reflects that this 'was a perfectly normal response, it just was all wrong for me. I didn't come from a normal family, I wasn't ready to get normal' (21).[8] In the final chapter of Bloom's second book, the novel *Love Invents Us* (1997), the narrator observes that 'Some people are your family no matter where you find them, and some people are not, even if you are laid, still wet and crumpled, in their arms' (Bloom 1997; 1998: 198). In 'Hold Tight', one of the stories from her third book, *A Blind Man Can See How Much I Love You* (2000), the narrator observes that her best friend Kay's parents are 'extremely normal', the oxymoron implying both that normality is a relative concept, whose parameters are contingent on particular social conditions, and that the narrator's own family will always exist outside these parameters (Bloom 2000; 2001: 133). Taken together, these three quotations suggest that Bloom's fiction challenges and subverts traditional, normative (Jewish) ideas of the family and (Jewish) family values. In the rest of this chapter, I want to explore some of the ways in which she does this in three stories from her first book ('Love Is Not a Pie', 'Song of Solomon' and 'Sleepwalking') and two from her third book ('Night Vision' and 'Light Into Dark').

In 'Love Is Not a Pie', Ellen describes the moment when, as a young girl, she discovers her mother in an embrace with Mr DeCuervo, a family friend:

> One night, I woke up around midnight and crossed the living room to get some water in the kitchen and see if there was any strawberry shortcake left. I saw my mother and Mr. DeCuervo hugging, and I remember being surprised, and puzzled. I had seen movies; if you hugged someone like you'd never let them go, surely you were supposed to be kissing, too. It wasn't a Mommy-Daddy hug [...] These two looked all wrong to me [...] like sister and brother [...] My mother's hands were under Mr. DeCuervo's white t-shirt.
>
> She must have felt my eyes on her, because she opened hers slowly [...] They had moved apart so quickly and smoothly I couldn't even remember how they had looked together [...] what I had seen was already being transformed into a standard good-night embrace, the kind my mother gave to all her close friends.
>
> (Bloom 1993; 1995: 9)

At first Ellen is confused and disturbed by what she sees: she instinctively recognizes that she has witnessed a moment of erotic intimacy, but when she tries to interpret it in terms of the cultural references available to her – love scenes from the movies, and the marital embraces of her parents – she finds that the empirical evidence does not conform to the conventions with which she is familiar. The embrace resembles those of movie lovers in its passionate intensity, but whereas in the movies such amorous moments are invariably accompanied by kissing, here the lovers stand 'cheek-to-cheek' and hence appear 'all wrong' to Ellen – more like siblings than lovers. She also notices an inversion of the dynamic of desire that she has observed in the 'Mommy-Daddy hug': whereas her father 'envelop[s]' her mother when he hugs her, in this encounter it is Ellen's mother whose hands encircle Mr DeCuervo. Unable to reconcile these conflicting signifiers, Ellen begins to distrust the visual evidence that she has been sifting ('I couldn't even remember how they had looked together') and then to reinterpret it as simply a 'standard good-night embrace'. But this revision of events provides only temporary reassurance, for the following night Ellen wakes with stomach cramps and, seeking out her mother, finds her 'spooned against my father's back, as she always was, and Mr DeCuervo spooned up against her' (15). Once again, Ellen is unsettled by the sight of something both familiar (her mother's embrace of her father) and strange (Mr DeCuervo's embrace of her mother):

> I stood and looked and then backed out of the bedroom. They hadn't moved, the three of them breathing deeply, in unison. What was that, I thought, what did I see? I wanted to go back and take another look, to see it again, to make it disappear, to watch them carefully, until I understood.
>
> (15)

Once again, she retreats, physically, from the scene ('I [...] backed out of the bedroom') and, psychologically, from its implications, (trying to erase the memory of it altogether by 'mak[ing] it disappear'). Whereas in the first episode, her mother and Mr DeCuervo are able to separate hurriedly, as the mother 'felt [Ellen's] eyes on her' (a phrase that transforms the act of seeing into a transaction palpable to the object of vision), in this case the three lovers are all asleep, their synchronized breathing reinforcing the impression of harmony implied by the positions of their bodies. What Ellen has seen, in fact, is quite straightforward: three adults contentedly sleeping together in one bed, each receiving comfort from the physical proximity of another. As was the case when she surprised her mother and Mr DeCuervo earlier, however, she cannot make sense of what her senses tell her, and so finds herself questioning both the nature of what she has seen ('What was that') and whether in fact she saw it at all ('what *did* I see?'; emphasis added). She also wishes to 'see it again', although she hopes, paradoxically, that such revision will not reinforce the image, but rather 'make it disappear'. Even as an adult, recounting this incident to her sister, Lizzie, Ellen feels unable to articulate what she has seen: 'I didn't know how to tell her about the three of them; that was *even less normal* than her having an affair [...] I couldn't even think of the words to describe what I had seen' (19; emphasis added). It's not so much that Ellen baulks at telling her sister the truth, but rather that the available discourse of love is too narrow, too conventional, too bound up with ideas of normality, to accommodate the particular kind of love shared by her parents and Mr DeCuervo. Instead of attempting to explain her actual experience, then, she substitutes for it a fabricated one that fits more easily into the available vocabulary of sexuality: 'I saw Mommy and Mr. DeCuervo kissing one night after we were in bed' (19).

However, Ellen eventually recognizes that her family is not 'normal' and that she herself is not 'ready to be normal'. With hindsight she sees that if the definitions of love available to her as a child were not sufficiently flexible to allow her to accept the evidence before her (namely, that her parents and Mr DeCuervo were involved in a consensual, loving triangular relationship), it is those definitions themselves that need to be revised, rather than the facts themselves. As the family assemble for the occasion of her mother's funeral, Ellen watches her father and Mr DeCuervo 'moan[ing] and rock[ing] together in a passionate, musicless waltz' (2). Their embrace revives memories of the embraces she witnessed as a child, but it is the enduring nature of their love for each other (later in the story the father announces that he and Mr DeCuervo are 'gonna lie down for a while', 20) that prompts Ellen to reconsider her future. 'Love Is Not a Pie' begins with Ellen deciding to break off her engagement to her fiancé, John Wescott, because 'I couldn't *see myself* in the long white silk gown Mrs Wescott had offered me' (1). As the story proceeds, it becomes clear that this is not simply a childish whim, or a question of aesthetics, but a genuine insight into her own values, an epiphany about the kind of person she is. In rejecting the image of herself in the white wedding gown, she is rejecting all that the gown symbolizes: a conventional definition of married love.

The *menage à trois* that Ellen unwittingly discovers as a child takes shape over the course of a summer when Mr DeCuervo and his daughter Gisela come to stay at the family cabin in Maine and is facilitated by the absence of Mrs DeCuervo. No one missed her, according to Ellen, since she was 'a professional mother, a type that made my sister and me very uncomfortable' (3). Whereas Ellen's mother 'had a few very basic summer rules [. . .] Mrs. DeCuervo was always amending and adding to the list, one apologetic eye on our mother, who [. . .] did things the way she always did' (3). What Ellen realizes at her mother's funeral, then, is that she, like her mother, does not want to conform to conventional ideas governing the behaviour of married women; she does not want to play the role of the professional mother and faithful wife. She wants to be free to make her own rules, to define herself in her own terms, to take love where she finds it. The final irony of the story is that it is John Wescott's decision not to attend Ellen's mother's funeral – out of a misguided belief that in doing so he is 'respecting [her] autonomy' – which convinces her that '[m]y mother would not have wanted me to marry this man' (1). Love, the implication is, is not to be found in symbols like a wedding gown or a piece of pie but rather in the instinctive sympathies of human beings. If Ellen's fiancé had truly loved her, he would 'have known that [she] was just being considerate' when she had said that he didn't have to come to the funeral from Boston (1). Indeed, he wouldn't have asked her whether she wanted him to attend in the first place but would simply have flown to her side.

There is no mention of the ethnic origins of Ellen's family in 'Love Is Not a Pie', but it seems to me that the story can be read as a parable about the parochialism of identity politics, a critique of the narrow boundaries used to circumscribe different ethnicities (for 'love' read 'race') and of the limitations of the discourses used to describe different cultures. Certainly, the story that follows it in the collection, 'Song of Solomon', gains resonance from such a reading.

'Song of Solomon' begins with what at first appears to be a thoroughly conventional, if not hackneyed, scene: a woman preparing to go out, agonizing over what to wear:

> Kate stood in front of the mirror trying on dresses. She could almost get into her black suit, but that couldn't be right for the New Year and it was almost eighty outside. She put on a yellow sleeveless dress with a white linen blazer and white sandals. Too summery but not bizarre.
>
> (Bloom 1993; 1995: 25)

As the paragraph continues, however, the expectations aroused by these opening lines are swiftly dispelled:

> Do they wear hats? In church women wear hats. Do Jewish women wear hats? Kate stared into the mirror, sweating in her slip, milk starting to come through the nursing pads.
>
> (25)

Kate is not a young free singleton but a nursing mother; she is not going to a New Year's party but to a religious service celebrating the Jewish New Year; her anxiety about her appearance has less to do with the vagaries of fashion than with ancient traditions (she wants to conform to the sartorial protocols of Jewish women attending synagogue, but does not know what these protocols are). Then again, as the story proceeds, it becomes clear that Kate *is* indeed dressing to impress a man: her obstetrician, Dr Sheldon. Moreover, she has planned her rendezvous with the physician like a military operation, producing a detailed schedule based on a reconnaissance expedition ('She had driven there [to the temple] yesterday and timed it') in order to ensure that she arrives at the right time (29). When she finally decides on what to wear, Kate 'dressed like a surgeon prepping, precise and careful in every movement' (29), and even those things over which she has no control seem to be conspiring in her favour, for her baby girl, Sarah, 'had fallen into one of her instant naps, from which she would emerge charming and alert but not yet hungry. Perfect for seeing Dr. Sheldon' (29). Again, Bloom's emphasis on seeing, both in the literal sense of receiving and processing visual stimuli and the metaphorical sense of imagining a scenario (seeing in the mind's eye), is present here in Kate's self-scrutiny in front of the mirror and in her envisaging of her imminent encounter with Dr Sheldon.

Yet in spite of all the care and attention that Kate expends on ensuring that everything is perfect for seeing, and being seen by, Dr Sheldon, what threatens to undo all her hard work and undermine all her romantic hopes is the fact that she is not Jewish. When they meet outside the temple, Dr Sheldon greets her with 'pleasure' and 'surprise': 'I didn't know we belonged to the same shul' (31). Kate overcomes this potential pitfall by thinking 'quickly, circling the strange word' ('shul', meaning 'synagogue') and answering ambiguously: 'I've never been here before, actually, but I've wanted to come here for a long time' (31). Careful not to lie, Kate admits that she isn't a member of the synagogue but is at the same time economical with the truth: she doesn't admit that she isn't Jewish. At this point all seems set fair for a happy ending:

> They squinted at each other in the September light, smiling and wondering what the other person saw. Dr. Sheldon thought Kate saw a pallid, overweight man sweating in an old navy blue suit, black-rimmed glasses sliding halfway down his big nose and wild gray curls floating around his bald spot. She didn't; she saw God. Kate thought he saw a slightly crazy woman, wild with exhaustion and loneliness, but he didn't see that. He saw that her dark blue eyes lit up when they rested on his face and that her hand lay tenderly, unconsciously, on his sleeve, like a lily. He saw that their house would have white flowers and bright plastic toys on the floor. He would not be alone.
>
> (31)

The fact that what Kate and Dr Sheldon see in each other is an idealized version of the truth, distorted by their own loneliness, is implied by the literal distortion of vision that can result from squinting. However, if squinting is often associated with myopia, it can result in a heightening rather than a blurring of vision (you may squint because you are short-sighted, but the act of squinting can help you focus more clearly). Whether Kate confuses Dr Sheldon with God, and is thus guilty of the sort of idolatry that Judaism regards as anathema, or whether she has an authentic revelation – an epiphany of sorts – when she looks at him is not clear. Equally ambiguous is Dr Sheldon's vision of domestic bliss: is it prophetic or self-deluding? Do these two really have more in common than their shared desire for companionship, as the repetition of the word 'wild' (used to describe both Sheldon's grey curls and Kate's exhaustion) might suggest, or is their attraction to each other based on deception and self-deception?

Certainly the precariousness of their relationship – and the possibilities for misunderstanding inherent in the differences between them (of age, social status, cultural background etc.) – is highlighted in the exchange that ensues:

> 'People are starting to go in,' he said.
>
> 'Oh.' She sounded wounded, which alarmed him. Had he offended her? Maybe she didn't want to sit with him.
>
> Dr. Sheldon shuffled backward, to show that he hadn't meant to intrude, and Kate's eyes filled with tears. How could he be leaving now, now that they were together?
>
> (31–2)

What Sheldon intends as an invitation Kate sees as a rebuff, and her disappointment he in turn misinterprets as a rejection. However, the situation is redeemed thanks to the unwitting intervention of Sarah:

> Sarah thrust one pink foot through her blanket, and they both looked at it, flexing in the air. Kate's face was so filled with loss and love that Dr. Sheldon reached out for her, and she pressed his hand to her hip as they carried Sarah up the temple stairs.
>
> (32)

It is possible to see this as either a sentimental story (Kate and Dr Sheldon overcome their misgivings and inhibitions and go on to live happily ever after) or a cynical one (Kate, a single mother in desperate circumstances, entraps a naïve, wealthy old man). The first of these readings might stress the evidence of mutual attraction (when they first meet Kate 'felt ethereally beautiful' and later he alludes warmly to her 'curls') and the role of the baby in bringing them together; the second, the degree of calculation that precedes their reunion and the way in which Kate repeatedly seeks to establish physical intimacy with the older man (what he sees as the 'unconscious' placing of her hand on his sleeve would, in this reading, become part of a deliberate strategy of seduction and the final image of Kate pressing the doctor's hand to her hip would be an escalation of this strategy rather than a moment of spontaneous tenderness) (30). Kate's non-Jewishness could also be pressed into service in either of these arguments: it could be seen as a potential obstacle to the love between her and Dr Sheldon that is triumphantly transcended by their common humanity; alternatively, Kate's failure to disclose her true identity could be seen as proof of her disingenuousness. There is, however, another way of reading the whole question of Jewish identity in this story that avoids either of these potentially tendentious lines of reasoning. The key to this third reading lies in the title of the story.

The biblical *Song of Solomon* is, of course (in)famous for its eroticism, an attribute generally apparent in holy scripture. Bloom's story contains verbal allusions to two of the most prominent images in the Old Testament poem: lilies (Dr Sheldon is charmed by the way Kate's 'hand lay tenderly, unconsciously, on his sleeve, like a lily') and doves (when Dr Sheldon 'bent his head toward Sarah to kiss the back of her round moist head, Kate felt so happy she thought her heart would break through her chest and fly around the temple, like a dove released') (31).[9] These allusions lend weight to a romantic reading of the story, in which the mutual regard of the principals in Bloom's story echoes the reciprocal structure of the lovers' tributes to each other in the biblical text. Apart from being the author of the *Song of Songs* (as the opening line of the song announces itself to be), however, Solomon is best known for two things: his wisdom (illustrated most notably by his judgment in the case of the disputed maternity of a new-born child) and his predilection for non-Jewish women.[10] It is unlikely to be coincidental, then, that Bloom's story features a new-born baby and a Jewish patriarchal figure – a pillar of the community – who finds himself drawn to a non-Jewish woman.

Whereas in the biblical account Solomon's taste for exotic women leads to a taste for exotic religions, with the result that he forsakes Yahweh, in Bloom's story the roles are reversed. Kate's reverence for Dr Sheldon encourages her to go to worship his God (indeed as we have seen she sees God *in* Dr Sheldon); it is she who is willing to forsake her Church-going tradition for the sake of her (potential) lover. If this makes Bloom's story sound as though it would qualify for inclusion in Ruth Wisse's or Andrew Furman's Jewish canons, then it is the role of the baby that would disqualify it. Kate goes to see Dr Sheldon in the first place because of his reputation as a compassionate, tolerant man, a champion of the 'weird, the dispossessed, the single mothers, the ones who wished they were' (29): a man, in other words, renowned for his *refusal to sit in judgment* over women who do not conform to moral and social norms. When Kate explains that 'she had only met the father once and hoped she never would again', Dr Sheldon doesn't 'purse his lips' in disapproval and when he meets Kate at the synagogue he hails her illegitimate daughter as 'an angel, a proof of God's goodness' (31). Unlike Solomon, whose stratagem to uncover the truth about the maternity of the baby brought before him relies on the threat of infanticide, for Dr Sheldon the paternity of the baby whom he delivers is irrelevant. The fact that Kate (and therefore, according to orthodox Jewish law, her baby) is not Jewish is likely to be of no more significance to such a man (shul-going or not) than the fact of his illegitimacy. Far from upholding the absolutist moral values of the Old Testament (in which adulteresses are condemned to death by stoning and children born out of wedlock to lives of ostracism), Dr Sheldon, like Ellen's mother in 'Love Is Not a Pie', endorses a pluralistic view of love and, by implication, of ethnic identity.

This pluralism is evident throughout Bloom's *oeuvre* and is often dramatized in the tension between seeing and not seeing. In 'Sleepwalking', another story from *Come To Me*, the narrator, Julia, and her stepson, Lionel, comforting each other after the death of Lionel's father (Julia's husband), find themselves drawn together by a strong sexual attraction. This erotic charge is signalled initially when Lionel is taking a shower and discovers there are no towels in the bathroom. When Julia brings him one,

> [a]ll I could see in the mist was a dark caramel column and two patches of dark curls, inky against his skin. I expected him to look away, embarrassed, but instead he looked right at me as he took the towel, and I was the one who turned away.
>
> (Bloom 1993; 1995: 42)

That night Lionel comes to Julia's bed and 'looked into my eyes, his own eyes like pools of coffee, shining in the moonlight [...] and then he kissed me and [...] I shut my eyes' (46). As his kisses become more urgent, Julia 'forc[es] [her] eyes open' (46) and she tries to resist, but then she submits and 'shut[s] [her] eyes again' (47). This dynamic relationship between looking and not looking, seeing and not seeing, and between dark and light, becomes a leitmotif not just in this story but in the others ('Night Vision' and 'Light Into Dark', from Bloom's third book, *A Blind Man Can See How Much I Love You*) that follow the lives of these two characters.

In 'Night Vision', Lionel has become the narrator and he is about to be reunited with Julia for the first time since their night together (after which Julia sends him away). The opening line of the story tells us that out of sight has not been out of mind: 'For fifteen years, I saw her only in my dreams' (Bloom 2000; 2001: 63). As a young boy of seventeen in 'Sleepwalking', Lionel 'charg[es] around the kitchen, bumping into chairs, blind' (49) when told to leave by Julia; as a thirty-three-year-old man in 'Night Vision' he stumbles around blindly in the dark, trying in vain to locate his glasses, breaking a water glass and a lamp and finally falling to the floor, 'hoping for no further damage and complete unconsciousness' (80). Hearing the commotion, Julia runs in and kneels beside her prostrate stepson 'so she could get a better look at me' and in this proximity Lionel 'could see her both more and less clearly than I would have liked' (80). In the following story in the collection, 'Light Into Dark', this time told in the third person, Lionel cross-examines Julia about a man with whom she may be having a relationship:

> 'Buster says you're seeing someone.'
> 'Well, "seeing." It's Peter, my neighbour down the road [. . .]'
> 'How old is he? White or black?'
> 'He's a little older than me. White.'
>
> (95)

The awkwardness of this conversation derives not just from the history between Lionel and Julia, but from Lionel's insistence on establishing the identity of Julia's lover in terms of strict categories of age and colour. Whereas his own relationship with Julia had transgressed conventional boundaries of family relations (he is her stepson), of colour (he is black, she is white) and of age (he was eighteen, she was thirty-nine), Lionel now wants to apply narrow, normative criteria by which to judge the suitability of Julia's lover. Nonetheless, he himself takes refuge in the euphemism 'seeing' (thus refusing actually to 'see' the sexual nature of the relationship), an evasion exposed by Julia's wry repetition of the word. When Lionel mislays his glasses and loses his balance while groping in the dark to find them, shattering the drinking glass and the lamp (a reflective, transparent object and an object designed to shed light, to enable night vision), he symbolically upsets the delicate balance between clarity and opacity that has governed his relationship with Julia, inverting their previous roles.

Whereas the lovers' vision in 'Sleepwalking' is sometimes blurred (by the mist of the shower, the darkness of Lionel's skin and the night itself), and sometimes sharpened (by the contrast between her skin and his, and between the moonlight and the darkness), in these later stories, as their titles suggest, there is a conscious attempt to cover things up, to forget the quasi-incestuous act that haunts them both, to revise history. Whereas in the first story it is Julia who doesn't know whether to look at Lionel or look away (to open or shut her eyes) and Lionel whose gaze is steady, in the later stories it is Lionel who doesn't know whether or not to avert his gaze (he can see Julia more and less clearly than he would like because he catches a glimpse of her 'breasts [...] in the hallway's dusty light') and Julia who examines him (and herself) unblinkingly (Bloom 2000; 2001: 80). What she sees is that neither of them has ever recovered from this episode, not because it was sinful but because it wasn't. When Lionel tells her that 'It didn't ruin me. It's not like we would ever be lovers now' ('Light Into Dark', 107), she is wounded rather than reassured, aggrieved that he can't 'figure out a nicer way to say that he no longer desires her [...] because she is too old now for him to see her that way' (108). Stung by his apparent indifference, she responds with a brutal revision of Lionel's term: 'We were never lovers. We had sex' (108). At this point, however, the narrator intervenes to record that 'this is not what she believes. They were lovers that night as surely as ugly babies are still babies; they were lovers like any other mismatched and blundering pair' (108).

Like 'Song of Solomon' and 'Love Is Not a Pie', the trilogy of stories involving Lionel and Julia celebrates the polymorphous perversity of sexual desire while at the same time acknowledging the difficulties it presents. Moreover, Bloom's representation of the relationship between Julia and Lionel exemplifies her preoccupation with, and subtle treatment of, ideas of vision and revision. By exploring their history from three different perspectives (Julia as narrator, Lionel as narrator, then a third-person narrator) Bloom emphasizes the multiplicity of possible perspectives that exist in any narrative; by focusing on the contingencies of the characters' own visions and revisions of their shared love, she draws attention to the provisional nature of these perspectives. It is no coincidence, then, that Bloom frequently revises her own previously published work. Her second book (and only novel), *Love Invents Us*, begins with a reworked version of one of the stories published in her first book, 'Light Breaks Where No Sun Shines' and much of the rest of the novel elaborates on material from another of the stories in that first collection, 'Semper Fidelis'. The title of her third book, *A Blind Man Can See How Much I Love You* (which is also the title of the opening story) first appears (in slightly different form, 'could' instead of 'can') as a line of dialogue in *Love Invents Us*. The closing story of *A Blind Man Can See How Much I Love You*, simply titled 'The Story', revises itself as it proceeds and is in fact an extended account of its own making. It is not, I think, modish self-reflexivity nor intellectual laziness that lies behind this self-revisioning, but rather the conviction that all stories are only possible, provisional interpretations of events: *the* story is only ever *a* story.

Many of Amy Bloom's stories have what might superficially be termed 'Jewish content': in her first book there is a trilogy of stories ('Hyacinths', 'The Sight of You' and 'Silver Water') which deals with some of the key events in the life of David Silverstein, a Jewish psychiatrist initially raised as a Presbyterian, and another of the stories from this collection, 'Faultlines', features Nathan, a novelist who writes 'about growing up Jewish in North Carolina' (Bloom 1993; 1995: 104). The heroine of 'Light Breaks Where No Sun Shines', 'Semper Fidelis' and *Love Invents Us* is Jewish, as is the narrator of one of the stories from her third book, 'The Gates Are Closing'. However, these stories are no more or less authentic as examples of Jewish-American fiction than Bloom's other stories. Rather, it seems to me that Bloom's heterogeneous, unorthodox *oeuvre* demands a revision of the Jewish-American canon, a redefinition of Jewish textuality based on a more inclusive, pluralistic vision of what Jewish literature might be and do.

Notes

1 The only story of Bloom's to be collected in an anthology of Jewish-American writing is 'Light Breaks Where No Sun Shines', which was published in Marks (1996: 24–32).
2 At the time of writing, the only article to have appeared on Bloom is a brief biographical piece by Anne Stockwell (2004).
3 This is the title of a bestselling collection of stories designed to warm the hearts of Jewish and non-Jewish readers alike, but which clearly alludes to the stereotype of the nurturing Jewish mother, see Canfield and Hansen (2000).
4 There are of course dissenting voices, notably Hana Wirth-Nesher and several of the other contributors to her edited volume of essays, *What is Jewish Literature?*, see Wirth-Nesher (1994a). In her introductory essay to this volume, 'Defining the Indefinable: What is Jewish Literature?', Wirth-Nesher rejects these paradigms and others, in favour of a more pluralistic approach, see Wirth-Nesher (1994b).
5 I am indebted to Bryan Cheyette's article 'On Being a Jewish Critic' for alerting me to Wisse's eccentric treatment of Malamud in particular, see Cheyette (2004) and chapter 2 in this volume.
6 She also includes brief sections on Abraham Cahan, Isaac Rosenfeld and Bernard Malamud, but only in order to dismiss their claims for inclusion in her canon for their failure to be faithful to their Jewish 'inheritance'.
7 As do Dickstein (2001) and Finkelstein (1992). Dickstein hails the emergence of the 'rapidly expanding group [of third-generation Jewish-American writers], which reflects a passionate new ethnicity', itself part of a larger American 'revival of ethnicity' (2001: 72, 75), while Finkelstein notes that '[a]mong writers of the earlier generation [...] to be a Jew means to have a certain origin, a certain relation to society, a certain set of cultural goals. For the following generation, all these conditions obtain, but in addition Judaism provides a relatively detailed intellectual infrastructure and a creative, formative idea as well as a unique social milieu' (1992: 18).
8 Bloom is interested in all her work in interrogating ideas of normality, as is clear from the title of her one work of non-fiction: *Normal: Transsexual CEOS, Crossdressing Cops, and Hermaphrodites with Attitude*, see Bloom (2002). In her preface to this book, Bloom explains that '*Normal* is about people widely considered not normal: female and male transsexuals, heterosexual cross-dressers, and the inter-sexed, sometimes known as hermaphrodites' (xiii).
9 Both doves and lilies recur throughout *The Song of Solomon*. The lover is addressed as a dove on three occasions (Sol 2:14, 5:2 and 6:9) and is said to have dove's eyes on three further occasions (Sol 1:15, 4:1 and 5:12). In the opening verse of the second chapter the female voice describes herself as 'the rose of Sharon *and* the lily of the valleys' and later in the same chapter she states 'My beloved is mine, and I *am* his: he feedeth among the lilies' (Sol 2:16), a line that is repeated later, with the first phrase inverted ('I *am* my beloved's, and my beloved *is* mine: he feedeth among the lilies', Sol 6:3). In addition, there are four other references to lilies in the poem (Sol 4:5, 5:13, 6:2 and 7:2).
10 Solomon is in a sense the prototype for Alex Portnoy and the many other Jewish men attracted to non-Jewish women in Jewish-American fiction, in that his transgressive sexual desires are associated with the rejection of Judaism itself: 'But King Solomon loved many strange women [...] For it came to pass, when Solomon was old, that his wives turned away his heart after other gods' (1 Kings 11:1–2).

Part IV

Changing centres, changing peripheries and spaces in-between

Jewish writing from the Anglophone diaspora(s) – Britain

8 Otherness and affiliation in Anglo-Jewish poetry

Peter Lawson

In this chapter I want to consider whether it is possible to speak of an Anglo-Jewish poetic tradition. Some people might argue that there are no thematic differences between poetry written by Gentiles and Jews in postwar Britain. Others may insist that poetry can only be Jewish if it is written in a Jewish language, such as 'Yiddish, Hebrew and Ladino' (see Wirth-Nesher 1994b: 5). Certainly, some reviewers of my anthology, *Passionate Renewal: Jewish Poetry in Britain since 1945* (2001), expressed such opinions.

Further, even if we concede that poetry written in English by British Jews is a species of Jewish poetry, we may be tempted to dismiss it as too marginal for serious study. Many scholars seem to think that post-Holocaust verse is only produced in Israel, the USA and the Continent of Europe. The British Isles are frequently overlooked in Jewish literary studies; possibly because the Nazis failed to invade and establish concentration camps there. If Anglo-Jewish poetry were geographically as well as historically post-Holocaust, it might be accorded more attention. Indeed, the Holocaust is crucial in understanding the critical reception of Anglo-Jewish poetry. Charles Fishman, for example, writing in *American Book Review*, grumbled that my Anglo-Jewish verse anthology lacked enough good verse about 'Israel and the Holocaust', 'Jewish victimhood and survival' (2002: 8).

However, my research into Anglo-Jewish poetry over the course of the twentieth century reveals a continuity of concerns which suggests more about the Jewish diasporic condition than the Holocaust. This is not to say that British Jewish poets are unaffected by the Shoah. Dannie Abse speaks for many secular British Jews when he confesses in 'White Balloon' (1990): 'Dear love, Auschwitz made me / more of a Jew than Moses did.' (34) Abse and others, such as Emanuel Litvinoff, Ruth Fainlight and Elaine Feinstein, are among many poets who have written about the Holocaust as a landmark event in their lives.

Still, what I want to do in this essay is consider diasporic continuities which span the twentieth century in Anglo-Jewish verse. Concerns with exile, 'orientalism',[1] extraterritoriality and a peripheral relationship with what Jon Silkin terms 'English and Jewish specifics' (1967: 22–4) are pertinent here. I will also look at commonly expressed tensions between otherness and affiliation. Otherness, I want to suggest, relates to what the First World War poet Isaac Rosenberg identified as the 'ungraspable' nature of poetry itself, and a prevalent sense of secular Jewish identity as similarly uncategorizable (1979; 1984: 151, 238).[2]

Countering such displacement is a common affiliation with the diasporic narrative of exile and deferred return to a textually imagined homeland. As Rosenberg writes in his sonnet 'Zion' (1906): 'she [Zion] fell, / And only left her story.' (1979; 1984: 3–4) This is the 'story' of the Hebrew Bible read as literature, and English literature which borrows from the Bible. Biblically-inspired poetry by John Milton, for example, engages Anglo-Jewish poets, as do Lord Byron's *Hebrew Melodies* (1815) and William Blake's *Jerusalem* (1804–20). Several Anglo-Jewish poets invoke nineteenth-century Romantic poetry for precisely its expression of biblically prophetic visions from the peripheries of conventional mores. Indeed, Anglo-Jewish poetry tends to follow a Romantic tradition. This is a universalistic tradition of affiliation with the outsider, the dispossessed and others passed over in silence. Further, Anglo-Jewish poetry evinces a struggle for Romantic transcendence of quotidian circumstances in order to be free of tensions in the diaspora.

In the twentieth century, Modernism continued the Romantic tradition of speaking for those marginalized by English literature and society. Indeed, it might be said that Modernist poetry was, in Terry Eagleton's phrase, produced by 'exiles and emigrés' (1970). Consequently, Anglo-Jewish poets who consider themselves exilic, such as John Rodker and Elaine Feinstein, self-consciously affiliate with Modernism. Isaac Rosenberg and Jon Silkin also engage with an exilic, Anglo-American Modernism.

America is particularly important to these poets, both as a country of immigrants, and as a relatively young country with a poetic tradition which scarcely predates nineteenth-century Jewish immigration to England. Rosenberg, for example, writes in 1913 of Ralph Waldo Emerson's verse: 'We have here no tradition – no tricks of the trade.' Instead, he discerns 'spontaneity, inspiration' (1979; 1984: 288–9). Jon Silkin is similarly keen to champion American poetry. In *The Life of Metrical and Free Verse in Twentieth-Century Poetry* (1997), Silkin applauds the distinction 'between English and American poetry, suggesting that the rhythms of the latter are more delicate, and subtle, than those in English poetry' (187). He goes on to praise Walt Whitman as 'great'.[3] Indeed, I suggest that Silkin and Rosenberg, like John Rodker and Elaine Feinstein, learn from the 'spontaneity' of American poets to challenge an English poetic practice which has not traditionally spoken for diasporic peoples.

Anglo-Jewish poets also look to Israel. Isaac Rosenberg and Siegfried Sassoon both write poems set in British Mandate Palestine. Indeed, Rosenberg's final trio of poems – 'The Burning of the Temple', 'The Destruction of Jerusalem by the Babylonian Hordes' and 'Through These Pale Cold Days' (1918; Rosenberg 1979; 1984: 115–7) – express a Zionist yearning for Jews to return to their ancestral homeland. By contrast, Sassoon's sonnet 'In Palestine' (1918) suggests an affiliation with Jewish identity located firmly in the Old Testament past. After the establishment of the State of Israel, Silkin and Feinstein wrote poems set in that country. Silkin also translated a collection of verse by the Israeli poet Natan Zach,

Against Parting (1967), and contributed to various Israeli journals and anthologies.[4]

Rosenberg was the first avowedly Jewish poet of the twentieth century to reach a wide English readership. Paul Fussell, in *The Great War and Modern Memory* (1975), identifies Rosenberg's 'Break of Day in the Trenches' (1916) as 'the greatest poem of the war' (250). Rosenberg's poetics were explicitly Jewish. He referred to the Old Testament for 'the exclusive atmosphere such as our literature possesses' (1979; 1984: 287). In other words, Rosenberg located his poetic roots in the Bible read non-theologically as *literature*. Like other Modernists, Rosenberg was mining ancient texts for their potential contemporary significance. Those texts he selected were primarily Jewish. Thus, Rosenberg was clear about writing within ancient Jewish as well as Georgian English literary traditions; and about fashioning something marginal, something eccentric. As he told his friend Ruth Löwy: 'G.B. [Gordon Bottomley] has urged me to write Jewish plays. I am quite sure if I do I will be boycotted and excommunicated, that is, assuming my work is understood' (247).

In his near-contemporaneous essay 'Tradition and the Individual Talent' (1919), T.S. Eliot expressed his contempt for literary 'eccentricity'. Indeed, Eliot terms eccentric poets 'perverse' (1919; 1966: 21). However, an eccentric is not merely whoever deviates 'from what is usual or customary', displaying 'oddity'. 'Eccentricity' also refers to a peripheral positioning, such as Anglo-Jewish poets occupied in twentieth-century English literature. According to *The Oxford English Dictionary*, the eccentric is not 'centrally placed'; and is defined, indeed, by his 'distance from the centre' (see OED 1989, 5: 49). The relationship between peripheral status and apparent perversity recurs in judgements made about Anglo-Jewish poetry and poetics.

Significantly, Rosenberg's trench poems are set *outside* England to present an Anglo-Jewish space *within* English poetry. In poems such as 'Break of Day in the Trenches' and 'Chagrin' (1915–16), Rosenberg *deterritorializes* English in order to write another, eccentrically-located kind of poetry. Once in the French trenches, I want to suggest, Rosenberg finally feels at home with his dynamic Anglo-Jewish inheritance. Rosenberg told his friend and fellow poet Joseph Leftwich in January 1918: 'After the war, if things go well – I doubt whether I'd live in London.'[5] Away from the metropolitan centre, Rosenberg finds his eccentricity is no longer out of place.

In Silkin's study of First World War poetry, *Out of Battle* (1972), the later Anglo-Jewish poet remarks:

> It is not possible in Rosenberg's *Moses* to determine what emphasis to put upon the ethnic impulse and what on the radical. For Rosenberg, one suspects that the two issues were in common. To be Jewish in England then was to be, in the main, working class.
>
> (1972; 1978: 263)

Silkin's point is that affiliation with both a 'perverse' ethnicity and a politically marginalized working class was in no way a contradiction for Rosenberg. Further,

Silkin edited *The Penguin Book of First World War Poetry* (1979) in which he fulsomely praised Rosenberg as the best of the war poets. According to Silkin, Rosenberg remains underrated as a poet because he writes a different sort of English: an eccentric English. Silkin states:

> The English that Rosenberg employs is not the English of [Wilfred] Owen, [Herbert] Read, [Siegfried] Sassoon, or yet [David] Jones. Whether it is better or worse is not quite the question here; it is more to do with the sense that English may have plural rather than singular standards. Rosenberg's language, at any rate, is exploratory; his poetry seeks to re-shape culture by introducing new ideas and alignments, and one might say that this aspiration is most apparent in Rosenberg's language.
>
> (1979: 36–7)

Rosenberg's English 'is exploratory; his poetry seeks to re shape culture by introducing new ideas and alignments.' Rather than looking to English 'form and tradition' (as Georgian poetics demanded) Rosenberg attempts to shape a poetry which will give voice to his Anglo-Jewish and working class experience.

Interestingly, Silkin's point concerning 'plural rather than singular standards' in English language and literature chimes with the notion of 'minor literature' proposed by Gilles Deleuze and Félix Guattari. In *Kafka. Toward a Minor Literature* (1975), the French critics ask:

> How many people today live in a language that is not their own? Or no longer, or not yet, even know their own and know poorly the major language that they are forced to serve? This is the problem of immigrants, and especially of their children, the problem of minorities, the problem of minor literature [. . .] How to tear a minor literature away from its own language, allowing it to challenge the language?
>
> (1975; 1986: 19)

Silkin affiliates with his Anglo-Jewish forebear Rosenberg (the child of immigrants) and to an eccentric project of challenging the English language. His stance is ethnically and, therefore, linguistically pluralistic. Silkin reads *Englishes* where tradition would inscribe a singular, monolithic *English* literature. Silkin understands that Rosenberg speaks with a minority voice in the literature of the majority. In effect, Silkin implies that he too, as an Anglo-Jewish poet, writes an eccentric 'minor literature' in English.

Indeed, I want to suggest that all Anglo-Jewish poets negotiate a minority relationship with England's 'major' literature – ratified by tradition and expectation across a certain geographical space – and, in so doing, produce what Deleuze and Guattari term a 'minor literature'. Further, I want to ask what Anglo-Jewish poets do with such marginality. How do they give it voice and make it speak for themselves as Jews, as well as for other, often overlapping marginal groups: such as women, regional peoples and more recent immigrants?

Marginality, I suggest, may be a blessing. It can confer freedom from the prescriptions of a 'major' literary tradition. Of course, it may also lead to silence born of neglect. As Elaine Feinstein remarks in *The Jewish Quarterly*: 'The danger of being at the periphery is that you never quite penetrate sufficiently not to disappear into darkness' (Lawson 2001: 65–9). Silkin, I suggest, displaces *his* Anglo-Jewish marginality to the North of England, where he finds a Jewish home, or 'new Jerusalem'. As he writes in 'The ship's pasture' (1986):

> Northwards,
> a new Jerusalem with the lamb lies separate,
> its shade dense and lovely.
>
> (1986: 84)

Moreover, Silkin empathizes with northern poets such as Geoffrey Hill and Basil Bunting. In *The Life of Metrical and Free Verse*, Silkin refers to Bunting's use of accentual poetry:

> [Accentual verse is] a form asking to be used, one capable of expressing rhythms with a radiating vitality, often a rugged one, different from the smooth confidence of a verse-line that counts stresses *and* syllables.
>
> (1997: 271)

Here Silkin deploys traces of a discourse which consistently informs his poetics, whereby 'rugged' vitality is associated with regional (particularly northern) accentual verse, and 'smooth confidence' is located elsewhere (particularly in London) side-by-side with accentual-syllabic verse ('a verse-line that counts stresses *and* syllables'). Unlike Rosenberg, Silkin *chooses* to stay in an eccentric relationship to the metropolitan centre. Rosenberg only *discovered* a similarly eccentric space in the trenches, as it were, by chance.

Interestingly, the spirit of the Cambridge University critic F.R. Leavis hovers over Silkin's poetics. As Francis Mulhern notes in Homi Bhabha's *Nation and Narration* (1990):

> The strategic prize in *Scrutiny*'s contention with the metropolitan elites was the status of 'centrality', which Leavis and his collaborators sought to invest with a strictly cultural, rather than 'social', meaning.
>
> (1990: 257)

Similarly in Silkin's schema, the regions become culturally central, while the metropolitan centre moves to a paradoxically parochial position. As Silkin remarks on the opening page of his autobiographical essay *The First Twenty-Four Years* (1987): 'No-one is so parochial as a Londoner, who, at the same time, adheres to an unshakeable belief that London is the radiating centre of Britain.' (243) Following a congruous line of reasoning, apparently peripheral Anglo-Jewish (and other minor) poetries begin to assume a culturally central place, while the 'hostile weight' (Silkin 1972; 1978: 271) of the major English literary tradition is radically de-centred.

To be sure, neither Isaac Rosenberg nor Siegfried Sassoon perceived themselves as culturally central. When Sassoon reflects on his youthful hunting days in *The Weald of Youth* (1942), he remarks: 'There were moments when I felt that I was an indecisive intruder who had no genuine foothold in either of those apparently incompatible spheres of activity ["Literature and Sport"]' (214). Feeling like a spectator of contemporary life, Sassoon characterized himself as peripheral: 'the *ruminant onlooker*'.[6] Unlike Rosenberg, who affiliated with a Jewish present and future, Sassoon located Jewishness in an ancient past. Rosenberg orientated his Jewishness towards a Modernist, politically radical future: socialist and Zionist. Conversely, Sassoon was only comfortable with his Jewishness when he viewed it nostalgically as '*in the past already*' (cit. Wilson 1998; 1999: 526). The Old Testament and Sassoon's ancestral 'Bagdad' (Sassoon 1983: 93) provided loci for the poet's articulation of a biblical and orientalized Jewishness. Such past and faraway Jewishness, I want to suggest, tapped into prevalent imperial and Christian discourses which, respectively, constructed the British Empire as the new 'Protestant Israel' (Colley 1992: 368–9), and the New Testament as superseding the Hebrew Bible. These discourses allowed Sassoon to displace his (old) Jewishness onto (new) England, while affiliating with the dominant social and literary mores surrounding him.

War is a recurrent theme of twentieth-century Anglo-Jewish poetry. Unsurprisingly, two world wars impinge on much poetry written between, and about, 1914–45. Moreover, I want to argue that a *particular*, though changing, embattlement is evident in this verse tradition. Before 1945, a significant cause of social and psychological embattlement was anti-Semitism. In *God Made Blind. Isaac Rosenberg, His Life and Poetry* (1999), Deborah Maccoby remarks that Rosenberg 'saw in the trenches his own symbolic world made real' (1999: 162).[7] Maccoby argues that Rosenberg was liberated by the Great War because social and psychological attacks were already familiar to him. Possibly for the first time in his adult life, Rosenberg did not feel marginalized because he was writing in a war environment. When Sassoon penned his preface to *The Collected Works of Isaac Rosenberg* (1937), he focused on Rosenberg's moral combativeness, praising the poet's verse as 'biblical and prophetic' (Rosenberg 1979; 1984: ix). However, it is Sassoon rather than Rosenberg who adopts the persona of a Hebrew prophet in several of his Great War poems. In 'The Poet as Hero' (1916), for example, Sassoon writes:

> But now I've said good-bye to Galahad,
> And am no more the knight of dreams and show;
> For lust and senseless hatred make me glad,
> And my killed friends are with me where I go.
> Wound for red wound I burn to smite their wrongs;
> And there is absolution in my songs.
>
> (1983: 61)

Here, Sassoon deploys Old Testament language to demand that the 'Galahad' of Christian chivalry ('knight of dreams') be put aside for vengeance ('Wound for red wound I burn to smite their wrongs'). Though Christian readings of the Old Testament presented Jewish values as vengeful, I want to suggest that Sassoon found in the Hebrew Bible a positive means of combating English complacency towards the First World War.

In the second half of the century, Jon Silkin began to construct an Anglo-Jewish poetics by harking back to First World War poetry. He wrote in a catalogue to an exhibition of Rosenberg's paintings at Leeds University (1959): '[Rosenberg] is the tension that exists between the two societies [English and Jewish], and in this, he is truly Anglo-Jewish' (3). As the editor of *The Penguin Book of First World War Poetry*, Silkin submits:

> Rosenberg's language then – this may seem strangely put – is more lived in than Owen's. Owen's language narrates or carries the ideas; Rosenberg's language is them, sensuously enacts them, and experiences them. So to this extent it shares some of the 'haecceity' (or thisness) of [David] Jones's language.
>
> (1979: 52)

According to Silkin, Rosenberg's language is more faithful to the world as it is ('more lived in') than Owen's. It resembles life to such an extent that it (more or less) becomes life ('sensuously enacts', 'experiences', 'shares some of the "haecceity" (or thisness) of Jones's language'). Apparently, Rosenberg affiliates with life through 'language'. He is text-based in his exploration of what 'is the mystical' in experience. In this, Silkin implies, Rosenberg is fundamentally 'Judaic',[8] and follows a Hebrew tradition of reverence for words. Indeed, Silkin appears to read Rosenberg's language as 'exploratory' and Jewish, while implicitly contrasting Owen's as formalistic ('narrates', 'carries the ideas') and Christian.

This dichotomy between Christian (classical) formalism and Jewish (Romantic) exploration can be traced back in England to the 1950s, when the *New Lines* (1956) and *Mavericks* (1957) poetry anthologies were published. The former, edited by Robert Conquest, launched what came to be known as 'the Movement'.[9] Kingsley Amis, Robert Conquest, Donald Davie, D.J. Enright, Thom Gunn, John Holloway, Elizabeth Jennings, Philip Larkin and John Wain were thus grouped together. Among the poems in *New Lines* was Larkin's 'Church Going' (1954). If there was such an entity as 'the Movement' (something several of its supposed members denied), 'Church Going' raised the question of its 'religious identity'. To be sure, Christianity held a powerful position in several of the poets' upbringings and university educations. As Blake Morrison explains in his 1980 study: 'The Movement writers tended to come from homes in which religion was still treated as a matter of seriousness and importance' (226–7). At Oxford University, where Larkin, Amis, Holloway, Jennings and Wain were all undergraduates in the 1940s, Christianity occupied a similarly central position. Morrison continues:

> Christianity exerted a powerful influence at Oxford in the 1940s: 'Everybody to whom an imaginative and bookish youth naturally looked up, every figure who radiated intellectual glamour of any kind, was in the Christian camp.' Wain adds that for him Christianity was intimately associated with the literature which he was reading at Oxford.
>
> (228)[10]

In discussion with the poet Anthony Thwaite in 1963, Silkin associates 'the Movement' with both Christianity and a 'formal' poetics (see Silkin and Thwaite 1963: 11). Silkin remarks that Larkin's 'Church Going' demonstrates that 'Larkin [. . .] is busy re-integrating himself with the Christian tradition.' He goes on to suggest that such formalism, or 'tradition', risks repetition of the injustices of the past, particularly persecution and murder of Jews. Silkin explains:

> I think that perhaps what I try to do – in my York poem ['Astringencies'] – exemplifies what I mean. Here is a situation of a massacre of Jews at York in 1190. At the end of the poem, an exact correspondence with what happened in York is implied with what happened in Europe in this century. And I'm asking, do we want this kind of thing to continue? If we don't then we have to change society.
>
> (Silkin and Thwaite 1963: 15)

Thus, the Holocaust makes the need for social change urgent, while the *poem-as-process* intimates such change through its language:

> In this poem-as-process you start off with a concept without knowing where it will lead you. Your concept is a reflection of a certain facet of reality that you feel involved with, but where that reality will lead you you don't know, but you explore it through the poem. The poets I can think of who work like this manage to release an enormous amount of energy in their work. Now Rosenberg would be a good example of a poet working through this 'in process' method.
>
> (11)

Silkin's perspective is European ('what happened in Europe in this century') and politically radical ('we have to change society', 'where that reality will lead you you don't know, but you explore it'). By contrast, poets associated with 'the Movement' tended to espouse an insular 'Little Englandism'[11] and political conservatism. As Dannie Abse remarked in a 1987 interview with Elaine Feinstein:

> I felt in opposition to 'the Movement' [. . .] There were also certain political undertones with the upraising of the English tradition. It was a feeling that, you know, 'wogs' began in Calais – that foreign poetry was no good [. . .] I didn't feel myself to be a Little Englander.
>
> (Feinstein 1987: n.p.)

Together with Howard Sergeant, Abse edited the *Mavericks* anthology in reaction to *New Lines*. Unequivocally, Abse espoused Romanticism:

> I suppose I am equating the romantic with the Dionysian and the Dionysian with that mysterious, permanent element in poetry that irradiates and moves us and endures [...] But if, for this reason, I am anti-movement, I'm certainly not opposed to discipline and form and style.
>
> (Sergeant and Abse 1957: 10)

Mirroring *New Lines*, *Mavericks* featured nine poets: Dannie Abse, Anthony Cronin, J.C. Hall, Michael Hamburger, Vernon Scannell, Jon Silkin, John Smith, W. Price Turner and David Wright. Of these, three were Jewish: Abse, Hamburger and Silkin. Indeed, I want to argue that Silkin's dichotomy – between a 'formal' language which 'narrates', and an implicitly 'romantic' language which 'sensuously enacts' – carries traces of a widely disseminated discourse distinguishing between a conservative, Christian Little Englandism and a radical, Anglo-Jewish Europeanism.

Like Abse and Silkin, Elaine Feinstein was shaped as a Jew by the Holocaust. She confesses in an autobiographical essay: 'When I read what exactly had been done to so many children, as young as I was, in the hell of Hitler's camps. You could say in that year I became Jewish' (1984: 219). Feinstein's poetry and novels express a cultural overshadowing by the Shoah. When she writes, for example, in 'Renaissance Feb. 7' (1971) of paradisaical 'golden hours' in a 'supernatural city' (1994: 66), she seems simultaneously to be fleeing 'the hell of Hitler's camps'. Certainly, Feinstein's verse gestures towards escape. As the speaker of 'Out' (1971) enquires: 'Who shall I take for my holy poet // to lead me out of this plain?' (1994: 27). Feinstein, I suggest, follows a Romantic tradition of transcendent poetry. Through art, she seeks to transform the social and psychological tensions of Anglo-Jewish reality into something like 'the daylight of the Duc de Berry's golden hours' (66). Her intoxicated 'flying' or 'rising' (8, 10), however, is counterbalanced by what she terms the 'baggage' of diasporic history (Feinstein 1994; 1996: 176). Consequently, lyrics such as 'To Cross' (1971) express both 'respite' from and affiliation with an embattled Jewish 'story', in a tense and ambivalent 'mad calm' (Feinstein 1994: 47).

Unsurprisingly, Feinstein also rejected 'the Movement'. To escape the restrictive formalism of 'the Movement', she became involved with an alternative group of poets, including Jeremy Prynne, Lee Harwood and Tom Pickard. Deborah Mitchell explains:

> Their main interest in common was the potential to British poetry in the practice of the Black Mountain poets; but Feinstein found the Cambridge group's insistence on its 'Englishness' incompatible with her growing awareness of the importance of her background to her work and left it after about six months.
>
> (1985: 118)

Whereas Feinstein looked to American poets such as Charles Olson and Robert Creeley at Black Mountain College for an extraterritorial way out of Little Englandism, the Gentile members of the group were intent on using the American model 'to explore the history of their particular Englishness' (Conradi 1983: 293). Indeed, Feinstein's family history of Russo-Jewish immigration and acculturation to England over fewer than a hundred years was passed over in silence. The Cambridge group prized an English insularity which excluded Anglo-Jewish, and other diasporic, experience in the twentieth century. To this extent, it bore a striking resemblance to the similarly insular 'Movement'.

Feinstein is one of several Anglo-Jewish poets who demand to be read against the grain of the dominant English literary tradition. Despite received critical opinion, there does appear to be a Jewish poetry in England. To be sure, there are diverse ways of writing about Jewishness. Still, diasporic tensions, and a sense of suspension between metaphorical exile and an imagined homeland, are evident in Anglo-Jewish poetry. What becomes clear is the sense of 'in-betweenness' shared by Anglo-Jewish poets. These poets do not express a common notion of origins or goals, but they do negotiate an ongoing 'story' which is always *in medias res*: in the middle of a diasporic narrative (Szirtes 2000: 15; Rosenberg 1979; 1984: 4).

Notes

1 See Said (1978; 1995: 73): 'I have been using the word [Orientalism] to designate that collection of dreams, images, and vocabulary available to anyone who has tried to talk about what lies east of the dividing line.'

2 In Rosenberg's verse drama *Moses* (1916), the eponymous hero speaks of fashioning the Jewish people into 'a thing, / Ineffable and useable' (line 464); and Rosenberg describes poetry similarly in a letter of 1916 to Gordon Bottomley as 'understandable and still ungraspable' (1979; 1984: 238).

3 Silkin (1997: 22): 'Whitman, like other great poets (America's only one, so far) has that interacting of opposites which makes, not a simulation of energy, but a living tissue of strength and delicacy.'

4 Zach (1967). See also, for example, Silkin (1989/1990: 166–76) and (2000: 174–7). See further Dor and Zach (1977).

5 Rosenberg, Letter to Joseph Leftwich, dated December 8, 1917 (1979; 1984: 267).

6 'Unpublished papers in the hands of a private collector', see Wilson (1998; 1999: 526, 582).

7 See further Phillips (1994b: 187): 'For Rosenberg [. . .] to enlist was to make vivid in a peculiarly literal way the dilemmas that constituted the struggle of his life.'

8 'In Judaic terms', Silkin (1979: 52) explains, 'although the soul may be nucleated by God's essences, humanity can only experience these through the body, that is, the total being; for in earthly life body and essences are inseparable.'

9 Morrison (1980: 3): '*New Lines* (1956), edited by Robert Conquest, contained the same eight poets [as D.J. Enright's *Poets of the 1950s* (1955)] and added one more: Thom Gunn. In the years since 1956, the term "the Movement" has come to be taken to mean these nine poets.'

10 Morrison quotes from Wain (1962; 1965: 142).

11 See Corcoran (1993: 84): 'The attitudinizing associated with a "little Englandism" in the Movement has always come under suspicion [in Silkin's oeuvre].' See further Conradi (1983: 293–4): '[Feinstein's] roots, if she had them and was not nomadic, were certainly not to be discovered in a nationalist version of "Little Englandism".'

9 Diasporic voices?

Second-generation Jewish authors in Britain

Oliver Groß

The aspect that is most striking when reading about diaspora(s) is the ubiquity of this only rather loosely defined concept in the fields of language, literature, religious and social studies, which makes it one of the longest-established, generic, yet also one of the most elusive terms in the history of scientific terminology. Of course it is always helpful, as a sort of lowest common denominator for all academic disciplines, to quote from the Greek original: 'diaspeirein', in its original meaning, might be translated as 'to disperse', 'to scatter seeds'. Yet diaspora seems to have come a long way from its ancient agrarian etymology and today seems to denote either an ethnic or religious community living outside its original homeland, the fact that a particular community has no homeland, or any of a series of host countries where such a community chooses to settle irrespective of whether it has a homeland or not.

How very apt, one might say, that the ominous word diaspora, which somehow includes the ideas of random movement, displacement and uprootedness, should itself have become a living proof of the standard Saussurean model of arbitrary signifiers and the fact that meaning tends to slip, to evolve or be irrevocably lost in the outer reaches of historical or geographic 'space'. Some sociologists/ethnologists indeed went so far as to suggest that the dreaded word should be dropped altogether, and 'diaspora' be replaced by the term 'transnational communities' (Rex 2002: 53–4). Others, instead, speak of 'third-time spaces', thus opting for an attractive aura of semantic sci-fi but perhaps ignoring the arduousness and the processes of disillusionment involved in the formation of diasporas, not to speak of the poverty, pain or persecution that prompted such displacement in the first place. In the context of the present chapter, 'diaspora' has been retained as a working term, since reference to it is still frequent and extensive in criticism and theoretical works, and since it has most of its roots in the history of the Jewish people, which makes it some sort of yardstick against which to measure the texts produced by young Jewish authors in Britain.

This should – hopefully – help to decide whether there is a visible difference between these texts and what has been conveniently labelled mainstream British literature. And, as a second step, this yardstick should also be expedient in helping to spot the difference, if any, between these younger authors and the previous generation of Jewish authors, the new arrivants of the 1920s and 1930s in Britain, perhaps including those who escaped the Holocaust, though this admittedly may stretch the idea of a single generation to its very limits.

Here then is one last definition of the word diaspora which is as useful as it is straightforward in terms of the palpable risks of diasporic life, and which has been borrowed for the purposes of this chapter from Gabriel Sheffer's book *Diaspora Politics. At Home Abroad* (2003: 78): 'ethno-national diasporas', Sheffer writes, 'are those groups that remain minorities in their host countries and thus potentially may face the possibility of expulsion, as well as social, political and economic hardships and rejection.'

This captures both the precariousness of a liminal existence and the assumption that members of these groups are more than just transient migrants, that they are here to stay, if only for lack of a better home. Their position of in-betweenness, of belonging and not belonging, is duly reflected in the tentative way in which younger authors have introduced Jewish themes into the English literary canon. Where Sander L. Gilman proudly claims that '[m]ore than Anglo Jewish or German Jewish writing, Jewish American culture is an example of how a successful multicultural presence in a national literature can be established' (2003: 172), Bryan Cheyette's words in his anthology of Jewish writing in the UK and Ireland seem to be tinged with rather more than the fair share of British resignation when he says that '[a]s Jewish writers are thought not to exist in Britain, the common reaction to my [Cheyette's] eccentric enthusiasms has been, until recent years, incredulity' (xi).

Diaspora politics seem to be running in the family, which may or may not operate as a shield against the outside world or, conversely, as an obstacle en route to acculturation. Daniel Boyarin subsumes this under the 'paradoxical power of diaspora'. 'On the one hand', he writes, 'everything that defines us is compounded of all the questions of our ancestors. On the other hand, everything is permanently at risk. Thus contingency and genealogy are the two central components of diasporic consciousness' (Boyarin and Boyarin 2002: 4). Family matters, the absence of eccentricity and an overbearing sense of blandness together mark out Jonathan Treitel's Anglo-Jewish story 'Selflessness; or Alexander and His Electric Work' (1998), an original contribution to Cheyette's aforementioned volume, as a case in point. Treitel's narrator, a young man nursing his mother – she is suffering from Alzheimer's disease – is summoned to the deathbed of his uncle Alexander. The uncle, who according to the narrator, 'had a profound sense of his own unremarkableness. He wasn't even remarkably unremarkable: just unremarkably unremarkable' (1998: 321–2), this uncle proceeds to utter his very last words, which turn out to be the seemingly incongruous story of how he had once bought an electric wok, switched it on at home, blown a fuse and thrown the whole thing away. While the narrator still muses about the deeper meaning of the wok episode, he discovers among the dead uncle's belongings a card with a lock of brown hair attached to it and signed in his mother's handwriting – proof of a clandestine affair between the uncle and the mother.

The metaphor of the wok, as complemented by the *billet doux* revelation, actually cuts both ways: in a sense, the wok as a commonplace pseudo-ethnic kitchen utensil signifies the uncle's failed pretensions in life as well as the degree of his acculturation, his wish to blend in with mainstream culture which is then duly exploded – just as all traces of his own existence are erased when the nephew hands back the 'trash bag' filled with his uncle's belongings to the hospital receptionist. And yet the wok story also serves as a vehicle to show up the ways in which the nephew misreads, through sheer ignorance, Alexander's identity and personal history and, by implication, his own. For he might well be the illegitimate son of that same Alexander whom he believes to have so entirely figured out and neatly pigeonholed as Mr Unremarkable himself. In telling Alexander's story, the nephew/son evinces an erratic mind as much as a tendency for self-effacement which can be traced back to the previous generation of uncle and mother: 'He recognized me as a fellow sufferer. He was urging me to break loose for once in my life' (328) is how the narrator finally makes sense of the uncle's message. As an exhortation of 'carpe diem', the wok story is both hilarious and heart-rending, transitory and transgressive as it is passed down from failing first-generation father to soul-searching second-generation son.

The disintegration of collective memory is also very much a dominant theme in Linda Grant's part biographical, part analytical book *Remind Me Who I Am, Again* (1998). Her case is infinitely more tragic as it is her own mother, the last of her generation in the extended Ginsberg and Haft families, who is gradually slipping away into senile dementia. Somewhere along the lines, the family had changed their name from Ginsberg to the much less obtrusive Grant, and Linda Grant herself, the elder of two daughters, has no qualms about showing her own youthful narrative self as having discarded all thought about her own dual identity: 'I had had my chance and I hadn't taken it', she writes. 'When I was younger I was bored stiff with my parents' reminiscences. I had no curiosity. I was living in a time when the past was going to be abolished' (1998: 27). Though being second- (or third-) generation in a family of Jewish migrants from rural Poland and from Kiev in Russia, she reinvents herself, along with so many others in the 1960s, as 'part of the first generation that was put on earth, [. . .] to be young and stay young forever.' Now, as a grown-up, she is painfully aware of the lacuna in her own personal memory, of how her self-inflicted cultural amnesia has deprived her of her roots, even as her mother's pathological amnesia ultimately prevents her from recuperating any of the long-lost family histories. 'Memory', she has come to understand whilst being faced with her mother's disintegrating personality and bodily functions, 'is everything, it's life itself' (17).

Grant's acutely felt cultural limbo, however, is not entirely of her own volition. She has perceived about her mother's generation a habitual secretiveness which she deems part of the precarious nature of the migrant condition and which only at a later stage seems to have been reinforced in her mother's individual case by dementia-induced oblivion. The mother's evasiveness when asked about past events of members of the extended family is infuriating to both daughters, and Grant comes up with a whole bundle of reasons for this particular sort of first-generation mnemonic defiance: it might be identified as 'mechanisms of repression, of covering up, of not letting on or giving yourself away', she suggests, in order to preserve one's own fragile identity *vis-à-vis* an encroaching host culture (25). It might have been a rudimentary survival instinct evoked by persecution in the so-called land of first settlement where, as Grant speculates, 'our parents imbibed with their mother's milk a deep distrust of bureaucrats, the representatives of power whom, with skill and cunning, they plotted to outwit [...] To them, a town hall clerk fell into the same category as the agents of a cruel and oppressive Tsar' (32). And, lastly, embarking on a new life somewhere in a different part of the globe can mean having to shed one's skin, reinventing oneself completely. This is an image makeover that affects both inside and outside and can as often as not be achieved only under false pretences or, as Grant puts it: 'All the lies and evasions and tall stories are what you must have when you are bent on self-invention' (156). To Grant, her mother's condition in old age seems no more than a continuation of what she had internalized as the perennial mindset of the migrant, resulting in a blur of cause and effect: a deranged and/or dislocated person (both senses are neatly captured by the German word 'verrückt') trying to pass herself off as 'normal'. Cheyette notes these inner workings of the migrant consciousness when he writes that '[t]he cultural amnesia engendered by the process of migration from one country to another results in a form of semiacculturation, a person who is neither "wild" nor "tame", neither Jewish nor English' (1998: xxii).

The blissful and utterly unspectacular normalcy of British middle class life has been effortlessly achieved by Natasha Kaplan, the protagonist of Elena Lappin's novel *The Nose* (2001). Natasha, an American-born editor of a Jewish literary magazine, has come to London to escape from her parents' huge personalities and zany artistic lifestyle as Jewish independent soft-porn filmmakers. And yet it is precisely here that she becomes entangled and fatefully implicated in her mother's mysterious past, which has – again – been kept under wraps for so long. Alice Kaplan's – the mother's – reticence to divulge the turmoils and the horrors of her own personal history to both husband and children adds yet another dimension to the failure in the transfer of collective memory from first to second generation. Here the mother's lips are sealed to prevent disaster from striking her family which rested at least in its formative stages on the fragile foundations of deceit, spying and voyeurism. Then again the mother's impenetrable silence has a self-serving aspect to it when she defies her children not to invade the unknown terrain of her long-guarded privacy. The mother figure in Lappin's novel is a professional actress who has perfected the art of disguise. It is not by accident that Lappin's book is prefaced by three mottos one of which, taken from William Maxwell's *Time Will Darken It* (1948), maintains that '[t]here is nothing so difficult to arrive at as the nature and personality of one's parents' (Lappin 2001; 2002).

Natasha's mother seems somehow compelled to re-enact her own life story as her husband's films expose her in her most intimate moments such as the birth of her first-born son, thus re-enacting the time when she was forced, as a pregnant young woman in Theresienstadt, to act in a Nazi filmmaker's cynical semi-documentary, losing her baby in the process. Alice Kaplan emerges unscathed, her personal integrity miraculously intact, yet her double standards seem highly questionable as she freely disposes of her children as star vehicles while not disclosing any of her really intimate secrets to them. Natasha herself is similarly bound to relive the past when she succeeds her mother's former lover as editor of *The Nose* magazine and is bribed by the Nazi documentary's director of photography with a £ 50,000 cheque to help her ailing publication. In the end, Natasha will have been, metaphorically speaking, the second innocent daughter sacrificed to serve her mother's hardening instincts of self-preservation. While she is, at the age of 30, made to listen to the exhortations from both her mother and the magazine's Jewish trustees that she is/was not only too young to have been there but also too young to know, Lappin's novel partly turns into an ardent plea for memory in Jewish survivors' families to be passed on, no matter how painful this may prove to be, from first to second generation as part of an historical legacy that must be shared, not lost.

Interestingly, if we compare Grant's and Lappin's texts with that of Bernice Rubens's *I, Dreyfus* (1999), which because of its author's age might arguably be classified as a first-generation novel though it was published as late as 1999, the onus in the communicative rift between the generations in the Rubens novel rests very much with the succeeding generation whereas in Grant and Lappin it is firmly placed onto the parents. It is not only that Rubens's long-suffering hero Alfred Dreyfus dared not ask, he is also consistently portrayed as being too strongly involved with his own career as a headmaster of British establishment schools to enquire into his parents' past. Rubens, towards the end of the book, makes him embark on a second cathartic journey to the memory-haunted places of what was once Nazi-occupied France, and to Auschwitz-Birkenau, whilst matching the exact timetable of his parents' last journey. This is meant to make him finally acknowledge his Jewish roots, so it seems. Yet Rubens's treatment of this ritual re-enactment is so uninspired, so summarily swift and, worst of all, staged so obviously as a self-castigation of and for Dreyfus that it fails to be more than a merely mechanical exercise. Lappin's heroine Natasha, when she undertakes a similar journey at her mother's insistence, is still occasionally put off by her mother's habitual intransigence, though once arrived at the original site of her ordeal, the latter seems to yield up much more readily to Natasha's probing questions. Grant's mother, when being told that her daughter has been to Poland, does not even care to remember whether this was her own birthplace or her husband's.

Amalgamating the ideas of Frantz Fanon and Edward W. Said, Sander L. Gilman has unravelled the formation of an Oriental other and its inscription into Western 'high' civilization. In *We're not Jews* he contends that

> [t]he Shoah defines a difference that is not merely victimhood but an odd sort of Orientalism, that casting of the exotic East as the place from which those who are inherently unassimilable come. What liminal characters share in the diaspora is their Oriental fate, that of victims.
>
> (2003: 174)

How this contention might chime in with 'authentic' Ashkenazi and Sephardic cultures and their duality of East and West, which perhaps are still much more of a presence in Europe than in the United States, is not fully clear. Yet though diaspora can also serve as a means to 'ameliorate the insistence on purity' championed by the nation-state, as Jonathan and Daniel Boyarin put it, there is a tendency that 'Jews see themselves and are seen as "white"' (meaning, presumably, WASP in the American context) which potentially affects 'Jewish self-constructions in the arena of ethnic politics' (Boyarin and Boyarin 2002: 32), an issue that is played on with much gusto and to surprising effects in Philip Roth's recent work *The Human Stain* (2000). In Rubens's text the character of Dreyfus can be seen trying to 'whiten' himself when in a series of blatantly obvious attempts he passes himself off as a Gentile in order to obtain a promotion. In the opening chapter of her novel Rubens presents Dreyfus in a state of contrition of almost biblical dimensions after having acknowledged his 'white lies' and longstanding deception of colleagues and neighbours which have led to a framed accusation of murder and landed him in jail. Bernice Rubens's moral rigour in dealing with her protagonist's timid self-negation as a Jew seems almost manichean if set against Lappin's and Grant's nonchalant approach towards similar assimilationist ploys. Natasha in *The Nose*, perhaps typecast as representative of American Jewry, is even less cagey about her Jewish identity than the finally well-adjusted Dreyfus, and mingles with ease in both Jewish and non-Jewish circles, though in the end even her Gentile husband, a British transport policeman, cannot save her from what Lappin describes as a 'terrorist attack on [. . .] the editor of a "kike journal"' (2001; 2002: 227). Thus anti-Semitism is very much in evidence in Lappin's text too, yet without her establishing any obvious correlation between the scale of anti-Semitic aggression and the more or less demonstrative self-representation of Jews. Ironically, Natasha, who had insisted on a Jewish wedding in order to make her partner understand that 'he and I are different people' (187), turns out not to be Jewish after all, in terms of the Halacha, as her mother confesses to having been the child of a mixed marriage. And when there is talk of a conversion in Lappin's book, it is more likely to be a loft conversion than the religious variant. Grant is equally forgiving when it comes to her family's name change, or her mother cutting down on what she sees as the three million rules of kosher cooking to a manageable one million and a half, but mentions her family's Christmas celebrations as an excuse for no-holds-barred consumerism, citing one particularly miserable case where the festive days seem to have been spoilt to an equal degree by her mother's mental aberrations and the uneasiness of all family members present with the emptiness, in religious terms, of that particular occasion.

When we take a brief look at Jeremy Gavron's debut novel *The Book of Israel* (2002), its most striking aspect is its ambitious, truly diasporic scope, encompassing at least five consecutive generations of the Dunsky family and shifting its setting in swift strokes from Riga to Leeds to Pretoria, then to London, Berlin, Haifa and back to London again, as if illustrating Bryan Cheyette's observation that instead of land, members of Jewish families have memories to pass on to each other, so that genealogy becomes their most precious asset. I would like to briefly focus on a passage in Gavron's novel where members of the Dunsky family shorten their name to the more English-sounding 'Dunn' (2003; 2003: 162), echoing what Grant recounts of the Ginsberg-Grant name change in her memoir. Grant alerts us to the fact that the name change device, though indicative of the migrant condition and the implications of a dual identity, and though it may indeed operate as a means of dissembling and evasion, an English-sounding sobriquet can also have been forced upon its reluctant bearers, speechless in a newfound land, upon first arrival. Grant writes about the family on her mother's side:

> The name wasn't Haft in Russia, but something else no one could remember. Like thousands of others, they were awarded a new name by a careless immigration officer who, unable to spell whatever it was he heard, wrote down the easiest word that sounded like it.
>
> (1998: 33)

This may well point to the fact that the migrants' old selves come under erasure as soon as they have set foot on the host country's soil. Yet Gavron tells a different story when in *The Book of Israel* the most recent in a row of male heirs to have inherited the ancestral name of Israel is persuaded after entering an English boarding school to drop this name and instead answer to the name of Jack, or Jack Dunn, in full. Gavron has the boy's father write home apologetically:

> Israel is the only Jew in a Christian school and Mr. Gimley's reasons for giving him a new name were to avoid him being teased and singled out. It is the same reason why we agreed to him going to daily chapel. I think Mr. Gimley was quite sensitive to choose Jack which you seem to have forgotten is a shorter form of Jacob which is another name for Israel in the Bible. Of course we don't want him to forget his real name or who he is.
>
> (2002; 2003: 172)

It is the sort of attitude that Cheyette sees as endemic to British Jewry and as effectively pandering to British nationalism. He insists that '[f]ar from being progressive, the privatization of Jewish identity left a homogeneous English nation unchanged and, worse still, essentially unchangeable' (1998: xv).

What are we to make of the fact that it is only the English branch of the Dunsky family in Gavron's novel, as opposed to the one in South Africa, who have recourse to such drastic assimilationist measures? Gavron leaves this essentially unanswered, yet in the ensuing chapter to the name change episode, under the heading of 'Proverbs', he lists a series of excerpts from British popular authors of the 1940s, including Graham Greene and John Buchan, in which the crudest anti-Semitic clichés are reiterated at length and, it must be presumed, to cater for an avid mass readership. If at that time, anti-Semitism in Britain was virulent though unacknowledged – '[b]efore the Nazis, anti-Semitism was "normal" and perfectly acceptable', writes Tony Kushner disparagingly about the situation in Britain, 'whereas after the war it was no longer "the done thing" to express it in polite company' (1998: 229) – if that was the case, a name change in the light of current wartime events might be held as no less than a vital and necessary precaution, though in the case of Gavron's Israel, it amounts to the ultimate betrayal of both genealogy and the family's legacy.

Affiliation with and assimilation to either the host country or Jewish minority culture in that country do not seem to figure prominently on the literary agenda of second-generation Jewish writers in Britain. From Gavron's acerbic presentation of the guests' tittle-tattle at the fringes of a Jewish wedding, about how it was de rigeur to 'live in Golders Green like everybody else' (2002; 2003: 222), or from the observation of one of Jack Dunn's business partners that his new acquaintance was 'Hebe [. . .], but not the mafia sort' (258), we are to infer that Anglo-Jewish establishment rules, if ever there were any, are consistently eschewed rather than embraced by second-generation authors like Gavron. What is more, as Cheyette assures us, British-Jewish writers 'defy the authority of England and the Anglo-Jewish community and disrupt the usual categories in which they have been authenticated' (1998: lxiv). While the narrative scope has been broadened to include the international sphere, domestic issues come to the fore in equal measure, prefigured by thematic strands like the preservation of personal and collective memory in extended families, conflicting expectations in mixed marriages and subliminal racism and its persistence in the British social environment. Where American-Jewish writers may turn out to be more assertive in pursuing Jewish themes, the voices of second-generation authors in Britain with their nuanced versions of liminal lives in the interstices between dominant and marginal cultures represent, in more than one sense, the positive side of diasporic writing – a highly advanced form, perhaps even transcending received notions of diaspora as we know them today.

Part V

Changing centres, changing peripheries and spaces in-between

Jewish writing from the Anglophone diaspora(s) – postcolonia

10 Postcolonialism and the Irish-Jewish experience

The novels of David Marcus and Ronit Lentin

Catherine Hezser

Irish-Jewish literature provides an interesting case in point for examining issues of postcolonialism.[1] Before the foundation of the State of Israel and the creation of an Irish Republic, Irish Jews were doubly affected by colonialism: both Palestine, the Jewish homeland, and Ireland, their place of residence, were under British rule. Zionism and the Irish nationalist movement were eventually successful in creating independent Jewish and Irish states. Yet certain legacies from the colonial period remain: modern Israel and modern Ireland even with its devolved government are threatened by the Middle East conflict and the Northern Ireland conflict, respectively.

In the following we shall examine how colonialism and nationalism are reflected in post-Second World War Irish Jewish writing.[2] The work of David Marcus, a native of Cork, whose novels *To Next Year in Jerusalem* (1954) and *A Land Not Theirs* (1986) thematize Irish Jewish life in the British Mandate period, and Ronit Lentin, a native Israeli and long time resident of Ireland, whose novel *Songs on the Death of Children* (1996) is set in Ireland and Israel of the 1990s, shall be compared in this regard. Special attention will be paid to the ways in which the novels' protagonists view and compare the Irish and the Zionist struggle for national independence, and how they perceive Ireland and Israel in the pre-state period and after the states have been established. Both David Marcus and Ronit Lentin wrote after 1948. Yet they differ considerably in their assessment of the Zionist enterprise.

Postcolonial writing is commonly considered a 'writing back', in which the formerly colonized challenge their colonizers' standpoints (McLeod 2000: 32). Whether and to what extent the novels under discussion here fit this description is doubtful, though. In all three novels the Jewish protagonists' identity problems arise from their minority status within an Irish Catholic rather than a British society. The Irish, with whom the protagonists are confronted, had experienced British colonialism themselves. The colonizers of Ronit Lentin's novel are not the British or Irish, but the Israeli settlers of the West Bank and Gaza Strip. Nevertheless, one may argue that the novels are postcolonial in that their authors write from the perspective of a Jewish and Irish state and thematize the practices and consequences of colonialism for both Jews and the Irish. The fact that these books are out of print and hard to find in Irish bookstores today indicates that the Jewish perspective remains marginal within postcolonial Irish society.

Postcolonialism and Zionism

It needs to be stressed at the outset that postcolonial criticism is not concerned with politics and factual history as such but with their representation in literature and art. Postcolonial criticism 'refuses the humanist assumption that literary texts exist above and beyond their historical contexts. It situates texts in history by exposing how historical contexts influence the production of meaning within literary texts, and how literary representations themselves have the power to influence their historical moment' (McLeod 2000: 38). That is, postcolonial analysis examines the effects of colonialism on literary production, the ways in which the texts react to the historical and political situations in which they are written and/or which they thematize (Ashcroft, Griffiths and Tiffin 1989; 2nd edn 2002: 2). Reappearing themes of Jewish and other postcolonial literatures in English are the topics of home (lessness), assimilation, displacement and identity (8–9).

Despite the literary focus of the postcolonial approach, it is necessary to mention that the question whether and to what extent Zionism can be compared with other anti-colonial or colonial movements has also been much discussed by Israeli historians and political scientists in recent years. This discussion can be presented only briefly here. Since the 1980s Gershon Shafir, Ilan Pappe, Baruch Kimmerling, Ronen Shamir and others have argued that the Zionist settlement in the Land of Israel can, from the time of the first *aliyah* onwards, be seen as a colonialist movement which eventually exploited and displaced the local Arab population (Bareli 2001: 99, with references). Gershon Shafir (1996) has stressed, however, that Zionist colonialism was not racist in nature and that it differed from other European colonialist movements in a number of regards. Unlike other colonial powers, early twentieth-century European Jews did not have a sovereign state which desired to expand its territory. They did not move to Palestine for economic reasons but because they considered it their ancestral homeland. Local residents were not pushed out of their farms, but land was purchased from Arabs with the owners' consent (230). According to Shafir, Zionist colonialism developed in a number of stages: it began as a so-called 'pure settlement colony' but eventually became exclusivist, with the aim of separation from Palestinians, in order to secure jobs for Jewish workers ('conquest of labor') (232–4). Shafir argues for continuity between the pre- and post-1967 situation: 'The 1967 War opened the door to the radicalization of Zionist colonisation' (237). He stresses that this was 'a transition not from rational universalism to exclusivism, but from economically justified to primordially legitimated forms of exclusivity' (239).

Other scholars have argued against categorizing pre-1967 Zionism alongside European colonialist movements. Avi Bareli has emphasized that Zionist immigration to Palestine should be seen in its proper perspective as part of a much larger Jewish emigration movement from Eastern Europe to escape anti-Semitism and various economic, political and social restrictions (2001: 100). Within Europe the Zionists – and Jews in general – were seen as 'aliens' of 'Semitic' or 'Oriental' origin. Would it not be only natural for these 'aliens' to move back to their ancestral homeland? (106). In addition, the Zionist settlers did not exploit the land in order to accumulate wealth; on the contrary, huge amounts of money and human energy were invested in the cultivation of land, while the pioneers themselves were usually poor and desolate (107). The goal was not exploitation of the Palestinian Arabs but separation between the Jewish and Arab realm (108).

On the basis of the situation of Jews in Europe at the end of the nineteenth and beginning of the twentieth century and the many differences between Zionism and European colonialism Derek J. Penslar has suggested to rather view Zionism as an anti-colonial movement, 'an act of resistance by a colonized people', and the foundation of the State of Israel as a postcolonial enterprise 'akin to state-building projects throughout twentieth-century Asia and Africa' (2001: 85). Like Shafir, he stresses that the *yishuv* before 1948 cannot be considered a colonizing state: 'From 1918 to 1948, the role of the colonizing state was played by Britain' (85). It was the British administration which 'developed Palestine's physical infrastructure, sanctioned mass Jewish immigration and fostered the development of Jewish autonomous political and even military institutions' (85).[3] Although the World Zionist Organization tried to emulate certain European colonizing practices, it was not successful because it lacked the necessary means. Palestine was not chosen 'for its strategic value, natural resources or productive capabilities, but solely because of the Jews' historic, religious, and cultural ties to the area known to them as the Land of Israel' (96). The goal was Jewish cultural renewal in one's historical land of origin. The Zionists 'were not wont to conceive of the Arab as an enemy to be expelled or a body to be enslaved for profit' (86). Therefore Zionist ideology was more similar to other anti-colonial national movements and the postcolonial states they created, showing 'aspects of hyperrational, utopian planning while pooling reservoirs of tribal solidarity and fury against the colonizer', certain distinctive qualities notwithstanding (91).[4]

Like a number of other scholars Penslar maintains, however, that after the 1967 war 'Israel's relationship with the Arab minority change[d] to a genuine form of colonialism', even though the subjugation of the Arab population in the so-called occupied territories should be seen as a side effect rather than the motivating factor of the conquest of land (97). In a much stronger fashion Rafael Reuveny criticizes Israel's settlement policy after 1967 as 'driven by [...] colonialism' (2003: 347). Israel's expansion beyond its borders and the establishment of Israeli settlements in the West Bank and Gaza Strip allegedly mean a practical annexation of the land, a development pushed forward by fundamentalist settler groups (347). Reuveny proposes that this situation can be changed only by withdrawal from the territories and the establishment of a Palestinian state (347). He hopes that this decolonization will eventually lead to peace, although it may not immediately solve Israel's security problems (376).

Irish Jewish literature, just as any other modern literary works which thematize Zionism and the foundation of the State of Israel, needs to be understood on the background of this ongoing debate.

David Marcus: Irish Jews in the British Mandate period

David Marcus's two novels, which are set in Ireland in the period of the British Mandate over Palestine, address issues which are typical for literary representations of colonialism: feelings of displacement and homelessness, problems of defining one's own identity, being seen as the 'Other' and internalizing this otherness, generational conflicts, a love–hate relationship with representatives of the majority group and the hope of eventually living a more fulfilling life in one's own homeland. In *A Land Not Theirs* (1986) Jewish Diaspora life in Ireland is presented as a life under British colonial rule in which Jews and Irish Catholics are siblings in the fight for national freedom. In *To Next Year in Jerusalem* (1954) the Irish Free State has already been established and Irish Jews eventually rejoice at the UN vote in favour of the creation of the State of Israel.[5] In both novels emigration to the Land of Israel is presented as the best solution for the young protagonists' identity problems.

The setting of *A Land Not Theirs* is the time when Ireland was under the regime of the so-called Blacks and Tans, a British auxiliary military force set up to suppress the Irish nationalist movement. After the Easter Rising of 1916 Sinn Fein gained in public support and won several elections. In 1919 the Irish Volunteers, known as the Irish Republican Army or IRA, began the 'War of Independence', and Sinn Fein proclaimed an independent Ireland. It seems that the Black and Tans did not stay in Ireland for long: they arrived in the spring of 1920 and left after the Government of Ireland Act at the end of the year. Yet they were remembered as a group of ruthless terrorists in the service of the British occupiers. In *A Land Not Theirs* Irish Jews are caught between the two camps: the British who let them settle in Ireland and who eventually lead a convoy of emigrants towards the ship that will bring them to Palestine; and Irish Catholics whose struggle for national independence they understand too well and compare with their own hopes for an independent homeland.[6]

A Land Not Theirs focuses on the life of the Cohen family in Cork, Iron Josh, a wealthy businessman and prominent member of the local Jewish community and his children Jacob and Judith. Iron Josh's father and Jacob's and Judith's grandfather is the community's rabbi. In the novel, Jews are seen as outsiders by the local Irish people and their own relationship to the Irish national movement is ambivalent. At the beginning of the novel, IRA men want to kidnap Iron Josh in order to redeem him for ransom. One of the kidnappers by the name Denis is sceptical, though: why kidnap an outsider and 'foreigner' who has nothing to do with Irish politics? (Marcus 1986: 28–9). A conversation between Iron Josh and the kidnappers on the subject of the Irish fight for independence ensues (60–2). According to Iron Josh, it is useless to fight against the British army because the British have already shown that they are more powerful. One can either choose to accept their rule or emigrate and settle elsewhere. He claims to have 'read your history', that is, he knows Irish history but does not identify himself with it. Similarly Denis claims that 'Ireland is our country', that is, the country of Irish Catholics, in which Jews are merely tolerated but not accepted as equals (63).[7]

Denis views Iron Josh's preference for non-resistance as typically Jewish. He, however, insists on the Irish people's fighting for their home (64).

This leads to a discussion on what 'home' means. Rosemary Marangoly George has emphasized the importance of the imagination of 'home' in postcolonial fiction: 'Imagining a home is as political an act as is imagining a nation. Establishing either is a display of hegemonic power' (1996: 6). For Joshua (i.e. Iron Josh), '[m]y home is myself, my body. I live in my body, in my family. That's my home' (Marcus 1986: 64). He refrains from identifying either Ireland, his country of residence, or Russia, his country of birth, as his home: 'What's that? A piece of land where I happened to be born…' (64). Denis therefore considers Joshua homeless, 'a wandering Jew, a refugee [...] He didn't have a country, so how could he understand what Denis felt for Ireland?' (64). When Denis asks Joshua whether he would fight for Palestine, Joshua rejects this possibility as well. He views Palestine as his spiritual home for which fighting is hopeless: 'The British rule it, just as they rule this country. How can we beat them? How can we even fight them? [...] We would have even less chance than you and your IRA. It would be madness' (64). There is a certain parallelism between the Irish and the Jewish predicament, then, but they are not seen as entirely equal. The IRA man lives in his own country and is ready to expel the British occupiers by force; the Irish Jew leads a Diaspora existence away from his ancestral homeland. For him, home has become a mere utopia whose liberation through active resistance seems impossible.[8]

Just as Joshua had suggested to Denis that the Irish who wanted to live in Ireland should tolerate British rule, likewise Jews might decide to realize their dream and live in Palestine under the British Mandate. Joshua's father, the local rabbi, plans to lead a small group of pioneers to Palestine.[9] The community is visited by Berel Karlinsky, a representative of the Jewish National Fund, in preparation of the emigration. The Jewish leader's visit strengthens the tiny Diaspora community's bonds with the worldwide Jewish community: '"All Israel are brothers" was what went through their minds' (77). Irish Jews' outsider status within the Irish Catholic environment is compensated for by the fact that they, too, are part of a larger ethnic and religious community which has its own homeland. Karlinsky's visit is described as a 'family meeting' which kindles the 'Zionist fever' (78), 'the harbinger of their Promised Land, their Jewish National Home'. Unlike the Irish, who are described as eager to launch a violent attack against the British, the Jewish pioneers appear as peaceful settlers who have collected money to purchase their land and are ready to cultivate the land under British rulership. Karlinsky stresses, however, that the British are not the owners of the land; they rather rule it 'as trustees for the League of Nations' (87). Since the Balfour Declaration they recognize the Jewish right to settle in Palestine.

The comparison between the Irish and Jewish hope for national independence reappears with the characters of Iron Josh's children Jacob and Judith who both fall in love with Irish Catholic freedom fighters. Jacob, who is studying medicine at College as a way to 'shake off ghetto restrictions' (48) regularly meets with his girlfriend Deirdre and accompanies her when she distributes the IRA newspaper (109).

Jacob cannot fully identify with the Irish national struggle, however. Like his father, he views Cork as his place of residence, not as his home. He tells Deirdre: 'You. Are. Irish. I'm not. Oh, technically, officially, I am. But I can't *be* Irish. I can't *feel* Irish' (112). He has no 'involvement, commitment' to Ireland; he has rather lived his life 'in a ghetto – Jewish people, Jewish friends, Jewish history, Jewish affairs, Jewish concerns, that's been my world' (112). Therefore Jacob does not feel that the Irish fight against the British 'has anything to do with me. It's not my fight' (113). Deirdre, on the other hand, thinks that the Jews owe Ireland something for letting them reside there, and that they should therefore participate in the IRA. Ireland is presented as the host country of a persecuted minority and the minority is supposed to feel grateful for the shelter provided. Accordingly, Irish Jews are seen by themselves and others as resident aliens with no hope of ever fully assimilating into Irish society. Deirdre tells Jacob what Denis had already remarked to his father: 'You're the proverbial Wandering Jew' (116).

The image of the 'Wandering Jew', which appears so frequently in the novel, is one of the most pervasive anti-Jewish stereotypes with a long history going back to at least the Middle Ages.[10] Various traditions, such as Cain's destiny of a 'fugitive and wanderer' as a Divine punishment for the killing of his brother Abel (Gen 4:12), and the Christian legend of an allegedly ill-inclined Jewish onlooker at Jesus' crucifixion who was predicted to walk the earth until messianic times, contributed to the myth (Anderson 1965: 3, 11–13; Rouart 1988: 7–8). By the seventeenth century the Wandering Jew was associated with Ahasverus as the representative of the eternally condemned Jews and infidels. This stereotype was reused in the German anti-Semitic propaganda of the nineteenth century (Anderson 1965: 275–7; Rouart 1988: 108–9). But Ahasverus also became a symbol of the tragedy of the Diaspora Jew, his homelessness and suffering from persecution. As such, some Jewish writers adopted the image and even identified with the Wandering Jew.[11] Especially interesting is the positive reinterpretation of the motif by Isaac Meyer Wise, the founding father of the American Reform movement. In his work *The Wandering Jew* he states that all Jews are 'wandering Jews' and as such have a distinctive role within modern civilization (referred to by Anderson 1965: 295). It seems that Wise connects the myth with the Reform notion of the worldwide 'mission of Israel' which gives a special positive meaning to Jewish Diaspora existence.

In David Marcus's novel the motif has entirely negative connotations. The self-identification of the Jewish protagonists as 'Wandering Jews' and eternal outsiders who conduct a ghetto life within the Irish cultural environment has to be understood in the context of (post) colonialist discourse in which certain stereotypes are adapted by the colonized themselves. Irish Jews such as Joshua and Jacob are seen as 'Wandering Jews' by Irish people, who thereby confirm their perpetual outsider status. They therefore see themselves in the image in which these others see them. The image of the 'Wandering Jew' was an ideological construct which served to justify the non-acceptance of Jews as equals by the European nations whose citizens they were.[12] What happens here is a discursive process in which 'the colonized subject [...] is forced into the internalisation of the self as an "other"' (McLeod 2000: 20). Instead of protesting against this ascription, Marcus's protagonists accept it, however, and this acceptance serves to foster their own ideology of Jewish nationhood.

As already mentioned above, the Cork Jewish community perceives itself as alien within the Irish environment but at the same time linked to the worldwide Jewish community, *Kellal Yisrael*. This community is presently dispersed but has its ancestral homeland to which at least some Jews will eventually return. Thus, the negative connotation of the 'Wandering Jew' and the image of Zion as the Jewish homeland relate to each other as two sides of the same coin. If the Cork Jews of Marcus's novel had assimilated more to Irish society and identified with the Irish cause (cf. Isaac M. Wise's positive American-Jewish adaptation of the motif), they would have had less reason to pursue their own project of national renewal and return to Palestine. David Lloyd notes, however, that assimilation is always a contradiction in terms:

> [T]he logic of assimilation resists its own ideal model: since the process is legitimated by the judgment of the essential inferiority of the colonized, its very rationale would be negated in the case of a perfect assimilation of colonized subjects without remainder. Therefore, it is at once the power and the weakness of assimilation as the cultural arm of hegemonic imperialism that a total integration of the colonized into the imperial state is necessarily foreclosed.
> (1993: 112)

Recognition of the eternal status of hybridity 'is a principal impulse to nationalism at the same time as it determines the monologic mode of nationalist ideology' (112–13).

Jacob and Deirdre eventually split up in recognition of their differences. Deirdre thinks that Jacob is unable to fully understand her dedication to fight for Ireland (Marcus 1986: 277). Judith's relationship to Denis eventually develops into a much closer bond. But here again the difference between the Irish readiness to fight against the British and the Jewish hope for a peaceful settlement in Palestine is emphasized. According to Denis, 'one thing is certain: The Irish won't get Ireland and the Jews won't get Palestine without a fight' (257). Judith's father continues rejecting the violent approach, an attitude which Denis cannot understand: 'Ireland is our land, our home; that's what they're fighting for. Sure aren't some of your own people going out to Palestine soon to *fight* for their land?' (370). Here, a direct parallel between the Irish and Jewish struggle for independence from the British colonial power is drawn. Iron Josh rejects the comparison, though: the Cork Jews who plan to move to Palestine are going there to settle, not to fight. Iron Josh eventually helps Denis to hide arms for the IRA in his workshop, and Judith helps him escape from the police and the Black and Tans.

At the end, Judith is destined to take her grandfather's place as the leader of the emigrants. Her initial scepticism against Zionism (could emigration to Palestine be a mere escape from the dissatisfying life in Cork?, see 50) has changed into an acceptance of the possibilities of national renewal which *aliyah* promises. In a way, then, she would be reunited with Denis in their pursuit of a similar goal: 'Where would he be, she wondered, while she was in *Eretz*, living in a *kibbutz*, helping to build a new Palestine? Would he still be trying to build a new Ireland? No doubt he would...' (406). She realizes that the reasons why Irish Jews would move to Palestine are identical with the reasons why Denis joined the IRA (412). Similarly Jacob finally admits that violence may be necessary to achieve the goal of an independent state; a homeland in Palestine may not be gained without fighting: 'Look what such a fight was costing the Irish. Centuries of time, thousands of lives!' (449). While Father McGiff preaches in his sermons that the Irish should take the local Jews as a model, who go to Palestine for 'farming and fighting' (119), similarly the IRA fighters are presented as models for young Irish Jews, to motivate them to fight for their own national homeland. Clearly Zionism is presented as an anti-colonial movement in analogy to the Irish independence movement here.[13]

Paul White has pointed to the significance of ambivalence in postcolonial discourse: 'Ambivalence toward the past and present [...] Ambivalence towards the future [...] Ambivalence towards the "host" society: feelings of respect, dislike or uncertainty. Ambivalence towards standards of behaviour: whether to cling to the old or to discard it, whether to compromise via symbolic events whilst adhering to the new on an everyday basis' (1995: 3–4). Such ambivalence is quite evident amongst the main characters of David Marcus's first novel, *To Next Year in Jerusalem* (1954). This novel is set in 1947, at the end of the British Mandate period and shortly before the UN vote in favour of the establishment of the State of Israel. The Irish had already received independence from Britain by then. Like the second novel, introduced above, this novel focuses on the life of one particular Irish Jewish family. This time the protagonists are not residents of Cork, however, but of Drumcoole, a small town in the Western part of Ireland with only ten Jewish men and five women, seen as 'the most western outpost of Jewish life in Europe' (Marcus 1954: 26). The community had been founded by Jewish refugees from Eastern Europe in the nineteenth century and had once been a relatively large and vibrant Jewish community (29). But most young people had moved away since then, so that the community was now threatened to perish with the death of its elderly members.

The novel focuses on Jonathan, the only young Jewish man who had stayed in Drumcoole and without whom there would not be a *minyan* of ten men needed for communal prayer. Jonathan is in love with Aileen, a young Catholic Irishwoman. He is torn between loyalty towards his family and the orthodox Jewish community and an assimilated life with Aileen and his other Irish Catholic friends. Despite his desire for happiness and marriage with Aileen, he knows, however, that his Jewishness will always separate them, no matter how hard they try. When they head home after having spend a two-week holiday together, Jonathan's musings are filled with ambiguity:

> Which is our real home [...] The guarded fortresses that encompass our respective rituals or the canopied honeymoon-bed in Mr. Forde's guest-house?

> Which is the right road home – the road ahead or the road back? Both lead home – one to the homes we have, the other to the one we want. And which is stronger? The claim which the homes we possess have on us or the claims we have on the home we want?
>
> (13)

Eventually the traditional ties prove stronger. Leaving their families and communities behind would cause suffering to others and they would 'pay dearly for our sins and our errors' (14). Crossing the boundaries of one's heritage and venturing into foreign territory, desiring a person who is of another religion and culture is seen as sinful and erroneous by both the protagonists themselves and the outside world here.

Robert J.C. Young has analysed expressions of 'colonial desire' and its relationship to hybridity and Diaspora existence. Colonial desire, that is, 'desire for the cultural other, for forsaking one's own culture' and merging – sexually or otherwise – with the culture of the 'host' country, must be seen as an important aspect of colonialism (1995: 3). It is not only felt by the colonized, but works both ways: the representative of the authoritative culture, in this case Aileen, feels that her culture 'lacks something, and acts out an inner dissonance' (3). The phenomenon that intermarriage is rejected as an option in both this and the previously discussed novel indicates that the Irish Jewish community projected here is in a state of uncertainty and insecurity, in which it feels threatened: 'Today's self-proclaimed mobile and multiple identities may be a marker not of contemporary social fluidity and dispossession but of a new stability, self-assurance and quietism. Fixity of identity is only sought in situations of instability and disruption, of conflict and change' (4). As we will see below, this insistence on the Irish Jewish community's clear boundaries also distinguishes David Marcus's novels from Ronit Lentin's writing in the New Ireland of the 1990s.

In the novel under discussion here David Marcus describes Jewishness in both religious and racial terms, as an acquired as well as an inherited otherness that separates Jews from Gentiles. Jonathan is convinced that mixed couples' relationships cannot be successful 'where both parties are rooted in their own beliefs as we are. There just doesn't seem to be enough common ground' (Marcus 1954: 16). They are 'members of two faiths which can be put together, sort of forcibly joined to each other as it were, but cannot ever really mix' (17). Religion is perceived as a 'fortress' here which is guarded by the communal leaders. Jonathan feels enclosed in this fortress and often dreams of escaping. At the same time, the fortress provides a 'home', a place where one can feel protected and safe (18). According to Jonathan, the barriers created by the Jewish and Catholic religions cannot be overcome. In between them there is an 'unbridgeable desert' in which one is destined to perish (24).

But it is not only the religious difference which separates Jonathan from Aileen. Although Jonathan had learnt the Gaelic language, played Gaelic football and appeared 'more Irish than the Irish themselves', he had different tastes and engaged in different leisure time activities, so that his Irish Catholic friends 'considered his apartness, both of thought and personality, from themselves as stemming from and being an aspect of his "foreignness"' (39). Jonathan attributes his otherness 'to his Jewishness, to his inheritance of a racial genius for adaptability, for fitting-in while still preserving originality and individuality, for being, in short, two things at the one time' (39–40). This racial definition of Jewishness subsequently becomes more explicit: 'A Jew was a member of a race as well as a religion, and that was where the anomaly arose' (40). The difference between Jonathan and Aileen is then perceived as 'something that might have had its origin in the blood, or the mind, or the soul, or maybe all three – and it was that something which provided the basic, vital, and ineradicable difference between himself and his Christian friends' (40). Like the notion of the 'Wandering Jew' mentioned above, the use of the racial definition of Jewishness may be seen as an internalization of common stereotypes against Jews which may have been prevalent in Ireland in the 1950s, when Marcus wrote the novel.

The racial definition of Jewishness also explains the strong opposition against intermarriage evident in the narrative: 'anxiety about hybridity reflected the desire to keep races separate, which meant that attention was immediately focussed on the mixed race offspring that resulted from inter-racial sexual intercourse' (Young 1995: 25). The fusion of separate entities was believed to create 'a radical heterogeneity, discontinuity, the permanent revolution of forms' (25). Jonathan is afraid of introducing his Irish Catholic girlfriend to his family but is at the same time disgusted by his own behaviour (Marcus 1954: 20). He can meet her only at the Catholic youth club of which he becomes the chairman. He is convinced, however, that just as his Jewish family is anti-Christian (123), every Catholic is an anti-Semite (150–1). Father Jim, the spiritual head of the club, can hardly convince him that this is not the case. Jonathan even suspects Father Jim and Aileen of anti-Semitism (167). He finally realizes that the only solution to his problems is to leave Ireland with his Roman Catholic girlfriend and to move to Palestine. With Jonathan, Marcus has created the image of a very insecure, threatened and vulnerable young Irish Jew who is unable to find his proper place within Irish and Irish Jewish society.

Marcus presents the Jewish community of Drumcoole as a community at the crossroads. A once vibrant Jewish community is about to perish, if one more male member dies. The synagogue building had to be given up already ten years ago, a loss which 'made them all feel the lurking presence of disintegration, the insecurity of their future as a community' (52). Although there is not much hope for continuity, ties between the community members are very close, creating a warm and familiar environment which the young experience as suffocating. Within the 'alien' Irish environment, the community constitutes a bulwark of orthodox Jewish ritual observance.[14] Marcus provides detailed descriptions of the communal celebration of the Sabbath and Jewish festivals. Gathering in a room at the back of the Lippman house, 'so people in the street would not hear the singing and the sounds of prayer' (54), an intimate atmosphere is created, 'and so the sensation of being physically as well as spiritually part of all the expressions of religious devotion was considerably strengthened and thereby rendered more satisfying than before' (56). Marcus's emphasis on the significance of communal rituals and symbols, on the presentation of the Drumcoole Jewish community as a separate entity within the Irish environment and on the connection between these small-town Irish Jews and the worldwide Jewish community very much conforms with representations of anti-colonial nationalism known from other postcolonial literatures as well. According to McLeod, 'a sense of mutual, national belonging is manufactured by the performance of various narratives, rituals and symbols which stimulate an individual's sense of being a member of a selected group' (2000: 69).

Whereas the older members of the congregation have accommodated themselves with the contradictions of Irish Jewish Diaspora life, with the notion of being 'smoothly absorbed and integrated as a separate and distinctive unit within its contrasting Irish environment' (Marcus 1954: 33), young people like Jonathan are unable to bear this tension (being 'two things at the same time', 40; the 'feeling of angst', 43) any longer and are searching for an escape, into marriage with a Catholic Irishwoman and total assimilation – or Zionism and emigration from Ireland.[15] Older people like Jonathan's grandfather consider themselves 'to have a stake in Ireland' (44). They were 'long settled, matured, and rooted in their Irish homes' (74). For them, Palestine can be a spiritual home only. Palestine 'was no longer a matter of life or death or home or need to these Irish Jews – they had life and livings and safe homes and, they thought, no need' (75). They nevertheless express their spiritual connection to Palestine by collecting money for the Jewish National Fund. Jonathan, on the other hand, becomes fascinated by the reports of the Zionist leader who visits the Drumcoole Jewish community, and he wants to participate in the fight for national independence. He 'would give anything, anything to go to Palestine' (112), and at the end decides to realize his dream.

In contrast to the pacifistic attitudes presented in *A Land Not Theirs*, in this novel the necessity of actively fighting for Israel's independence is readily acknowledged. This is probably due to the different time setting: by 1947 various Jewish underground organizations were attacking British installations in Palestine because the British had restricted Jewish immigration and not fulfilled the promise of free settlement stated in the Balfour Declaration. In the European press these freedom fighters are presented as 'terrorists', as the Zionist representative explains (82). At this point a parallelism between the Irish and Jewish fight for national freedom is drawn: it had taken Ireland eight hundred years to rid itself of British domination, and the Irish were already living in their own land, so how could the Jews hold out? (78). Some of the Jewish listeners 'had taken part in the fight for Irish independence' and therefore sympathized with the Jewish freedom fighters (84). Jonathan sees the fight for Palestine as a fight for the real (spiritual and physical) home he lacks in Ireland (113). He is supported by Father Jim, the leader of the youth club, who is also the first one to mention the eventual British retreat from Palestine to Jonathan: 'Your boys have made it unbearable for them in Palestine so they're getting out. The same as we beat them here in Ireland, you've beat them there' (207). Mr MacDonagh, Aileen's father, also sympathizes with Jonathan's Zionist affiliation. He introduces himself as an Irish nationalist who once served as a staff officer in the IRA (221). At a time when Irish national independence had already been gained as a consequence of the IRA's fighting, the Jewish fight for an independent homeland in Palestine was considered entirely legitimate as well: 'Now, soon, it would all be changed and the wandering would be ended' (297).

In this novel David Marcus presents Zionism as an anti-colonial movement which is analogous to the (already successful) Irish struggle for independence from the British. In this struggle the use of arms is considered perfectly legitimate. Although they pursue separate causes, Irish Jews and Irish Catholics understand and support each other in their striving for national freedom. At the same time Jews are presented as a distinct religious and ethnic group who cannot truly participate in Irish nationhood. They share their loyalties with a worldwide Jewish community whose ancestral homeland is Palestine. Jewish immigration to Palestine is presented as a return to one's roots in a country from which Jews had been dispersed a long time ago. Diaspora existence is seen as a condition one can become used to, but which will always be characterized by ambiguity and contradiction. The in-betweenness of Diaspora life has a clearly negative connotation. Especially at a time when Irish Jewish communities are declining, for Jews true happiness can be found in the Land of Israel only.[16] For young Irish Jews home, which the older generation had conceived of as a mere mental space, has become a physical reality.

Ronit Lentin: Irish Jews and Israel in the 1990s

Ronit Lentin wrote her novel *Songs on the Death of Children* in the 1990s, at a time when the so-called post-Zionist debate took place amongst scholars in Israel and elsewhere.[17] Post-Zionists were not anti-Zionist but dissatisfied with certain aspects of Israeli politics which they criticized. They especially complained about the treatment of the Palestinians by the Israeli military and about the settlement policy in the so-called 'occupied territories', that is, the areas which were added to Israel as a result of its victory in the 1967 war, areas which were populated by Arabs until then. Ronit Lentin's presentation of Israel and Irish Jewish identity fits well into the context of this post-Zionist debate and has to be understood on its background.

Like the main protagonists of David Marcus's novels Ronit Lentin's Patricia is an Irish Jew in search of her identity, who hopes to find a solution to her problems in Israel. Frustrated in Ireland both privately and professionally, Patricia travels to Israel to interview Palestinian women for a book project. In contrast to David Marcus, who likened pre-state Zionism to the Irish independence movement, Lentin compares the State of Israel with the colonial practices of the British. This is already evident at the beginning of her novel when Patricia's suitcases are searched by Israeli security guards at the airport. Annoyed, Patricia is reminded of Northern Ireland: 'Just like the North. Soon they'll want to strip search me' (Lentin 1996: 4).

In Ireland Patricia had led a very assimilated life. Not the fact that her lover is non-Jewish but that he is her boss is considered problematic. She is not religious, and neither were her parents. As the daughter of German Holocaust survivors who came to Dublin in the 1950s, her Jewish identity is mainly related to the Holocaust, although her parents never talked much about their experiences and erected a wall of silence between themselves and their daughter. They 'decided to keep ourselves to ourselves and didn't join the Jewish establishment' (27). As secular German Jews they stood alone in a no-man's-land between the Irish Jewish and Irish Catholic communities. That they had gone to Britain first and obtained British citizenship may have separated them from the Irish as well. In Germany before the Holocaust their secularism and socializing with non-Jews had not prevented Patricia's parents from being 'proud Jews' (27). They had considered Germany their homeland and defended 'German values and German decency' (25) even after their experiences under the Nazis. In Ireland her parents never went to a synagogue, yet Patricia always considered them being 'so Jewish. So different from anyone else' (32). She feels burdened with the weight of her parents' past, a certain pain, the only remnant of her Jewish identity.

When Patricia arrives in Israel, her comparison of the Middle East conflict with the Northern Ireland conflict continues: 'Everywhere there is this kind of war, there are old men sitting on fences and saying it will all come to pass . . . ' (36). On the one hand, she sympathizes with the Palestinians, whom she sees as victims harassed by the Israelis; on the other hand, she feels guilty as an Irish Jew who lives in safety while Israelis fight: 'To my surprise, all this made me feel guilty. You live in safe, grey old Ireland while young Israelis and Palestinians fight over this place' (36). Patricia appears in the role of an onlooker and visitor who views Israeli society from a certain distance without identifying herself with it. When she accompanies soldiers into the 'occupied territories', associations of Northern Ireland arise in her again: 'Masses of black smoke filled the air with an appalling stench, the likes of which I remembered from trips to Derry and Belfast. Burnt rubber, the smell of anger and hatred' (38). In a conversation she says: 'Don't even mention British fairness to me [. . .] There is little difference between what's going on in Northern Ireland and here, let me assure you' (52). The comparison between Israel and Northern Ireland is very common in Ireland today.[18] That Patricia, an Irish Jewish journalist, repeatedly makes this comparison seems to indicate her high level of assimilation to Irish society. Whether and to what extent this comparison is valid is not further reflected here, though.[19]

Ronit Lentin's Patricia is a very left-wing, politically correct feminist who did not come to Israel for Zionist reasons. She rather went there to escape a bad relationship and to distract herself after the death of an abused girl whose case she documented. In Israel she takes up the cause of the Palestinians and even defends Palestinian terrorism against Israel. When comparing the PLO with the IRA she finds it hard to understand how a Palestinian can approve of the PLO but criticize its terrorist tactics: 'I had heard of these arguments before. Love the IRA but detest their actions. Approve of a United Ireland, but not at any price' (57). Whereas the Irish Jews of David Marcus's novels compared the IRA with the

Zionist freedom fighters and were doubtful whether force should be applied to liberate Palestine from colonialist British rule, the Irish Jewish woman of Ronit Lentin's novel associates the Palestinians with the IRA and seems to approve of their violence against the allegedly colonialist Israeli society.

Patricia's rather one-sided pro-Palestinian stance is linked to the Holocaust experience of her parents: 'Sitting there with this confident and positive [Palestinian] woman I couldn't but feel humble about being a Jew, member of a conquering nation, past victim turned occupier' (57). The terms 'conquering nation' and 'occupier' clearly associate Israel with the European colonial nations of the past. The assumption is that the Jewish experience has turned from one extreme to another, from suppressed to suppressor, without any middle ground. It is her friend Rachel who explains to Patricia that both of these images are myths rather than accurate descriptions of historical reality: 'If you're honest, which many of us are not, you'll find most of your presuppositions shattered. The myth of the Jew as victim, the opposite myth of the invincible Israeli, the myth of justice, the myth of the Greater Israel – all vie with each other, but they're nothing but myths' (79). What remains are many contradictions.

Nevertheless, a short time later, the Holocaust survivors are partly blamed for the present situation. Daniel, Patricia's Israeli boyfriend whose mother is a Holocaust survivor too, maintains that in their victimhood the Holocaust survivors were the real heroes, 'not us, beating up helpless Palestinians' (104). Since they experienced victimhood themselves, however, his parents educated him to be a strong boy, 'a boy who would never have gone to the ghetto without putting up a fight' (104). That is, the experience of suppression allegedly turned the suppressed into suppressors themselves rather than teaching them compassion and humility. Although there may be some psychological truth in the notion that someone who suffered violence may promise him- or herself to never show weakness again, the way in which this notion is generalized and used to explain the conflict between Israelis and Palestinians does not do justice to the complexities of Middle East history.

In a conversation with Shifra Sharlin, Ronit Lentin talks about her own upbringing and political standpoint which bear certain similarities with the protagonists of the novel. Her parents had come to Israel from a German-speaking part of Rumania and had tried hard to educate their children to be Israelis rather than Old World Jews (Sharlin 1990: 48). Since the Eichmann trial she had 'been obsessed with the Holocaust' and identified with her parents' Rumanian past (49). After having been delighted initially with Israel's victory in the Six-Day War of 1967, she subsequently 'joined the most extreme left-wing group for a while' and 'was very outspoken against Israel' (49). But when she came to Ireland she noticed that her Israel-critical statements were used by the Irish, that she had become 'their token critical Israeli' (49). The Israel-critical Irish (wo)men lacked a proper understanding of Israeli history and the Middle East conflict, 'they were thinking in clichés' (49). Lentin was caught between being an outspoken critical Israeli and providing ammunition for Irish anti-Israel propaganda. With her very left-wing and pro-Palestinian protagonist Patricia she seems to be caught in this dilemma too: one may assume that with its political correctness and Israel criticism the book would please an Irish Republican readership.

At the end of the novel Patricia finds it impossible to return to her former life, but we do not know whether she has found a home in Israel and solved her identity problems. The open ending suggests that this is rather not the case. After nine weeks in Israel Patricia still feels like an outsider (Lentin 1996: 137). In Ireland she loved the Sabbath dinners at her friend Marianne's home, a religious ritual which her own parents refused to practice (159–60). There is no evidence that she would feel tempted to adopt a Jewish religious identity in Israel, but Israel would give her the opportunity to be secularly Jewish and *not* feel like an outsider on that account. She begins to feel 'weary of Israel's inhospitality' (182) and muses about her parents' 'disconnected life among Irish Catholics and my purposeless life, the wrong relationships, the searching, always feeling out of place, always feeling shame' (182). When she finds her long-lost sister in Israel (who turns out to be the wife of her boyfriend Daniel!) this disconnectedness may eventually end. Or perhaps not. Ronit Lentin quotes – and seems to identify with – Isaac Deutscher who was asked about his Jewish identity and answered: 'Nationally? No, I'm an internationalist. Religiously? No, I'm a secular Jew. It is the common fate' (Sharlin 1990: 51). This common fate includes both the Holocaust and the Middle East conflict.

Conclusion

David Marcus and Ronit Lentin provide very different accounts of Irish Jews' relationship to Zionism, Israel and Jewish identity. They write from different perspectives and thematize different time periods in their novels. David Marcus's novels feature orthodox Zionist Jews who live in Ireland at the time of the British Mandate over Palestine. The Zionist struggle for national independence and a Jewish homeland is presented as an anti-colonial movement analogous to the Irish fight for freedom from the British.[20] Ronit Lentin's novel, on the other hand, presents a very assimilated, left-wing and feminist Irish Jewess who travels to Israel in the 1990s and is very critical of Israeli politics, so much so that Israel is likened to the colonialism of the British in Northern Ireland. These different depictions fit in well with recent scholarship on Zionism introduced above. There seems to be a general trend in scholarship to see pre-1967 and especially pre-1948 Zionism as an anti-colonial or postcolonial movement which strove to create a homeland for dispersed and persecuted European Jews in the land of Israel which was historically and religiously associated with Jews and Judaism. During the so-called post-Zionism debate from the 1990s onwards, however, some scholars compared the Israeli settlement practices in the West Bank and Gaza Strip after 1967 with the European colonialism of the first half of the nineteenth century. Whether such a comparison is appropriate is subject to further debate and cannot be discussed in this context. It is evident, however, that Ronit Lentin's novel needs to be understood in the context of this discourse. It provides a very left-wing position which criticizes alleged Israeli colonial practices towards the Palestinians.

Despite these differences, David Marcus's and Ronit Lentin's presentations also have a lot in common. Both present the situation of young Jews in Ireland in rather negative terms. On the one hand, there is the traditionally orthodox, close-knit Jewish community of David Marcus's novels which provides a warm and familiar atmosphere but is also experienced as stifling. And then there is the constant threat of too much assimilation, intermarriage and the loss of Jewish identity, a possibility which David Marcus rejects as an option for his protagonist and which Ronit Lentin takes as a given. For both Marcus and Lentin the best option is the escape from Ireland and move to Israel.

Both authors seem to see cultural hybridity as problematic, as a situation which causes suffering to their protagonists and which they strive to overcome. Neither Jacob and Judith nor Jonathan and Patricia are able to live the tension between their Jewish identity, however sparsely defined, and the Roman Catholic or secular Irish environment. The positive connotations of cultural hybridity and 'unhomeliness' stressed by Homi K. Bhabha, and the cross-cultural possibilities which they provide, are obviously not envisaged here (1994: 4–5, 9).

An alternative approach is provided by James Joyce: Being of mixed ethnic and religious origin and identity, Leopold Bloom, the Irish 'Jewish' protagonist of *Ulysses* (1922), is the hybrid personality *par excellence*.[21] Kathleen Richard Ferris has suggested that Joyce deliberately based *Ulysses* on the myth of the Wandering Jew, a paradigm he himself identified with too (1989: 61–3).[22] Irish and Jewish nationalisms are neither approved of nor criticized here. Both thematically and stylistically Ulysses constitutes an 'adulteration' which 'undermines the stable formation of legitimate and authentic identities' (Lloyd 1993: 108). The novel 'insists instead on [...] a stylization of the hybrid status of the colonized subject as of the colonized culture, their internal adulteration and the strictly parodic modes that they produce in every sphere' (110). Neither Irish nor Jewish culture are presented as uniform and stable, that is, mutually exclusive entities here. Both are rather seen as 'adulterated', that is, they have incorporated 'alien' elements. The positive depiction of hybridity makes all kinds of too eagerly pursued nationalism suspect. Therefore Joyce may be seen as the representative of a utopian state beyond nationalism and colonialism, in which cultural hybridity is acknowledged and appreciated.

Notes

1 See also Hezser (2005).
2 On Irish Jewish history see Hyman (1972), Keogh (1998) and Rivlin (2003).
3 The importance of considering the British role in Palestine is also stressed by Golan (2001: 131–40), where he provides a detailed analysis of the British use of Zionists as collaborators in their imperialist enterprise.
4 See also Golan (2001: 140), who sees Zionism as a 'national liberation movement that developed in eastern and central Europe'.
5 The Irish Free State was established in 1921. In reaction to this event an interesting article by the title 'Die Lehren von Irland' [The Lessons of Ireland] appeared in the journal *Der Jude* 5 (1921–2) 265–7: The foundation of the Irish Free State is seen as advantageous for Zionism, since it allegedly shows that the British are inclined to give autonomy

to their colonial subjects in recognition of local realities. In Palestine these local realities include the Arabs. The author [M. b. M.] of the article suggests that Jews need to come to terms with the Arabs ('Der Ausgleich mit den Arabern ist eine immer dringlicher werdende Forderung'; 'Statt Polemik und Anklagen müsste endlich ernsthaft daran gegangen werden, uns für ein Zusammenleben mit den Arabern vorzubereiten'), rather than rely on the British in this regard.

6 Sheffer (2003: 232) notes that British Jews were expected to show loyalty towards the British during the British Mandate period. They had 'to pursue a cautious strategy of dual loyalties' and had to be careful with regard to expressing their Zionist affinities.

7 See Sheffer (2003: 2): Host societies usually 'viewed the presence of ethno-national diasporas as a marginal and temporary phenomenon'.

8 See George (1996: 11): 'Home is also the imagined location that can be more readily fixed in a mental landscape than in actual geography'; and: 'Home in the immigrant genre is a fiction that one can move beyond or recreate at will' (200).

9 According to Hyman (1972: 194–5), in 1893 several Dublin Jews decided to purchase land in Palestine. Ten thousand dunams of land were bought and forty families were supposed to emigrate. The emigration was eventually postponed and the plan later given up.

10 On this image see especially Anderson (1965), who provides a detailed survey of the historical development and variant versions of this myth; see also Rouart (1988), who focuses on the usage of the myth in the nineteenth century; see also Körte (2000) and Hasan-Rokem and Dundes (1986).

11 See Anderson (1965: 283–4), who points out, however, that the Jewish adaptation of the myth did not occur frequently in the second half of the nineteenth century; see also Rouart (1988: 101–4).

12 In the Nazi period Joseph Goebbels commissioned an anti-Semitic propaganda film by the title *Der ewige Jude* which was first shown in November 1940 and meant to justify the deportation of Jews from Germany. On this film see Hornshoj-Moller (1995).

13 On anti-colonial nationalism which is a liberationist and anti-imperialist movement see Barker, Hulme and Iversen (1994: 198).

14 On the formation of 'defensively clustered social networks' amongst ethnic minorities see White (1995: 11).

15 On this tension amongst children of migrant families see also White (1995: 12) with regard to an Algerian novel reflecting 'the complexities of a generation who move between identities, experiencing the exile's desire to retain cultural roots, whilst at the same time being drawn to assimilation and the abandonment of "otherness"'.

16 Interestingly, David Marcus did not consider immigration to Israel a solution for his own identity problems. In his autobiography, he admits that he has never even visited Israel: 'I have never desired to go there, a reluctance based on two opposing fears: that I would like it and that I wouldn't' (2001: 249–50). Even if he would like it, however, 'I cannot see myself as feeling it to be my home', claiming that his 'ghetto gene' would rebel at the idea (250).

17 On the post-Zionist debate, which has been introduced briefly above, see also Kelman (1998), Nimni (2003), Sharan (2003), Matta (2003) and LeVine (1996).

18 See Cleary (2002: 6–7), who provides examples: in Tom Clancy's popular novel *Patriot Games* 'Irish republican and Middle Eastern "terrorisms" are closely identified' (Cleary 2002: 6). Some Republican wall murals in Northern Ireland 'have shown Irish and Palestinian guerillas as comrades in arms' (Cleary 2002: 6). On these murals see Rolston (1991: 38–9, 80, 94–5).

19 Many books and articles have been written on similarities and differences between Ireland and the Middle East conflict, usually by very left wing scholars who are ready to associate the Irish Catholics with the Palestinians, see, for example, Cleary (2002), a work which originated from a PhD thesis supervised by Edward Said; Howe (2000); Lustick (1993).

20 Cleary (2002: 6–7) points to an Israeli film from 1955, *Giv'a 24 Eina Ona* [*Hill 24 Doesn't Answer*], which provides a similar comparison: during the 1948 war four fighters, one of them an Irishman, defend a strategically important hill outside Jerusalem together. This shows the film's 'desire [...] to suggest that Zionism was not a regressive colonial settler nationalism but a revolutionary anti-colonial national liberation struggle which, like the Irish counterpart, deserved international sympathy and support'. On this film see Shohat (1989: 58–76).

21 On Joyce's depiction of Leopold Bloom and Judaism see Davison (1996), Reizbaum (1999) and Nadel (1989).

22 Joyce seems to have been familiar with the legend, since he had several versions of it in his library in Trieste: 'The image of the wanderer is one with which Joyce, the exile, identified with throughout his adult life' (Ferris 1989: 72).

11 Jewish writers and postcolonial choices in South Africa

Margaret Lenta

Thabo Mbeki, second post-democracy president of South Africa, in a speech on the occasion of the adoption of the 'Republic of South Africa Constitution Bill' on 8 May 1996, defined the identity 'South African' inclusively: the San, the Khoikhoi, the Nguni peoples, the Sotho and other black groups, the immigrants from India who arrived in the nineteenth century and the two waves of whites, Dutch and British, were all mentioned. Implicit in his definition is the condition that the descendants of these people, despite the diversity of their origins, will accept this country as their permanent home, acknowledging that it is the focus of their primary political loyalty, and recognizing the obligation to work for the material, moral and cultural welfare of the whole South African community.

Acceptance of this inclusive postcolonial South African identity means for many white people, including South African Jews, the severance or at least the weakening of ties to communities elsewhere. No doubt this is the case in any post-colonial country: increasing national autonomy must gradually weaken ties to the metropolis. In South Africa, however, where colonialism has been a prolonged process – over three hundred years from beginning to end – and the maintenance of segregation and division has been for most of that period the endeavour of its rulers, the task is especially urgent.

Jewish writers in this country, like many other whites, often have strong ties with the rest of the world, especially Israel, Britain, Canada, the USA and Australia – the first world, with all it can offer writers. They have in addition to their identity as South Africans, and to different degrees depending on their circumstances, the identity of 'Jew'. From the middle of the twentieth century at least (the establishment of the state of Israel in 1948 may stand as a marker) until the present day, they have been considering what these identities mean and how they relate to each other. The answers to which they have come have been different, partly because the claims of 'Jewishness' and 'South Africanness' have differed over time, and partly because of their individual temperaments and situations.

An important determinant of Jewish identity as it is perceived by Jews and Gentiles alike, from 1948 to the present, has been the existence of Israel, emigration to which was presented by Gordimer in *The Lying Days* as well as by others[1] as a brave choice. But Israel, hard put to it to find allies, at times offered aid to the apartheid government in South Africa. Since 1994 the governing party in South Africa has been the African National Congress (ANC), which has strong links with the South African Communist Party,[2] which has always had a large Jewish membership. Since the Palestine Liberation Organization supported the ANC in its years of exile from South Africa, the party retains a pro-Palestinian ethos, often expressed as anti-Zionism, even by Jews. Since the conflict between Lebanon and Israel in 2006, the anti-Zionist sentiments in the ANC have intensified.

In the selective and partial account of post-apartheid Jewish writing in South Africa which follows, there are two necessary provisos: the one, that the voices of the ultra-orthodox community in this country are missing, since its members do not write for the larger South African community, and their numbers are not sufficiently large to support literary production for themselves. The second proviso is that the line between writers and non-writers in this country is blurred by the fact it is difficult to make a living by writing here, and even established writers tend to spend most of their time working at other things. How many published works make a professional writer, as opposed to someone who has once ventured into print? I have avoided this question, and other embarrassments related to omissions, by focusing on a relatively small number of writers who, I shall claim, represent some of the positions which Jews have occupied as writers.

In the 1990s all South Africans, including Jewish writers, had to understand that the declining years of apartheid had left the country in economic disarray. Restrictions on the opportunities for blacks in the professions and in white-collar employment generally since the 1950s, though these restrictions had been relaxed in the 1980s, necessitated an affirmative action employment policy which disadvantaged white applicants, especially males, who had been privileged under the old regime. What this seemed to mean for young whites, and perhaps especially for young Jews, was that for at least a generation, and perhaps longer, their educational and professional opportunities would be narrower than those of their parents. What seems to have occurred in response is not an exodus of established writers, but a movement elsewhere of young people who might have become South African writers.

In the period of political uncertainty between 1990 and 1994, the date of the first elections in which South Africans of all races took part, violent local conflicts between ANC supporters, supporters of the Inkatha Freedom Party (IFP), and a mysterious and murderous 'third force' damaged national and international confidence in the ability of South Africa to transform itself peacefully. There were many people, both inside and outside of the country, who did not believe that so radical a change could be made without causing economic chaos. Everyone knew that the privileged position of whites would have to yield at least to equality and perhaps to a regime in which whites would become an underclass – it was difficult not to transfer the template of the past on to the future. Many middle class whites, including Jews, left in this period and after because of the continuing violence in urban areas. Farms too were attacked and murders took place, and the urban Jewish community was hard hit by robberies and murderous attacks of all kinds.

For all South African writers the 1990s was a period when they had to rethink their subject matter. Apartheid had been a great unifier, and after the Soweto

Uprising in 1976 until the 1990s it was difficult to write a book without reference to it. Few writers had supported the apartheid regime: 'Black writers are regarded as enemies, and most white writers as well, because we all oppose the state. You won't find *one* writer who will covertly or overtly defend apartheid', said Nadine Gordimer (1990: 260). The result in the 1990s when opposition to a regime already being dismantled was irrelevant was that a certain kind of subject matter had gone dead, in a way which raised questions about its liveliness in the past. In 1991 Tony Morphet published a review of four 'struggle' novels in which he wrote:

> The political break of 1990 has undercut [the novels] no less sharply than it has everything else. Two years ago these stories would have been able to count on 'history' (or a version of it) to subdue and direct their readers; to keep them within some fairly strictly defined bounds of literary duty and political morality. But now readers have been released.
>
> (1991: 166)

With little sense of what the new dispensation might be, South African writers had to re-examine the national reality and ask themselves how they should engage with it. Reconstruction and its problems, especially those of racial integration and the accompanying changes in previously exclusive groups, were likely to be part of that reality, as were the enormous problems arising from economic inequalities in a society where the poor were close to destitution.

When Jewish writers moved in the 1990s 'beyond solidarity' to other subject matter it seemed unlikely that they would focus strongly on the Jewish community, aging and diminishing in the period. A side-effect of Mbeki's speech had been to throw doubt on the possibilities for literatures of immigrant communities in the present day. Would it be possible, for example, to sell novels which focused on the lives of Jewish immigrants in South Africa in the first half of the twentieth century, like Rose Zwi's *Another Year in Africa* (1980)? The answer to this question appears at first sight to be 'Yes, if they are well written – and explore a theme of change'. Dan Jacobson's *Time and Time Again*, admittedly published in Britain, appeared in 1985, and deals with life in Kimberley from the perspective of a Jewish child and adolescent. His later works, *The Electronic Elephant* (1994) and *Heshel's Kingdom* (1998) also have South African components, but are distinctively the work of an author of South African birth who has established another national home. Lyndall Gordon's *Shared Lives* (1992) deals with a group of young Cape Town Jewish women from the 1950s, who transcend their parents' narrow ambitions for them and go elsewhere. Both of these authors are long-term residents in Britain where they are established writers. Though neither is insensitive to the changes in the South African community, they feel no obligation to explore a post-liberation South African identity.

Two important Jewish literary figures have died in the period after the first democratic elections, Barney Simons, dramatist and short-story writer, and Lionel Abrahams, poet, novelist and editor. Both worked to help younger writers, especially black writers, to realize their potential. It may well be that the state and the parastatal organizations which it has set up will take over the roles which they played, though it will be difficult to transmit the combination of experience and generosity which was such a feature of their informal teaching.

In the matter of a postcolonial white South African identity, Gordimer has been the trail-blazer: she has for most of the period of apartheid been aware that not only Jews but all white South Africans would eventually be faced with the necessity of accepting that they were African. 'For me, the formative thing has been being a white African' she said in 1987 (Bazin and Seymour 1990: 297).

In accepting such an identity she has explained how little in her case was abandoned. She presents the colonial world of her childhood as 'a society removed from all danger, that had made itself comfortable with injustice' (Gordimer 1995: 115). Her physical context in Springs, a gold-mining town near Johannesburg, was culturally impoverished, and the social barriers between white and black and even between poor white Afrikaners and middle class English-speakers made it particularly bleak for the English-speaking child of non-practising Jewish parents.

Gordimer says that she was 'brought up on English picture books of lush meadows and woods' (116) which made her see the landscape of mine dumps around her as ugly. She learnt at school that the focus of patriotic sentiment should be England, but also that 'it was so remote, that England, that Northern Hemisphere we learnt about in geography class. In the 1920s and 1930s it was four weeks away across the seas. We were at the bottom of the map; we did not count, had little sense of ourselves beyond the performance of daily life' (117). The conclusion to which the adolescent came and which the mature writer can formulate is that she was '[t]he one who belongs nowhere' (120), and must make her own identity.

The definition of a white South African has changed greatly over the half-century in which Gordimer has been writing, but one option she marked at an early stage in her career as closed to her was that of being a Jew of the petty bourgeois shopkeeping group to which her father belonged. She sums him up in an interview in 1986:

> He had been brought up in exactly the way the majority of Africans are brought up here. His mother was a dressmaker and his father was a shipping clerk; both parents worked in the city of Riga and the old granny in the village brought up all the children [...] Although he had a normal Jewish village religious upbringing, my mother more or less forced him to abandon all that. We kept the Day of Atonement: he had a new suit about every two years and off he would go to fast – and my sister and I would be sitting in our shorts in the car, waiting for him, looking at these people coming out of the synagogue! [...] I remember his attitude towards blacks was that they were beyond the human pale, an extraordinary attitude for someone who had fled from Tsarist oppression.
>
> (Gordimer 1990: 248)

Gordimer writes of 'the usefulness to the regime of the poor immigrant's opportunity, at last, to feel superior to someone, and thereby support the regime's policy of keeping the indigenous population decreed inferior' (1995: 123). She recognizes, however, that many Jews in South Africa behaved differently: 'it was the Jewish Socialists and the British Labour Party that started the Communist Party[3] in South Africa in 1921. Some people's struggles in life produce a strong political awareness; in others struggle produces merely a desire to get what you can and just hang on to a cosy life' (1990: 248).

Stephen Clingman (1986) has traced the relationship between Gordimer's work and the events of the period. She has been preoccupied throughout her writing life with the question of what role a South African white can play. Since *The Lying Days* appeared in 1953, when the Nationalist government was beginning to introduce its programme of racist and separatist legislation, she has offered in her fiction a number of answers, recognizably time-bound, since they were in each novel shaped by immediate circumstances. 'Nothing that I write here in this essay will be as true as my fiction' (Gordimer 1990: 260) is one of her wellknown statements, and it is legitimate to look at her novels in order to understand her responses to events. The decline of the colonial world and the painful emergence of a new dispensation is her major theme. *A World of Strangers* (1958) marks the end of what South African readers think of as the *Drum* or Sophiatown era,[4] when it seemed that an urban, multiracial society of writers and other artists might evolve. *The Late Bourgeois World* (1966) is a representation of the new black militancy in the post-Sharpeville massacre period. *Burger's Daughter* (1979) narrates the movement of revolutionary whites from centre stage to the margins of the struggle in the 1970s, before and after the Soweto Uprising.

Gordimer has not chosen to focus strongly on Jews in her writing, and the first novel in which she has a Jewish protagonist, Hillela, is *A Sport of Nature* (1987). She has commented that she did not intend to indicate attachments to the Jewish group in this choice. Hillela's parents have abandoned her; she is tolerated or rejected at different times in her aunts' households. 'Her Jewishness doesn't really play much part in her life, and that's the only connection with my own' says Gordimer (1990: 297). Her aunts Olga and Pauline represent two different middle class South African women's roles: Olga rich, self-indulgent and politically indifferent, Pauline with her 'progressive opinions' (293) and life of service. In contrast to both of them, Gordimer says, 'I really wanted [Hillela] to be stripped, in a sense, and she is; she's stripped of all the middle class, all the bourgeois trappings that Olga could have given her, and she is stripped of all the support of decent, middle-of-the-road opinions that [...] she could have got from Pauline' (293). Hillela finds by trial and error the role which suits her, that of consort to an African president.

'Stripping' as a necessary prologue to the adoption of a new identity and the vagueness in the novel about what follows marks Gordimer's uncertainty in the period about the positives which would characterize the white African of the future. At the end, the new Hillela is known to us only by the fact that she is the wife of the President of the OAU and that on a great occasion she wears 'the striped, hand-woven robes and high-swathed head-cloth that is the national dress of the President's country' (Gordimer 1987: 339); she has become 'a public face'.

In 1994 Gordimer published *None to Accompany Me*, a much more detailed investigation of what it might mean to be a white African. Her protagonist, Vera Stark, (who is given no declared subgroup allegiance, though Stark is a well-known South African Jewish name) is a lawyer who works in Johannesburg, in a foundation which offers aid to and negotiates on behalf of the homeless. At the beginning of old age Vera breaks the ties of married life. Her husband, knowing himself meaningless to her, moves to England; her son lives there already, and her daughter and her partner live in the Cape. She sells the house which has symbolized her family life and rents a garden cottage from the black man who owns the main house. The central image of the novel is of Vera dancing alone (Gordimer 1994: 306).

To interpret this novel as representing the choices of secular Jews in the post-apartheid period would be unjustifiable, except to the extent that Gordimer believes that they have the obligation to investigate in their own lives what it means to be a white African. It is a study of a particular individual, a passionate but emotionally detached professional woman who finds her husband's dependence on her intolerable. Partly because her professional work brings her into contact with the leaders of the black community, she can envisage herself as occupying a domicile and a social position which will relate to her age and choices, rather than to her white skin.

Of Gordimer's later novels, *The House Gun* (1998) shows violence permeating South African society and *The Pick-up* (2001) deals with a white woman's move from affluent white society in Johannesburg to a poorer, unspecified Moslem country. Both bear on her interest in the white African, but seem unconnected with the particular conditions in which Jews make their decisions about national identities.

The Jewish socialists whom Gordimer mentions as the founders of the South African Communist Party are represented in South African letters today, or at least their descendants are. In 1990 F.W. de Klerk announced the unbanning of the ANC and the Communist Party, which allowed an important group of Jews, including three authors of memoirs, Joe Slovo, Ronnie Kasrils and Albie Sachs, to return to South Africa. Until this point, the secular and socialist part of the community, which as Gordimer points out had made an enormous contribution to South African life, had been in exile or silenced for almost thirty years.

Of those who returned (a considerable number did not return permanently), Sachs has published several books and has always had a strong interest in the arts. Slovo and Kasrils seem to have written memoirs because they believed that their life experiences were important, and had no doubt that they were too little known in South Africa. Before 1990, the laws relating to banned persons meant that their writings and utterances of all kinds could not appear in South Africa.

All three men are secular Jews of eastern European descent. Slovo, who died in January 1995, was born in Lithuania and Kasrils and Sachs are the descendants of immigrants. All three have played important roles in South Africa since their return. It is plain from Slovo's and Kasrils' memoirs that in their childhoods both were part of working-class groups which in a fairly anti-Semitic society were composed entirely of young Jews and as young men they were influenced by fellow-Jews who were socialists. Sachs is the son of prominent communists.

All three men demonstrate in their texts that in the long years of exile, their feeling for fellow-Jews was necessarily tempered by another, that between fellow-workers in the struggle. Committed to a multiracial state, and welcoming young people of different origins into the ANC – in many cases seeing them die in the struggle – they have not rejected their Jewish past, but see the future differently. In *The Soft Vengeance of a Freedom Fighter* (1990; 2000) Sachs talks about the fusion of individual diversity into a unified group:

> This is what the ANC is, we do not wipe out our personalities and cultures when we become members, rather we bring and share what we have, Zuma's African-ness, his Zulu appreciation of conversation and humour, is mingling with my Jewish joke, enriching it, prolonging and intensifying the pleasure. We are comrades and we are close, yet we do not have to become like each other, erase our personal tastes and ways of seeing and doing things, but rather contribute our different cultural inputs so as to give more texture to the whole. This is how one day we will rebuild South Africa...
>
> (118)

Sachs does not go further to discuss the truth as it applies to South African residents in the post-apartheid period, that these desirable interactions must further hybridize the individuals involved in them. It is of course true that a hybridization process began at the moment of the colonial encounter, and that the descendants of the Jews who came from Lithuania to South Africa in the late nineteenth century are very different from their ancestors. But the collapse of apartheid marked the end of a period in which difference was strongly maintained in this country. The period of national reconstruction in which South Africans now live is one in which they are inclined to emphasize what they have in common. In the rebuilt South Africa to which Sachs looks forward, and of which Mbeki speaks, the constituent groups are likely to downplay their cultural differences even if this means losing a part of their inheritance. In this phase of the process of hybridization, South African literature, especially the literature of particular ethnic groups, is likely to change its character.

Sachs's most recent work, *The Free Diary of Albie Sachs* (2004) can be seen as part of a trilogy which began with *The Jail Diary of Albie Sachs* (1966; 1990) and continued in *The Soft Vengeance of a Freedom Fighter* (1990; 2000). The first volume describes his 168 days in solitary confinement in 1963 under the law which permitted prisoners to be held for ninety days without being tried or charged with an offence. This could extend into an indefinite period, since at the expiry of each period of ninety days the order could be renewed. At the mercy of jailers and security police, alone and for much of the time without reading or writing materials, interrogated and threatened, he preserves what is most valuable to him in his personality. The politicized Albie is in these circumstances almost irrelevant; what matters is the man who holds on to his humanity in contrast to the brutality which surrounds him, and who treasures evidence that humane people constitute the norm of the world outside.

From one extreme experience to another: *The Soft Vengeance of a Freedom Fighter* records the car-bombing in which Sachs suffered the loss of an arm and eye, and his long process of rehabilitation. To summarize the work in this way is not to do it justice: it is a gripping narrative, as is *The Jail Diary*, of an exciting process which the reader does not, even knowing the ending, ever take for granted.

The Free Diary does not deal with such extremes. Sachs has several times said that he and his comrades have fought to bring about a 'boring' South Africa, though to its present-day inhabitants, including himself, 'boring' does not seem the right term. The view of South Africa here is long-range and contemplative, since *The Free Diary* deals with his travels in Europe, and is an invitation to get to know the post-democracy Sachs, co-framer of the South African constitution and now a Constitutional Court judge. Looking at a restored synagogue near the centre of Berlin, he dislikes the secularity which follows from the fact that it is 'a touristy memorial site' 'rather than a place of living worship' and this leads him to think of what it means to him, a freethinker since his childhood, to be a Jew:

> The Jewishness which is an integral part of me does not link up spontaneously with formal religion (even though I am tempted to say that some of my best friends are rabbis) or with temples of worship, but rather with something to me more primordial, a millenarian, historically created spiritual and cultural urge towards freedom, and what I'd like to think of as an unquenchable striving for justice in the world.
>
> In the mysterious way that the Lord is said to perform His or Her wonders, it was my participation in the secular struggle for freedom that led to my reading the Bible from cover to cover. During my solitary confinement it was for a long time the only book I was allowed to have, and reading it was the sole activity other than staring at the wall that was permitted to me. I found two completely different themes running through the Old Testament. The one that horrified me and left me bereft in my cell was the inward-looking one, which proclaimed the existence of a divinely protected Chosen People, for whose benefit genocidal punishments were meted out to all enemies, homes were razed, men and women slain, oxen slaughtered, plagues visited and first born sons exterminated. The one which filled my heart with beautiful courage was the lyrical, poetic and prophetic one, which spoke of an outward-looking people's participation in the affairs of the world and offering it the richness of their songs, psalms and visions of justice.
>
> (Sachs 2004: 103–4)

Rejection of a part of his religious past (and that of most religions) is therefore part of what Sachs sees as his obligation as a Jew in the present day. The part which he rejects is tribalism, which sets group survival – even group supremacy – so far above human rights that genocide becomes possible. The learning process which has been his life has also led him to reject Communism: 'I came to be a member of the biggest party in the world, the party of ex-communists, which is full of bewildered people from every continent' (67), he says, explaining that he strives as a member of the constitutional court to avoid the imposition of orthodoxies of behaviour or belief by the state.

Slovo, whose autobiography, *Slovo*, was left unfinished at his death, writes of his young life of poverty in Doornfontein, on 'the lowest rung of the Jewish residential ladder' (1995: 14). His life was soon rendered more difficult by the death of his mother and the failure of the family greengrocery business. His younger sister went to an orphanage and he and his father moved into the first of two boarding houses in which he passed his adolescence. The second of these he describes as having

> many of the characteristics of a Sholom Aleichem East-European *shtetel.* Yiddish was the official language... Apart from the occasional excursion to the left-inclined Jewish Workers Club (burnt to the ground by Grey Shirts during the war), social life for the inhabitants was restricted to the double-storey house which was ringed by a large stoep.
>
> (20)

He describes the boarding house as 'a colourful oasis of immigrant life', and the phrase is significant of his pleasure in these memories. But like Gordimer he is aware that many of the immigrant Jews with whom he associates see no connection between their aspirations towards social justice and the plight of black South Africans:

> My leaning towards left socialist politics was also formed partly by the bizarre and paradoxical embrace of socialism shared by most of the immigrants who filled the boarding houses in which we lived. I say 'bizarre' because they tended to combine a passionate devotion to the Soviet Union with Zionism and vicious racism towards the majority of the South African population.
>
> (22)

The group to which he belongs in his youth is one that he has to transcend, but the ideological inconsistencies of his early associates no doubt help him to do so. He begins work at the age of fourteen and comments:

> I immediately commanded mature African men (some of whom had worked there for many decades) who called me 'Baas'. No black could be a member of our union branch so long as it remained registered under the Act. Our picket line was manned by whites only and the negotiated settlement which ended the strike referred only to the white staff; in law no agreement which

> included Africans was enforceable. This was the objective reality of the law, but unfortunately it was also a reality which would have been defended by the overwhelming majority of my white fellow-workers.
>
> (25)

The South African Communist Party, which he joins as a probationary member in 1942 when he is sixteen, is also, as he experiences it, heavily Jewish. He mentions Issy Wolfson, General Secretary of the Tailoring Workers Union, Solomon Buirski, Fanny Klennerman and Benny Weinbren, and it is through these people that he eventually becomes acquainted with black workers.

Kasrils' introduction to socialism also took place through friendships with fellow-Jews: he remarks that when he first joined the Movement[5] he was surprised to discover that none of his early associates in the group was Jewish. 'I had laboured under the illusion that Jews were the only whites concerned about the racial oppression of blacks' (2004: 23).

In 1995, when Slovo died, the need to declare oneself, as a member of the ANC, pro-Palestinian was much less strong than it is today. Kasrils, in the 2004 edition of his memoir *Armed and Dangerous* (1993), which is described as 'updated',[6] has felt the need to explain his attitudes. He identifies himself early in the book as non-religious, but respectful of Jewish observances: when, for example, his father dies in 1963, he regrets that in exile he cannot say Kaddish for him, and when, many years later, after his return from exile, his mother dies at the age of 94 he recites Kaddish at her funeral. He is always happy to identify himself as Jewish and to claim a relationship with another Jew, greeting an astonished Russian doctor with 'Shalom'. His explanation of his attitudes to Israel links them to his opposition to apartheid:

> I had never in my adult life regarded my Jewish origin as guaranteeing uncritical support for the state of Israel. From the time I joined the liberation struggle I had viewed the idea of a mono-ethnic, exclusivist Jewish state as akin to apartheid and an injustice to the Palestinian people. The reservation of special rights for Jews consigned non-Jews to an inferior status and smacked of apartheid's race classification. Israel had come into existence as a settler state through the forceful dispossession of the land of a people who had lived there for centuries.
>
> (Kasrils 1993; upd. Edn 2004: 340–1)

He goes on to enumerate some of the distinguished South African Jews who oppose the present policies of Israel: Gordimer, Denis Goldberg, Lea Bethlehem, Steven Friedman, Anton Harber, the political cartoonist Zapiro. His point that to be Jewish and to be Zionist are different matters must be taken seriously, though he understands that this is 'difficult for many Jews to concede, given their emotional ties to Israel, the nightmare of the Nazi holocaust and the threat to the existence of Israel' (341). He makes it clear that he does not want to sever his ties with the Jewish community in South Africa, though he writes of the 'venom and distortion' (342) which the opinions of the non-Zionist group attracted. He and the chief rabbi, despite their differences, have found it possible to have 'an amicable chat' and to shake hands. The moment is significant, in that it is a recognition on both sides that disagreement even on a matter so crucial does not dissolve the bond between them.

Two of the younger generation of writers, Karen Press and Damon Galgut, poet and novelist respectively, both of whom began to write in the 1980s when apartheid was crumbling but was at the same time at its most violent, may serve as indicators of the literary preoccupations of our time. Though both are of Jewish descent, they take it for granted that their subjects must be South African and secular, and to different degrees seem to have become what J.M. Coetzee has called 'people in this country who have become detached from their ethnic roots [...] and have joined a pool of no recognizable *ethnos* whose language of exchange is English'. Coetzee goes on to hope that 'as the pool has no discernible *ethnos*, so one day I hope that it will have no predominant colour [...] a pool, I would hope, in which differences wash away' (1992: 342). This hope seems to be shared by both Press and Galgut, both of whom emphasize the extent to which blacks and whites of different origins have always coexisted in South Africa.

Galgut's novels are for the most part concerned with what life has been, and in the case of *The Good Doctor* (2003), still can be, for a white man in South Africa. This latest novel is set in a dilapidated hospital in a former 'homeland',[7] where a demoralized white doctor has been working in a subordinate position since his divorce. The corruptions for which 'homelands' were notorious survive close to the surface of daily life, the hospital is being gradually stripped of equipment and furniture, and into this uneasy stasis comes another white doctor, an ignorantly idealistic young man, who believes that he can change things for the better. The plot may sound familiar to readers of Graham Greene's novels, but the portrayal of the cynicism and despair of professional people, black and white, in this situation and the unheeded misery of the poor is telling. In addressing the multitudinous problems of post-apartheid life in South Africa, the situation in rural areas, and perhaps especially in the former homelands has tended to be neglected by government and the general public. Galgut has been inspired by a real sense of obligation to these forgotten communities.

Press, who has published seven collections of poetry in all, has brought out three since 1998: *Echo Location. A Guide to Sea Point for Residents and Visitors* (1998), *Home* (2000) and *The Little Museum of Working Life* (2004). Sea Point, a suburb of Cape Town, is a holiday resort which is the home of an old (by South African standards) Jewish community. Press gives voice to many of the people who live and have lived there. Found poems, which use public notices, captions on photographs, local history and newspaper reports, give tone as well as information. The destitute speak as well as the middle class residents, trades people and their customers. There are moments of imaginative entry into Jewish experience. 'Single Passage' for example, looks compassionately at the old men whose children have emigrated:

The old men
had not expected to be abandoned.

Striding alone on the patterned stones
spattered with sea scum like foamy brains
they experimented with being
young again, at the edge of a new home

and found it didn't work.
They were old, and had never learnt
to be sentimental about landscape.

They had the choice of playing cards
with each other, arguing about politics
or folding silently inside a nurse's shadow.

Just ships some gene was using
to get from Vilnius to Perth. You could see
the thought flickering in their eyes:
bloody long detour.

(1998: 24)

There is a similar diversity of subjects in *Home*: in one of the most poignant poems, 'Days' (2000: 44), the voice is that of a destitute meths drinker. 'Freedom's Hostage' (45) is an exploration, in the metaphors appropriate to different South Africans, of the huge burden of expectation placed on Nelson Mandela on his release. But in the poem 'Ancestors' there are 'clues' (her word) to the origins of this particular woman:

Outside it snows
and horsemen ride in with guns.
An old man in a prayer shawl
sips tea through a sugar cube.
If he had looked up
he would have seen through the doorway
a small child standing in the sunlight far away
waving to him: he might have waved back.

(25)

In *The Little Museum of Working Life* there are no such such 'clues' to origins. Diversity is even more characteristic, and whatever textual 'room' we enter, the invitation is to look at working lives. Press shows us our strategies of resistance to understanding of the work of others in 'The Room of Pigeonholes' and 'The Room of 'These Things Happen'. The demand is often that we understand as 'work' something which we know differently: clearing up after a bus crash in which children die, a man's presence in a house where a child depends on him. The book as a whole demands that we look afresh and question our understanding of other's lives.

The work of these two productive and professional authors must provoke the question of whether Jewishness, in the sense which it might have had in the early decades of the twentieth century, is ceasing to matter in this postcolonial state. Part of the answer must be that Jews are now free to live where and how they like, and that most are secular and remote in time and interests from the ancestors for whom their identity as Jews was primary. The special pressures of an immediately postcolonial state and of national reconstruction are strongly felt by Galgut and Press, as the pressures of life in the ANC in exile were felt by Sachs and his comrades. It seems that the remaining Jewish writers, and probably those of the future, are likely to continue to feel the pressure to be 'white Africans' – but they may feel other pressures, and other attractions, too.

Notes

1 Rose Zwi's *Exiles* (1984) is an example of such presentation.
2 The South African Communist Party dissolved itself in 1950, in anticipation of the Suppression of Communism Act which was passed in the same year. In the same year, J.B. Marks, a communist, was elected president of the Transvaal ANC. The ANC was banned in 1960 and many of its leaders fled abroad to establish resistance movements in exile.
3 The Communist Party was the first multiracial party in South Africa and had a membership which included many Jews, including Ronnie Kasrils, Albie Sachs and Joe Slovo, whose writings are discussed here.
4 *Drum* was a magazine produced in Johannesburg, which in the 1950s employed a group of black writers which included, amongst others, Es'kia Mphahlele, Bloke Modisane and Can Themba. Sophiatown was a multiracial Johannesburg suburb where many of these black writers lived. It was bulldozed in 1955 on the orders of the Nationalist government, and a white suburb named Triomf was established on the site.
5 A collective term used in the period for the ANC and its allies.
6 The first edition appeared in 1993 and contained three sections: 'Beginning, 1938–63', 'Exile, 1963–89' and 'Home, 1990–93'. Since then there have been two other, revised and extended editions, published in 1998 and 2004.
7 'Homeland' was the term applied to the territories within the borders of South Africa which under apartheid were designated autonomous black states, and were the official homes of the various black groups, where alone black people could vote and be permanently resident.

12 Jewish literature in Australia[1]

Elisa Morera de la Vall

As a geographical, or even political entity 'Australia' is fairly uncomplicated. Less straightforward are the two remaining denominators referred to in the title of this chapter: Who is a Jew? And what can be considered Jewish literature? William D. Rubinstein writes:

> Most contemporary Jews would agree that Judaism is the central expression of Jewishness [. . .] but in all likelihood most would also agree that it is quite possible (if not desirable) to be a good Jew, even a great one, without manifesting any Jewish religious fervour, and that secular expressions of Jewishness are perfectly valid if not primary.
>
> (1991: 35)

Orthodox Judaism has an unequivocal definition of who is or is not a Jew: a Jew has to be born to a Jewish mother or to a woman converted to Judaism by an Orthodox rabbi. To Reform Judaism a Jew would be anyone born to a Jewish mother or father, or else converted to Judaism by any rabbi. But in a wider context, not determined by religion, conceptions of Jewish identity are less clear-cut. Rubinstein points out that 'Jewish identity is particularly difficult to define precisely, because of its religious, ethnic and cultural components' (1995: 13). And Leon Yudkin, referring to the interrelation of the religious and the secular, considers that 'the place of Judaism within Jewishness is [. . .] problematic' (1982: n.p.).

Of course, there are many more definitions of what makes a Jew,[2] and it is unlikely that a generally accepted or even satisfactory definition may ever be agreed upon.

What, then, about the second question: What can be considered Jewish literature? Just any literature written by Jews or about Jews? Gael Hammer (1988: 11) argues that, if that were the case, *Das Kapital* would be considered Jewish writing as well as Shakespeare's *The Merchant of Venice*. The suggestion being, of course, that neither is, really, 'Jewish'. The vexing question is explored in ample detail also in Hana Wirth-Nesher's classic collection *What is Jewish Literature?* (1994) in which is given voice to authors as diverse as Cynthia Ozick, Robert Alter, David G. Roskies or Saul Bellow.

Because an undertaking like the present survey requires some fixed criteria of inclusion and exclusion, this chapter will deal with halachically Jewish authors whose work expresses their Jewishness and who live in Australia.

Despite characteristics possibly common to all Jewish literatures, Australian Jewish literature has traits of its own, because the space and time influencing it make it distinct from that elsewhere. Thus, it has been remarked that Australian Jewish literature is significantly different from the much better known American Jewish literature. Helen Bersten suggests that these differences result from the different cultural backgrounds of both countries: The American Founding Fathers had a great dream which they took with them to the new land, but there was no such dream at the foundation of Australia (1997: 713). Rubinstein argues along similar lines when he observes that Australia, like America, received several waves of Jewish migrants, but that, while they found 'a land of boundless achievement and opportunity, a natural ethos of success' in America, in Australia the situation was rather different, as were the migrant waves themselves, composed of 'convicts, British migrants with the more formal British patterns of behaviour, refugees and Holocaust survivors' (1991: 325). It is hardly surprising that all this is reflected in literature:

> Both the Australian and the Australian Jewish traditions are, compared with their American counterparts, narrower in horizon and outlook, more inward-looking, closer to tragic and unpleasant events, and always more remote. From the point of view of literature these need not be disadvantages: on the contrary, these could well prove to be the seedground of great literature more surely than the optimistic environment of America.
>
> (325)

There is, however, no general consensus on the dissimilarity between American and Australian Jewish writing. Writer and editor Yvonne Fein, for instance, highlights some traits she perceives to be shared by all Jewish literatures. She claims that from her university years, she has been able to recognize Jewish writers in general: 'For me, their flavour was so strong, so distinctive, that I could have identified them in my sleep', further adding: 'Although Goldhar and Waten might set their stories on this side of the Pacific and Bellow, Singer and Malamud on the other [. . .] they shared the same heritage and the Holocaust made them grapple long and hard with what their Jewishness meant to their lives' (1993: 13–14).

If literature reflects reality, it is undeniable that Australian Jewish literature cannot but reflect tragic realities. The Shoah looms large in many autobiographies, poems and fictional works. Rubinstein says:

> These works are invariably agonizing to read and convey the sheer horror and tragedy of that unspeakable event far more directly than most serious historical accounts, for, in Stalin's perceptive if infamous phrase, the death of one person is a tragedy while the death of millions is a statistic.
>
> (1991: 333)

There are, however, some differences between first and subsequent generations of Holocaust writers. Alan Berger sees first generation Holocaust authors as 'seeking to restore a moral universe', whereas subsequent generations are intent on passing on the memory of the tragedy so that it is never lost (1998: 171–3). There is often a sense of guilt in these generations for the suffering they did not share with their parents, as well as a distressing sense of family loss. Fein mourns those grandparents, uncles, aunts, unborn cousins that she never had a chance to meet or play with, and reckons that her development as a writer was largely influenced by her pain (1993: 13–18).

Certain subjects are common to both Jewish and non-Jewish writers in Australia, yet the Jewish authors cannot be simply labelled as migrant writers. There is something distinctly Jewish in their work, in the way they transmit the pain of exile and the nostalgia for a home forever lost. The new land is a far cry from the envisaged Land of Milk and Honey. And it is in this difficult, alien environment that the Jewish identity and heritage must be preserved. Hand in hand with this, we may find an anguished self-questioning on the meaning of life, on suffering and death. Moreover, although there are elements in Australian Jewish literature common to other peoples, the Jews have the honour of having been the forerunners in producing in Australia a literature about themselves as a group. In 1949 Judah Waten claimed:

> It is a fact that, of all the groups of people from non-British countries residing in Australia, only the Jewish people have even the beginnings of a literature about themselves that has become a part of the general literature of the country.
>
> (1949: 96)

This 'literature about themselves' began with Nathan Spielvogel (1874–1956) who was born in Ballarat, Victoria, the son of an Austrian father and a Polish mother, both orthodox Jews. Hilary Rubinstein says that 'Spielvogel was the product of an intensely Jewish home and of parents who were able to transmit their heritage' (1991: 328). Besides being a vocational schoolteacher, he became well known as a writer. According to Waten, '[u]ntil the thirties [...] Mr Spielvogel was an unusual phenomenon in Australia, a writer who wrote of Jewish life. Until that time it would have been absurd to speak even of the outlines of a Jewish literature...' (1949: 94). Spielvogel wrote in English for a specific Jewish audience which kept growing and eventually incorporated Yiddish speakers (Yiddish was the language of most Jewish immigrants in those days) and, despite writing in English, he shows the influence of the Yiddish literary tradition in his work.

Spielvogel offers a rather rosy picture of the struggle of the first and second generation of Jewish settlers in Ballarat to survive without loss of identity. His short stories reveal his pride in his Jewishness, his authentic religious beliefs and his moral values (see Spielvogel 1956). But '[m]ost are frankly sentimental, avoiding the sense of form and subtle analysis of motives found in the masters of the art' (Fredman 1956: i). Yet, if Spielvogel is more a storyteller with a touch of sentimentality than a psychological writer, this may be attributed in part to the Yiddish oral tradition, while his profession as a teacher may account for the didactic purpose which is obvious in some stories and for his succinct style. The optimism shown in stories that were written between the 1930s and the 1950s but are set well before, is puzzling. The Jewish society that the author describes had been blossoming but, by the time the author depicted it, that society no longer existed and the present was dismal. Another eminent Jewish writer visited Spielvogel in Ballarat in the 1940s and was upset and depressed by the decay he witnessed. This writer, who had a different story to tell about Ballarat and its Jewish community, was Pinchas Goldhar. In Spielvogel's private museum Goldhar perceived the smell of death: 'It struck me suddenly that Spielvogel personifies our Jewish fate. We are dying out. In Europe we get exterminated by Hitler, and elsewhere we just dwindle away slowly and painlessly…' (cit. Brezniak 1967: 14).[3]

Unlike Nathan Spielvogel who was born in Australia, wrote in English and was a confirmed optimist, Pinchas Goldhar (1901–47) was an immigrant, wrote in Yiddish and was essentially pessimistic. Born in Poland, Goldhar arrived in Australia in 1928. He had left behind a promising career in literature and a lively literary and artistic Yiddish environment. He found in Melbourne the reverse of the coin: a society persuaded that the best policy for the country was that of cultural homogeneity and showing little sympathy to non-British immigrants (Maclean 1987: 128). Goldhar, however, was befriended by artists and writers like Noel Counihan, Vic O'Connor, Vance Palmer and Alan Marshall. The establishment, in 1931, of a Yiddish press, a determining factor in the publication of Yiddish authors, was made possible by the enthusiasm of the printer David Altshul and Goldhar's tenacity. Goldhar was persuaded that Yiddish was *the* Jewish language and should be preserved if the Jewish culture was to survive, and defended his convictions in passionate essays. Much against his wishes English would eventually win the day, yet the heritage was not lost, as the work of later Anglophone Jewish writers in Australia testifies.

Although Goldhar had started by writing poems in his native country, the hardships he experienced in Australia matured him and changed him inwardly. The poet gave way to the realist fiction writer to reflect the disappointing reality of Jewish life around him (Maclean 1995: 31). His career was short but fruitful. Hyam Brezniak comments that in his nineteen years in Australia, Goldhar 'laid the foundations of the now substantial literature of Jews in this country' (1967: 13). His stories reveal his concerns: the misery resulting from mixed marriages; assimilated Jews in Nazi Germany; the plight of young pioneering Jewish men unable to escape marrying out; the tensions between the recent immigrants from Eastern Europe and the well established, Anglicized Jews, who had adopted Gentile customs. Goldhar's best known story is 'Café in Carlton' (1946), translated by Waten. In this story, a survivor of Nazi persecution finally succumbs to madness when he meets with anti-Semitic graffiti in Melbourne, thus giving Nazi hatred the final victory over him. William D. Rubinstein praises the author for his 'characterisation and his technique' (1991: 326) and Pam Maclean remarks: '[H]e might be referred to as a multicultural writer before multiculturalism: as a writer whose work explicitly explored the issues of cultural disjunction in Australia before there was any general acceptance for or means of conceptualising such an approach' (1987: 129).

Yiddish literature did not become extinct in Australia the day Goldhar died. He was survived by another Yiddish writer, Herz Bergner (1907–70). Born in Poland, Bergner arrived in Melbourne in 1938, leaving behind, like Goldhar, a career as a writer. Once in Australia he first wrote stories set in the old world but he would, in later stories, show his preoccupation with the problems inherent in the lives of Jewish immigrants in the new land. In 1946 he was awarded the Gold Medal of the Australian Literary Society for a poetic, symbolic short novel, *Between Sky and Sea* (1946), a striking forerunner of Holocaust writing, in which Bergner seems to anticipate the anguish and horror that later Jewish writers would expose more openly. The bunch of doomed refugees on board an old Greek ship have escaped one hell only to fall into another. Symbols become very powerful and parallels can be established with Coleridge's *The Rime of the Ancient Mariner* (1798). According to Waten, responsible for the superb translation, 'Bergner's novel [. . .] is one of the most powerful war books that has appeared from the pen of a Jewish writer' (1949: 96).

In an early story, 'The Actor' (1955), Bergner had approached the topic of migration with the ensuing loss of language and culture through assimilation. In his novel *Light and Shadow* (1963), he would expand on this topic. He would also dwell on Holocaust issues since his characters have escaped it physically but not spiritually. The scope of the novel is challenging, as is the attempt to follow the adventures and misadventures of the Zeling family for over twenty years in less than four hundred pages. This might explain why Bergner does not go into deep characterization, as critics have pointed out. Another reason could be the influence of Yiddish literature where the story had place of honour over character building. Bergner's style is more uneven than Goldhar's but he is also less pessimistic. The title *Light and Shadow* is suggestive of the author's balanced vision of a reality where positive and negative elements are inextricably woven into a whole.

'Death of Pioneer Author' read the headline of Judah Waten's obituary in the *Australian Jewish News* of 2 August 1985. Waten had died on 29 July, precisely on his seventy-fourth birthday, and the press had unanimously voiced regret at the disappearance of the first major writer who had dealt with migrant experiences. Goldhar and Bergner had been concerned with similar experiences and their writings influenced Waten but, as critics commonly agree, he surpassed them both. Judah Waten (1911–85) was born in Odessa into a Russian Jewish family and, although his parents left Russia when he was only eleven days old (first for Palestine, then, when young Judah was three years old, for Australia), his work shows the influence of Russian authors. This may partly be due to his mother's passion for Russian writers. 'My mother', he wrote, 'actually liked Chekhov even more than Sholem Aleichem, saying that he was the deeper writer, only second to

Count Leo Tolstoy who was the deepest of them all' (1984: 115). Waten's voracity for books would make him discover the Russian writers for himself at an early age. They were not the only major influence in his work. Waten's life and literary career were permeated by his political convictions. He was a staunch Marxist, devoted to the Communist cause despite many reasons for disillusionment. David Carter sees the mother's influence here, too: 'She [...] taught him independence and rebellion' (1996: 121).

Influenced by Goldhar's advice on his writing, Waten decided: 'I would write about people I knew, real people as it were [...] about my parents and their friends and my own associates and myself, the migrant world I had grown up in, from 1914, when we arrived in Australia, onwards' (1981: 17). As a result, the pages of his first successful book, *Alien Son* (1952), are filled with his mother and the progressive alienation between her and her son, as it explores issues of migration, assimilation and politics. The author described the book as 'a kind of novel without architecture' (1971a: 87), a brilliant paradox considering how skilfully this 'novel' was built. June Factor has observed that, besides being alienated from his mother, the son also feels distanced from the land at times, when he senses the hostility or rejection of some Australians. Factor praises the title 'for it suggests the double alienation which is the difficult birthright of so many children of immigrants' (1982: 4).

After the success of *Alien Son*, Waten wrote a novel about a migrant Jewish family in Australia, *The Unbending* (1954), which was also an account of the bitter political and social strife over the issue of conscription during the First World War. Much controversy followed its publication and many critics have argued that Waten's political bias was detrimental to his art. Nevertheless, the novel has many positive values and is an interesting document on a number of socio-historical issues such as political manipulation, the horrors of war, pacifism, jingoism, or state education. In a later novel, *Distant Land* (1964), the author reworks the topic of an immigrant Jewish family, but this time the background is not politically explosive. The novel begins in Tsarist Russia before the First World War and ends in Australia well after the Second. The topics, which include the Holocaust, bear a certain affinity with Bergner's *Light and Shadow* but the treatment is quite different, more artistic; situations are better developed and characters better construed. The main male character, Joshua, is very idealistic while his wife, Shoshanah, is an ambitious woman who makes the family's fortune. Like the mother in *Alien Son*, and like Hannah in *The Unbending*, she is a rather formidable person. Following the models of his own mother and father, Waten portrays gentle, easy-going husbands, in contrast with 'unbending' women. On the subject of intermarriage, discussed in the novel, Shoshanah formulates this question to justify her intransigence: 'Do Catholics believe in inter-marriage?' (1964; 1978: 177). Waten would approach this question again in another novel, *So Far No Further.*

So Far No Further (1971), set in Melbourne in the 1960s, is what appears to be a faithful depiction of the university unrest and of the social background out of which it emerged. The connecting thread is the love story of a Jewish girl,

Deborah, and a Catholic boy, Paul, who feel irresistibly attracted to one another despite their often conflicting views and their respective families' abhorrence of intermarriage. The amorous conflict is interwoven with the conflicts of other characters and the political tensions affecting university life. Holocaust traumas are still present in the lives of the Jewish characters, often, if not always, buried deeply. The main conflict is left unresolved as Paul insists on marriage and Deborah, another of Waten's formidable women on the make, is adamant in refusing marriage if not their relationship. Talking to Yvonne Fein in mid-1984, Judah Waten summarized his effort: 'I've really written [...] almost a chronicle of Jewish life from about 1914–15 till the early seventies. So far... no further' (Fein 1988: 5).

Polish-born Maria Lewitt (b. 1924), has been living in Australia since 1949. As an adolescent, she was caught in the turmoil of the Second World War. The assistance of non-Jewish relatives, faked papers and her own looks, allowed her to pass as an Aryan and survive. When she arrived in her new land she already had a desire to write but did not have a word of English, so her literary career had to wait. Her autobiographical novel, *Come Spring*, was awarded the 1978 Alan Marshall Prize and was a great success. Its sequel, *No Snow in December*, won the 1986 NSW Premier's Literary Award. Lewitt has also written a novella, *Just Call Me Bob*, as well as many short stories on themes like the Holocaust, Jewish refugees or alienation.

In *Come Spring* (1980) Lewitt 'wanted to preserve the time which was as seen through the eyes of a young girl' (Fremd 1984: 4). The historical perspective is, thus, limited to the 'I' narrator but, as she has said, she also wanted to fictionalize history: 'Somehow, fiction and facts blend together [...]. What I did in *Come Spring* was taking the liberty to manipulate events and people... ' (Fremd 1984: 4). Actually, she did more than that, she effectively used literary devices to make her narrative more appealing. Annette Corkhill writes: 'The need to give expression to former grief and loss is the primary impetus behind the writing of [...] Maria Lewitt'. She adds that 'Lewitt turns to the past [...] as an inferno which must be exposed in order to be vanquished' (1994: 154). Yet, the past in this novel is not exclusively an inferno, as the author incorporates into it elements of an ordinary existence; some joys intertwine with the many sufferings and there are glimpses of humour. Towards Angelika, Fremd the novelist asserted: '*Come Spring* is a book about people set up at the time of the war. I don't see it as a book about the persecution of the Jews only, but rather about the human spirit and how people managed to live under impossible conditions' (Fremd 1984: 5).

In *No Snow in December* (1985) Lewitt describes a Polish Jewish family (immigrants in Australia after the Second World War) coming to terms with their new environment, in a struggle that ends successfully, although it will take Irena, the protagonist, a long time, and many efforts to accept as a beloved home the disappointing Australia of her early dreams. There is gentle irony in the description of Australia as first perceived by immigrants and the silly mistakes they make in the use of their new language. The novel is also a Holocaust and post-Holocaust story in two ways: in Irena's recollections and in the traumas lived by other survivors whose haunting experiences are far worse than Irena's. Considering that it comes from a first generation Holocaust survivor, Lewitt's writing, if tinted with grief and anguish, is not devoid of humour, the appreciation of beauty and the joy of living.

Serge Liberman (b. 1942) was nine years old when he first set foot in Australia, the land that he would soon learn to love as his own. The son of Polish–Jewish parents, he had been born in Soviet Russia and had experienced life in a Displaced Persons' camp in Germany before the family could migrate to a new world. Although milk and honey did not await them in the 'Promised Land', it offered them freedom, hardly any anti-Semitism and the assurance of work. But for Liberman's parents it meant endless hours of toil and – especially for the mother – a perennial nostalgia for a past which could not be retrieved and for a home forever lost. Years later the author would recreate their arrival and those early times in some of his stories, like 'Greetings Australia! To You Have I Come', 'Two Years in Exile', 'Home' and others.

Liberman, a vocational physician besides being a vocational writer, acknowledges that his medical practice has provided him with themes. His general practice is in Carlton, an inner suburb of Melbourne that used to have a large Jewish population, which is now moving to other suburban areas. But he had ample opportunities to meet immigrant patients, survivors of the Holocaust, and could even talk to them in Yiddish. They gave him a penetrating insight into their traumas that would prove a powerful inspiration for his stories. He felt compelled to tell their tales for the sake of future generations. Liberman is aware that he cannot write as a primary witness, but only as a witness of the Shoah trauma as lived by survivors and their children. This would include his own parents and himself. He acknowledges that his mother's negativity was transmitted to him. On the other hand, he acknowledges the literary and philosophical influence of authors like Chekhov, Kafka, Camus, Sartre, Russell and Kierkegaard. He is intensely preoccupied with the interplay of free will, determinism and chance, and often explores questions of illness, age and mortality, the purpose of life, as well as the possibility of a secular redemption from an anthropocentric perspective. Richard Freadman has commented that Liberman's humanism is of a kind 'that leaves open – wide open – the possibility of a spiritual dimension, and of human participation in that dimension' (2000: 6).

The titles of his five volumes of collected short stories are eloquent: *On Firmer Shores* (1981), *A Universe of Clowns* (1983), *The Life That I Have Led* (1986), *The Battered and the Redeemed* (1990) and *Voices From The Corner* (1999). He has won the Alan Marshall Award three times and he was also given the NSW Premier's Literary Award for Ethnic Writing. Although Shimon Cowen argues that 'the Jewish writer [...] must have a genuine depth of religious Jewish experience' (2000: 4), which he finds lacking in Liberman, the author himself proclaims his Jewishness:

> I do regard myself very much a Jewish writer. I am born Jewish; many of my themes and characters and literary concerns are Jewish; there are instances in

> which I use Yiddish terms and Yiddish speech in my stories [. . .] while I believe that the ethics and principles in my stories and what I like to think is a humanism that I try to convey are very Jewish. . . .
>
> (1987: 2)

Peter Kohn, born in Melbourne in 1955 to Jewish parents who had emigrated from Vienna, is one of the second-generation children who have gained an insight into the horror of the Holocaust through their parents and parents' friends. In his first novel, *Rachel's Chance* (1987), Kohn tells the story of those Jews who survived by spending the war years in Shanghai. Unlike other parents who were reluctant to speak up, Kohn's parents were willing to talk about their past because, in a way, they were fortunate. Although they had to suffer the Japanese occupation and disease during their sojourn in China, they were not rounded up and taken to Auschwitz, they escaped extermination (Kohn 1996). *Rachel's Chance* could be considered to belong to the same genre as Thomas Keneally's *Schindler's Ark* and should, therefore, be counted as 'fact'ion' (Elliott 1987: 7). According to Anton Herman with his novel Kohn fulfilled the wish of the Jewish historian Simon Dubnow, who had been murdered outside his home in 1941: 'Remember, and record it!' (1988: n.p.).

In the foreword of *View from a Sandcastle* (1998), a sequel to *Rachel's Chance*, Kohn states: 'This novel was inspired by my experience of growing up in Melbourne's suburbs, but it is not autobiographical. Its heroes and villains are composites, allowing events which involved large numbers of people to be played by a manageably small cast of fictional characters' (1998: vii). The motivation to publish the book was to be found in 'the rise of the One Nation Party and the Howard Government's response to a variety of multicultural and indigenous issues' (Gronow 2000: n.p.). The author exposes the xenophobia experienced in Australia in the sixties, as a result of the 'White Australia' policy – a policy that personally affected him and his parents – by using a narrator who is only five when the story begins and an adolescent when it ends, matured by the experience of abuse but secure in the confidence of his Jewish education and religious beliefs, an adolescent, moreover, happy that the family are leaving their creamy brick house (a perishable sandcastle) in an unsympathetic neighbourhood, and moving to more congenial, more Jewish, surroundings.

Arnold Zable (b. 1947), although born in New Zealand, was taken to Australia at a very early age and may therefore be counted among Australian Jewish writers. His family settled in Carlton and it was there that Zable discovered the Yiddish Theatre and developed his passion for it. Years later this passion was expressed in a bilingual (English-Yiddish) book: *Wanderers and Dreamers: Tales of the David Herman Theatre* (1998). Zable has always sympathized with marginalized people, arguably a Jewish characteristic. He has travelled extensively and spent years living abroad. One of his journeys took him to Europe. This time he was driven, like many other children born of Holocaust survivors, by a powerful desire to find his ancestors' roots. The quest, fictionalized, resulted in a novel, *Jewels and Ashes* (1991). 'The fragmentary material with which the writer works tends to blur distinctions between memory, or fantasy, and actual experience', writes Marcelle Freiman (1995: 38). The author refers in the text to his elders as those who 'left a legacy of fragments, a jumble of jewels and ashes, and forests of severed family trees which their children now explore and try somehow to restore' (Zable 1991: 23–4). The novel was very well received by critics, has been reprinted in the USA and several times in Australia, translated into Yiddish and been given five literary awards.

Cafe Scheherazade (2001) has been another very successful novel. The 'Author's Note' states that it is 'a homage to the power of storytelling' (Zable 2001a: 222). The healing power of storytelling emerges in the lives of those octogenarians, survivors of the Holocaust and Melbourne citizens for over fifty years, who patronize the Cafe Scheherazade in Acland Street. All of them are storytellers and their stories keep the young narrator entrapped night after night. Zable's lyrical prose redeems the horror of those stories. Ivor Indyk has commented on the luminous moments in the novel: 'The radiance cast by these moments sustains and invigorates those who experience it' (2001: n.p.). And if 'there is something beyond our endless recycling of words' (Zable 2001a: 220), as the narrator wonders, that something is silence. Zable has pointed out that 'the book ends with silence, a positive silence, like the calm after the storm' (2001b: n.p.). Once the story has been told the storyteller can rest and be silent, as Scheherazade did every daybreak after her tale had succeeded in seducing her king one more night.

'[His] ability to see the beauty of the ordinary in a world obsessed with the extraordinary informs every aspect of Zable's writing', says Helen Elliott (2002: n.p.) of yet another successful book of Zable's, *The Fig Tree* (2002). This book is a collection of ten stories about his family and that of his wife, about the (unjustly) forgotten Yiddish writers, and about voyages. It is set in Australia and in the Greek islands, in the present and in days gone by. It is, again, a poetic book and, as Susan Varga remarks: 'He reminds us gently, and without too much overt moralising, of the present-day refugees against whom so many people have hardened their hearts' (2002: n.p.).

Zable's latest book so far is the equally celebrated *Scraps of Heaven* (2004). Set in Carlton in the late 1950s, this novel is more than the story of the childhood years of a Jewish boy, marked by the trauma of his parents. The gallery of characters is varied, showing how quickly Australia was becoming multicultural. Carlton comes alive in detail. As Sam Lipski says: 'the suburb itself is a main character in the book', adding: 'It is a tribute to the storyteller's craft [. . .] a wonderful tale, to savour and read again' (2005: n.p.).

Often, but not always, the stories of the eight Australian Jewish writers discussed here are related to migration and the hardships that go with it, but often, too, they touch on other topics. The eight writers are indeed non-Anglo-Celtic writers. They could be called ethnic-minority writers, although this might imply that the national literature of Australia is the literature of an ethnic majority, a politically incorrect assumption. In their own singular ways, all but Spielvogel deal with the Holocaust. All of them are heirs to the long, rich Jewish history and there is a profound sense of Jewishness underlying their works.

The stories that first-generation migrant writers – Bergner, Goldhar and Lewitt – tell their readers originate in their personal experience. The two Yiddish writers had escaped the Holocaust themselves, but it had destroyed their families, friends, everything that made up their former life. In Goldhar there was an intense fear that the Jewish life they had known would come to an end, as in his days assimilation posed a serious danger to the Jewish community in Australia. Bergner's stance was more balanced, life was neither completely infused with light nor immersed in shadow. Lewitt's personal testimony is captivating as it is sincere and youthful. The wish of second-generation children to give voice to the horror of the Holocaust and the trauma of its survivors is patent in Liberman, Kohn and Zable, even in the latter's most recent works. Nathan Spielvogel differs from all the writers mentioned above in that he chose to depict Jewish life in his community in an almost idyllic way, avoiding any form of pessimism.

Much has been written about Judah Waten, not least about his role as mediator between the dominant culture and the migrant milieu, because he was both an outsider and an insider. His command of English allows him to play with it and inflect it with subtle foreign nuances, as when he makes his characters think in terms of Jewish proverbs or when he construes sentences which denote a Yiddish speaker. Yet he wanted to be considered as an Australian writer and, in being accepted as one, he was clearing a space within mainstream Australian literature for other Jewish writers and non-Anglo-Celtic writers in general. The non-Anglo-Celtic literature in Australia should not be read as a marginalized literature produced by 'the Other', but as part of a heterogeneous whole and, since mainstream literature has determinedly shed its colonial past and any temptations to be monolithic, there is surely room for other projects.[4]

Since Jewishness is not akin to uniformity all the authors surveyed here are unique, having construed themselves as Jewish authors in their own individual way. Thus, Spielvogel is unique in his optimism; Bergner in his poetic symbolism; Goldhar in his pessimistic insight in Jewish life; Waten in his balanced position between cultures; Lewitt in her non-melodramatic stance and courage; Liberman in his philosophical questioning of God, the meaning of life and of suffering; Kohn in his denunciation of racism, rich in symbolic suggestions; and Zable in his lyricism and perception of beauty, not in evil, but in spite of it. All of them are realist writers. They are not transgressive if we give the term a meaning of resistance to the host culture. They want to be heard not as coming from the margins but as part of a multicultural national literature. If literatures written in languages other than English in Australia are doomed after the first generation, this is not the case of the non-Anglo-Celtic literatures written in English, like Jewish literature in Australia nowadays. As Goldhar had feared, Yiddish and Yiddish literature, although not dead, will not flourish again, but they have influenced the language and the storytelling of the anglophone authors.

Australian Jewish literature has evolved and is more complex now, in depth and aesthetic dimension. The question is: Which way now? Is the Holocaust likely to engage the energies of Jewish authors further? On the one hand, authors wish to tell the story which must not be lost for future generations; on the other hand, they might wish to leave the Holocaust trauma, and the implicit sense of guilt for not having been its direct victims, and move on, to write about other topics. If those topics or their treatment are not Jewish the authors may well be labelled as Australian writers who merely happen to be Jewish, but many will find – or have already found – in their own imagination and creativity, even in the ordinary life of any Jewish person, the inspiration with which to produce compelling literature with a Jewish content.

Notes

1 This chapter is based on my unpublished PhD thesis: 'A Contribution to the Study of Jewish Writing in Australia' (2002).
2 See, for example, the introduction to this volume and chapter 7.
3 See also W.D. Rubinstein (1991: 1).
4 For a comprehensive study on Judah Waten, see Carter (1997) and, for a discussion of the concepts summarized above, especially chapter 8: 'A Jewish Australian Writer'.

13 Contemporary Jewish Canadian plays on the Canadian stage

Albert-Reiner Glaap

This chapter is a small segment of a comprehensive project. Of the twenty-two contemporary Canadian plays from the pen of Jewish writers, which I have so far come across, only a few, written by survivors, reveal an immediate connection with the Holocaust, while the majority have been written with the benefit of hindsight by second or third generation Canadian playwrights. There has been a remarkable development from documentations of what happened in Hitler's time to reflections on the aftermath of the Holocaust and on Jewish life in Canada in our day and age. With reference to four plays, I will point to diverse facets of this development. For a start, however, some background information – in terms of a few dates and figures – would be useful.[1]

Canada, with over 350,000 Jews, has the sixth largest Jewish population after the United States at about 5.6 million and Israel at 4.3 million, and is ahead of the United Kingdom at 300,000. Most Canadian Jews are of Eastern European origin, but we also find Jews from the Middle East, North Africa and Ethiopia, from South Africa and Israel. Jews in Canada are 90 per cent Ashkenazi, i.e. Central and East European, in origin (Ashkenaz being an older Hebrew word for German).

Holocaust survivors have played a pivotal role in the cultural development of the Jewish community, especially in Toronto. They were defined – in census terms – as persons who were born before 1945 in countries which were occupied by the Nazis and immigrated to Canada after 1939. (But there are limitations to this definition; for instance, there are persons who left Germany for the United States in 1928 and did not arrive in Canada until 1951!) In 1991, there were over 27,000 Holocaust survivors in Canada. Jews are both a religious and ethnocultural group, with a large variety of cultural traits, and – needless to say – they are not a race. Therefore, the term 'Jewish-Canadian' (similar to 'African-Canadian' or 'Asian-Canadian') plays is basically a misnomer. Their authors are rather Canadian playwrights who write about Jewish topics or issues.

Kindertransport – a child's journey

Goodbye Marianne by Irene Watts was first produced in Vancouver in 1994. 'The play is dedicated to the memory of [the author's] grandfather who perished in Theresienstadt Concentration Camp in 1944.' It is a one-act play, set in Berlin in 1938, primarily addressing young audiences. The date of 9 November 1938, referred to as 'Kristallnacht', the 'Night of Broken Glass', saw the unleashing of the government-planned anti-Semitic pogrom when '191 synagogues were burned', 'hundreds of Jewish businesses' destroyed and the rights of citizenship for the Jews of Berlin and all of Germany eroded.[2] Irene Watts herself, at the age of seven, was one of ten thousand children who travelled to England by the so-called 'Kindertransports', 'the lifeline created by the British government' to rescue Jewish children from Germany during the ten months before the outbreak of the Second World War (Watts 1994; 2001: n.p.).

The central character of *Goodbye Marianne*, which opens on 15 November, six days after 'Kristallnacht', is Marianne Kohn, aged 11, a Jewish girl. At the beginning of the play, when finding the front door of her school locked, she knocks loudly and is then confronted with a secretary who wears an armband with a swastika on it and reads aloud the notice on that door: 'As of today, November 15, 1938, Jewish students are prohibited from attending German schools' (16). What is more, Marianne's father is in hiding and is later taken to Sachsenhausen Concentration Camp, 'where they took away all their clothes and made them stand naked in the prison yard for 24 hours' (26). Her mother 'has to step in the gutter when they are walking on the sidewalk, so no one can say she's taking up any room' (32), and Marianne is told that 'from now on your name is Sara' (31). The play develops into a moving portrayal of Marianne's last four days in Germany before joining one of the first 'Kindertransports' to Britain. The audience gain some revealing insights from Marianne's outspoken criticism of the Nazis and the discussions with Ernst, her friend, who is a true 'Aryan German' and a convinced member of the Hitler Youth. But finally, when Marianne gets an exit visa to England and then halfway across the world to Canada, he realizes that Marianne is Jewish. Before rushing off without looking back he professes his friendship by leaving a card on which he has written: 'Berlin. December 2, 1938. We are not all the same. Goodbye Marianne. From your friend Ernst' (40). The friendship with Ernst is a bright spot in the otherwise drab and frustrating reality of Marianne's life. What happens to her in England and Canada is the subject of *Remember Me* (Watts n.d.), a sequel to *Goodbye Marianne*: She is desperate, misses her mother terribly but realizes that she has to stand on her own feet. This play for Young Audiences is, at a different level, also a universal story of children in general who leave their home country and yearn for a better life.[3]

A few years ago, Roman Herzog, former President of the Federal Republic of Germany, claimed that now, with only a few survivors and witnesses of the Holocaust still alive, all adolescent boys and girls should be taken to a former concentration camp – just to realize and remember what happened during Hitler's time. On a smaller scale *Goodbye Marianne* may also serve that purpose.

Should the cry for justice fade or resonate?

Past Imperfect by Emil Sher is a radio play which was broadcast on *Sunday Showcase* on 14 December 1997 (Sher 1998). It is not a play about the Second

World War or the Holocaust, but about an after-effect of an actual event that had happened in those times. The incident made national headlines in Canada in 1997 as the Jean-Louis Roux affair. The public figure in question, a veteran Québec actor, had to resign as Lieutenant Governor of Québec when he admitted in an interview that as a university student he had worn a swastika on his laboratory coat and participated in an anti-conscription demonstration that turned into an anti-Semitic riot during the Second World War.

In a letter Emil Sher sent me, the playwright explains what it was that made him start from this affair when writing his radio play *Past Imperfect*:

> I was drawn to this story because it posed a very interesting question: To what degree, if any, should we be held accountable for the actions we took in our youth. I took great liberty with the Jean-Louis Roux affair, as I felt the dramatic stakes had to be increased. I created a fictitious character, Michel Beauchemin, who is highly respected for all his humanitarian works. But an incident from his youth comes back to him. So I had Beauchemin become part of a mob in which a Jewish shopkeeper was killed.

Roux being a wellknown actor – he was 74 when he stepped down – was asked by James Roy, the CBC's producer of Sher's play to take over the part of Michel Beauchemin. Roux read the play, thought the offer over and finally agreed to do it – a courageous decision, considering that appearing in a play triggered by the incident would certainly bring up the incident itself. Roux was aware that, for his role in the play, he would be accused of something he never did in real life, i.e. of throwing stones against Jews, and in particular the killing of Aaron Farber, an elderly Jewish merchant. His main concern was that the listeners on the radio might confuse him with his role. But the politics of the Jean-Louis Roux case were different from the politics in Sher's play in that they were federal-provincial as opposed to taking place within the Jewish Council which was about to give Beauchemin an award. What is more important is that the Roux affair merely provided a launching pad for examining larger issues, such as prejudice, fear, forgiveness, moral sensibilities: the central question of this play is, in reviewer Hal Doran's (1997) words: 'Does one act of violent youthful bigotry forever condemn someone as a racist? Or should a person's character be judged on the acts of a lifetime?'

There are two scenes in which this conflict comes particularly to the fore. There is Beauchemin's discussion with his Jewish wife Evelyn, who cannot cope with the fact that her husband kept 'dark secrets' from her, that he never told her that he had been involved in the riots: 'I will not live in a house filled with half-truths and white lies. Do you understand me?' (Sher 1998: 125). More than any other scene of the play it is the powerful long monologue at the end that encapsulates what Emil Sher's play is about. Michel Beauchemin addresses a hostile crowd in front of a synagogue, asking for understanding. He has learned how to come to terms with himself about his past. Whether or not the audience agrees is left to each individual person. Beauchemin's last words are:

> I knew Aaron Farber could not forgive me. And so I decided the best way to honour him was to live honourably. I have tried my best to do just that. (*Pause.*) This morning, I visited a Jewish cemetery for the first time in many, many years. I walked for a long while. I got lost. I kept walking until I found what I was looking for. I picked up a handful of stones and placed them on the tombstone, one at a time.
>
> (137–8)

Past Imperfect is the title of the play. Terminologically, the word 'imperfect' (as opposed to 'perfect') does not simply refer to actions in the past, but '*im*perfect' also points to something that has flaws or problems. Sher's play is about how we might or should cope with the things that went wrong in our past. By increasing the dramatic stakes the way he did, the playwright Emil Sher has developed the Jean-Louis Roux case into a thought-provoking and moving radio play, which otherwise could easily have meandered towards a plain documentary or a morality play. *Past Imperfect* is not about how human beings, Jews in particular, tried to save their lives in the 1930s and 1940s as in *Goodbye Marianne*. Rather it raises questions about how one can come to terms with one's Nazi past in our day and age – be it in Germany, in Canada or elsewhere. Should the cry for justice fade or resonate?

A neo-Nazi skinhead and a Jewish lawyer

In David Gow's play *Cherry Docs* (1998), Danny, one of the two characters starts the play with the following words:

> My wife and I both come from mixed backgrounds. We are both of us made up of a bit of this and a bit of that. I'm a genuine Canuck. I'm an English, Irish, Scots, Belgian Jew. The question I always get is, 'How Jewish does that make you?' Or if I say I'm Jewish, then I get, 'How Jewish does that make you?'
>
> (15)

Mike, the other character delivers his first monologue in a solitary prison cell. He says: 'I wear Cherry Docs, eighteen hole, steel shank, steel toe, original-air-cushioned, acid, oil, detergent and [...] waste-resistant sole. Combat Model. Combat tread. These boots were developed by a leading German orthopaedic specialist' (17). The name *Cherry Docs* is derived from the firm producing these boots: *Doc* Martens, and '*Cherry*'(-red) refers to their colour.

Michael Downey is a neo-Nazi skinhead in his twenties, who is accused of a racially motivated murder. He is defended by Daniel Dunkelman, a liberal, court appointed Jewish lawyer. In Gow's tight 'two-hander' these two contrasting characters reluctantly agree to work together, and pay a high price for the consequences of their decision. What actually makes them work together is that Mike thinks that he may gain something from having a lawyer who is Jewish, and Danny calculates that defending a skinhead as a Jew might be helpful for his career. But soon they realize that more than their beliefs is at stake, that they are stuck in their self-destructive stances, that their exchanges of arguments increasingly become 'wrestling matches' between good and evil. Danny gives Mike the dossier and tells him that he has to get special permission for Mike to have it. 'You're giving me this?' asks Mike. 'I'm lending it to you, for now. We'll see how it goes. [...] And you'll come up with a strategy... I want your brain out of neutral. I want you engaging life on some level' (40–1). What starts off as a juxtaposition of an intelligent neo-Nazi and a lawyer, who is by no means pussy-footing, develops into an examination and exploration of hate politics, ideologies and personal beliefs.

While the skinhead slowly develops into a thinking human being, Danny, by delving more and more deeply into the ramifications of his 'mission', neglects his family and friends. His marriage breaks up. The potential violence which seems to come to the surface in each of their meetings 'is informed not just by the aftermath of one savage act, but by the memory of a thousand years of hatred' (Ferguson 1998: 11). It impacts on Danny's private life and poses the general question of how each of us may contend with the hatred to which no one is immune. By defending the skinhead, however, he is also thrown back on his Jewish roots.

Danny succeeds in making Mike become conscious of what is evil. Mike realizes that revenge cannot really be the answer to what has gone wrong in one's life, while the lawyer feels he must reassess the limitations to his liberalism. The two, who began as opponents, almost become a team, and *Cherry Docs* is ultimately also a play about discovering oneself, enabling others to discover their selves, and giving every individual a chance to become a human being again. And the references to the etymological meanings of the names 'Michael' and 'Daniel' made in the epilogue written on screen somehow epitomize the different positions of the characters in *Cherry Docs*.

Michael: An archangel whose name is a rhetorical question meaning 'Who is like God?' Michael is sometimes thought to have fallen, to have been bound to the Devil and later released. Michael is called upon by Daniel in the book of Daniel: 'Michael stand up.'

Daniel: Whose name means: 'God is my judge.' He is representative of the idea that we might change the world through righteous prayer. Daniel is thrown into a Den of Lions and is entirely unharmed. Daniel interprets the dreams of his king and saves his king from insanity.

(Gow 1998: 86)

Structurally, this play is a combination of dialogue and monologue, i.e. the explosive discussions of the accused and the defender. Monologues – from one or the other – are spoken in spotlights, unheard by one another, but establishing connections with the audience.

A true tale of resistance

The Danish Play by Sonja Mills was first produced (by Nightwood Theatre at Tarragon Theatre's Extraspace) in Toronto in 2002. It is not about what happened either in post-war Canada or in Nazi Germany during the Second World War, but set in Nazi-occupied Denmark, focusing on Agnete Ottosen, a member of the Resistance against the Nazis in Aalborg in the 1940s. The author of this play is Ottosen's grand-niece Sonja Mills, a non-Jewish writer, who inherited her great-aunt's diaries from her mother and translated the work into English. She also conducted interviews with other Resistance members and went to the two concentration camps that Ottosen survived. However, the play is not a dramatized biography; it draws more on Ottosen's own poems than anything else. Apart from her, all characters are fictional. The play's subtitle reads 'A true *tale* of Resistance' (not 'A true *story* of Resistance', which was the subtitle when it was produced). 'I didn't want to get into trouble with anyone for telling a largely fictional story and calling it "true,"' Sonja Mills tells me in a letter, and 'a "true tale" seemed the perfect thing to call a story which is both a parable *and* based on true events.' The playwright considers the topics of her play to be also relevant to our time: patriotism, nationalism, borders, personal freedom and justice.

The action begins in 1962 with a reunion of four former Resistance fighters who reminisce about the old days and draw us closer to Agnete Ottosen (who is absent!), her courage, struggle and sufferings. Flashbacks bring us forward to the Second World War, when Germany ended its non-aggression pact with Denmark and invaded the country. Ottosen joined the Resistance when the war broke out. She organized the smuggling out of Denmark to Sweden of 7,000 Jews, wrote articles for an underground newspaper, fell victim to gynaecological experiments and was tortured by the Gestapo. But she refused to give evidence, let alone betray her comrades. Mills's play, in reviewer Kate Taylor's (2000) words, 'appears at first as a rather conventional tale of wartime heroism [. . .]. But by the time the evening is through, it has emerged as the deft and subtle account of a story set in Nazi-occupied Denmark'. It is the tripartite approach to the topics of the play – flashbacks to the events of the 1940s, the contextualization of those events into the reunion of the Resistance fighters in 1962, and the contemporary perspective of the playwright – that gives thought-provoking insights into Agnete Ottosen's life during and after the war and makes us see the dangers of nationalism. 'It is about the fact', writes Sonja Mills, 'that flag-waving leads to war, and war leads to flag-waving, which leads to more war, which leads to . . . [. . .] War is not the answer (even to insane problems).'

The Danish Play is certainly also about gender and sexuality. Agnete knows well that there is much she has been kept from doing. Mills' favourite line in the play is when the judge (in Scene 22) asks Agnete: 'Miss? It is Miss, isn't it?' and she responds: 'Miss, Misses, Mister' (Mills 2002: 25). Mills also points out that she 'didn't want to write a big flag-waving feminist play', but 'a play about inequity in our weird male-centric society.' Agnete was determined to have a child but not a husband. There is the scene with the Judge in Act II in which Agnete threatens to name the Judge himself as the father of her child: 'You're the father. Put your name down. What difference does it make?' (94). She is fined 50 crowns for this.

The Danish Play, as we read in a paper published by Nightwood Theatre, 'reflects upon the conflicts of nationalism, patriotism, and the role of women as good citizens; all relevant in our own time when the world once again careens towards an uncertain political future.'

One of Ottosen's poems, which Sonja Mills has Agnete recite in her play, reads like this:

> Rising up from every hut and house and home
> before us,
> All believers burning prayers combine in mighty
> chorus.
> One proffers to Krishna, another prays to Christ,
> One praises Jehovah, one says Allah is right.
> [...]
> A thousand souls, a thousand tongues, a thousand
> different prayers,
> Imploring each their almighty God for an end to
> their despair.
> Buddha, protect us! Grace us, Madonna! And see to
> us in our stead,
> One asks for luck, another for glory, another for daily bread.
> [...]
> I ask for only this:
> Through suffering will I find my true wish.
> My pain do not spare me, and end to grief don't give,
> My wretched burdens do not take, just let me with
> Sorrow live.
>
> (25)

The plays compared and contrasted

The four plays discussed here deal with different issues seen from different angles. *Goodbye Marianne* is totally concerned with the past, i.e. the author's personal experiences in Nazi times mirrored in the 'Kindertransports'. In *Past Imperfect* it is but one dark moment in the past which, however, impacts greatly on later life. It problematizes the process of coming to terms with one's past. *Cherry Docs* seems to be uncoupled from the past. The central character is a young man of our times in his twenties. He is accused of a racially motivated murder and makes us sense how an unreflected Nazi-ideology has impinged on the skinhead. On the other hand, he brings to the surface that his Jewish lawyer has to examine his liberalism. *The Danish Play* comes full circle in that this play is – like *Goodbye Marianne* – based on documentary material. But it is not about an author's personal experiences, rather an examination of the nature of nationalism, of freedom, justice and borders – based on Agnete Ottosen's diaries: a play as a parable.

As regards the structures and the makings of these four plays, what they have in common is that there is no subdivision into acts in any of them; they consist of sequences of scenes. But they are different. *Goodbye Marianne* is documentary fiction. *Past Imperfect* is a radio play drawn on national headlines that caused passionate debates. *Cherry Docs* is a two-hander, an alternation of dialogue and monologue. Its structure is underlined by specific visual images for each of the different scenes which stretch over seven days – images and titles which appear on a screen, such as 'A nearly bare tree' for 'Winter Solstice' (First day), 'Crocuses in bloom, on brown grass' for 'Passover' (Fourth day) or 'A full field of wheat' for 'Mid July' (Sixth day). *The Danish Play* is characterized by flashbacks to events in the 1940s put into the context of the 1960s, and the contemporary perspective of the author.

The plays reviewed

Plays are written and staged for audiences in theatres. The following brief excerpts from reviews put in a nutshell the impact that productions of the four plays discussed in this chapter have or may have on the audience.

> *Goodbye Marianne*
> For children, who may not know much about Nazi Germany, the play offers a touching story about their fellow kids. For adults, it answers questions most of us never thought to ask before: What would it have been like to be a Jewish kid in 1938 Berlin? Would you go to school? Would you play with your friends? Would you have fun?
> Hitler's evil is a perfect contrast to the innocence of youth and Goodbye Marianne is a sober and heartfelt reminder that there's always hope for the future – and that our children's purity is what gives us that hope.
> (Snider 2000)

> *Past Imperfect*
> The play asks: Does one act of violent youthful bigotry forever condemn someone as a racist? Or should a person's character be judged on the acts of a lifetime? Sher offers no simple answers, even though he has dramatically heightened the conflicts in the play to more dramatic black-and-white levels than the real-life facts concerning Roux's participation in the rally 56 years ago.
> (Doran 1997)

> *Cherry Docs*
> Gow skilfully transcends the obvious clichés and crafts an engaging dialectic of ideas. Though each side fights to win, each is affected by the other. Danny begins to worry about the limits of his own tolerance, while Mike begins to see the responsibility he has to find a constructive response to the hatred in himself and in society. [...] This play speaks convincingly not only in portraying the hatred that infects some young people in our society but also in addressing the problem of how we might deal constructively with this hatred in order to build a better future.
> (Rivers 2001)
>
> *The Danish Play*
> The Danish Play, written by Sonja Mills and produced by Nightwood Theatre, is a moving work about Denmark's resistance to Nazi aggression and occupation. [...] Mills has crafted a subtle, though harrowing, drama whose shifting chronology gradually brings us forward in time from 1940, and draws a portrait of Agnete's anguished decline. At the same time it suggests unsettling parallels between past and current nationalisms.
> (Ormsby 2002)

As pointed out at the beginning, the plays discussed here are only four examples of how multifaceted the Jewish experience is, which presents itself in contemporary Canadian plays, that are far from being mere documentaries of what happened before and during the Second World War. They are increasingly becoming plays on universal issues seen through Jewish eyes and are an integral part of today's theatre in Canada.

Notes

1 For detailed information see Weinfeld (2001).
2 A play titled *Kristallnacht* was first performed by the University of Lethbridge Department of Dramatic Arts in 1985, see Epp (n.d.).
3 *Kindertransport* is also the title of a play by English playwright Diane Samuels, which was first performed by the Solo Theatre Company at the Cockpit Theatre, London, in April 1993, see Samuels (1996).

14 The Anglo-Israeli writer: double identities in troubled times

Karen Alkalay-Gut

English writers in Israel, although in no way integrated into the artistic society of Israel, are nevertheless a part of its cultural life, and their literature reflects, and dialogues with, the daily life and culture. It is generally a one-way dialogue, because the Israeli readers and Israeli society are not exposed to these writings. Because of the central importance of the Hebrew language in the concept of establishment of a culture in a new state, rarely are English books written in Israel reviewed in the local papers, nor are English writers centralized in culture through participation in festivals, interviews on literature programmes or talk shows. Nevertheless, the constant references to and evaluation of Israeli culture, politics and daily existence indicate that the Anglo-Israeli writer is very much involved in life in a chosen civilization.

The three categories of English and Writer and Israel have become extremely amorphous in recent years, and are increasingly problematic to isolate and identify. Numerous English writers, for example, frustrated with their inability to reach a local audience, have turned to multimedia, or poetry with music and painting, to amplify their poetic efforts. Elazar Larry Freifeld, whose socio-political and lyrical poems have been expanded into multimedia, is one of many who have expressed little interest in writing verse in recent years and have turned to art. Others have expanded into rock music, poems integrated into clothing and poems in match boxes,[1] augmentations to their texts. Furthermore, because of the growing cosmopolitanism of Israeli culture, the borders of language have become blurred. Thus one may identify oneself only as a 'writer', refusing to accept the limitations of a specific language, and may choose to obscure the identity of the source language and/or the nature of the linguistic process of writing. Native Hebrew-speaking writers, for example, not only seek translation actively, but sometimes prefer to publish first in English.[2] Although his native language is Arabic, for example, Osama Massarwa chooses to write in English as a 'bridge language', a mutually foreign language to Hebrew speakers, and common ground for both. His opening poem of *Quest for Peace of Heart* (2003), 'If', illustrates this:

> If you had the right magic word,
> We'd absolutely vanish,

If we had it or the right code,
Your existence we'd ravish.
But because neither you nor we
Have that magical skill think
What the alternative will be –
Peace, otherwise we all sink

(3)

The very forced grammar and rhymes here illustrate the non-native speaker, and highlight the nature of his message. And Osama's use of the foreign language is not uncommon. Ada Aharoni, founder of the 'International Forum for the Literature and Culture of Peace', writes numerous poems directly stating the need for dialogue through poetry, addressing 'My Arab sister' (1997), and it is clear that the use of English makes it far more possible for these potential dialogues to occur. Aharoni, born in Egypt, might also have written in Arabic, but the neutrality of English is part of the message.

There may not always be so direct a reason for exchanging Hebrew for English, and the goals may be antithetical – not to clarify and repair their local identity, but to expand it, and to allow a wider potential audience to comprehend the complexity. In a multilingual country such as Israel in which there is a tradition of literacy in more than one language, these options are available, and sometimes increase the linguistic potential as well as the audience options for the writer. Moshe Benarroch, a Hebrew poet who later changed to English and Spanish, has discussed the extraordinary acceptance he received in English after reception to the same poetry had been tepid in Hebrew, and explains, 'I feel that English has opened a door to the world, to the outside world. I found readers. I don't feel like an outsider in English, although it is a language I have never lived in' (Alkalay-Gut 2003: n.p.).

The lure of a universal audience, or at least a universal potential audience base, is great in a small country of only six million people who do not always share a common language. But other reasons than audience reception are also common. Some writers do not acknowledge their current or past place of residence in their writing, seeing it as a distraction from the work which may not be concerned with nationality, or too politically charged an identity to 'write over', and they seek identification only as an author. These writers do not identify themselves as Israeli so as not to focus interest on the element that is not central to their writing. Others may defy categories because they divide their residence with other countries. Orit Kruglanski, a native Hebrew-speaking poet, living in Barcelona and using English as her base language, describes herself as 'an Israeli born (interactive) poet and writer' (22 March 2005). Her texts, which would not be identifiable as non-native English to any reader, are only part of the multimedia interactive work. Nevertheless it is clear she can be categorized as an Israeli-English writer.[3]

Another manifestation of the use of English in literature in Israel in recent years is the position of the English writer as communicator and interpreter from Israel to the world outside. In this environment, the role of the native English speaker is increased and made more complex and demanding. Robert Rosenberg, a journalist who came from Boston to live in Israel in 1973, found that his English language profession imposed upon him such a sense of responsibility that he abandoned his successful fictional career to focus primarily on news and reportage, writing a daily column on 'the situation', and editing a poetry section on his web journal www.ariga.com until his recent death. In a society in which every element of daily life is influenced by the news, this concentration on the political and physical environment is inevitable. Even the subject of much writing in English is located in place, and poet Linda Zisquit, who has written extensively of extremely personal issues, appeared in various universities in the United States in 2004 with scholar Sidra Ezrahi under the title *Writing Jerusalem*.[4] A recent article, 'The Secret Life' aimed at explaining her Jewish heritage and almost not concerned with politics, reveals nevertheless the basic feeling.

> Most of my poems begin in the cracks of my life where opposing forces collide, in the tensions I experience between ritual and desire, tradition and freedom. In poetry I am free to play with the material of my life, to use whatever I find that helps me see my way through the disorder to some coherence. Yet anxiety and doubt often inform the pleasurable process.
>
> (2004b: n.p.)

This search for meaning and order coupled with anxiety and doubt characterizes much poetry of today. A special issue of the American-based Jewish feminist journal *Bridges*, entitled *Amid Grief* (2004), is dedicated to 'Writings by Israeli Jewish Women on Peace Seeking'. Containing poems by major English-Israeli poets, Sharon Kessler, Linda Zisquit and Rachel Back, they illustrated the complex grief, pride and confusion at being Israeli. Zisquit, whose previous poetry has emphasized family and Biblical themes, uses an image from her experiences with her art gallery in 'Lines of Defense'. 'I don't let the news in at dawn', the poem begins, as if choosing to escape into the world of 'lines', of 'art', from the immediate environment of terror-torn Jerusalem. But the ultimate goal in her concluding lines is to write a poem like her friend's painting, 'a sensation of having/something in my control' (Zisquit 2004a: 45). Rachel Back addresses the issue more directly, and illustrates the need to encompass the complexities of the situation,

> in the Huleh valley around the reflooded
>   swamp of the north where
> I walk   October 2001
>   one year after
>   the women of Sakhnin first
>
> buried their faces
>   in the rough wind-dried still
>   sweet smelling clothes of their
> dead sons.
>
> (2004: 43)

'Huleh' identifies the Israeli setting, significant in the history of Zionism. The Huleh valley was created when the Huleh lake was dried in order to create rich farming land in the 1960s. This project, promoted as another example of Israeli redemption of the wasted land, emerged as misguided and was reversed in recent years.

Sakhnin is an Arab village in the Galilee, where Israeli police, in a confused attempt to quell a political demonstration in 2000, killed two of the demonstrators, both young men. Even the basic orientation and setting of the poem is charged with tragic history that reverses both direction and meaning.

These poems bridge cultures through their language as well as their subject matter, and their power depends in part on the intimacy of the involvement, the fact that the speaker has a great personal stake in every detail of the self. But the perspective enabled by the language is equally powerful, enabling the transcendence so necessary to the solution of the situation.

Since all these relatively new blurring and critical examinations of categories are also figured in the contemporary universal crisis with identity and ideology, it would be as irrelevant to discuss its manifestations in this context alone as publishing an examination of the wagging of the tail of a dog with no information and recognition of the dog itself. The historical and sociological study of this situation can only be acknowledged in these pages and not completely investigated.

By limiting this study to the genre of poetry, however, it is possible that some of these manifestations, unique to the situation in Israel, can be delineated and clarified in these pages. And poetry indeed seems to be spearheading some kind of change.

In October of 2003, Shiri Lev-Ari of the *Ha'aretz* daily newspaper reported: 'Something is happening to poetry in Israel: While prose drowses, poetry is responding rapidly to political reality and new groups are emerging: religious poets, including residents of settlements in the territories, Arab poets who no longer write in emotional, nationalist tones, and immigrant Russian poets.'[5] Although the rest of the article deals with the example of a new immigrant poet who writes in Russian in Israel, Lev-Ari passes over the fact that the change of which she is enamoured is emerging from marginal writers, those who, only a few years before, would have been considered betrayers of their people because they did not write in Hebrew and were therefore not helping to create a renewed culture. In this failure to identify the phenomenon, the article, seemingly foregrounding marginal poetry, is instead a testament to the national transparence of the foreign language writer.

Furthermore, the subject of the contemporary politicization of poetry, to my knowledge, has not been taken up again,[6] although its pervasive ubiquitousness – in the writing of authors who do not write in Hebrew – is unique and overwhelming. The universal response of non-Hebrew poets to the political situation since the breakdown of the peace talks in 2001 is a complete genre unto itself. A 'reality' medium, poetry became to be preferred precisely because it did not tell the 'whole story', but mirrored the sense of the narrative uncertainty of the times, the feeling that any narrative could end in the middle with no shape or plot with a single shooting or bombing, that poetry could deal with the land antithetically, could be the perfect form for a concise political statement. When reality and the grasp of future changes from day to day, even from minute to minute, poetry is a far more useful tool in reflecting this situation. A poem by Elazar Larry Freifeld, mirrors this:

> FANTASTICA
> the small effects of small people are large
> the large effects of large people are small
> 600 million people watch CNN
> but that's only really 20% of the world's population. So
> what can the matter be further to sell coca-cola to the coolies
> they're all the same East of Eden
> waiting for the fibre-optic connection for
> instantaneous E of overall informational networking sensibility
> for upgrading tri-annually
> additional bucks for all
> and a world that goes to sleep with one eye open.
> (22 March 2005: n.p.)

Paradoxically, poetry is also a handy form for the utterance of 'universal truths'. Consider, for example, the ironic concision of Ricky Friesem's 'History':

> Dust
> Clay Sod Earth
> Fields Meadows Pastures
> Land Property Country Nation
> Motherland Fatherland Homeland
> Realm Dominion Kingdom Empire
> Dust
> (2004: n.p.)

From all the spectrum of the political arena, poetry is used to summarize an opinion, and the quantity of poems written in English is a subject for study in itself. In brief, poetry in English in Israel is at times related to the need to 'explain' to another culture what is happening in the one in which the poet exists, a factor which is simply redundant to the native Israeli writing to a local audience. The Hebrew scholar, Hanan Hever, has recently noted that 'the Occupation becomes not only Israeli culture's social survival net, something to fall back on, but also that which forms its daily life, the main element which constitutes and constructs its language; its social behaviour; its political make-up; its moral discourse; its consumerist habits; its economic rationale; its understanding of childhood, of youth, of old age; its production and consumption of culture, including the most elite, canonical literary writings' (2003: n.p.). A situation in which daily life is so infiltrated by a political situation can also make the expression of it difficult. Poetry which simply mirrors the news, particularly tragic news that infiltrates every element of daily life, and in the same language as the news, is too painful, too close to home to be evaluated as poetry. A foreign language helps to provide distance, perspective.

There is an additional attraction for English poets to this subject. The political element of poetry in English writing is also related to the extreme popularity of politics and 'testament' in contemporary English poetry in the world, particularly in its manifestions on the Internet. From Carolyn Forché's groundbreaking anthology *Against Forgetting* (1993) to Sam Hammill's ongoing website anthology protesting the US involvement in Iraq (http://www.poetsagainstthewar.org) inspiring other poetry sites such as that of the film, *Voices in Wartime* (http://www.voicesinwartime.org/VoicesInWartime/Film/Movie.aspx), poetry has been recording public events in recent years. The Internet has proven a particularly fertile ground for this kind of work, and since 11 September 2001, has blossomed. After 11 September, many poetry sites around the world perceived their role as accumulators of testament and saw their function as inclusive and democratic, welcoming in particular poetry from around the world.[7] For Israel, physically isolated by neighbouring enemy countries, the Internet has the additional advantage of providing a meeting ground, in English, for dialogue. This of course takes place primarily in non-literary environments,[8] but its influence is felt everywhere.

In contrast, Hebrew poetry seems to deal much less with the immediate political and military situation. As Michael Gluzman points out with the title of the first chapter of his book, *The Politics of Canonicity* (2003), 'The National Imperative: Writing the Nation, (Un)writing the Self' (12), the history of the establishment of the nation demanded the erasure of the personal. Contemporary Hebrew poetry has been strongly influenced by the movement in the sixties away from these previous political and ideological subjects. Hebrew poets of the early twentieth century, such as Natan Alterman and Uri Zvi Greenberg, saw their role in Hebrew culture as partially pedagogical, and the rebellion against them, the 'confessional' movement that altered American poetry with Sylvia Plath and Robert Lowell, took very strong hold. The tone of the poetry of these writers also changed, emphasizing the personal and lyrical rather than the collective experience, and moving away from the subject of the nation. The lyric preference among editors continues to influence opinion against poetry of overt political relevance, although poets such as Yitzchak Laor and Aharon Shabtai have recently provided alternative political poetry in Hebrew.

Hebrew poetry, like Israeli society, may in general disdain direct explanation and clarification, seeing political and social issues as a kind of degradation of the lofty genre of verse, a dragging down of the muse to the language of the newspaper reportage, but non-Hebrew poets have a built-in linguistic division that liberates them. And the foreignness of the English language in Israeli society seems to help provide a sense of perspective, allowing the poet to deal with material otherwise too painful and intimate, and yet so taken over by the common social discourse as to be unwieldy. Schulamith Chava HaLevy, a poet who usually writes in Hebrew, found herself penning a poem in English when she was abroad and the immediate tension under which she had been living in Jerusalem was abated sufficiently for her to write. Full of the immediate expectation of a terrorist attack, the poem, entitled 'Let Not Suddenly Boom' begins:

> Let not suddenly boom!
> then silence and then
> the screams and cries
> and the wailing sirens
> with flashing red and
> blue lights
>
> (2003: 36)

The prayer, an imprecation to the Divinity so unlike the prayers of Hebrew in which very little is asked, and only praise is given, describes the entire process of the 'cleaning up' of the remains of the victims from the point of view of the anticipated victim, a subject that would certainly be too disturbing for readers trying not to think of that very visualization. With its detailed account of the quieter hours of clean-up, and its modified type of prayer, linguistic defamiliarization enables the wrenching subject to be addressed and somehow managed.

For the writer in English, linguistic defamiliarization is not a chosen technique, but a way of life, since almost all of these writers exist and experience the matter of their poetry in the Hebrew language, but verbalize it in English. In some cases, the English becomes as sparse as the limited Hebrew vocabulary of the immigrant used in the actual experience. Lois Michal Unger's 'Suicide Bomb at the Carmel Shuk', for example, registers shopping in the market in Hebrew, in simple English terms.

> I don't buy from that cheese counter I said
> as if that would assure my life
> and anyway
> I did not buy cheese that morning
> I bought
> lettuce
> and tomatoes
> and saccharine
> and oh yes
> I tried on boots
> they were size 41
> and the man said
> get them
> even though I wear 39
> the blast occurred
> an hour later

a suicide bomber
age 16
blew himself up
and three people
buying cheese
or vegetables
or olives

(unpublished; with permission
of the author)

The use here of simplistic reportage enables the sense of an experience lived, not analyzed. The sense of the fragility of life, which frames the experience and the poem, almost seems to disappear in the unsubordinated description, but is actually central to the experience.

Yet as can be perceived from the subject of the previous poem, Israeli society is not distant and removed, but interfering and intrusive by nature. Not only is every citizen immediately and completely affected by events in the news, but the culture is also intimate by character. This linguistic defamiliarization coupled with a physical intimacy often enters into the thematics of contemporary poetry. Rochelle Mass, who moved to Israel from Winnipeg, Canada, in 1973, writes a great deal about the physical situation of living a 'normal' suburban Israeli life within view of the Palestinian town of Jenin. The following poem by Mass, entitled 'Hands on a Gun', illustrates the subject of intimacy and strangeness.

The soldier has slipped onto my shoulder again, his breath skips
with the road. His head falls to my chest; I straighten,
tightening the part of my back that usually goes sore
on rides long as this. His knee hits mine, then flips
away as the bus rolls, returns to mine, stays there.
I feel his muscles.

Hills are drying in the June sun. Goats and two camels
pass on my side and dark children sell eggplants
from plastic crates. The soldier's head falls almost
into my arms; I lift his face. His hands stay on the gun,
a scar goes from the thumb up the arm. Swollen and red.

The bus makes a sharp turn. The low area between the hills
is filled with black tents; wide women herd sheep and children
to grass left after winter. The soldier has slipped again;
I lift his face, saliva runs on my hand, then I touch his hair.
The bus stops.

Three soldiers push duffel bags in. The last eats cherries,
spits out the stones. An old lady with parsley in her lap
shouts at him, the next stone rolls under her skirt. The bus
revs up, and my soldier shakes himself like a dog out of water.
Shalom, he says.

Shalom I say and feel the sweat each time
I raised his head. *Where are we?* he asks and leans over
to see more tents and goats. *Almost there?* and answers
long way yet.
I want to look straight at him but study his hands on the gun want to know if
he's afraid. There's so much more I want to say
but you can't talk like that
to a man you hardly know.

(22 March 2005: n.p.)

Except for 'Shalom' the speaker here does not speak in any language. The soldier asks and answers his own question. And yet the two share not only the experience of physical intimacy but also the unmarked road in an Arab countryside and the uncertainty of the conclusion of their journey. Nevertheless it is the speaker who is conscious, awake, aware of the intensity not only of this experience but also of the complexity of the soldier's existence and of the weight of his burden. Although there is no political evaluation here on the part of the speaker – she neither praises and encourages the soldier nor criticizes nor pities him – there is a maternal sense of responsibility for him as well as an erotic fascination.

The distance and relation is everywhere apparent in the works of writers in English in Israel. Riva Rubin, who moved to Israel from South Africa during the sixties because of the political situation there, insists upon an aesthetic transcendence in her political perspective of the situation.

WALL
– *Kfar Kassem*

But, I said to him, can't you
see? This broken wall is breathtaking.
Its big square stones were daubed
with bitumen long ago and now
the natural granite is grinning through
so each uneven row throws light
in a different way.
So? he wanted to know. Well, I said
can't you see…
See what?

(2006: n.p.)

Kfar Kassem, an Arab village whose name is charged with guilt in Hebrew and connected with a massacre of forty-seven villagers that took place on 29 October 1956 because the villagers coming home from the fields had not heard of the shoot-to-kill curfew imposed at the sudden onset of the Sinai Campaign, was given literary resonance in S. Yizhar's story 'Hirbat Hiz'ah' ['Hiz'ah in Ruins'] (1949) that relates to this issue, and in writings by other literary figures of the time such as Natan Alterman. This resonance can only be lost in English and in a non-Israeli context.

And yet here the setting of Kfar Kassem infuses the entire poem with significance. Coupled with the title and the subject 'Wall', which in turn is electric with political controversy, there is a powerful argument to transcend the political history and all their symbolic and historical references through the clear vision of aesthetics. 'Let's go beyond the walls broken by some historical battle', she seems to say, 'Let's look at the beauty'. Yet her partner is incapable even of understanding the nature of her argument.

It is the linguistic position that allows Rubin the transcendent perspective here, even though it is the physical and emotional intimacy with the stones, the walls and the history, that must be known and understood in order to be transcended.

For others the linguistic and cultural perspective renders the poetry almost too thick to be decipherable, and there is a need for notes to transmit the multicultural sources. One of Rachel Tzvia Back's most haunting works, from *Azimuth* (2001), is rendered more complex and meaningful by the author's notes. One passage:

> I, half stranger
> at a stone
> of loss
>
> spoke for no one.
>
> I am the one
> who now speaks
>
> (I have been to the barbed North)
>
> in translations:
>
> (the tel
> is still
> mined)
> all I could carry.
>
> (72)

To contextualize this and the preceeding passage, the poet explains in the notes:

> The passages 'What happened really happened…' and 'distant bell…' are from T. Carmi's *At the Stone of Losses*, translated by Grace Schulman (JPS 1983). Carmi's 'Stone of Losses' – and hence my use of the image also – refers to the following passage from *Baba Metsia* (28b): 'There was a Stone of Losses in Jerusalem. Whoever found an object went there, and whoever lost one did the same. The finder stood and proclaimed, and the other called out the identifying marks and received it back.' The passages 'We travel like other people…', 'Speak speak…' and 'country of words…' are from Mahmoud Darwish's poem 'We Travel Like Other People' in *Modern Poetry of the Arab World* (Penguin 1986).[9]

So that when the speaker of the poem claims to have been silent and now speaks 'in translations' she is being quite literal, for speaking through her are many identical and antithetical civilizations. But, as Back claims here, only through this experience is there a possibility of being found. Back, the author of two poetry collections, *Azimuth* and *The Buffalo Poems* (2003), has also written a groundbreaking study on the American poet Susan Howe, and this multiple cultural vision is not limited to Jewish and Arab considerations.

When it is not the lens through which the contemporary scene is viewed, or the infusion of the poet, the multiple perspective is often the subject. Shirley Kaufman moved to Israel in 1973 from the United States and soon after began to deal with her dual identity. Involved in the San Francisco poetry scene in the 1960s and 1970s, Kaufman's transition to a relatively conservative and provincial poetry environment must have been a harsh one. But she immediately began to act as a bridge between the two cultures, publishing books of translations of Israeli poets such as Abba Kovner, Amir Gilboa, and, most recently, Meir Wieseltier and co-editing with Galit Hasan-Rokem, and Tamar S. Hess a volume of Hebrew feminist poems entitled *The Defiant Muse* (1999). A bilingual anthology, this monumental work presented for the first time in any language the poetry of women in Hebrew culture, and in some sense, helped to introduce feminism in a dialogue of redefinition of Hebrew culture.

As the title of an earlier collection of hers indicates, she perceives herself as having 'Roots in the Air' – belonging neither to here nor there. But Kaufman has apparently found various complex strategies for transcending this situation. One is to live with the 'hyphen', as she calls it. Even an innocent poem from her recent book, *Threshold* (2003), about her Seattle past reflects this sense of being between two places:

Jump

Sundays. Sun-narrowed eyes. My father
in the leaky rowboat unties the frayed rope
from its peg, raises his arm from the oar
he steadies and holds out his hand. My job
is to bail out the water when the dinghy leaks.
One foot in the boat, one foot on the dock:
the lake quickly widens under my crotch.
When he cries Jump, I jump, and fall in.

I've narrowed the distance, reach for him
now in his vagueness, honey on his tongue
and the songs of Zion. What did he know
about this hot wind breathing down my neck
like the future – stripping the sand from the desert.
A bright face blown off. Out there in the light
as far as my eyes can see there is only
what's happened.

If I could scoop out of the water
with my small can. I am filled with intentions.
My father says Jump. When I get to one side
what I want most is on the other.

(101)

In 'Sanctum', Kaufman shows the complexity of this hyphen. Her desire to be 'nowhere', initially might be perceived as one of escape, of going beyond the imperative of a city with thousands of years and the imperatives of times past.

Sometimes I need to be nowhere. A place
without history.
A life of wandering
like the desert generation of Moses.
The wandering Jew

(129)

But this desire becomes an awareness that there is no escaping 'history' and the imperatives of identity that living in both countries has taught her. Her own history as an American, her present history as an Israeli, have combined in her identity as Jew.

But that brings me
back into history.
Sealed rooms. Windows
criss-crossed with tape so the glass won't shatter.
A dark noose of memory around my neck.
Coffins covered with flags and flags
burning. I need to be nowhere.

(129)

Even when her poetry does reflect the immediate environment of Jerusalem there is a palpable hunger for simplification, a sense of the weight of this environment:

> The little line that has become a bridge between America and Israel has begun to sway and swing like the Golden Gate Bridge, suspended on cables between San Francisco and Marin County, and even though the wind is strong coming in from the ocean and over the bay, I begin to find my balance on it. I discover that, after all, it does connect me... I am learning to make a virtue of it.
>
> (Katz 2002: 113–14)

The need to be nowhere, to escape the imperatives of place, is not unique to Kaufman's poetry, and can be seen in many of the poets discussed. The consequences of the imperatives of place can also be felt, in varying degrees, in the work of most of the poets I have discussed.

And yet the antithesis may also be argued. From many of the poets discussed it may also be seen that the imperatives of places are not only pervasive but also have formed the sense of poetic identity. This centrality may be seen in the fact of recent publications. In 2005 three significant English literary journals in Israel have appeared: The *Jerusalem Review* and *Arc*, which halted publication four years previously for lack of funding, and *Maggid* (22 March 2005), a new literary journal from Bar Ilan University published by Toby Press. The *Jerusalem Review*, edited by Hebrew writer, critic and doyen, Gabriel Moked, Haim Marantz and myself, deals with world literature in any language but particularly encourages English writing in Israel. The tremendous transcultural success of its first four issues did not elicit a similar response in the Israel government or individual donors, and the journal has only recently succeeded in recuperating, publishing the fifth issue in November 2006. *Arc*, the journal of the Israel Association of Writers in English (IAWE 22 March 2005), was also halted in 2002 due to government withdrawal of support for official literary organizations and began to reappear only through individual efforts of members to renew publication. *Maggid*, edited by Michael Kramer, is part of a new general programme at Bar Ilan University, which includes an MA in creative writing in English. *Arc*, published since 1980, has not only highlighted all English literature in Israel, but also publishes occasional translations from other languages and English literature from other countries.

These journals are in addition to continuing publications of the previously mentioned *Ariga*, and *Voices* (22 March 2005), an annual journal of poetry, that has been in continual publication since 1971. This sudden appearance and reappearance of English literary publications reflect a sense of the need and desire to share Israeli experience with the English-speaking world. But it also exhibits a new awareness and secure sense of identity.

Notes

1 Albeit with much internal conflict as to the academic validation of this, I speak here of my own work including an alternative rock disk entitled *Thin Lips* (Pookh records) and a line of clothes containing poems with Israeli fashion house *Comme-Il-Faut*. Also Sharon Kessler has marketed a series of poems contained in tiny decorative boxes.

2 One example: The long-standing journal, *Modern Hebrew Literature*, has recently been given a long-awaited push through new and promising distribution with the Toby Press, www.tobypress.com/books/mhl.htm (accessed 22 March 2005) The Toby Press is also publishing Hebrew literature in translation. Although the subject is outside the range of this essay, this new interest in a world audience is worthy of further study.

3 For more information on Kruglanski's work with alienation and defamiliarization see Utterback (2004).

4 The talk is billed as 'A conversation on loving Jerusalem and loving in Jerusalem, on remembering and forgetting, on planting domestic stakes on the shore of eternity, on Hebrew and English as a quarrelling couple, on stones that feel pain and people who don't' (Tikkun 2004).

5 The fact that this article was written in Hebrew and anonymously translated is indication in itself of the lack of linguistic integrity.

6 The first critical work specifically on this subject, by Yochai Oppenheimer, was published in 2003 and did not include the second intifada.

7 See also Alkalay-Gut (2005).

8 See, for example, Talya Halkin's (2005) discussion of groups and dialogues in English.

9 These notes do not appear in the book of poems but are published only on the web, see Back (26 January 2006).

Part VI

The ‘loquation’ of Jewish culture

15 Voices of identity

Language in Jewish-American literature

Pascal Fischer

The 'multilingual turn in American Studies' that Werner Sollors (1997: 13) and Marc Shell (2002: 19) have promoted has gained some momentum in recent years. Michael Moon even calls it 'one of the most promising, and so far most productive, directions in comparativist literary studies of North America' (2004: 683). Whereas the growing research in this field has often fallen short of including texts in languages other than English, it has profitably explored the linguistic contact zones represented in English language literature.

Current studies in linguistics have drawn fresh attention to the close connection between language and ethnic identity (Joseph 2004: 162–93). In the case of Jewish-American writing in English, it is very rewarding to take the issue of language into account. I want to argue that particularly for authors of the immigrant period language played a major role in constructing and signalling identity. This holds true in spite of the fact that the ability to speak a certain language is no prerequisite for being a Jew. It is certainly harder to be French, English or German without the respective knowledge of French, English or German than to be a Jew without knowing any 'Jewish language'. While some ethnic identities are primarily defined by language, Jewish identity is primarily defined by a complex relation between ancestry on the one hand (child of a Jewish mother) and religion on the other. On a secondary level, though, language is connected to both of these criteria. In America it has mostly been Yiddish, the *mamaloshen* ('the mother tongue'), that is associated with ancestry and Hebrew, the *losh kodesh* ('the holy tongue'), that is associated with religion.

John Myhill has recently argued that the language Jews use for secular purposes has traditionally not been a central component of their identity (2004: 10). The importance some have nevertheless ascribed to language was, according to him, due to the influence of a non-Jewish view on language. Although his well-founded thesis, which challenges much twentieth-century scholarship, throws new light on many long-term developments, it has the disadvantage of working on the premise that the two cultures are strongly polarized. A Jewish existence devoid of non-Jewish influences is, after all, only a theoretical construct. According to the concept of transculturality, as developed by Wolfgang Welsch, cultures should neither be imagined as uniform in the inside nor clearly delineated toward the outside (1999: 195). Despite the fact that Myhill generally doesn't see any great significance of Yiddish for Jewish self-definition before the second half of the nineteenth century, he concedes that 'at least among secular eastern European Jews between about 1880 and 1930, Yiddish really did play a central role in defining Jewish identity' (2004: 159). In the process of modernization, language was now taken as a substitute for a traditional definition of Jewish existence.

In late nineteenth-century Europe as well as in America, Yiddish was certainly more than a means of communication; it clearly marked the identity of its speakers. While the status of Yiddish as a language separate from German was not commonly acknowledged and some continued to refer to it as Judeo-German or as a German dialect (Myhill 2004: 127–36; Weinberg 1982: 253–90), it was obvious that it was only Jews who spoke this 'dialect' as a mother-tongue. Moreover, the Hebrew-Aramaic alphabet is an indigenous Jewish letter system, not only used for Hebrew and Aramaic, but also for other Jewish languages like Yiddish, Judeo-Arabic and Ladino. Here again Myhill does attribute some importance to language, since the Hebrew-Aramaic alphabet 'must be taken as a significant, though secondary, component of Jewish identity' (2004: 24). The Yiddish word ייִדיש *yidish* has the double meaning of 'Yiddish' and 'Jewish' and many considered the ability to speak the language one of the hallmarks of Jewishness. Since it was only Jews who spoke Yiddish, the language served to secure the distinctiveness of the group of immigrants in America. Where Jewish-American literature deals with the question of identity, it very often does so with recourse to language.

After a few remarks about the importance of the immigration of Yiddish-speaking Jews from eastern Europe for Jewish-American culture and literature, I will examine the immigrant authors' choice of language as a literary medium. It is, after all, not natural for people to write in a language other than the one they were brought up with. Then I want to consider the different languages involved in the fictional worlds and the way they are presented including their functions and connotations. In a further step, I want to briefly outline the development of the perception and presentation of languages in later periods of Jewish-American writing, when the immigrant experience no longer captivated the imagination as it had before. Such an investigation that focuses on the linguistic dimension of the literature of an ethnic minority group can provide valuable insights into different narratological techniques and draw attention to its transnational and transcultural character. Looking at the multiplicity of languages used in much Jewish-American literature helps us to understand to what great extent Jewish-American culture has been 'characterized by mixes and permeations' and therefore most clearly fulfils the criteria Welsch outlined for 'transculturality' (1999: 197).

When in the years following the assassination of the Russian tsar Alexander II in 1881 almost two million Jews fled discrimination and persecution in the Russian 'Pale of Settlement' for the New World, a new chapter in Jewish-American history opened. The preceding waves of immigration by the Sephardim in the seventeenth and eighteenth centuries and by the German Jews in the nineteenth century had been considerably smaller. By its sheer numerical strength the eastern European immigration altered the cultural make-up of the Jewish community in America decisively. While it is notoriously difficult to arrive at a definition of Jewish-American literature, most scholars agree that it was first and foremost shaped by this group of immigrants.[1] Richard Tuerk expresses the widely-held view: 'It was [. . .] the new immigrants and their children who began what we today think of as Jewish-American literature' (1983: 137). Accordingly, the experience of immigration and assimilation initially constituted the thematic centre of gravity.

One should be careful not to imagine eastern European Jewry as homogeneous. The immigrants did not only come from regions that were far apart geographically, but also from diverse social and cultural backgrounds. Although most of the Jews who were prepared to emigrate had not been unaffected by modernity,[2] there were vast differences between secularized Jews in the cities of Russia or the eastern part of the Austro-Hungarian empire and those in the provincial small town communities, the *shtetlekh*. But in spite of these differences there was a unifying element that kept the immigrant group together: the Yiddish language. Except for a few completely Russified or Germanized Jews almost all eastern European Jews spoke Yiddish in one of its regional varieties, as is documented in the Russian census of 1897, when 98 per cent of the Jewish population stated that Yiddish was their mother tongue (Harshav 1990: 87; Fishman 1991: 86). Lacking a homeland of their own, this group of eastern European immigrants was to a large extent bound together by language. The Jews did not come from one home country they could call their own, but they did come from a large territory where in certain places people spoke a language they could call their own. In his eulogistic poem 'Yiddish' the poet Avrom Reyzen, who emigrated to America in 1914, doesn't only refer to his mother tongue as 'the wonder of my existence' but also calls it 'my home in every place' (Shandler 2003: 133).

Most of the Jewish immigrants initially adhered to their native language in the immigrant quarters of New York, Boston or Chicago, as Sol Steinmetz remarks: 'Yiddish [. . .] was the principal language of American Jews at home and in the streets from the late 1880s to the late 1920s' (1986: 17). The fact that the immigrant quarters were teeming with Yiddish speakers from all dialect areas fostered people's awareness of language in general and of its identity function in particular: 'Never before had so many Yiddish-speaking Jews been forced to rub shoulders with other Jews from different regions and speaking different dialects' (Roskies 2003: 70). Instead of effacing regional allegiances amongst the Jewish immigrants, the American experience initially strengthened the consciousness of belonging to a particular dialectal and cultural group like the *litvaks*, the *rumener* or the *galitsyaner*. According to David Roskies this unique historical situation also led to a heightened awareness of the three basic components of Yiddish, the Germanic, the Slavic and the Hebrew elements. Yiddish writers in America like Morris Rosenfeld, Moyshe-Leyb Halpern, Lamed Shapiro and Sholem Asch exploited the 'triangular structure' of their native language in new ways (2003: 71–2).

If one bears in mind that Yiddish publishing 'exploded' in America around the turn of the century and Yiddish literature continued to enjoy great popularity (Berkowitz 2003: 19), the very decision of some of the immigrant writers to use

English as a medium of artistic expression instead of their native language is especially noteworthy. Writers like Abraham Cahan, Anzia Yezierska, Mary Antin, Elias Tobenkin and Ezra Brudno had been born in eastern Europe and had to learn the English language under difficult circumstances.

In his autobiography, Cahan recalls how he started to learn some bits of English aboard the *British Queen* with a dictionary he had bought in a harbour in England, a stop-over on his way to the New World (Marovitz 1996: 15). In the Lower East Side of New York, where most Jewish immigrants settled after their arrival, Cahan was known as a proponent of Yiddish. As a convinced socialist and newspaper man, he stressed the necessity of using Yiddish to reach the masses. According to his comrade Bernard Weinstein, Cahan was the first to deliver a Yiddish socialist speech in America (1924: 44). In view of the fact that there was hardly any Jewish leader who was more deeply immersed in the Yiddish culture of the Lower East Side, it is indeed remarkable that Cahan became the pioneer of Jewish-American writing in English. It was certainly partly due to the success of his early fictional works in Yiddish that Cahan decided to address a wider audience by the use of English. Further encouraged by William Dean Howells, who had read Cahan's first short story published in English, 'A Providential Match', he started writing his first English novel *Yekl. A Tale of the New York Ghetto* (1896). Apart from serving his desire to transcend the confines of the Jewish immigrant community and become part of the wider culture, Cahan's use of English can also be interpreted as an attempt to explain the Jewish immigrant experience to the American public and thus to act as a mediator between the two cultures.[3] While the portrayal of his Jewish characters in *Yekl* contains some critical remarks, it is nevertheless an appropriate means to promote a better understanding of the cares and troubles of immigrant life. In an article entitled 'The Russian Jew in America' (1898) Cahan seeks to present the Jewish immigrants as positively as possible. Countering the arguments of the opponents of immigration, he puts particular emphasis on the ambition of his fellow immigrants to learn the English language and their gift for doing so (132–3). The very fact that the article is written in immaculate English serves as an implicit but irrefutable proof of his argument.

Gert Buelens has shown that Jewish-American immigrant narratives should be seen as active interventions in the debate about the restriction of immigration and the ability of the immigrants to assimilate, rather than as mere reflections of the immigrant experience (1994: 89). Only by using the English language could Jewish authors convince sceptics of the willingness of the Jews to assimilate. The use of English by authors like Mary Antin, Elias Tobenkin and Ezra Brudno was not only a prerequisite but also served as an example in their campaign for the acceptance of Jewish immigrants in America.

One should, however, not underestimate the immigrants' true fascination with English, a language containing the promise of belonging to a culture many eagerly embraced. When the protagonist in Mary Antin's autobiographical novel *The Promised Land* (1912) describes her love for the English language, we sense that the author is giving a true account of her own feelings: 'I shall never have a better opportunity to make public declaration of my love for the English language [. . .]

It seems to me that in any other language happiness is not so sweet, logic is not so clear' (1912; 1997: 164).[4]

Whereas the prestige of English was high, many held Yiddish in low esteem around the turn of the century. Benjamin Harshav outlines the common stereotype of the time: 'Yiddish had to defend itself against the double accusation of being a "jargon," a distorted and poor form of German, and an unprincipled hodge-podge of words stolen from various languages' (1990: 28). The accusation that Yiddish was an inferior dialect was not only levelled against it from outside the Jewish community but also from inside. In eastern Europe it was particularly the Jewish enlightenment, the *Haskalah*, that looked on the language with disdain: 'for many followers of the *Haskalah*, the language epitomized all that was wrong with traditional Jewish life' (Shandler 2003: 128). But also in America many continued to refer to their own language as a 'corrupted German dialect', as Morris Hillquit did in his memoirs *Loose Leaves from a Busy Life* (1934: 17), and the term 'jargon' was common currency in the Jewish quarters of the American cities (Bluestein 1989; 1999: xxiv).

Even Abraham Cahan, who was emotionally much attached to his mother tongue, had reservations about the language and initially published his Yiddish works under a pseudonym. He later pointed out that at the turn of the century the term 'Yiddish Literature' was something of a joke (Chametzky 1977: 54). The Yiddish tradition was an oral one and the use of Yiddish as a literary language still relatively new. According to John Myhill, the very idea that Yiddish was capable of developing a formal written register was due to Gentile influences (2004: 8, 130). If we accept this argument, the decision of Jewish authors to write in English rather than in their mother tongue is perfectly in line with traditional Jewish views on language.

Whatever their individual reasons for writing in English were, most Jewish-American authors of the immigrant period acknowledged the importance of Yiddish for Jewish self-definition in their novels and short stories. The narrator of Samuel Ornitz' novel *Allrightniks Row* (1923) remembers how the Jews of the Lower East Side conflated 'Yiddish' and 'Jewish' in their perception of fellow immigrants. When one day immigrants from the Balkans, whose native language was Ladino, moved into a house in the Jewish quarter, 'the neighbours thought they were not Jews because they did not speak Yiddish' (1923; 1986: 44). A similar connection between the Yiddish language and Jewishness is evident in Henry Roth's novel *Call it Sleep* (1934). When the young immigrant child David, who is growing up in the Lower East Side of Manhattan, is asked in Yiddish by an old woman if he is Jewish, his reaction is surprise: 'For a fleeting instant, David wondered how he could have understood her if he hadn't been a Jew' (1934; 1970: 318).

While most Jewish authors of eastern European descent stress the unifying aspect of Yiddish,[5] Sidney Nyburg, who came from a German-Jewish family, emphasizes the dangers of defining Jewish identity too strongly in linguistic terms. When in Nyburg's novel *The Chosen People* (1917) the posh Rabbi Graetz, the head of an established German reformed congregation, comes to the bed of a dying Jewish immigrant from Russia, whose Yiddish he doesn't understand, he is contemptuously called a 'goy', a non-Jew, by the Russian immigrant (1917; 1986: 64–5). The language barrier symbolizes a cultural barrier within the Jewish community that can only be overcome with considerable difficulty.

Jewish-American writers have not only used Yiddish to mark the boundaries of the Jewish community, but have also described it as an element that connects the community with other cultures. The fact that Yiddish is a mixed language is proof of its historical evolution and continuous exchange and interaction. The strong consciousness of the composite character of the language with its Germanic basis, Hebrew elements and Slavic influences, which characterized the Yiddish language in America at the beginning of the twentieth century and which Roskies has observed in Yiddish writing, is reflected in some Anglophone works as well. In Elias Tobenkin's novel *Witte Arrives* (1916), the immigrant Masha Witkowski and her children are 'cheered to the marrow' when they realize that the conductor of their train speaks German: 'With a man who spoke German they felt kinship. Masha even took it as a good omen. She put her questions in the most cosmopolitan Yiddish she could summon to her command' (1916; 1968: 3). Here, the effort to modify the Yiddish language in the direction of the German standard has the very practical aim of improving intelligibility. Mamie, a character in Cahan's novel *Yekl*, however, exploits the kinship of the two languages to elevate her own language by drawing on the prestige of German. The narrator – and by extension Cahan – does not seem to be very keen on this strategy and disparagingly refers to Mamie's 'affectedly Germanized' Yiddish (1896; 1970: 49).

While the immigrant authors usually see Yiddish as an integral part of Jewish life, some nevertheless betray their own doubts about the language's value in their works. When Cahan refers to Yiddish as the 'omnivorous Jewish jargon' (1896; 1970: 38) to illustrate the language's readiness to integrate new words, he evokes an unpleasant or even threatening image and – maybe inadvertently – reveals his own repulsion. In Brudno's *The Fugitive* (1904) the Russian-born first-person narrator tells us about the first days he spends in New York after having lived in central and western Europe. That he has to use his native Yiddish in the Jewish quarter again amounts to an atavistic relapse for him: 'Again I was babbling the Jewish jargon as in the beginning of my miserable childhood' (1904: 290).

Considering the importance of Yiddish for Jewish life in the immigrant quarters, it does not come as a surprise that most Jewish authors writing about the immigrant experience tried to represent Yiddish speech in their fictional works. Yet the strategies they pursued differed widely. Sidney Nyburg probably chooses the least difficult way: whenever his characters converse in Yiddish the narrative voice changes into indirect speech and simply tells his readers that the original language was Yiddish. But the German-Jewish Nyburg is an exception, as he was not too familiar with the language of the eastern European Jews. Portraying the Russian immigrant community from the outside, he adopts the role of cultural as well as linguistic interpreter for his implied German-Jewish readers. It is, however, not only in the case of indirect discourse that Yiddish speech is presented in translated form. In his later novel *The Rise of David Levinsky* (1917), Cahan renders Yiddish for the most part as Standard English direct speech.

The same is done by Elias Tobenkin in *Witte Arrives*. In the following example the word *yiddish* is tellingly translated as *Jewish*: 'I always talk Jewish to mama' (1916; 1968: 25).

While most Jewish-American authors translate the Yiddish of their characters, they do not translate it into immaculate idiomatic English, but into a kind of English that reminds the reader of the source language. Authors like Cahan, Yezierska, Ornitz or Brudno regularly intersperse their passages of direct speech with a few Yiddish words. These can be interjections that are stereotypically associated with Jewish discourse like *Nu*, *Ach* or *Oi weh!* or lexical words expressing concepts that are part of Jewish culture like *shadkhan* ('Jewish marriage broker'), *cheder* ('Hebrew primary school') or *tzimess* ('a desert made of carrots, honey and raisins'). Whereas the use of these words can be explained by the lack of satisfactory English counterparts, this explanation does not apply to all Yiddish words. In his novel *Yekl* Cahan uses words like *poritz* and *panenke* in the main text and supplies the English equivalents *nobelman* respectively *young nobelwoman* in footnotes. These concepts are definitely not particularly Jewish and the Yiddish words are dispensable. Although Cahan could have used the English words *father*, *papa* or *dad* in Gitl's exclamation to her son 'Yosselé, look! Here is *taté!*' (1896; 1970: 35), he preserves the Yiddish original, in this case even without the English translation. With this kind of 'devised translational interference' (Sternberg 1981: 227) the author certainly wanted the reader to experience some elements of the language his characters are speaking. The fact, though, that the Yiddish elements appear most frequently in the speech of the least assimilated character, the young immigrant woman Gitl, shows how close the connection between the Yiddish language and Jewish identity was perceived by Cahan. Gitl's language is a metonym for her identity: it cannot be completely translated into English, just as her identity cannot be completely assimilated into America.

As some authors of the immigrant period wanted their readers to experience more of the character of Yiddish, they even presented a few lines of transliterated Yiddish in their novels. After her positive experience with the German-speaking conductor, Masha Witkowski in Tobenkin's novel tries her luck in addressing a policeman: '*Sprechen Sie Deitsch?*' But the policeman retorts: 'no Dutch' (1916; 1968: 7). In a scene at the immigration office in Henry Roth's *Call it Sleep*, the newly arrived Genya asks her husband Albert, who has already spent some time in America, shortly after their reunion:

> 'Gehen vir voinen du? In Nev York?'
> 'Nein. Bronzeville. Ich hud dir schoin geschriben.'
> (1934; 1970: 154)

As the direct presentation of transliterated Yiddish hinders communication with the Anglophone reader, one usually does not find much of it. The next words we hear from Genya in the novel are already given in very poetic English.

In the same way as Genya remains fairly isolated from the wider American culture, her Yiddish remains virtually unchanged. Her son David, conversely, has assimilated his language in the direction of English while roaming the streets of the Lower East Side of New York, a fact noticed by his mother: 'Your Yiddish is more than one-half English now. I'm being left behind' (154). Yiddish had always been very open to adopting new vocabulary from other languages, but the influx of words was extraordinarily high in America. This reality is also given special attention in *Yekl*. For Cahan it is even important to distinguish between different levels of English influence in Boston and New York. We learn that the Yiddish spoken in Boston is 'more copiously spiced with mutilated English than is the language of the metropolitan Ghetto in which our story lies' (1896; 1970: 2).

Most Jewish immigrants did, of course, not content themselves with using a few English words in their Yiddish, but wanted to really learn the new language. English was, after all, a presumably infallible sign of Americanization. The first-person narrator in Cahan's *The Rise of David Levinsky* is highly motivated: 'I threw myself into my new studies with unbounded enthusiasm' (1917; 1993: 129). While this ambition as well as the mental training that his Talmud education had given him facilitate his progress, he cannot suppress an amusing remark about the new language: 'English impressed me as the language of a people afflicted with defective organs of speech' (130). That learning the language was a difficult process is shown again and again in Jewish-American immigrant literature. The stories of Leo Rosten are legendary for the awkward attempts of their title figure Mr Kaplan to acquire the rudiments of the new idiom (Ross 1937). When the young teacher Sara Smolinsky in Yezierska's novel *Bread Givers* (1925) does pronunciation exercises with her pupils, she cannot help slipping back into the immigrant language herself only to be corrected by her colleague Mr Seelig, a Jewish immigrant as well (1925; 1999: 271–2).

The Jewish immigrant dialect of English is sometimes referred to as *Yiddish English* or *Yinglish* and Jewish-American authors frequently made an enormous effort to depict it in their works. Whereas some authors restrict themselves to employing a slightly different word order in the speech of their characters, others try to convey the immigrant speech as realistically as possible on all linguistic levels. Generally, novelists have at their disposal a wide variety of possibilities to represent deviations in the fields of phonetics, morphology, syntax and on the textual level. Understandably enough, the problems are greatest in phonetics and graphemics, as the English spelling system is not strictly phonographic. It is therefore sometimes hard to decide which pronunciation an author had in mind when he gives a non-standard spelling for an English word.

The literary dialect employed in Jewish-American literature was influenced by the vogue of 'local colour writing' in America at the beginning of the twentieth century. In contrast to the regional variants in the works of this literary movement, authors like Cahan, Yezierska, Rosten, Ornitz and Henry Roth rendered a dialect[6] that was to a large extent determined by interference or language transfer from the native language. Cahan acknowledges this fact explicitly in his novel *Yekl*, where the narrator informs us that the English spoken in the dancing school of the

Jewish immigrants was 'broken and mispronounced in as many different ways as there were Yiddish dialects represented in that institution' (1896; 1970: 17). The heightened awareness of the different Yiddish dialects characteristic of the early immigrant period is documented by Cahan's efforts to make these dialects accessible to the reader through the filter of English. What is most salient is Cahan's reproduction in English of a pronunciation feature that is typical of the North-Eastern (or Lithuanian) Yiddish dialect. That the protagonist of the novel is unable to pronounce the English voiceless alveolar fricative correctly and instead uses the palatal fricative in words like *beeshnesh* (business) or *shent* (cent) is a consequence of his native Yiddish dialect, where these two sounds are not in phonological opposition. Furthermore, since Lithuanian Yiddish doesn't distinguish between long and short vowels, Yekl hardly pays attention to vowel length in English, for instance when he pronounces the English words *pitch*, *kick* and *mister* as *peetch*, *keeck* and *meester*. His peculiar accent marks Yekl as a Lithuanian Jew or *litvak*, a provincial type much laughed about at that time. With Yekl, Abraham Cahan presents a character who parades his assimilation by speaking English, but the way Yekl pronounces English exposes the *litvak* in him and indicates that he still partly belongs to the Old World. Yekl's colleague Mamie, who speaks 'in the dialect of the Polish Jews' (49), never makes Yekl's mistakes, because in her Central Eastern variant of Yiddish, the contrast between the alveolar and the palatal sibilants as well as the length of vowels are of phonological value. It was obviously one of Cahan's main objectives to portray his group of immigrants as heterogeneous and diverse. His depiction of completely different personalities is supported by his use of different linguistic varieties. By illustrating that Jewish culture is neither uniform in the inside nor clearly delineated toward the outside, Cahan's Yinglish encapsulates the transculturality of immigrant America.

Although Yiddish plays a much more central role than Hebrew in Jewish-American literature at the beginning of the twentieth century, some authors nevertheless acknowledge the importance of the 'holy tongue', which was traditionally reserved for written and religious purposes. With Hebrew they usually accentuate the religious dimension of Jewish identity. As in the case of the vernacular, some authors were not satisfied with making metalinguistic remarks about its use, but actually tried to render the language in their novels and short stories.

In his novel *The Island Within* (1928), Ludwig Lewisohn, another author with a German-Jewish background, sometimes provides a transliteration of individual sentences in Hebrew followed by a Standard English translation, as in the following example: '*Rachmonim bnei rachmonim* – we are the merciful children of merciful parents' (1928; 1997: 8). In other sentences he leaves out the original altogether and gives only the translation, however, mostly not in contemporary English, but in archaic English. The curse 'may their names be blotted out' (16), which an old Jewish couple in the novel put on apostates, is taken directly from the translation of Psalm 109:13 in the *King James Version* of the Bible. The same

Christian Bible translation is made use of in Cahan's novel *The Rise of David Levinsky*, where the title hero recites Psalm 104 from his Hebrew prayer book while crossing the ocean on his way to the new world:

> Thou who coverest thyself with light as with a garment, who stretchest out the heavens like a curtain: who layeth the beams of his chambers in the waters: who maketh the clouds his chariot: who walketh upon the wings of the wind.
>
> (1917; 1993: 86)

The role of a Christian Bible translation for rendering Ashkenazic Hebrew by Jewish-American authors is a powerful example of cultural permeations and demonstrates the transcultural status of their literature.

Whereas Lewisohn presents just a small sample of transliterated Hebrew, Henry Roth supplies us with a longer passage in his novel *Call it Sleep*. The English reader experiences the 'holy tongue' as the pupil David does, who is not yet able to understand its meaning. Since it is the sound that matters to Roth, he does not provide a translation:

> 'Beshnas mos hamelech Uziyahu vawere es adonoi yoshav al kesai rum venesaw, vshulav malaiim es hahahol. Serafim omdim memal lo shash kanowfayim, shash kanowfayim lawehhad, beshtayim yahase fanav uvishtayim yahase raglov uvishtayim yaofaif.'
>
> All his senses dissolved into the sound. The lines, unknown, dimly surmised, thundered in his heart with limitless meaning, rolled out and flooded the last shores of his being.
>
> (1934; 1970: 343)

Again language seems to be at the centre of Jewish identity.

From the 1940s onwards the thematic focus of Jewish-American literature widened from the immigrant experience to a broader horizon. As Jews had to a large degree become submerged in the American mainstream, the subject of linguistic assimilation consequently also lost in importance. Yet, the fact that authors of the second and third generation, who often had English as their mother tongue, regarded Yiddish to a lesser extent as a part of their existence, does not mean that it became insignificant. After the holocaust and the foundation of the State of Israel, the connotations and functions of Yiddish and Hebrew changed considerably. Yiddish was increasingly associated with the victims of the holocaust while Hebrew – apart from retaining its religious meaning – became linked with the image of the self-assured Israeli.

Saul Bellow's controversial novel *The Victim* (1947), published just two years after the death camps had been liberated, while portraying a problematic Gentile-Jewish relationship, does not yet make Yiddish the language of the victims. One of the few Yiddish sentences that are given in transliteration refers to the old stereotype of the Jew as a 'money grubber' and thus indirectly addresses the question of anti-Semitism. The Jewish protagonist Asa Leventhal remembers with discomfort and shame a verse his father had often spoken:

> *Ruf mir Yoshke, ruf mir Moshke,*
> *Aber gib mir die groschke.*
> (Bellow 1947; 1984: 98)

The fact that Bellow gives the English equivalent of the proverb refutes the prejudice that it is indicative of a particular Jewish mindset: 'Call me Ikey, call me Moe, but give me the dough.' (98–9) While Yiddish doesn't play a prominent role in this early work, it seems to possess great significance for the title figure in *Herzog* (1964), probably Bellow's most Jewish novel. It is particularly in the interior monologue of the rambling protagonist that Yiddish words and proverbs appear – an indication of how strongly his identity is still controlled by the immigrant past, in spite of his ostensible rootlessness. His antagonist Valentine Gersbach, on the other hand, employs the language as mere affectation and crudely uses and misuses individual words to exploit ethnic solidarity. But although the narrator comments that 'Herzog's Yiddish background was genteel' (1964; 1984: 60), this doesn't meant that his Yiddish is always respectful and polite. The curses of Herzog and his aunt Zipporah live up to Bellow's characterization of Yiddish in *Him with His Foot in His Mouth and Other Stories* (1984): 'Yiddish is severe and bears down without mercy. Yes, it is often delicate, lovely, but it can be explosive as well' (16).

In Bernard Malamud's novel *The Assistant* (1957), the Jewish protagonist Morris was still born in Russia and speaks the Jewish immigrant variant of English. Although his Yinglish is rendered by a literary dialect that does not have recourse to respellings, it is clearly reminiscent of Yiddish. The Yiddish grammatical and lexical elements contribute much to the claustrophobic atmosphere that makes *The Assistant* a good example for what Emily Miller Budick has called 'holocaust-inflected' literature, works that only allude to the holocaust (2003: 216).

The connotation of suffering is also characteristic of Yiddish in Philip Roth's short story 'Eli, the Fanatic' (1959), in which the insecurities of the assimilated Jewish American middle class are exposed by the arrival of a few traditionally clad holocaust survivors from eastern Europe. In a kind of pseudo-Whorfian speculation, the newcomer Tzuref ingenuously asks one of the assimilated Jews: 'You have the word "suffer" in English?' (265) In contrast to this, Yiddish in Roth's *Portnoy's Complaint* (1969) is not evocative of the holocaust. The author, who grew up without any deeper knowledge of Yiddish, just intersperses a few dirty words of lowly immigrant life as part of the generally raw language of the novel.

Writers like Roth are targeted by the Yiddish poet Edelshtein in Cynthia Ozick's 'Envy; or Yiddish in America' (1969):

> *Jewish* novelists! Savages! The allrightnik's children, all they know is to curse the allrightnik! Their Yiddish! One word here, one word there. *Shikseh* on one page, *putz* on the other, and that's the whole vocabulary! [...] They

know ten words for, excuse me, penis, and when it comes to a word for learning they're impotent!

(1969; 1971: 79–80)

When Sarah Blacher Cohen writes that this diatribe 'does not apply to Cynthia Ozick [. . .] the Yiddishe Mama of Jewish-American letters' (1994: 47), she is only partly right, because she overlooks that Ozick's own story is sprinkled with untranslated Yiddish words. This irony is actually a key to the interpretation of the story, as it shows the author's distance to her protagonist. While we sometimes feel impelled to mourn the death of Yiddish with Edelshtein, his attempts at linguistic purity appear ridiculous.[7]

In 1970 Ozick advocated the creation of a 'New Yiddish', but although James Loeffler holds that what she wanted was a 'new Jewish language corresponding to Yinglish' (2002: 151), it is doubtful that she primarily had a linguistic mix in mind. Her ideal to 'pour not merely the Jewish sensibility, but the Jewish vision, into the vessel of English' (Ozick 1970; 1983: 176) remained hazy – probably a reason why she abandoned the whole idea as a 'literary conceit' later (152). When Ozick in a personal letter observes that in her time 'murdered Yiddish begins to take on some of the holiness of liturgy and hallowed Hebrew becomes workaday mamaloshen' (cit. Cohen 1994: 48) this characterization does not describe her own literature, where Hebrew is still the 'holy tongue'. This is particularly evident in her *Puttermesser Papers* (1997), in which Hebrew appears to Ruth Puttermesser 'not so much a language for expression as a code for the world's design' (5). After the title figure has formed a female golem from earth, she visualizes and then pronounces the word השם *hashem* ('the holy name') and thus breathes life into her creation (40). That Ozick wrote the word in Hebrew characters attests to the fascination this alphabet still exerts.

Philip Roth in his novel *The Counterlife* (1987) documents the functional and connotation transformation Hebrew has undergone as a result of Zionism. In one version of the kaleidoscopic postmodern story, which is retold in several forms, the assimilated Jewish dentist Henry Zuckerman from New Jersey enters an *ulpan*, a Hebrew school, in a Westbank settlement, to establish a new identity for himself. It is, however, not so much a spiritual rebirth he is looking for, but masculine self-assurance. The character Shuki summarizes the connotation of Hebrew as opposed to Yiddish when he talks about the feelings American Jews have when they see bearded Jews with weapons in Judea: 'The Beards to remind them of saintly Yiddish weakness and the guns to reassure them of heroic Hebrew force' (Roth 1987: 75). Apart from forming the masculine counterpoint to an ostensibly feminized Yiddish culture, Hebrew for some Jews in the novel also represents the normalcy of Israeli life in contrast to a precarious Diaspora existence. While Hebrew has metamorphosed from the holy tongue to a means of every-day communication, Yiddish, the traditional vernacular, is sanctified. On the other hand, Henry's brother Nathan, a novelist who resembles his creator Philip Roth in many respects, is not too preoccupied with the question of Jewish languages: '– not the semantic range of classical Hebrew but the jumpy beat of American English was what excited me' (53).

Even though many Jewish-American authors today are again much involved with questions of Jewishness and Judaism, Nathan Zuckerman's position is probably representative of the majority of them. They occasionally quote a Yiddish phrase to evoke the old homeland, the immigrant experience or the holocaust and they sometimes use a few Hebrew words to emphasize their religious ties or their attachment to Israel, but it is the English language they use most naturally to voice their thoughts on different aspects of Jewish identity.

Notes

1 This holds true in spite of the recent interest in the writings of Sephardi and German Jews before the mass influx of eastern European Jews around the turn of the last century. See e.g. Kramer (2003).

2 Charles S. Liebman challenged the older notion that most of the immigrants who came to America were strictly orthodox. According to him, their decision to leave the traditional communities in eastern Europe was a consequence of enlightenment influences (1965: 27–30).

3 Aviva Taubenfeld (1998: 148) has shown that Cahan adopted a different voice in the Yiddish translation of his novel, which he published after he was initially unable to find a publisher for *Yekl*; see also Chametzky (1977: ix).

4 See also Wirth-Nesher (1998: 214).

5 In *The Rise of David Levinsky*, Cahan, however, mentions some assimilated Jews in Russia who did not only wear Gentile clothes but spoke Russian instead of Yiddish. The first-person narrator remembers his unequivocal verdict on them: 'To me they were apostates, sinners in Israel' (1917; 1993: 42).

6 I use the term *dialect* in a wide sense, comprising regiolects, sociolects, ethnolects as well as learner languages.

7 This ambiguity towards her characters is typical of Ozick, as Hillel Halkin has recently pointed out: 'Often in Ozick's fiction, indeed, the characters that intellectually seem most designed to be repudiated are the ones to whom, experientially, we are most drawn' (2005: 52).

16 The words to say it

The loss of language and power in Cynthia Ozick's 'Envy; or, Yiddish in America'

Miriam Sivan

God made man because He loves stories.

Yiddish proverb

In Cynthia Ozick's 58 page long short story, 'Envy; or, Yiddish in America', Hersh Edelshtein is desperately seeking a translator. Though he is forty years in America, he continues to write in Yiddish, his *mamaloshen* – mother tongue – for he admits he is no Kosinski or Nabokov (Ozick 1969; 1971: 52). He will always remain green inside (52) and therefore outside of English. But it is not merely that he cannot, technically, compose good poetry in his adopted English. Yiddish, as *mamaloshen* and the literature it has inspired since the 1500s, is his 'substitute for religion and statehood, it [is] a State in itself, "Yiddishland"; to abandon it [is] to abandon the whole culture' (Harshav 1990: 136). This would be, for Edelshtein, an act of unconscionable treason, tantamount to patri- or, as some may insist, matricide.[1]

For many millennia books have helped define the landscape of Jewish nationhood. In Heine's phrase, *das aufgeschriebene Vaterland*, the scripted fatherland, was fundamental to the forging of the identity of a stateless, landless people. Even the Bible, the fundamental text for Jewish civilization, was composed and incorporated into their culture when Israel was in the Sinai desert, still in a state of exile, though no longer enslaved. And yet from the time of the Roman conquest, when the kingdom of Israel was destroyed and its people scattered for the most part throughout the Middle East, North Africa and Europe, local tongues were used for everyday life. Hebrew became the privileged language, the one used for ritual and recital, the container of national memory and the outline of their idiosyncratic history (Yerushalmi 1982: 11). Of all the diasporic languages and dialects, Yiddish, which means Jewish in the language itself, was the most popular (Goldsmith 1997: 30). Incomparable sacred and secular 'Jewish' literature was produced in it (28).

Born and raised in the Yiddish culture of Russia, Edelshtein cannot but continue to contribute to the rich and unique literary tradition in which he was nurtured. In fact, for Edelshtein, knowledge of Yiddish is the accurate measure of a person's familiarity with Jewish culture. He derides Jewish American writers as

' "*Amerikaner-geboren.*" Spawned in America, pogroms a rumour, *mamaloshen* a stranger, history a vacuum' (Ozick 1969; 1971: 41). He is critical of those Jewish American writers who sprinkle Yiddish among their prose, as one would a dull paprika on a casserole, to give it some colour without adding real flavour. As an avid reader of these Jewish American novelists, Edelshtein says they 'know ten words for, excuse me, penis, and when it comes to a word for learning they're impotent' (80). For them, Yiddish is a kind of hip kitsch, a way of gaining entry into a savvy ethnic humour which had 'a soul of its own [and was] a way of excluding the gentile mainstream which formerly enslaved, oppressed, and finally tried to exterminate the Jews' (Damon 1991: 14).

Benjamin Harshav has cited Max Weinreich's observation that while Yiddish may have an unimpressive selection of names for flowers, it has three words for 'question': *frage* – derived from German, *kashe* – from Aramaic, and *shayle* – from Hebrew (1990: 4). The culture and language which placed such emphasis on the power of the intellect, on the inevitability of open-endedness,[2] on the necessity of a discerning humour, is what Edelshtein feels is being eclipsed with these flip sprinklings of bawdy language.

And he is enraged by those Jewish American writers who claim to have no cultural, let alone religious, affinity with Jewishness. He rants that he wants to remind Norman Mailer 'what F. Kafka, rest in peace, said to the German-speaking, already very comfortable, Jews of Prague, Czechoslovakia: "Jews of Prague! You know more Yiddish than you think!" ' (Ozick 1969; 1971: 52). For Edelshtein, to know Yiddish is to be Jewish.[3]

Yiddish, as a diasporic language of a displaced migratory people, is a uniquely hybrid tongue. Medieval German, Jewish dialects of Old French and Old Italian, Slavic languages and Rabbinic Hebrew have been, over time, incorporated into it. As a language which enabled Jews in Europe to 'mediate between their daily lives and the Hebrew religious and educational heritage on the one hand, and the languages and beliefs of the surrounding Christian world on the other', Yiddish is a quintessential language of resistance. 'It [is] the extraterritorial enclosure which kept the separate social and religious network of the Jews within its own possible world' (Harshav 1990: xiii). Its very construction reveals how, in Homi Bhabha's words, 'social articulation of difference, from a minority perspective, is a complex, on-going negotiation that seeks to authorize cultural hybridities that emerge in moments of historical transformation' (1994: 2).

And it is this language, this deliberation of a minority culture, which Edelshtein is trying desperately to salvage as he searches in vain for a translator. Rendering his poetry into English is his only recourse for unlike other languages, Yiddish has been 'lost, murdered. The language – a museum. Of what other language can it be said', Edelshtein muses, 'that it died a sudden and definite death, in a given decade, on a given piece of soil? Where are the speakers of ancient Etruscan? Who was the last man to write a poem in Linear B? Attrition, assimilation. Death by mystery not gas' (Ozick 1969; 1971: 42). When one-third of the Jewish people perished in the concentration camps and in the woods of Eastern Europe, Edelshtein lost his readers. This slaughter was followed by

Stalin's purges which brought to a decisive halt any literary productions in Yiddish in Russia. For a while Yiddish speakers in America maintained their cultural and linguistic connection to Eastern Europe. But not for long. The price of American Jewry's successful assimilation into the mainstream culture came at the expense of Yiddish. Young American readers and intellectuals 'spit out the Yiddish that had bred them for the sake of Western Civilization' (45). Like Edelshtein's fellow poet, Baumzweig, their sons complete doctoral degrees on *Sir Gawain and the Green Knight*, on Carson McCullers (45).

Without a Yiddish readership, without someone who is willing and able to translate his work into English, Edelshtein is threatened with an extinction similar to those readers whose lives ended prematurely during the Second World War. And to let Yiddish die is to violate Emil Fackenheim's ' "614th commandment," forbidding Jews to give Hitler posthumous victories' (1982; 1994: xix). Edelshtein has no choice but to seek translation, for like other contemporary writers, as George Steiner wrote, he looks to 'English translation for his window on the world' (1975; 1981: 468).

English is the language of common currency, not only in Edelshtein's home town of New York, but the world over. Even Kwame Anthony Appiah acknowledges that postcolonial intellectuals in Africa 'are almost entirely dependent for their support [...] [on] the Euro-American publisher and reader' (1991; 1996: 63). And yet English remains 'one of the [languages] least translated into' (Venuti 1988: 160).

For Edelshtein the thought that his hated rival, Yankel Ostrover, should be the only Yiddish writer translated and published in English, and by default 'the only evidence that there was once a Yiddish tongue, a Yiddish literature? And all others lost? Lost! Drowned. Snuffed out. Under the earth. As if never' (Ozick 1969; 1971: 51), was almost as intolerable to him as the idea of not writing in Yiddish at all.

For the narrator of the story says: 'The difference between [Edelshtein] and Ostrover was this: Ostrover wanted to save only himself, Edelshtein wanted to save Yiddish' (56). And in order to save Yiddish from oblivion, Edelshtein is convinced that he needs to have his poems translated into English. His unsuccessful search reflects André Lefevere's analysis of the politics inherent in this co-creative act: 'Translation has to do with authority and legitimacy and ultimately, with power' (1992: 2). Lawrence Venuti writes that

> asymmetries, inequities, relations of domination and dependence exist in every act of translating, of putting the translated in the service of the translating culture. Translators are complicit in the institutional exploitation of foreign texts and cultures.
>
> (1988: 4)

For Edelshtein, any potential translator holds all the power. Etymologically, to translate means to 'carry across', and without this, his work will never cross the cultural divide for publishers will not even consider his poems until they are presentable in English. And the pool of individuals who not only know Yiddish, but also know literary Yiddish, and not only know literary Yiddish, but also know literary English, is tiny and fickle. Ostrover's main translator, a woman born in Russia and educated at Vassar, is a rare breed. She calls herself a 'cultural hermaphrodite' (Ozick 1969; 1971: 55) and claims that it is her literary and not merely linguistic talent that transforms Ostrover's traditional Yiddish prose into what is lauded as modern English.

Ostrover's translator prevails over the language not so much by raising the original into a higher and purer linguistic air, as Walter Benjamin claimed translations were wont to do (1923; 1969: 75), but by domesticating the text, by dehistoricizing it, and working it until it conforms to the local market's aesthetic values (Venuti 1988: 67). Her claims of simplifying the language, of 'tak[ing] out all the nice homey commas he sprinkles like a fool' (Ozick 1969; 1971: 55), are criticized by Edelshtein and Baumzweig. Not because these boasts enforce Venuti's claim that often translations are intent on 'suppressing the linguistic and cultural differences of the foreign text, assimilating it to the dominant values in the target-language culture' (1988: 31). They object to the translator's self-aggrandizement. She claims Ostrover is great because of her. Because of her, the English reader is able to identify with the text and ensure its lack of censure. Because of her he is modern. Not that Edelshtein doubts that Ostrover's work is benefiting greatly from the face-lifts, from the attention he receives at the hands of his translators. But Edelshtein protests against one woman taking all the credit for this Frankensteinian transformation. He knows too well that 'Ostrover's translators, unhappy pairs of collaborators he changed from month to month, never satisfied' (Ozick 1969; 1971: 47), are all responsible for this literary hocus-pocus. And he wonders, 'What does it require to make a translator?' (84), as if one could conjure up such a person, as Ruth Puttermesser does her messianic golem in Ozick's narrative, 'Puttermesser and Xanthippe' (1997).

And indeed, this idea takes hold in Edelshtein as his frustration grows, yet it suffers a poignant reversal as well. In the beginning of his search, while still hopeful and cognizant of his power as a poet, he wonders how to make a golem. As it becomes clearer to him that he will not so easily find or make someone perform this voodoo for him, he is willing to give up all power and become the golem himself: 'Breathe in me! Animate me!' (Ozick 1969; 1971: 94) he challenges Hannah, a potential translator, rendering himself putty, literally, in her hands. To no avail. Hannah is not interested in breathing life into Edelshtein's inert matter. She is only interested in Ostrover's so-called modern prose. Edelshtein, wild with envy, does not understand

> [w]hy does the world pick up an Ostrover, instead of an Edelshtein or even a Baumzweig? What occult knack, what craft, what crooked convergence of planets drove translators to grovel before Ostrover's naked swollen sentences with their thin little threadbare pants always pulled down? Who had discovered that Ostrover was a 'modern'.
>
> (51)

The double title of the story indicates that the two themes which are unfolding here are connected. Edelshtein's rageful jealousy of Ostrover's success as a published and lauded writer is compounded by the sorry state of Yiddish in late twentieth-century America. The same cultural and political forces which raise up an Ostrover, hold down an Edelshtein, spawning an envy so fierce that Edelshtein seems to be, like Vorovsky, on the verge of losing control of his faculties. Vorovsky, who in addition to becoming one of Ostrover's cadre of translators, is a Berlin trained mathematician. His life's project, the writing of a bilingual German-English mathematical dictionary, lies rejected, collecting dust in boxes in his apartment. Vorovsky's despairing descent into madness is a warning to Edelshtein that even if he is translated, even if he 'gets where [he] wanted to reach, that's when [he would] realize that's not what [he] wanted to reach to' (65). Edelshtein may in the end succeed in finding a translator only to discover that, like Don Quixote, he exists in a world which does not care for his impossible dreams. And 'reaching is impossible' (65), Vorovsky warns Edelshtein in a moment of clarity.

But it is as if Edelshtein cannot help himself. Though he experiences the double (and one is tempted to say the triple) consciousness which W.E.B. DuBois (1903; 1994: 5) claimed haunted African-Americans and which haunts Edelshtein as well, for he is a Jew and European, and then some sort of American Jew, and though he simultaneously experiences the internal colonization which Gayatri Spivak described (1990: 792), being both in a coercive oppressive diaspora and eventually internalizing the negative image of himself as a despised Other, he will not surrender his point of view. Edelshtein is aware that this, that his, drama occurs against the backdrop of a history of forced Jewish assimilation into the majority culture. But he refuses to become a Crypto-Jew. He will not proclaim his Yiddish in whispers and insists on vocalizing his protestations. He is not ashamed nor is he afraid of the Gentiles and their biases. For him, the Yiddish language, the determination to have its literary produce see the light of day[4] is embedded in the Jewish relationship to 'the vision and experience of the book', what Steiner called 'the syllabus of the Judaic' (1996: 315).

There is a bitterness and sweetness in 'Envy; or Yiddish in America' which pervades many levels of the story. First, it is reflected in the actual language or tone Ozick employs. For example, a missionizing Christian says to Edelshtein: 'You pray in a debased jargon, not in the beautiful sacramental English of our Holy Bible', and Edelshtein responds sarcastically, 'That's right, Jesus spoke the King's English' (Ozick 1969; 1971: 100). The bittersweetness is reflected in the character of Edelshtein himself, who oscillates between being 'the fearful little man of the shtetl who has a Chaplinesque sense of himself as the accidental and insignificant creature barely surviving in the hostile world [. . .] [and] has the hauteur of the high priest of Yiddish culture' (Cohen 1994: 288). Throughout the narrative, the tragicomic spirit of Eastern European culture is animated. It is this spirit which, like Yiddish itself, provides not only relief but is itself a mechanism by which Jews are able to survive as a nation despite the recurring onslaughts. Vorovsky, the mathematician cum translator cum madman, laughs himself uncontrollably into fits and spasms. Edelshtein watches his friend guffaw his way into a deeper madness and pleads with Vorovsky's niece, Hannah, Edelshtein's potential saviour, the young literary American who miraculously knows Yiddish fluently, that it is she who has the skill and talent, if not the will, to translate Edelshtein and so lift himself and Yiddish out of the ghetto (Ozick 1969; 1971: 94), out of the omnivorous jaws of historical oblivion. When she parlays her final insult at him, saying that in the end he just does not interest her, Edelshtein turns to a befuddled, broken Vorovsky and says, 'What distinguishes men from the beasts is the power of ha-ha-ha' (99). It is the ability, demonstrated over and over in Yiddish literature, to laugh at oneself, to use what Maurice Samuel calls 'the humour of verbal retrieval, the word triumphant over the situation' (1945: 186), which is what continually provides Edelshtein with a life raft when despair threatens to drown him.

Hannah, the representative of Jewish American youth, shares no sense of the tragicomedy of Jewish culture and history. She lacks the compassion inherent in a sense of humour. Ozick herself, in her story 'Usurpation (Other People's Stories)', cites the Talmud: 'All that is not Torah is levity' (1976: 141). It is not just that the 'all' which is not about law and morality is frivolous, rather, that this 'all' is an essential part of existence, it is the 'truth that is found at the end of every incident' (141–2).

In the figure of Hannah, the potential translator, we see Edelshtein's (and also Ozick's) critique of American indifference and a willed amnesia.[5] Like the evil son at the Passover Seder who asks what this exodus narrative and ritual retelling has to do with 'you' and therefore not with him, Hannah also deliberately removes herself from the collective experience of the Jews and their celebratory and mournful relationship to Yiddish when she jibes Edelshtein: 'All you people want to suffer' (Ozick 1969; 1971: 92). She is referring to *all* the old people who are seeking to preserve something from the hundreds of years of European Yiddish culture. For her they are ghosts of the past who bring with them, like an odour on their clothes, the smell of musty shtetl homes, the smoke of the camps. For her they represent Jewish powerlessness, weakness, a defeatist exile posture. And when Edelshtein picks up on this 'you' she retorts by even further disassociating herself from him by clarifying what she means, 'You Jews' (92).

Softly, he asks her how can one, as if, avoid suffering when suffering comes from history. And she retorts that 'History's a waste' (92). Edelshtein needs no more proof than this but that America has produced a generation of indifferent amnesiacs and that there is little chance that this thin thread of hope which she contains in her linguistic skills will be strong enough to provide him a way out of the labyrinth of obscurity.

Hannah though defends her interest in Ostrover by claiming he appeals to contemporary tastes, he is in the world (94). He writes of demons and sexuality, of complex human relationships, of debauchery and treachery. 'Even in Yiddish Ostrover's not in the ghetto. Even in Yiddish he's not like you people' (94), Hannah reiterates. And so the power of the translator comes to full light. Much has been written about the authority of the actual words employed by a translator and Ostrover's great success is in no small measure a reflection of his translator's creative licence. But Ozick's story reflects the power inherent in the total silencing of a text when it will not come to light, however transformed and manipulated, through the vehicle of translation. Benjamin wrote that 'translation is so far removed from being the sterile equation of two dead languages that of all literary forms it is the one charged with the special mission of watching over the maturing process of the original language and the birth pangs of its own' (1923; 1969: 73). Edelshtein and his poetry never stand a chance then. Not only is Yiddish fixed in time, and so unable to mature as a living language does, but Edelshtein's inability to procure a translator sounds the final death toll for his withering tongue. With Yiddish, Benjamin's special mission experiences a total eclipse. 'Translations give life, life both beyond that of the original text itself and beyond that of the original author' (Chesterman 1997: 29). Edelshtein experiences only the process of dying and is bombarded with death at every turn. 'To speak of Yiddish [is] to preside over a funeral' (Ozick 1969; 1971: 43), he acknowledges.

Hannah's rejection of him is the most recent, and also the most poignant, in a long line of silencers whom he catalogues in the story's last sentences. In this finale, Edelshtein is seen seeking shelter in an inadequate phone booth on a snowy New York morning after wandering the stormy streets for hours, oscillating between strategizing how to nevertheless convince Hannah to take on this life-saving project, and accepting that Yiddish, and so he, have reached their final denouement. He decides to call a phone number he picked up during a previous phone booth interlude. We hear him engaged in a telephone conversation, and one needs to add ridiculously so, with a vituperative Christian missionizer. What begins with the standard script instructing Edelshtein to accept Jesus and be saved, quickly deteriorates into the man spouting anti-Semitic justifications for the millennia of persecution and murder. 'You are a bone in the throat of all mankind' (100), the missionary shouts. 'Who gnaws at bones? Dogs and rats only' (100), Edelshtein responds acerbically. This only ignites the missionary Christian even more and he resorts to calling Edelshtein a kike and a yid. Finally Edelshtein shouts back:

> Amalekite, Titus, Nazi! The whole world is infected by you anti-Semites! On account of you children become corrupted! On account of you I lost everything, my whole life! On account of you I have no translator!
>
> (100)

One cannot help be struck by the painful listing of the villainous murderers of Jews and the almost comedic association Edelshtein draws between the attempted historical genocides and his personal inability to find someone who will help him bridge the abyss which lies before him and mainstream western culture.

One of the painful ironies is that Yiddish, as an osmotic diaspora tongue and the Jews, as a people who have always lived with bi- and trilingualism, is very generous towards other languages. Andrew Chesterman described the dubbing of movies as the 'preferred policy in nationalistic cultures which resist the foreign'; subtitling, on the other hand, 'is used more in weaker cultures that are readier to accept the foreign' (1997: 38). In Israel, where foreign language films are always subtitled and not dubbed (except children's movies for the targeted audience is not literate), this reflects, in my opinion, a strength, not a weakness, and is part of the traditional openness to other cultures and languages endemic to Jewish civilization. Hence the double insult experienced by Edelshtein: he cannot secure for himself the openness that he is more than willing to give to other tongues and cultures.

Under the rubric of post-colonial theory it is sometimes possible to find the silver lining in the intermingling of cultures which colonialism forced both upon native populations and among the colonizers. There is an analysis of the so-called contemporary universality of displacement which both reflects historical facts and which can, conceptually, be seen as a liberating force from the parochialism of a society with fixed boundaries. Aijaz Ahmad has responded to this pollyannaish view of displacement by writing that

> most individuals are not free to fashion themselves anew with each passing day, or do communities arise out of and fade into the thin air of the infinitely contingent [...] Most migrants tend to be poor and experience displacement not as cultural plentitude but as torment; what they seek is not displacement but, precisely, a *place* from where they may begin anew, with some sense of a stable future. Postcoloniality is also, like most things, a matter of class.
>
> (1995; 1996: 289)

For the Yiddish speaking Jews of Eastern Europe, displacement was a way of life. It was viewed as a torment, rife with violence and loss. But it also gave rise to Yiddish, the rich language of fusion.[6] If postcolonialism is 'in broad terms, an oppositional stance, concomitant with a celebration of the marginal', if this oppositional ethic 'forms the desire for resistance and difference' (Paolini 1999: 52), then the Jewish experience certainly fits this definition. First, the ancient kingdom of Israel was colonized a number of times, the last and most devastating being by the Roman Empire which subsequently destroyed its autonomy and exiled its citizens most effectively. Then, being a constant minority among majority cultures, the Jews experienced much of the same external and internal oppressions analysed in post-colonial theory – physical brutality, psychological disfigurement, spiritual murder.[7] Similar to a great many post-colonial narratives and hence, critiques, Yiddish culture and literature developed in relationship and reaction to the European hegemony; Yiddish and its productions became a literature of resistance.

The rise of the Yiddishist movement in the early decades of the twentieth century, the decades in which Edelshtein was born and reared,

> represented the serious attempt of a major portion of Jewry to confront itself, as well as the world of the twentieth century, as a modern 'normal' nation [...] It set out to relieve the unbearable psychological pressure and tension that the Jew experienced as he emerged from a segregated world of outcasts into the spiritual and mental climate of twentieth-century Europe.
>
> (Goldsmith 1997: 264)

Edelshtein himself acknowledges this when in one of his imagined missives to Hannah he writes:

> The liberated slave who is not forgetful and can remember when he himself was an artifact, knows exactly the difference between God and an artifact. A language also knows whom it is serving at each moment [. . .] Of course you see when I say liberated I mean self-liberated. Moses not Lincoln, not Franz Josef. Yiddish is the language of auto-emancipation.
>
> (Ozick 1969; 1971: 86)

Yet the pressure to self-liberate and assimilate, while maintaining a distinctive cultural identity, is only augmented in the post-Shoah world where Edelshtein cannot even convince one of a trinity of potential translators to 'carry fathers and uncles into the future' (74). With great ambivalence he accepts that 'whoever uses Yiddish to keep himself alive is already dead' (69). He is intrigued by the power of western civilization, even admits to his infatuation: 'he coveted mythologies, spectres, animals, voices. Western Civilization his secret guilt' (96). This is an attraction to privilege, a desire to assimilate which would then eliminate the need to always proclaim difference, to always resist. Yet Edelshtein, on the edge of madness though he may appear to be at the story's end, has an epiphany:

> He saw everything in miraculous reversal, blessed – everything plain, distinct, understandable, true. What he understood was this: that the ghetto was the real world, and the outside world only a ghetto. Because in actuality who was shut off? Who then was really buried, removed, inhabited by darkness? [. . .] Talmud explains that when the Jews went into Exile, God went into Exile, also. Babi Yar is maybe the real world, and [. . .] New York with all its terrible intelligence, all fictions, fantasies. Unreality.
>
> (96)

There is a kabbalistic idea that in messianic times, there will be no need for translation for God and so all separate languages will no longer be in exile. They will return to their common source, a pre-Babel state in fact. The 'profound philosophic, ethical and magical import' of translation will no longer be necessary (Steiner 1975; 1981: 64).

But living as we are in a world of nationalism, regionalism, tribalism and cultural and linguistic competition, Yiddish as a language unnaturally and brutally vanquished reminds us of the horrors of genocide, of the brutality of Othering. Edelshtein, a loud mourner, recalls how the Talmud says that if you save one life it is as if you have saved the world. He expands on the idea: 'And if you save a language? Worlds maybe. Galaxies. The whole universe' (Ozick 1969; 1971: 83).

When Isaac Bashevis Singer won the Nobel Prize for Literature in 1978, it was greeted as the great recognition Yiddish had been seeking since the Czernovitz Language Conference in 1908 when Yiddishists sought to make Yiddish and not Hebrew the national language of the Jewish people. By the time Bashevis Singer received these accolades, the mass of Yiddish speakers had been murdered, first by Hitler's designs, then by Stalin's. A profound reversal of fortune made Hebrew and not Yiddish the vernacular national language of the Jewish people. The few who continued to write in it, like Edelshtein in Ozick's 'Envy; or Yiddish in America', appeared to be quaint relics from a past too quickly forgotten by the new Jew who seemed to find nourishment in English and fortune on American soil.

Unlike Edelshtein, Bashevis Singer remained optimistic in his assessment of Yiddish's future. To his audience in Stockholm he said:

> Yiddish has not said its last word. It contains treasures that have not been revealed to the eyes of the world. It was the tongue of martyrs and saints, of dreamers and cabalists – rich in humour and in memories that mankind may never forget. In a figurative way Yiddish is the wise and humble language of us all, the idiom of the frightened and hopeful humanity.
>
> (1985: 172)

Unlike Edelshtein, Bashevis Singer had a translator.

Notes

1 Historically, Yiddish and Hebrew were once cast into oppositional gender roles, with Yiddish as *mamaloshen* being the language of domesticity, of common life, of common folk and sacred Hebrew inhabiting the domain of authority, formality, of learned texts and of privilege; Seidman (1997) discusses this relationship extensively.

2 Mel Alexenberg, an American artist and academic, has written in *Aesthetics in Judaism*, that the open-ended spiral is the form which best expresses a Jewish perspective. For him, the Torah scroll which resembles 'a Moebius strip' (1989: 21) and the *tzitziot*, the knotted spirals, which 'rip open the corners' (22) of the rectangle corners of the prayer shawls, are strong examples of the freedom Judaism seeks and insists on from the enslavement of a closed form and/or system (22).

3 This remains true today in Israel with the influx of over 800,000 Jews from the former Soviet Union since 1990, of which a great percentage are not technically Jewish according to Jewish law (they may be married to Jews, or have one Jewish grandfather). When a Russian knows Yiddish, and in fact many of the people in their forties and above do, Yiddish remaining a way for Jews in Russia to maintain their distinctiveness, it is as if this individual has 'passed' the litmus test of authenticity.

4 In Hebrew and in Yiddish, the verb to publish is literally 'to bring out into the light'.

5 This can also be seen in Ozick's novella, *The Shawl* (1989; 1990). Here Americans are loathe to give their attention to the stories Rosa, a death camp survivor, needs to share.

6 Max Weinreich coined this phrase (1959: 563).

7 Patricia Williams, writing about the African American experience, said: 'Only one form of spirit murder is racism – cultural obliteration, prostitution, abandonment of the elderly and the homeless, and genocide are some of its other guises' (1991: 73).

17 Ricki Lake in Tel Aviv

The alternative of Orly Castel-Bloom's Hebrew-English

Karen Grumberg

התיישבתי. זה היה TOO MUCH.

היא נשמעה, במקרה הטוב, בדיוק כמו המטיפים האלה בערוצים הרחוקים של הטלוויזיה, שכל הקהל מהנהן אחריהם ואומר YEAH YEAH ALL RIGHT.

> I sat down. This was *too much*. She sounded, at best, exactly like those preachers on the distant television channels, where the whole audience nods in agreement with them and says *yeah yeah all right*.
>
> (Castel-Bloom 1995: 48)[1]

The irrelevance of English

The quotation above from *Hamina lisa* (1995) offers a humorous glimpse at Orly Castel-Bloom's practice of interspersing English phrases within her Hebrew. It also, however, demonstrates the easy intersection between television and the real world. American English is the *lingua franca* that connects these two realms. More specifically, the type of English popularized by television asserts itself as a valid possibility of expression even within the heroine's Hebrew world, elements of which are described in terms of a television show. Of course, English varies from one type of show to another. The English spoken on a talk show is not the same English spoken on news broadcasts. To organize these various types of television-speak, I use Mikhail Bakhtin's notion of 'speech genres'. He writes that 'each sphere in which language is used develops its own *relatively stable types* of these utterances. These we may call *speech genres* [. . .] [Each] sphere of activity contains an entire repertoire of speech genres' (1986: 60). If television is one such 'sphere', then newspeak or sitcom-speak are only two of its characteristic 'stable types', or 'speech genres'. The English used here has a 'generic nature' (64) that is clearly linked to the sphere of television. In Bakhtin's formulation, '[even] in the most free, the most unconstrained conversation, we cast our speech in definite generic forms' – that is, all spoken language is subject to the speaker's choice of speech genre (78). The emphasis on choice is significant: if the speaker can choose to express herself using a particular speech genre, then the consistent use of any genre reveals as much about the speaker as does the content of her expression. As the opening quotation demonstrates, the type of English present in much of Orly Castel-Bloom's work is distinguished from other foreign languages because of its function as a distinctly generic linguistic style.

The literary critic Sidra Ezrahi has written that 'English in Israel has always been somewhat beside the point' (2000b: 71). She elaborates:

> Not a combatant in the 'language wars' where Yiddish was the sparring partner. Not a participant in the territorial wars, where Arabic continues to be the contender. Not even part of the Eurocentric culture wars where German, Russian, and French have been the heavyweight challengers. English has only a bit part to play in the drama of ingathering those 'Lost Tribes' who, by their own admission, speak Kurdish, Yemenite, Amharic, and, most anciently and recently, the Bantu of the Lemba. Of course there was the Mandate[2] [...] But the more ubiquitous it is, the more English – and in particular its American stepchild – have been regarded not as a contender for but as a pollutant of whatever enterprise you happen to subscribe to. In socialist eyes, Coca-Cola and Microsoft are the icons of capitalism, engraved on every signpost and storefront. In the ears of religious puritanism, English rings discordantly as the language of liturgical compromise. Even postzionists, postcolonialists and expatriates guard Hebrew zealously as the bedrock of their identity[3] when all the other idols have been smashed.
>
> (71)

English, in other words, does not occupy the Israeli consciousness in the same way as other languages that are associated with the experiences of emigration and immigration. In this respect, it is largely irrelevant to the formation of Israeliness.

This decided irrelevance is precisely that which makes the ubiquity of English in some Israeli fiction so striking. Orly Castel-Bloom, one of the most controversial and provocative young writers in Israel, uses English consistently in her short stories and novels. The reasons behind this tendency, though, and the manner in which the English is used, are not in themselves consistent. Her relationship to English – and the relationship of Israel in general to English – differs from the relationship to other languages that have distinct cultural and historical links to Israeli Jews. Moreover, the *type* of English she chooses to use is the American English of consumerism and slang, of television and cinema, of technology and mass reproduction.

In this chapter, I examine Castel-Bloom's use of various genres and influences of television-English as a means of representing Israeli apathy, both social and cultural. Moreover, I seek to demonstrate that, ironically, the uniformity of this apathy in its representation through hollow Hollywood English displaces the imposed homogeneity of Israeli Hebrew. First, I consider the central ideological markings of Castel-Bloom's style and use of language, and the critical interpretation of these elements. Next, I evaluate the multiculturalist reading of some of her work, questioning its validity in the context of English. I then seek an alternative understanding of her response to the dominating and homogenizing tendency of Hebrew. Finally, I turn to several examples from her novels.

A brief background: Castel-Bloom's style

Since the publication of her first collection of short stories, the Hebrew of Orly Castel-Bloom has provoked wildly disparate critical reactions. The highly regarded Hebrew literary scholar Gershon Shaked asserts that her distinctive style has done 'nothing less than change the face of Hebrew fiction' (2000: 241). Her 'thin Hebrew' (*ivrit raza*), a term initially intended to be derogatory and eventually embraced as positive by some critics, was a central point of critical debate in the literary supplements of Israeli newspapers as she rose to prominence in the 1990s. Along with her use of slang juxtaposed with literary Hebrew, Castel-Bloom's 'thin Hebrew' was at the crux of the debate of her literary merit, not least because it resembles what could be called 'thin English' prevalent in so many television shows imported from the United States. Is her style literarily worthy? Is it a passing fad? Will it leave an indelible mark on Hebrew literature? Such questions dominated the discussions of her work. Her language has driven some critics to despise her for what they call stylistic games and others to adore what they dub her innovation.[4] In a review of *Hamina lisa*, Ariana Melamed marvels at what she claims is an unprecedented disagreement among literary critics regarding any writer's work: 'I do not know another instance of such enormous controversy, and also of such enormous interest, forming around an author who lives and works here all the while his books are being published' (1995: 80).

With time, the praise of those members of the Israeli literary establishment who had embraced Castel-Bloom from the start, including the important writer S. Yizhar and influential critics like Dan Miron and Yigal Schwartz, surpassed the harsh criticism that had lamented her 'corruption' of the Hebrew language.[5] Dan Miron, in a laudatory article, refutes the oft-repeated categorization of her Hebrew as 'thin', claiming that it is more 'dead' than 'thin', in its accurate portrayal of the unthinking and lifeless linguistic combinations that characterize contemporary spoken Hebrew (1989: 19). While some of the most famous American authors wrote in a similar linguistic register already in the first half of the twentieth century (Hemingway, for example), producing a 'dead' English, Castel-Bloom's 'dead' Hebrew of the 1980s and 1990s provides a stark contrast to the language used by her literary predecessors in Israel. In his discussion of the earlier literary generation known as the New Wave (*Gal hadash*), the critic Avraham Balaban emphasizes the 'search for a lost wholeness' and the use of refined Hebrew that characterize the works of writers such as A.B. Yehoshua and Amos Oz (1995: 70, 19). Such 'pure' language is associated with Zionist ideology because of its contribution to and reflection of the Zionist project of reviving Hebrew. Castel-Bloom, on the contrary, dilutes her language, signaling her rejection of such nostalgic dreams and ideologies, and, ultimately, her acceptance of the fragmentary and chaotic nature of the world.

It is not just the thinness of her Hebrew that marks her work ideologically, however, but also her use of English. English is omnipresent in her novels, yet the many reviews and critiques of her work have mentioned this phenomenon only in passing. In a review of *Hasefer hehadash shel orly kastel-bloom* [Orly Castel-Bloom's New Book] (1998), Yoram Meltzer (1998) writes that her use of English is one of the problems in her style in that it creates a confusing doubleness: 'The English that appears here and there pulls confusingly to North as well as South Tel Aviv[6] and more.' Ariel Hirschfeld's (1992) insistence that he is not troubled by 'the entrance of Americanisms' into Castel-Bloom's Hebrew glaringly highlights the belief that there is something troubling about it. Other critics' discussions of her English are limited to the praise or condemnation of her liberal use of slang, much of which is derived or directly transliterated from American English.

Whether it is lauded or disparaged, Castel-Bloom's use of English seems to be taken for granted as one element within the project of representation: it is part of the Israeli consciousness. Castel-Bloom's tendency to use often untranslated English has generally been glossed over as an accurate rendering of an anthropological phenomenon: the development (or corruption, depending on who is asked) of Hebrew among the younger, television-watching, English-speaking generation. This is Israeli Hebrew as it is really spoken in the streets of Tel Aviv. Categorized safely within the postmodern, Castel-Bloom can shake off the constrictions of 'literary' language, which is barred from the newest Hebrew-English words and phrases. It is unlikely that Amos Oz, for example, has used even the common word 'cool' in his writing. However, there has been little critical attention devoted to the significant ideological implications of Castel-Bloom's intermingling of English in her Hebrew, and to the various levels on which English operates in her work. Moreover, while the influence of television, cinema and other media on her work has been duly noted by several critics,[7] its link to her use of English remains largely unacknowledged.

Identity politics?

In a recent study, Deborah A. Starr discusses Castel-Bloom's use of language in the context of Israeli identity. Starr argues that

> Pairing a multilingual narrative texture with a range of characters drawn from all walks of Israeli society, Castel-Bloom attempts to broaden the base of Hebrew expression in order to acknowledge the presence of Israel's repressed languages and identities [...] Castel-Bloom, herself the daughter of Francophone Jewish immigrants from Egypt, seeks to reverse [the normalizing trend of Hebrew's displacement of diaspora languages] that threatens Israel's multilingual heritage.
>
> (2000: 224)

In other words, Castel-Bloom is (re)instating the 'linguistic hybridity' (in the words of the critic Yitzhak Laor 2001: 215) that has been repressed by the Hebrew literary establishment. Like Laor, Starr argues that Castel-Bloom seeks to disrupt and subvert the unifying pretensions of Hebrew. Starr mentions Bakhtin's notion of *polyglossia* as useful in revealing 'the potentially subversive impact of Castel-Bloom's critique of language usage on the national myth of a unitary Israeli Jewish identity' and claims that Castel-Bloom seeks to upend what Bakhtin calls a 'unitary and totalizing national myth' (Bakhtin 1981: 65; Starr 2000: 225). This 'slow death of the myth' (Bakhtin 1981: 65) parallels similar linguistic revolutions in hyphenated American literature, which incorporates non-English words to assert its cultural legitimacy and multiple understandings of Americanness. Henry Roth's *Call It Sleep* (1934), for instance, provides a classic example of *polyglossia*, incorporating a veritable symphony of various immigrant languages, as well as accenting the English with a heavy Yiddish.[8]

As Starr points out, Castel-Bloom, too, has used non-Hebrew words in some of her novels and short stories in order to convey the multi-dimensional cultural landscape of Israel. In the short story 'Ummi Fi Shughl'[9] [Arabic; My Mother's At Work], in the collection *Sipurim bilti retsoniyim* [Involuntary Stories] (1993), a woman sits on a bench and, upon suddenly feeling a sting, discovers an elderly woman under the bench. Their short conversation, in which the old woman insists that she is the younger woman's mother or sister, is conducted in Arabic. Castel-Bloom provides a translation for this brief exchange, a choice which not only reflects her confidence that her average Israeli reader does not know even the most basic Arabic, but also the importance that the author places on the reader's understanding of these few sentences, the repetition of which makes up the bulk of the story. While this story is unarguably Castel-Bloomian in its fantastic flight from realism, the use of Arabic as a distinct political reminder of Israel as part of the Middle East – in its cultural heritage, its geographical placement and its intricate entanglement with the Palestinians – is unusual for the author. Embedding Arabic in the Hebrew here is similar to the use of Spanish or Chinese in American works: it announces a certain cultural loyalty to the identity represented by that language. There is nothing particularly innovative about this use of foreign words. Like the American project of multiculturalism, it encourages a reclamation of the culture (and the language that represents it) that has been sacrificed in favour of the new culture and language.

However, Castel-Bloom's first novel, *Heykhan ani nimtset* [Where Am I] (1990), which contains French words and expressions, shifts the dynamics between Hebrew and the foreign language. The unnamed heroine's French aunts arrive in Israel for a visit. They do not speak Hebrew, and our heroine's French is so rusty that she responds to her aunt by saying 'qui' instead of 'oui' (Castel-Bloom 1990: 32). Other French words and phrases punctuate the novel in a similarly comical vein. Again, these foreign words are used to convey a cultural forgetting, in this case clearly instigated by the acquisition of Hebrew. While the forgetting is not politically charged here as in 'Ummi Fi Shughl', it nevertheless points to the potency of Hebrew, which distorts or erases the language that preceded it culturally.

While 'Ummi Fi Shughl' much more consciously participates in the by now conventional endeavour of cultural reclamation, however, *Heykhan ani nimtset* simply mocks it. The young woman in 'Ummi Fi Shughl' understands Arabic and can communicate in it; the young heroine in this novel informs the reader twice that she speaks 'extremely clumsy' French (Castel-Bloom 1993: 30, 31). This information is offered without any contextualization or apology. Indeed, her attempts to speak and understand French are designed to evoke our laughter. And, unlike the Arabic passages in 'Ummi Fi Shughl', the French passages here are left untranslated, and thus their content is rendered unimportant. One reason for this difference, of course, is that the relationship between Hebrew and Arabic is utterly different than the one between Hebrew and French. Arabic is related to Hebrew formally, geographically, culturally, historically, politically; French is not. However, even though the mother and family of the heroine speak French, and even though her mother sometimes addresses her in French, she feels no special connection to that language (30). This is particularly intriguing since Castel-Bloom herself was raised in a home in which French was spoken. French is not devoid of significance for her. Yet, far from attempting to reincorporate it into the heroine's linguistic reality, she rejects it.

Castel-Bloom's use of foreign words is not rooted in the concerns that preoccupy Yoel Hoffmann, whose characters in *Kristus shel dagim* [Christ of Fish] (1991), for instance, wallow and dream and live in other languages, redeeming their dying European cultures in the Middle East. Nor does it resemble that of Erez Biton, who sprinkles Arabic throughout his Hebrew poems, thereby constructing a distinctly Mizrahi space within Israeli literature. These and other authors who intersperse their Hebrew with foreign words do so in the service of a present that defines itself according to the past. Castel-Bloom rejects the necessity of relying on the past, opting instead for a 'detached presence' that is utterly independent. Her Hebrew, saturated in the English of television and film, looks only to Hollywood for its legitimization. While in the two examples above, Arabic and French are both used, at least to some degree, to convey a specific link to the heroines' personal cultural histories, English never plays such a role in Castel-Bloom's works.

The role of English

Yitzhak Laor[10] examines the overtly political dimension of Castel-Bloom's Hebrew, though he does not do so in the context of her use of Americanisms. Indeed, he dismisses the impact of Americanisms in the perceived 'corruption' of Hebrew. He writes:

> The enemy that occasions such active protection of the [Hebrew] language is not the Americanisms, for example, which have penetrated into every language of the world, and that occasionally elicit anger. [...] The enemies of the language that necessitate fierce defense are not those who toss in an occasional colloquialism from outside the language, but, rather, those who do not speak 'proper' Hebrew in the 'proper' way.
>
> (2001: 224)

Although Laor is discussing Americanisms in the spoken (not necessarily the literary) context here, it should be reiterated that this chapter examines the use of

English not in the form of 'the occasional colloquialism' but rather precisely in its capacity to transform 'proper' Hebrew into 'improper' Hebrew. In a review of *Hasefer hehadash shel orly kastel-bloom*, Laor describes a scene in which a linguist named Shimon explains that he supports the official acceptance of common mistakes in Hebrew. Laor uses the scene to support his claim that Castel-Bloom 'shoots at the elitism of Hebrew' ('Sefer'). This trenchant image provides the twofold metaphorical basis for my analysis of her use of English: she shoots hegemonic Hebrew with a loaded gun, and also with a loaded camera.[11] She aims not only to destroy the exclusivity of Hebrew, but also to provide a snapshot of its replacement. This alternate linguistic domination that she represents – that of Hollywood English – reflects the hollowness of contemporary Israeli society.

Much as Laor dismisses English as having a minimal impact on the undoing of the cultural hegemony of Hebrew, Starr discusses the use of English in Castel-Bloom's *Hamina lisa* as no more than a 'ludic tendency' (2000: 225). Almost as an afterthought, she adds that Castel-Bloom's 'inclusion of banalities mocks both Mina, an upper-class housewife, and the faddishness English has come to denote in popular culture' (225). The significance of Castel-Bloom's use of English in her writing, however, connotes much more than mere faddishness. Indeed, it is one of the deadliest weapons in her arsenal, to extend Laor's metaphor.

While Bakhtin's *polyglossia* can account for Castel-Bloom's use of Arabic and even of French, it does not account for her use of English.[12] On the contrary, it creates a *monoglossia*[13]: English, as the oft-reproduced language of the media, is established as the unifying language, thus enacting a highly ironic displacement of Hebrew. This generic, hollow language that springs from Hollywood but is beamed all over the world ultimately unifies Castel-Bloom's characters, and throws into sharp relief the inability (or unwillingness) of Hebrew to do so. The television-English in Castel-Bloom's works demonstrates a pervasive culturally imperial endeavor: the reign of emptiness, represented by television and other forms of mass cultural media.

Shooting Hebrew

In a note preceding the English translation of the novel *Doli siti* [Dolly City] (1992), the translator, Dalya Bilu, proclaims that 'American expressions have been retained by the author in the English translation of *Dolly City* in order to keep the flavour of the language created by the American orientation in Israel, especially in the Tel Aviv area.' Considering that the only available English translation of *Doli siti* was published by Loki Books in England in an unmistakably British English, the need to maintain a specifically 'American orientation' which is represented by particular genres of American English is intriguing. The use of English in this novel is not just about language but also about culture. American culture, as represented by American English, plays an important role in Castel-Bloom's construction of this modern dystopia and its generic, anonymous culture.

Castel-Bloom uses English terms transcribed in Hebrew letters throughout the novel: 'monkey business' (Castel-Bloom 1992: 22), 'non-stop' (29, 46, 59), 'trick' (59), 'show-off' (76), 'oh my God' (79), 'this show-must-go-on... bullshit' (83). She sometimes inserts English phrases in Latin letters: 'do it', an echo of Nike's ubiquitous advertising campaign, for example (58). The use of television-speak sets the flat, apathetic tone of the novel. Draped in such English, the Hebrew language loses all ideological significance. On the level of theme, too, Americanisms dominate, leaving their indelible mark on the inhabitants of Dolly City: 'Everyone has a crooked mouth from all the times they'd hissed the black market rate of the dollar, everyone has a mouth in the shape of an S to identify with the $', Dolly, the protagonist, tells us (84).[14] The importance of capitalism and material wealth in the wretched Dolly City is expressed through the Latin letter S, which is inscribed bodily onto the inhabitants' mouths, and which is the basis for the symbol $. The letter S has been reduced to its capacity as a dollar sign, a symbol that is inextricably linked to America and its rampant consumer culture, but is universally comprehensible.

In another section, Dolly wonders why, when the Israeli government cannot control the Arabs in the Occupied Territories, she should be expected to control her own 'occupied territories' (written in English) (74). The English term 'occupied territories' is readily identifiable with the distinct genre of international news jargon. Moreover, it is a term that was initially controversial in Israeli discourse, since it takes for granted that the territories belong to another people and are being occupied by Israel. Indeed, the Hebrew term commonly used today is *shtahim kvushim*, or 'conquered territories', a term which conspicuously neglects to mention the continuing act of occupation. Not only those on the far right of the Israeli political spectrum but also some of the political mainstream take offence at this nomenclature and insist on referring to these areas as 'Judea and Samaria', their biblical designation. When Dolly chooses to refer to this land using the by now hackneyed phrase 'occupied territories', she appropriates this tired media-speak in the context of herself as an individual – thereby not only risking a trivialization of her personal situation, but also rendering the larger ideological implications of the term meaningless.

Clearly, then, the so-called 'American orientation' in Dolly City that the author wishes to preserve is based on more than simply the use of English colloquialisms. The American orientation is a cultural designation – or, rather, a signifier of the *lack* of such a designation. The television-English creates a sense of cultural impoverishment that is reinforced by the dollar signs marking the inhabitants of Dolly City like scarlet letters. The American consumerism that brands Dolly City is testament to its hollowness. The use of English news-speak suggests the transformation of a heated, emotional political and ideological debate into a broadcast item that can be reproduced literally as well as recycled to fit a different context.

The use of English in *Hasefer hehadash shel orly kastel-bloom* can be divided into several different categories: the use of English slang; the use of English words instead of their Hebrew equivalents; and, finally, the syntactic reformulation of Hebrew as English.

Almost every page of the novel is punctuated by phrases such as 'take it or leave it' (Castel-Bloom 1998: 11), 'business as usual' (37), 'super-duper' (113), 'full gas' (80). These phrases are imposed in untranslated and untransliterated English into Castel-Bloom's Hebrew text and her heroine's Hebrew world. Arguably, these phrases are untranslatable, since they are used as slang in English as well. Particularly in this novel, which is about the ceaseless obsession with trends that permeate Israeli society, the use of English slang is relevant thematically: it is just another trend to be picked up or discarded.

However, the narrator also uses English words when they seem completely unnecessary, in place of equivalent Hebrew words. 'Peach' (41), 'pistachio' (40), 'trash' (50, 105), 'obvious' (54), 'definitely' (60), 'slogan' (83), 'issue' (97), 'favorite' (104), 'fame' (108), 'job' (114), 'rejection' (128) – the list goes on and on. Unlike the slang phrases above, for instance, which cannot be accurately rendered in another language, these words have no special cultural value, yet they are used throughout the novel in place of their Hebrew counterparts. Our narrator, who is not presented as especially intelligent or erudite, has clearly been exposed to a great deal of English, to the extent that she feels comfortable enough with it to use it even when she does not need to. The facile interchangeability between Hebrew and English mocks the notion of any one language being imbued with ideological value, at the same time as it reflects the powerful presence of television and other mass media.

Perhaps the most striking use of English, however, is that which adapts English to the characteristics of Hebrew grammar and syntax. '*Ha-reputation sheli on stake achshav*', proclaims the narrator ['My reputation is at stake now'] (132). In this half-Hebrew, half-English sentence (transcribed in Hebrew letters), the Hebrew definite article *ha* precedes the English noun 'reputation', and is necessary to maintain the Hebrew structure, which, unlike English, requires the definite article even though the possessive pronoun is present. The possessive pronoun *sheli* (my) follows 'reputation' as it would if the sentence were in Hebrew. The use of 'on stake' rather than of the correct 'at stake' reveals that, although the narrator feels comfortable peppering her speech and thoughts with English, her knowledge of the language is far from polished. Nevertheless, this example demonstrates the extent to which English can permeate the Hebrew language without disrupting its structure as *Hebrew*.

Another example reflects a different phenomenon, a veritable Anglicization of Hebrew. Our nameless heroine and narrator discovers that someone has won the enviable prize of Lancôme make-up for life on a quiz. She responds thus: '*ze atsar oti. ani mitkavenet, lankom lehol hahayim?*' (142). The literal translation into English would be: 'That stopped me. I mean, Lancôme for life?' What is fascinating in this example is that the English translation that I have just provided is actually the *source* of the Hebrew, the original from which the Hebrew was created, even though the sentence is rendered entirely in Hebrew, both in its words and in its letters. The structure is duplicated from English, in a form that does not exist in Hebrew, except as the literal translation of American slang. Though *ani mikavenet* sounds much more literal in Hebrew than in English, it is used here as common linguistic currency that connects the two languages.

Inadvertently, perhaps, Castel-Bloom has managed to render quite faithfully the speech patterns that have become the common lot of many Israeli immigrants to the United States. The intimate intermingling of Hebrew and English in these cases has created an Anglicized Hebrew that epitomizes the 'corruption' of the Hebrew language – and, by extension, of the despicable *yored* (Hebrew; an emigrant from Israel), who has chosen to abandon the spiritual and physical superiority of Israel for the glittering dollar signs that lure to the United States only to twist one's mouth into an S. It is worth noting in this context that the terms for emigration from and immigration to Israel are related hierarchically: while *aliya*, immigration to Israel, means literally 'ascent', *yerida*, the term for emigration from Israel, means 'descent'. In one of the more memorable moments of Israeli patriotism, Yitzhak Rabin, when he was prime minister between 1974 and 1977, called *yordim*, emigrants, *nefolet shel nemoshot* (roughly translated as 'pile of cowardly weaklings'). The term *yored* and its various forms continue to exude repugnant disapproval. Castel-Bloom's Anglification of Hebrew enacts a defiant *yerida* on a linguistic level. This *yerida* is inscribed both on the level of individual words – the use of English words when Hebrew has words that express precisely the same thing or idea – and on the level of structure and syntax, when English and Hebrew are braided to create sentences that function sometimes according to the grammatical rules of Hebrew, and sometimes to those of English, without any hierarchical categorization of either type of sentence.

It is interesting to compare this process to an incident that took place in 1977, when a Jewish American named Tal Brody led Israel's Maccabi Tel Aviv basketball team to the European Cup Championship and, in his post-game euphoria, coined a new phrase in Hebrew: *anahnu al hamapa* ['we are on the map']. Brody, an American immigrant to Israel whose native language is English, translated a common American phrase literally into Hebrew – and it caught on. The circumstances of this particular example were instrumental in the success of this linguistic success. Brody had just led Israel to its first European basketball championship, a feat that was considered to place Israel on 'the map' not only because it was a victory, but because it was a decidedly *physical* victory, indisputable proof of the realization of the Zionist dream of the 'Hebrew' or the 'New Jew'. Indeed, Brody went on to say that Israel was on the map 'not only in sports, but in everything'. On both the individual and the national level, it represented the normalization for which Zionism yearned, proof that the Jew is physical and that the Jewish State is a state like any other. Brody is a Zionist who still lives in Israel. His Americanized Hebrew was considered charming since it issued from the mouth of an American who had chosen to leave the 'golden land' to come to the Promised Land. All these factors contributed to the immediate embrace of this newly-coined phrase and to its adoption into the Hebrew lexicon. These same factors, of course, distinguish Brody's Anglicized Hebrew from Castel-Bloom's – her characters are not Zionists, nor do they exemplify any sort of Zionist ideal. Quite to the contrary, they are apathetic drifters, postmodern specks unconnected to any real system of values or beliefs. Hebrew, for them, is a mode of communication easily replaceable by the emptiest system of symbols. The connection between language and place, which is so crucial to the Zionist construction of Israeliness, is disregarded entirely by Castel-Bloom's narrators.

A final example from *Hasefer hehadash* illustrates this point. Our heroine has crash-landed a Cessna plane on an island and decides to send a fax 'HOME' (transcribed in English), which, she informs us, 'is also a key on the keyboard' (Castel-Bloom 1998: 177). This observation connects the intimate, welcoming place that wards off the condition of exile to one of dozens of keys on a keyboard, replicated on millions of keyboards around the world, stripping the word 'home' of its value. On one level, this act exemplifies Castel-Bloom's humour. At the same time, though, it raises serious questions regarding the Zionist insistence that Israel is the only home for Jews, and that any other place is exile. If home can be infinitely replicated, if all it requires is the press of a button, then the significance of this insistence is disparaged.

In Castel-Bloom's recent novel, *Halakim enoshiyim* [*Human Parts*] (2002), the role of English takes on a new dimension. English words like 'okay' and 'cool' continue to pepper the text as in the other novels and stories. However, in this novel, American English and its direct association with television is a principal theme. Tasaro Tasama, one of the major characters in the novel, is an Ethiopian who immigrated to Israel in her childhood. Her most fervent dream is to speak Hebrew 'just like a regular Israeli' – that is, without her Amharic accent (Castel-Bloom 2002: 152). This not uncommon desire of immigrants to perfect the language of their new land is given a distinctly Castel-Bloomian spin. The narrator explains the development of Tasaro's Hebrew:

> If there was anyone in the world that Tasaro had to thank for her knowledge of Hebrew, which wasn't at all bad, it was Ricki Lake. Tasaro had an overwhelming desire to understand what they were all yelling about, both the studio audience and the guests on the show. A lot of blacks of all shades and features came to the *Ricki Lake Show*. Tasaro liked looking both at the whites and at the blacks, because it was only on this show that she had the opportunity to see such a wide range of colours and features in both races at once. [. . .]
>
> Thanks to Ricki Lake, Tasaro had also mastered writing and spelling. Her Hebrew was the Hebrew of movie subtitles, to such an extent that sometimes when she was talking, even in the most trivial conversation, she would first see the white letters at the bottom of the screen, as if she were reading from a written text. Thus she was able to say the words in the right order, even if she didn't always get the pronunciation right.
>
> Tasaro's dream was to get rid of all traces of a foreign accent, and to speak just like a regular Israeli [. . .] [She] chose to apply herself to the study of Israeli culture. As a result, she would often use the same expression over and over again, *ad nauseam*.
>
> (161–2)

The language that is common to these people of different shades on the *Ricki Lake Show* is, of course, English. They are Americans. Significantly, they are Americans of a very specific socio-economic affiliation. The type of English that Tasaro hears on *Ricki Lake* differs from other genres of television-English, such as the formal news-speak encountered in *Doli siti*, but both spring from the same ubiquitous medium. The irony of learning Hebrew by watching a popular show in English is echoed later, when Tasaro urges her younger siblings to improve their Hebrew by watching subtitled Spanish language *telenovelas*, or soap operas. Tasaro, however, is not only attracted to *Ricki Lake* because it teaches her Hebrew, but also because it teaches her the possibilities of Israeli culture through the many shaded reality of American culture. The fact that the United States remains segregated culturally, socially and geographically is unimportant, because the *Ricki Lake Show* becomes America to this Ethiopian woman watching television in her Tel Aviv living room. When Tasaro watches Ricki Lake, she is fascinated and hopeful about her own uncertain future with her white boyfriend Adir.

Several forces are at work undermining the unifying claims of Hebrew. The notion of learning Hebrew through another foreign language places it on the same level as other languages and deprives it of its claims of exclusivity. The idea that television and cinema, rather than literature or *ulpanim* (intensive language programs for new immigrants), provide the basis for a solid 'Israeli' Hebrew reinforces this positioning. Another element revealed in this passage is the extent of the ethno-cultural impoverishment that someone like Tasaro feels so strongly in her 'homeland' of Israel, which fuels her fascination with the glimpse that *Ricki Lake* provides of the interaction of blacks and whites.

The postmodern representation of reproduction and multiplicity plays an integral role in Tasaro's acquisition of Hebrew. The television show is a medium that is, by definition, reproduced *ad infinitum*, as Tasaro reminds us when she ponders that Ricki Lake's guests reveal their feelings and humiliate themselves 'in front of the whole of the United States of America, and indeed, the rest of the world, too' (160). But this multiplicity functions on a linguistic level as well, in Tasaro's own repeated use of the same expression 'over and over again' (162). The acquisition of language is thus mechanized. Tasaro's determination to learn Hebrew, which she believes will eventually allow her to enter the realm of authentic 'Israeliness', bypasses books and teachers and relies instead on an un-Israeli cultural phenomenon that is streamed to Israel and the rest of the world through technological processes of reproduction. Tasaro herself multiplies these reproductions in her robotically repeated phrases, until Adir tells her 'to talk normally' (162).

Indeed, to talk normally is all Tasaro wants. Her hope that talking normally will lead to her acceptance in Israel, and that this acceptance will lead to Adir's agreement to marry her, is what drives her. It is what she perceives as her family's refusal to learn Hebrew – and by extension their refusal to become integrated into Israeli culture – that disgusts and shames Tasaro. The mixture of Amharic and Hebrew that characterizes her siblings' speech embarrasses her. Meanwhile, her own culturally generic English-derived Hebrew is perfectly acceptable, since it does not betray any other national or ethnic allegiance. Tasaro desperately wants to fulfil the Zionist dream through the perfection of her Hebrew, but we know (since the narrator tells us) that Tasaro has re-written her own history. She has forgotten that it is her beauty that has enabled her to progress in Israeli society. Indeed, because of her accent, she has not been allowed to speak in the commercials in which she has appeared. The ultimate mockery of Tasaro's dream of perfect Hebrew comes when, to her elation, she is selected to be the Lotto Girl – the woman who pronounces the winning lottery numbers on television each week – partly because of her good Hebrew. This is her reward for perfecting her language. This is the realization of her dream: To become herself a televisionic reproduction, perhaps a role model for Ethiopian youths aspiring to reach the heights of success, to achieve the 'Israeli Dream' that Zionism promises downtrodden immigrants in its mythology of Jewish unity and Israeli homogeneity. Castel-Bloom ridicules the notion of the Hebrew language as the crowning jewel of Israeli unity. In doing so, she collapses the very foundation of the myth of Israeliness.

Hebrew becomes a means to an end, a language to be conquered on the path to acceptance by the majority to which the immigrant wants desperately to belong. From a certain perspective, this is a fulfilment of the Zionist desire for normalcy – Hebrew is to Israeli immigrants what English is to American immigrants and what French is to French immigrants. But, on the other hand, it also destroys the claim of Hebrew's uniqueness: if Hebrew can be interchanged with English, if it can even be learned through English, then what is so special about it? The pervasive language of the mass media is presented as Hebrew's most powerful challenger for cultural supremacy. Castel-Bloom's representation of this displacement of Hebrew forces an awareness of a cultural emptiness that is nothing less than terrifying.

Insofar as it represents the superficial culture that erases difference and heterogeneity as much as does standard Hebrew, Castel-Bloom's use of English is much more than an attempt at replicating authentic contemporary Tel Aviv speech. Clearly, too, she does not use English to participate in a project of cultural reclamation, a concern that is largely irrelevant in the context of English. Castel-Bloom is not interested in reconstructing the present on the basis of the past. Rather, she establishes, through her use of various genres of television-English, an utterly hollow *presence*, that 'detached presence' which is unencumbered and unconcerned by the past. She thus depicts an Israel that is largely apathetic and de-historicized, a one-dimensional place wallowing in social and cultural indifference. Such a defiantly un-ideological use of English as a universalizing language serves as an ironic and cynical photographic negative of the Zionist hegemony which has moulded 'Israeliness' largely through the imposition of a standard, univocal Hebrew.[15] She attacks not only the linguistic fortifications of the Zionist ideals of the State, but also Israelis' unthinking embrace of Hollywood as an alternative. Her work defies the myth of shared culture – rather than attempting to preserve or reclaim it – by mockingly replacing it with a force that is as powerful as it is shallow. In doing so, it disrupts the fundamental Zionist objective of a national unification which demands cultural and ethnic erasure.

Notes

1 The translations from Hebrew in this chapter are mine, except those from *Halakim enoshiyim* [*Human Parts*], which I quote from the English edition. While *Doli siti* [*Dolly City*] is also available in an English translation, for the purposes of my analysis I cite from the original Hebrew, which contains elements not retained in the translation.

2 The linguist Ghil'ad Zuckermann (2003: 217) writes that, while British English influenced Hebrew in the early twentieth century (a result of the British Mandatory presence in Palestine), the influence of American English on Hebrew dates to the late twentieth century (a result of 'American as the global language'). He adds that Americanization 'is also apparent in more established languages' (220), confirming the a-historicity of the link between Israeli Hebrew and American English. For specific examples of the entrance of foreign words into Hebrew, see his Chapter 6.

3 There are notable exceptions to this statement. A few Israeli writers, such as the Iraqi-born Samir Naqqash, have rejected Hebrew altogether as the language of their literary expression. Naqqash continued to write in his native Arabic until his death in 2004, though he lived in Israel for most of his life.

4 For instance, although Batya Gur (1995) writes that *Hamina lisa* is 'probably the most complete and wittiest' of all of Castel-Bloom's books up to that point, she claims about Castel-Bloom's writing that '[its] power is immediate, contemporary, and short-lived. Her devotion to the enjoyment of the game in linguistic patterns and word combinations chokes the sorrow and dread in her works' ('realizem mugaz'). Ariana Melamed (1995), on the other hand, maintains that Castel-Bloom is 'a genius'.

5 The publication of *Heykhan ani nimtset* [Where Am I], as Melamed notes, initiated the turning of the critical tide in Castel-Bloom's favour, a process that was completed with the publication of *Doli siti*. This development opened the doors to discussions of other issues in Castel-Bloom's work, including her representation of the Israeli reality, her role as a woman writer and her postmodern tendencies.

6 The distinction between North Tel Aviv and South Tel Aviv is an ethnic and socio-economic one that is common knowledge in Israel: North Tel Aviv is predominantly Ashkenazi (European) and upper middle class, while South Tel Aviv is the impoverished home of Mizrahim (North African or Middle Eastern Jews), new immigrants and legal and illegal guest workers from countries like the Philippines, Thailand, Nigeria and more. These differences have created a vast cultural chasm between North and South Tel Aviv.

7 The following are some examples of the fascination with this notion: Adia Mendelsohn-Maoz (1996) emphasizes the role of film in her discussion of Castel-Bloom and Etgar Keret. Smadar Shifman (2002) points out that 'a dominant factor common to all the characters in [*Halakim enoshiyim*] is the tendency to see their lives in televisionic terms [. . .] The sense of familiarity awakened by the novel flows not only from its closeness to our lives, but also from our closeness to representations of this reality, representations to which we have become so accustomed that we tend to interchange them with reality itself'. Kobi Nissim (1992) writes that Castel-Bloom's Hebrew is the Hebrew of 'written (newspapers) or spoken media (television)'. Tali Schwartzstein (2002) notes that 'the media is woven into the characters' lives'. Batya Gur (1992) compares the experience of reading *Doli siti* to that of watching absurdly violent cartoons. David Gurevitch (1990) writes of *Heykhan ani nimtset*: 'It is clear to me that everything is linked [. . .] to a kitschy, overdone, and "romantic" example of that same reality, as it is reflected in the Hollywood melodrama'. In another article about postmodernist Israeli writers (including Castel-Bloom), he writes (1996) that postmodern language 'is manifested in a metaphor of the matrix screen: the television screen, the computer screen, the screen of photographic reproduction'.

8 For more on the language of Roth's *Call It Sleep*, see Sollors (1996).

9 I am using Starr's transliteration of this Arabic title (which Castel-Bloom provides in Hebrew transliteration).

10 Laor (2001) provides an insightful analysis of the 'cleansing and purification of the [Hebrew] language of all foreign elements' (214) and of the resultant 'alienation in Hebrew prose from spoken language' (215).

11 My double use of the verb 'to shoot' is, of course, limited to English. The Hebrew verb that Laor uses, *yara*, is used only for weapons.

12 It is interesting to note that Starr adds a note to her brief discussion of the use of English in *Hamina lisa*, in which she cites rates of linguistic assimilation among English-speaking immigrants in Israel, and then writes that 'in recent years English has made great inroads into Hebrew' (2000: 243). The assumption that the presence of English-speaking immigrants is related to the tremendous presence of English in Hebrew undervalues the immeasurable impact of American television, films and music, focusing instead on the same analytical model that can be applied to other languages, such as Arabic and French, which are imported to Israel by the immigrants who speak them.

13 *Monoglossia* is Bakhtin's term.

14 In the English edition, the sentence is translated thus: 'They've all got crooked mouths from all the times they've hissed the black market rate of the dollar out of the corner of their mouths; all their mouths are shaped like dollars' (Castel-Bloom 1992; 1997: 125). While the link between excessive consumerism and the United States is maintained, the symbolic value of both the 'S' and the '$', so conspicuous in the original Hebrew, is lost in this translation.

15 See Laor (2001).

Anglophone Jewish writers

The following list of Anglophone Jewish writers is long but not, of course, exhaustive. It is meant to provide aid for further study, to sketch a 'geography' of Anglophone Jewish writing and to convey a feeling for its diversity. Wherever possible, migratory movements of Jewish writers within the Anglophone diaspora and to or from Israel have been indicated in brackets following individual entries.

Aaronson, Lazarus Leonard (UK)
Abish, Walter (USA)
Abraham, Nelson Ahlgren (writes as Nelson Algren) (USA)
Abraham, Pearl (ISR/USA)
Abrahams, Lionel (RSA)
Abse, Danny (UK)
Acker, Kathy (USA)
Afterman, Allen (AUS)
Aguilar, Grace (UK)
Aharoni, Ada (ISR)
Alexander, Goldie (AUS)
Algren, Nelson (see Abraham, Nelson Ahlgren) (USA)
Alkalay-Gut, Karen (UK/ISR)
Altman, Phyllis (RSA)
Alvarez, Alfred (UK)
Antin, Mary (USA)
Apple, Max (USA)
Armstrong, Diane (AUS)
Asimov, Isaac (USA)
Atlas, Zygfryd (AUS)
Auster, Paul (USA)

Back, Rachel Tzvia (USA/ISR)
Baitz, Jon Robin (USA)
Baker, Mark Raphael (AUS)
Baron, Alexander (UK)
Bart, Lionel (UK)
Barwin, Victor (RSA)
Baumbach, Jonathan (USA)
Beck, Mordechai (UK/ISR)
Becker, Jillian (RSA)
Becker, Robin (USA)
Behrman, Samuel N. (USA)
Beker, Ruth (USA/ISR)
Bell, Daniel (USA)
Bell, Marvin (USA)
Bellow, Saul (CAN/USA)
Benarroch, Moshe (ISR)
Benatar, Isaac (RSA)
Bensusan, Samuel Levy (UK)
Berkoff, Steven (UK)
Bermant, Chaim (UK)
Bernstein, Hilda (RSA)
Birstein, Ann (USA)
Blay, Anna Rosner (AUS)
Bloom, Amy (USA)
Braude, Sandra (RSA)
Brauner, David (writes as Robert Morris) (UK/ISR)
Brett, Doris (AUS)
Brodky, Harold (USA)
Broner, E.M. (USA)
Brooker, Anita (UK)
Brown, Rosellen (USA)

Brudno, Ezra (USA)
Bukiet, Melvin Jules (USA)

Cahan, Abraham (USA)
Calisher, Hortense (USA)
Chabon, Michael (USA)
Charles, Gerda (UK)
Chertok, Haim (USA/ISR)
Chester, Roberta (ISR)
Clouts, Sydney (RSA)
Codish, Edward (USA/ISR/USA)
Cohen, Bernard (AUS)
Cohen, Jack Sidney (ISR)
Cohen, Leonard (CAN)
Cohen, Matt (CAN)
Collins, Alan (AUS)
Cykiert, Abraham (AUS)

Danby, Frank (see Frankau, Julia) (UK)
Davidson, Lionel (UK)
Dayan, Yael (ISR)
Dean, Macabee (USA/ISR)
Disraeli, Benjamin (UK)
Doctorow, E.L. (USA)
Dowse, Sara (AUS)
Dubnow, Eugene (ISR)
Dudai, Nomi (ISR)
Dworkin, Andrea (USA)

Edelman, Maurice (UK)
Edelstein, Hyman (CAN)
Elazar (see Freifeld, Larry) (USA/ISR)
Elgrably, Jordan (USA)
Elisha, Ron (AUS)
Elkin, Stanley (USA)
Eprile, Tony (RSA)
Epstein, Leslie (USA)
Epstein, Seymour (USA)
Eve, Nomi (USA)

Fagan, Cary (CAN)
Fainlight, Ruth (USA/UK)
Farhi, Morris (UK)
Farjeon, Benjamin (UK)
Fast, Irving (USA)
Federman, Raymond (USA)
Fedler, Dov (RSA)
Feinstein, Elaine (UK)
Ferber, Edna (USA)
Fiedler, Leslie A. (USA)
Fierstein, Harvey (USA)
Figes, Eva (UK)
First, Ruth (RSA)
Frankau, Julia (writes as Frank Danby) (UK)
Frankel, Rudy (RSA)
Frankel, Zygmunt (ISR)
Freedman, Shalom (USA/ISR)
Freedman, William (USA/ISR)
Freifeld, Larry (writes as Elazar) (USA/ISR)
Fried, Erich (UK)
Friedman, Bruce Jay (USA)
Friedman, Florence Louie (RSA)
Friedman, Graeme (RSA)
Friend, Robert (USA/ISR)
Friesem, Ricky (ISR)
Fuchs, Daniel (USA)

Galgut, Damon (RSA)
Gavron, Jeremy (UK)
Gershon, Karen (UK)
Ginsberg, Allen (USA)
Glanville, Brian (UK)
Gleitzman, Morris (AUS)
Gold, Alan (AUS)
Gold, Herbert (USA)
Goldberg, Rifkah (UK/ISR)
Golding, Louis (UK)
Goldreich, Gloria (USA)
Goldstein, Rebecca (USA)
Gollancz, Sir Victor (UK)
Goodman, Allegra (USA)
Goodman, Paul (USA)
Gordimer, Nadine (RSA)
Gordon, Gerald (RSA)
Gordon, Lyndall (RSA/UK)
Gordon, Samuel (UK)

Gorenberg, Gershom (USA/ISR)
Gottlieb, Phyllis (CAN)
Goudvis, Bertha (RSA)
Gow, David (CAN)
Grant, Linda (UK)
Green, Jeffrey M. (USA/ISR)
Greenberg, Joanne (USA)

Hacker, Marilyn (USA)
HaLevy, Schulamith Chava (ISR)
Halperin, Lami (writes as Lami) (USA/ISR)
Halter, Alona (UK/ISR)
Hamburger, Michael (UK)
Harris, Emily (UK)
Harris, Norman Y. (USA)
Harwood, Ronald (RSA/UK)
Hastings, Michael (UK)
Hecht, Ben (USA)
Helfgott, Barbara (USA)
Heller, Joseph (USA)
Hellman, Lillian (USA)
Helprin, Mark (USA)
Hemley, Robin (USA)
Hobsbaum, Philip (UK)
Hollander, John (USA)
Horovitz, Michael (UK)
Howe, Irving (USA)
Howland, Bette (USA)
Hurst, Fannie (USA)

Israels, Isaac (writes as William Luscombe Searelle) (RSA)
Izak, Gretti (ISR)

Jacobs, A.C. (UK)
Jacobson, Dan (RSA/UK)
Jacobson, Howard (UK)
Jhabvala, Ruth Prawer (UK/USA)
Joelson, Annette (RSA)
Johnson, Joyce (USA)
Jong, Erica (USA)
Josipovici, Gabriel (UK)
Julius, Lila (ISR)

Kadmon, Jean (USA/ISR)
Kalman, Judith (CAN)
Kaplan, Johanna (USA)
Karmel, Ilona (USA)
Kasrils, Ronnie (RSA)
Katz, Steve (USA)
Kaufman, Bob (USA)
Kaufman, Shirley (USA/ISR)
Kazin, Alfred (USA)
Kersch, Gerald (UK)
Kessler, Sharon (USA/ISR)
Kirchheimer, Gloria (USA)
Kirsch, Olga (RSA/ISR)
Klein, A.M. (CAN)
Klepfisz, Irena (USA)
Koestler, Arthur (UK)
Kohn, Peter (AUS)
Konecky, Edith (USA)
Kops, Bernard (UK)
Kosinski, Jerzy (USA)
Kramer, Lotte (UK)
Kramer, Mordechai (ISR)
Kreisel, Henry (CAN)
Kriel, Maja (RSA)
Krouse, Matthew (RSA)
Kruglanski, Orit (ISR/ESP)
Kumin, Maxine (USA)
Kunitz, Stanley (USA)
Kushner, Tony (USA)

Labensohn, Hudy (ISR)
Lami (see Halperin, Lami) (USA/ISR)
Lappin, Elena (UK)
Layton, Irving (CAN)
Lazarus, Emma (USA)
Leavitt, David (USA)
Lentin, Ronit (ISR/IRE)
Lerman, Rhoda (USA)
Lerner, Laurence (UK)
Leventhal, Ann Z. (USA)
Leverson, Ada (UK)
Levine, Norman (CAN)
Levinsky, Nehemia (RSA)
Levinson, Mark L. (USA/ISR)
Levy, Amy (UK)

Lewin, Hugh (RSA)
Lewisohn, Ludwig (USA)
Lewitt, Maria (AUS)
Liberman, Serge (AUS)
Lichman, Simon (UK/ISR)
Lipshitz, Fay (RSA/ISR)
Litvinoff, Emanuel (UK)
Louvish, Simon (UK/ISR/UK)
Ludman, Barbara (RSA)
Ludwig, Jack (CAN)
Luscombe Searelle, William (see Israels, Isaac) (RSA)

Magun, Carol (USA)
Mailer, Norman (USA)
Majzels, Robert (CAN)
Malamud, Bernard (USA)
Malpede, Karen (USA)
Mamet, David (USA)
Mandel, Eli (CAN)
Mandel, Jerome (USA/ISR)
Mankowitz, Wolf (UK)
Mann, Emily (USA)
Mann, Stanley (USA/ISR)
Marcus, David (IRE)
Margolis, David (USA/ISR)
Markfield, Wallace (USA)
Markowitz, Arthur (RSA)
Martin, David (AUS/UK)
Mass, Rochelle (CAN/ISR)
Massarwa, Osama (ISR)
May, John Henry (see Schlosberg, H.J.) (RSA)
Mayne, Seymour (CAN)
Mendes, Moses (UK)
Merkin, Daphne (USA)
Merrick, Leonard (UK)
Metzger, Deena (USA)
Michaels, Anne (CAN)
Mikes, George (UK)
Miller, Arthur (USA)
Miller, Betty (UK)
Miller, Ruth (RSA)
Millin, Sarah Gertrude (RSA)
Mirvis, Tova (USA)
Misheiker, Betty (RSA)
Montefiore, Charlotte (UK)
Morgan, Robin (USA)
Morris, Robert (see Brauner, David) (UK/ISR)
Moskowitz, Faye (USA)
Moss, Celia (UK)
Moss, Marion (UK)
Moss, Rose (RSA/USA)
Motro, Helen Schary (USA/ISR)

Nassauer, Rudolf (UK)
Nemerov, Howard (USA)
Neugeboren, Jay (USA)
Nissenson, Hugh (USA)
Nochomowitz, Molly (RSA)
Nyburg, Sidney (USA)

Odets, Clifford (USA)
Olsen, Tillie (USA)
Oppen, George (USA)
Ornitz, Samuel (USA)
Ostriker, Alicia (USA)
Ozick, Cynthia (USA)

Paley, Grace (USA)
Parker, Dorothy (USA)
Pascal, Julia (UK)
Pastan, Linda (USA)
Pelletiere, Marcia (USA)
Perelman, Sidney J. (USA)
Piercy, Marge (USA)
Pinero, Sir Arthur Wing (UK)
Pinkus, Denny (ISR)
Pinsky, Robert (USA)
Pinter, Harold (UK)
Poliakoff, Stephen (UK)
Potok, Chaim (USA)
Press, Karen (RSA)
Prose, Francine (USA)

Radzyner, Marc (AUS/ISR)
Ragen, Naomi (USA/ISR)
Rakosi, Carl (USA)
Ralph, Nathan (CAN)

Raphael, Frederic (USA/UK)
Rapoport, Nessa (USA)
Ravvin, Norman (CAN)
Redhill, Michael (CAN)
Reich, Tova (USA)
Reisner, Gabriel (ISR)
Reznikoff, Charles (USA)
Ribalow, Reena (USA/ISR)
Rich, Adrienne (USA)
Richler, Mordecai (CAN/UK/CAN)
Riding, Laura (USA)
Robson, Jeremy (UK)
Rodker, John (UK)
Roiphe, Anne Richardson (USA)
Rosen, Norma (USA)
Rosenbaum, Thane (USA)
Rosenberg, Isaac (UK)
Rosenberg, Robert (USA/ISR)
Rosenblatt, Joe (CAN)
Rosenfeld, Isaac (USA)
Rosten, Leo (USA)
Roth, Henry (USA)
Roth, Philip (USA)
Rothenberg, Jerome (USA)
Rothman, Claire (CAN)
Rubens, Bernice (UK)
Rubin, Riva (RSA/ISR)
Rudolf, Anthony (UK)
Rukeyser, Muriel (USA)

Sachs, Albie (RSA)
Safransky, Rosa (AUS)
Salinger, J.D. (USA)
Samuel, Maurice (USA)
Samuel, Naomi (see Shmuel, Naomi) (ISR)
Samuels, Diane (UK)
Sanchez, Raquel (ISR)
Sarah, Robyn (CAN)
Sassoon, Siegfried (UK)
Schaeffer, Susan Fromberg (USA)
Schlosberg, H.J. (writes as Henry John May) (RSA)
Schoenbrun, Adam (ISR)
Schwarts, Lynne Sharon (USA)
Schwartz, Delmore (USA)
Segal, Arthur (RSA)
Segal, Lore (UK/USA)
Self, Will (UK)
Sendak, Maurice (USA)
Setton, Ruth Knafo (USA)
Shaffer, Anthony (UK)
Shaffer, Peter (UK)
Shapiro, Karl (USA)
Shapiro, Lionel (CAN)
Sharon, Reva (USA/ISR)
Shaw, Irwin (USA)
Sher, Emil (CAN)
Sherman, Kenneth (CAN)
Sherman, Martin (USA)
Sherwin, Richard E. (USA/ISR)
Shmuel, Naomi (writes as Naomi Samuel) (ISR)
Sidgwick, Cecilly (UK)
Silk, Dennis (UK/ISR)
Silkin, Jon (UK/ISR)
Silverman, Dov (USA/ISR)
Simms, Norman (USA/NZ/ISR)
Simon, Barney (RSA)
Simon, Lilian (RSA)
Simon, Neil (USA)
Simon, Oswald John (UK)
Sinclair, Clive (UK)
Sinclair, Jo (USA)
Sivan, Miriam (USA/ISR)
Skillman, Judith (USA)
Slesinger, Tess (USA)
Slovo, Joe (RSA)
Solotaroff, Ted (USA)
Sontag, Susan (USA)
Sowden, Lewis (RSA)
Spark, Muriel (UK)
Spiegelman, Art (USA)
Spielvogel, Nathan (AUS)
Stavans, Ilan (USA)
Stein, Gertrude (USA)
Steiner, George (USA)
Stendig-Lindberg, Gustawa (ISR)
Stern, Gladys Bronwyn (UK)
Stern, Steve (USA)

Sternburg, Janet (USA)
Stevens, Wallace (USA)
Stollman, Lev Aryeh (CAN/USA)
Stone, Michael E. (UK/ISR)
Stoppard, Tom (UK)
Styron, William (USA)
Sukenick, Ronald (USA)
Sutro, Alfred (UK)
Swados, Elizabeth (USA)

Tarn, Nathaniel (UK)
Taylor, C.P. (UK)
Tobenkin, Elias (USA)
Treitel, Jonathan (UK)
Trilling, Lionel (USA)

Unger, Lois Michal (USA/ISR)
Uris, Leon (USA)
Uys, Pieter-Dirk (RSA)

Waddington, Miriam (CAN)
Wallant, Edward Lewis (USA)
Wandor, Michelene (UK)
Wasserstein, Wendy (USA)
Waten, Judah (AUS)
Watts, Irene (CAN)
Wayman, Tom (CAN)
Weissbort, Daniel (UK)
Wesker, Arnold (UK)
West, Nathanael (USA)
White, Roger (CAN/ISR)
Whitman, Ruth (USA)
Wiesel, Elie (USA)
Wilentz, Amy (USA)
Wilson, Jonathan (UK/USA/ISR/USA)
Wiseman, Adele (CAN)
Wolf, Emma (USA)
Wolfe, Humbert (UK)
Woolf, Leonard Sidney (UK)
Wouk, Herman (USA)

Yankowitz, Susan (USA)
Yezierska, Anzia (USA)
Yglesias, Helen (USA)

Zable, Arnold (AUS)
Zangwill, Isaac (UK)
Zeldis, Chayym (USA/ISR/USA/ISR)
Zisquit, Linda (USA/ISR)
Zukofsky, Louis (USA)
Zwi, Rose (RSA/AUS)
Zwicky, Fay (AUS)

Bibliography

Further reading, reference works and study aids (some suggestions)

Alkalay-Gut (2002)
Bernstein (1960)
Biale, Galchinsky, and Heschel (1998)
Braude (2001)
Brauner (2001)
Cheyette (1996)
Cheyette (1998)
Cheyette (forthcoming)
Cheyette and Marcus (1998)
Cohen (1997)
Ezrahi (2000a)
Freedman (2000)
Fried (1988)
Furman (2000)
Hammer (1988)
Hollinger (1995)
Kalechofsky and Kalechofsky (1984)
Kerbel (2003)
Kramer and Wirth-Nesher (2003)
Lenta (2001)
Liberman (1987; 2nd edn 1991)
Myhill (2004)
Raz (1998)
Rubin (2005)
Rubinstein (1996)
Sarna, J.D. (1986)
Shatzky and Taub (1997)
Wirth-Nesher (1994a)
Wirth-Nesher (2006)
Wisse (2000)

Cited works

Aarons, V. (2005) *What Happened to Abraham? Reinventing the Covenant in American Jewish Fiction*, Newark: University of Delaware Press.

Abrahams, P. (1950) *Wild Conquest*, New York: Harper and Brothers.

Abse, D. (1990) *Remembrance of Crimes Past*, London: Hutchinson.

Adamson, W. (1980) 'To Be or Not to Be (a Jew)', *Melbourne Chronicle*, April–May.

Aharoni, A. (1997) 'A Bridge of Peace', *Not In Your War Anymore*. Online. Available HTTP: <http://www.iflac.com/ada/peace-p.html> (accessed 22 March 2005).

Ahmad, A. (1995; 1996) 'The Politics of Literary Postcoloniality', in P. Mongia (ed.) *Contemporary Postcolonial Theory. A Reader*, London, etc.: Arnold.

Alexenberg, M. (1989) 'Aesthetics in Judaism', *Wellsprings*, April–May: 18–22.

Alkalay-Gut, K. (2002) 'Double Diaspora: English Writers in Israel', *Judaism*, 51: 457–68.

Alkalay-Gut, K. (2003) 'An Interview with Moshe Benarroch', *Archipelago*, 7.1. Online. Available HTTP: <http://www.archipelago.org/vol7-1/recommend.htm> (accessed 22 March 2005).

Alkalay-Gut, K. (2005) 'Poetry of September 11 – The Testimonial Imperative', *Poetics Today*, 26: 257–79.

Alter, R. (1968; 1994) 'Jewish Dreams and Nightmares', in H. Wirth-Nesher (ed.) *What is Jewish Literature?*, Philadelphia: The Jewish Publication Society, 53–66.

Alter, R. (1982; 1986) 'The Jew Who Didn't Get Away: On the Possibility of an American Jewish Culture', in J.D. Sarna (ed.) *The American Jewish Experience*, New York: Holmes & Meier, 269–81.

Anderson, G.K. (1965) *The Legend of the Wandering Jew*, Providence: Brown University Press.

Ang, I. (1998) 'Can One Say No to Chineseness? Pushing the Limits of the Diasporic Paradigm', *Boundary 2*, 25: 223–42.

Anonymous (2003) 'Wingate Literary Prize: Zadie Smith and Sebastian Haffner win top literary prize', *The Jewish Quarterly*, www.jewishquarterly.org/050803b.shtml (accessed 6 June 2004).

Antin, M. (1912; 1997) *The Promised Land*, New York: Penguin.

Appiah, K.A. (1991; 1996) 'Is the Post- in Postmodernism the Post- in Postcolonial?', in P. Mongia (ed.) *Contemporary Postcolonial Theory, A Reader*, London, etc.: Arnold, 55–71.

Arendt, H. (1951; 5th edn 1973) *The Origins of Totalitarianism*, New York: Harcourt Brace Jovanovich.

Armstrong, J. (1992; 2nd edn 1998) 'The Disempowerment of First North American Native Peoples and Empowerment through Their Writing', in D.D. Moses and T. Goldie (eds) *An Anthology of Canadian Native Literature in English*, Toronto: Oxford University Press, 239–42.

Arnold, M. (1865; 1962) 'On the Study of Celtic Literature', in R.H. Super (ed.) *Lectures and Essays in Criticism*, Ann Arbor: Michigan, 291–395.

Arnold, M. (1869; 1965) *Culture and Anarchy: An Essay in Political and Social Criticism*, R.H. Super (ed.), Ann Arbor: Michigan.

Arnold, M. (1993) *Culture and Anarchy and other Writings by Matthew Arnold*, ed. S. Collini, New York: Cambridge University Press.

Ashcroft, B., Griffiths, G. and H. Tiffin (1989; 2nd edn 2002) *The Empire Writes Back. Theory and Practice in Post-Colonial Literatures*, London, New York: Routledge.

Ba'al Makhshoves (1918; 1994) [i.e., Israel Isidor Elyashev] 'One Literature in Two Languages', trans. H. Wirth-Nesher, in H. Wirth-Nesher (ed.) *What is Jewish Literature?*, Philadelphia: The Jewish Publication Society, 69–77.

Back, R.T. (2001) *Azimuth*, New York: Sheep Meadow Press.

Back, R.T. (2003) *The Buffalo Poems*, Sausalito, CA: Duration Press.

Back, R.T. (2004) 'Two Northern Poems', *Bridges*, 10.1: 43.

Back, R.T. (26 January 2006) www.partnersforpeace.org/pressreleases/db200601260

Bakhtin, M. (1981) *The Dialogic Imagination: Four Essays*, trans. C. Emerson and M. Holquist, M. Holquist (ed.), Austin: University of Texas Press, 1981.

Bakhtin, M. (1986) *Speech Genres and Other Late Essays*, trans. V.W. McGee, C. Emerson and M. Holquist (eds), Austin: University of Texas Press.

Balaban, A. (1995) *Gal aher basiporet ha'ivrit: siporet ivrit postmodernistit* [A Different Wave in Hebrew Fiction: Postmodernist Hebrew Fiction], Jerusalem: Keter.

Bareli, A. (2001) 'Forgetting Europe: Perspectives on the Debate about Zionism and Colonialism', *Journal of Israeli History*, 20: 99–120.

Barker, F., Hulme, P. and Iversen, M. (eds) (1994) *Colonial Discourse/Postcolonial Theory*, Manchester, New York: Manchester University Press.

Bartels, A. (1903) 'Das Judentum in der deutschen Literatur', in *Kritik und Kritikaster*, Leipzig: Avenarius, 102–24.

Bauman, Z. (1987) *Legistlators and Interpreters*, Ithaca, NY: Cornell University Press.

Bauman, Z. (1991) *Modernity and Ambivalence*, Ithaca, NY: Cornell University Press.

Bauman, Z. (1998) 'Allosemitism: Premodern, Modern, Postmodern', in B. Cheyette and L. Marcus (eds) *Modernity, Culture and 'the Jew'*. Cambridge: Polity, 143–56.

Bazin, N.T. and Seymour, M.D. (eds) (1990) *Conversations with Nadine Gordimer*, Jackson, London: University Press of Mississippi.

Beckett, S. (1955) *Waiting for Godot: A Tragicomedy in Two Acts*, London: Faber & Faber.

Belloc, H. (1922) *The Jews*, New York: Houghton Mifflin.

Bellow, S. (1947; 1984) *The Victim*, London: Secker & Warburg.

Bellow, S. (1963; 1994) 'On Jewish Storytelling', in H. Wirth-Nesher (ed.) *What is Jewish Literature?*, Philadelphia: The Jewish Publication Society, 15–19.

Bellow, S. (1964; 1984) *Herzog*, London: Secker & Warburg.

Bellow, S. (1984) *Him with His Foot in His Mouth and Other Stories*, New York: Harper & Row.

Benjamin, W. (1923; 1969) 'The Task of the Translator', trans. H. Zohn, in H. Arendt (ed.) *Illuminations*, New York: Schocken, 69–82.

Benjamin, W. (1940; 1969) 'Theses on the Philosophy of History', trans. H. Zohn, in H. Arendt (ed.) *Illuminations*, New York: Schocken, 253–65.

Berger, A.L. (1998) 'Memory and Meaning: The Holocaust in Second Generation Literature', in Z. Garber and A.L. Berger (eds) *Methodology in the Academic Teaching of the Holocaust*, Lanham, MD: University Press of America, 171–89.

Bergner, H. (1946) *Between Sky and Sea*, trans. J. Waten, Melbourne: Dolphin Publications.

Bergner, H. (1955; 1984) 'The Actor', in R. and R. Kalechofsky (eds) *Jewish Writing Down Under: Australia and New Zealand*, Marblehead, MA: Micah, 63–70.

Bergner, H. (1963) *Light and Shadow*, trans. A. Braizblatt, Melbourne: Georgian House.

Berkowitz, J. (2003) 'Yiddish Writing in the 20th Century', in S. Kerbel (ed.) *Jewish Writers of the Twentieth Century*, New York: Fitzroy Dearborn, 17–22.

Bernstein, E. (1960) *Jewish Writers in South Africa*, New York: Jewish Book Council of America.

Bernstein, M.A. (1994) *Foregone Conclusions: Against Apocalyptic History*, Berkeley: University of California Press.

Berquist, J.L. (1995) *Judaism in Persia: A Social and Historical Approach*, Minneapolis: Fortress Press.

Bersten, H. (1997) 'Review of *Stelle e Strisce e Estella Di David Nella Croce del Sud (Stars and Stripes and the Star of David in the Southern Cross)* by Rosanna Rosini, Coopstudio scrl, Trieste, 1988', *Australian Jewish Historical Society Journal*, 13: 710–15.

Bhabha, H.K. (1994) *The Location of Culture*, London, New York: Routledge.

Bhabha, H.K. (1998) 'Foreword: Joking Aside: The Idea of a Self-Critical Community', in B. Cheyette and L. Marcus (eds) *Modernity, Culture and 'the Jew'*. Cambridge: Polity, xvi–xx.

Biale, D. (1998) 'The Melting Pot and Beyond. Jews and the Politics of American Identity', in D. Biale, M. Galchinsky and S. Heschel (eds), *Insider/Outsider. American Jews and Multiculturalism*, Berkeley: University of California Press, 17–34.

Biale, D., Galchinsky, M. and Heschel, S. (eds) (1998) *Insider/Outsider. American Jews and Multiculturalism*, Berkeley: University of California Press.

Bible JPS (1917) *The Holy Scriptures According to the Masoretic Text. A New Translation with the Aid of Previous Versions and with Constant Consultation of Jewish Authorities*, Philadelphia, PA: The Jewish Publication Society of America.

Bible NOAB (1977) *New Oxford Annotated Bible: An Ecumenical Study Bible*, ed. H.G. May, New York: Oxford University Press.

Birnbaum, R. (2000) 'Interview: Amy Bloom'. Online. Available HTTP: <http://www.identitytheory.com/people/birnbaum2.html> (accessed 24 June 2005).

Biton, E. (1979) *Minha maroka'it* [Moroccan Gift], Tel Aviv: Traklin.

Bloom, A. (1995) *Come to Me*, London: Picador.

Bloom, A. (1996) 'Light Breaks Where No Sun Shines', in *Nice Jewish Girls: Growing Up in America*, ed. Marlene Adler Marks, New York: Plume, 24–32.

Bloom, A. (1998) *Love Invents Us*, London: Picador.

Bloom, A. (2001) *A Blind Man Can See How Much I Love You*, London: Picador.

Bloom, A. (2002) *Normal: Transsexual CEOS, Crossdressing Cops, and Hermaphrodites with Attitude*, New York: Random House.

Bluestein, G. (1989; 2nd edn 1998) *Anglish/Yinglish. Yiddish in American Life and Literature*, Lincoln: University of Nebraska Press.

Borowski, T. (1948; 1967) *This Way for the Gas, Ladies and Gentlemen, and Other Stories*, trans. B. Vedder, London: Cape.

Boyarin, D. (2000) 'The Colonial Drag: Zionism, Gender, and Mimicry', in F. Afzal-Khan and K. Seshadri-Crook (eds) *The Pre-Occupation of Postcolonial Studies*. Durham, NC: Duke University Press, 234–56.

Boyarin, D. and Boyarin, J. (1993) 'Diaspora: Generation and the Ground of Jewish Identity', *Critical Inquiry*, 19: 693–725.

Boyarin, J. (1992a) *Storm from Paradise: The Politics of Jewish Memory*, Minneapolis: University of Minnesota Press.

Boyarin, J. (1992b) 'Reading Exodus into History', *New Literary History*, 23: 523–54.

Boyarin, J. and Boyarin, D. (2002) *Powers of Diaspora. Two Essays on the Relevance of Jewish Culture*, Minneapolis: University of Minnesota Press.

Brah, A. (197) *Cartographies of Diaspora. Contesting Identities*, London: Routledge.

Braude, C.B. (ed.) (2001) *Contemporary Jewish Writing in South Africa*, Cape Town: David Philip.

Brauner, D. (2001) *Post-War Jewish Fiction: Ambivalence, Self-Explanation and Transatlantic Connections*, New York, Basingstoke: Palgrave Macmillan.

Brenner, M. (2002) 'Jewish Culture in Contemporary America and Weimer Germany: Parallels and Differences', *Jewish Studies at the CEU (Central European University). Yearbook II, 1999–2001*. Online. Available HTTP: <http://www.ceu.hu/jewishstudies/pdf/02_brenner.pdf> (accessed 8 December 2006).

Brenner, R.R. (1980) *The Faith and Doubt of Holocaust Survivors*, New York: Free Press.

Brezniak, H. (1967) 'Pinchas Goldhar', *The Bridge*, 3: 13–15.

Brooks, P. (1994) *Psychoanalysis and Storytelling*, Oxford: University of Oxford Press.

Brudno, E. (1904) *The Fugitive: Being Memoirs of a Wanderer in Search of a Home*, New York: Doubleday, Page & Company.

Budick, E.M. (2001) 'Introduction', in E.M. Budick (ed.) *Ideology and Jewish Identity in Israeli and American Literature*, Albany: State University of New York Press, 1–22.

Budick, E.M. (2003) 'The Holocaust in the Jewish American Literary Imagination', in M.P. Kramer and H. Wirth-Nesher (eds) *The Cambridge Companion to Jewish American Literature*, Cambridge: Cambridge University Press, 212–30.

Buelens, G. (1994) 'The New Man and the Mediator: (Non-)Remembrance in Jewish-American Immigrant Narrative', in A. Singh, J.T. Skerrett, Jr. and R.E. Hogan (eds) *Memory, Narrative, and Identity: New Essays in Ethnic American Literatures*, Boston, MA: Northeastern University Press, 89–113.

Butler, J. (1997) *Excitable Speech: A Politics of the Performative*, New York: Routledge.

Cahan, A. (1896; 1970) *Yekl. A Tale of the New York Ghetto*, in *Yekl and The Imported Bridegroom. And Other Stories of Yiddish New York*, with a new introd. by B.G. Richards, New York: Dover Publications, 1–89.

Cahan, A. (1898) 'The Russian Jew in America', *The Atlantic Monthly*, July: 128–39.

Cahan, A. (1917; 1993) *The Rise of David Levinsky*, New York: Penguin Books.

Canfield, J. and Hansen, M.V. (eds) (2000) *Chicken Soup for the Soul: Stories that restore your faith in human nature*, New York: Vermilion.

Carter, D. (1996) ' "Mother" (Excerpts from a biography of Judah Waten)', *Westerly* (Summer): 114–22.

Carter, D. (1997) *A Career in Writing: Judah Waten and the Cultural Politics of a Literary Career*, Toowoomba, QLD: ASAL Literary Studies Series.

Castel-Bloom, O. (1990) *Heykhan ani nimtset* [Where Am I], Tel Aviv: Zmora-Bitan.

Castel-Bloom, O. (1992) *Doli siti* [Dolly City], Tel Aviv: Zmora-Bitan.

Castel-Bloom, O. (1992; 1997) *Dolly City*, trans. D. Bilu, London, Paris: Loki Books/UNESCO Publishing.

Castel-Bloom, O. (1993) *Sipurim bilti retsuyim* [Involuntary Stories], Tel Aviv: Zmora-Bitan.

Castel-Bloom, O. (1995) *Hamina lisa* [The Mina Lisa], Jerusalem: Keter.

Castel-Bloom, O. (1998) *Hasefer hehadash shel orli kastel-bloom* [Orly Castel-Bloom's New Book], Jerusalem: Keter.

Castel-Bloom, O. (2002) *Halakim enoshiyim* [Human Parts], Tel Aviv: Kinneret Publishing.

Castel-Bloom, O. (2002; 2003) *Human Parts*, trans. D. Bilu, Boston: Davide R. Godine.

Chametzky, J. (1977) *From the Ghetto: The Fiction of Abraham Cahan*, Amherst: University of Massachusetts Press.

Chanes, J.A. (1999) 'Beyond Marginality', *Judaism. A Quarterly Journal of Jewish Life and Thought*, 48: 387–90.

Chariandy, D. (2006) 'Postcolonial Diasporas', *Postcolonial Text*, 2. Online. Available HTTP: <http://postcolonial.org/index.php/pct/article/viewArticle/440/159> (accessed 24 June 2005).

Chesterman, A. (1997) *Memes of Translation: The Spread of Ideas in Translation Theory*, Amsterdam, Philadelphia: John Benjamins.

Cheyette, B. (1996) 'Englishness and Extraterritoriality: British-Jewish Writing and Diaspora Culture', *Literary Strategies*, 12: 21–39.

Cheyette, B. (2003) 'Diasporas of the Mind: British-Jewish Writing Beyond Multiculturalism', in M. Fludernik (ed.) *Diaspora and Multiculturalism: Common Traditions and New Developments*, Amsterdam, New York: Rodopi, 45–82.

Cheyette, B. (2004) 'On Being a Jewish Critic', *Jewish Social Studies*, 11: 32–51.

Cheyette, B. (ed.) (1998) *Contemporary Jewish Writing in Britain and Ireland. An Anthology*, Lincoln: University of Nebraska Press.

Cheyette, B. and Marcus, L. (eds) (1998) *Modernity, Culture and 'the Jew'*, Oxford: Polity Press.

Cheyette, B. (forthcoming) *Diasporas of the Mind*, New Haven, CT: Yale University Press.

Clancy, T. (1987) *Patriot Games*, New York: Putnam.

Cleary, J. (2002) *Literature, Partition and the Nation-State. Culture and Conflict in Ireland, Israel and Palestine*, Cambridge: Cambridge University Press.

Clendinnen, I. (1999) *Reading the Holocaust*, New York: Cambridge University Press.

Clifford, J. (1994) 'Diasporas', *Cultural Anthropology*, 9: 302–38.

Clingman, S.R. (1986) *The Novels of Nadine Gordimer: History from the Inside*, Johannesburg: Ravan.

Coetzee, J.M. (1992) *Doubling the Point: Essays and Interviews*, ed. D. Atwell, Cambridge, MA; London: Harvard University Press.

Cohen, R. (1997) *Global Diasporas. An Introduction*, Seattle: University of Washington Press.

Cohen, S.B. (1994a) *Cynthia Ozick's Comic Art. From Levity to Liturgy*, Bloomington: Indiana University Press.

Cohen, S.B. (1994b) 'Cynthia Ozick: Prophet for Parochialism', in J. Baskin (ed.) *Women of the Word: Jewish Women and Jewish Writing*, Detroit: Wayne State University Press.

Colley, L. (1992) *Britons: Forging the Nation 1707–1837*, London: Yale University Press.

Conradi, P. (1983) 'Elaine Feinstein', in *Dictionary of Literary Biography 14: British Novelists Since 1960, Part 1: A–G*, Detroit: Gale, 292–7.

Cope, J. (1955) *The Fair House*, London: MacGibbon & Kee.

Corcoran, N. (1993) *English Poetry Since 1940*, Harlow: Longman.

Corkhill, A.R. (1994) *Australian Writing: Ethnic Writers 1945–1991*, Melbourne: Academia Press.

Cowen, S. (2000) 'There is Whom to complain to: a look at religious themes in the writing of Serge Liberman', unpublished address to a seminar in Melbourne (29 September 2000): 1–5.

Cowley, J. (2001) 'The Tiger Woods of Literature?', *New Statesman & Society*, 29 January: 57.

Damon, M. (1991) 'Talking Yiddish at the Boundaries', *Cultural Studies*, 5: 14–29.

Dash, J.M. (1996) 'Psychology, Creolization, and Hybridization', in B. King (ed.) *New National and Post-Colonial Literatures: An Introduction*, Oxford: Clarendon Press, 45–58.

Davison, N.R. (1996) *James Joyce,* Ulysses, *and the Construction of Jewish Identity. Culture, Biography, and 'the Jew' in Modernist Europe*, Cambridge: Cambridge University Press.

de Lange, N. (2000) *An Introduction to Judaism*, Cambridge: Cambridge University Press.

Deleuze, G. and Guattari, F. (1975; 1986) *Kafka: Toward a Minor Literature*, Minneapolis: University of Minnesota Press.

Derrida, J. (1978) *Writing and Difference*, trans. Alan Bass, Chicago: University of Chicago Press.

Derrida, J. (1982) 'Signature, Event, Context', in *Margins of Philosophy*, Chicago: University of Chicago Press, 307–30.

Dershowitz, A.M. (1996) *The Vanishing American Jew. In Search of Jewish Identity for the Next Century*, Boston, MA: Little, Brown.

Dickstein, M. (2001) 'The Complex Fate of the Jewish American Writer', in E.M. Budick (ed.) *Ideology and Jewish Identity in Israeli and American Literature*, New York: State University of New York Press, 57–78.

Docker, J. (2001) *1492: The Poetics of Diaspora*. London, New York: Continuum.

Dor, M. and Zach, N. (eds) (1977) *The Burning Bush: Poems from Modern Israel*, London: W.H. Allen.

Doran, H. (1997) 'A man's fascist past exposed: art meets actuality in radio play', *The Ottawa Citizen*, 14 December.

Doward, J. (2004) 'Madonna's Mystics Target British Kids', *Observer*, 29 August. Online. Available HTTP: <http://www.guardian.co.uk/religion/Story/0,2763,1293279,00.html> (accessed 2 February 2005).

DuBois, W.E.B. (1903; 1994) 'Of Our Spiritual Strivings', in *The Souls of Black Folk*, New York, Avenel, NJ: Gramercy Books, 2–8.

Eagleton, T. (1970) *Exiles and Emigrés: Studies in Modern Literature*, London: Chatto & Windus.

Eliot, G. (1876; 1988) *Daniel Deronda*, ed. G. Handley, Oxford: Oxford University Press.

Eliot, T.S. (1919; 1966) 'Tradition and the Individual Talent', in *Selected Essays*, London: Faber & Faber, 13–22.

Elliot, H. (2002) [Review of: Zable, A. (2002) *The Fig Tree*], *Australian*, 25 May.

Elliot, R. (1987) 'Long passage to a new land, and new life', *Canberra Times*, 3 December, 14.

Epp, R. (n.d.) *Kristallnacht*, Toronto: Playwrights Guild of Canada (typescript).

Epstein, L.J. (2001) *The Haunted Smile: The Story of Jewish Comedians in America*, New York: Public Affairs.

Ezrahi, S.D. (2000a) *Booking Passage. Exile and Homecoming in the Modern Jewish Imagination*, Berkeley: University of California Press.

Ezrahi, S.D. (2000b) 'Opening the Letters', *Tikkun*, July–August: 71–5.

Fackenheim, E.L. (1982; 3rd edn 1994) *To Mend the World: Foundations of Post-Holocaust Jewish Thought*, Bloomington, Indianapolis: Indiana University Press.

Factor, J. (1982) 'Individual and Community in Commonwealth Literature: three explorations of the immigrant experience in Australia', *Melbourne Chronicle*, 33, August–September: 3–6.

Fanon, F. (1952; 1967) *Black Skin, White Masks*, trans. C.L. Markmann, New York: Grove Press.

Fein, Y. (1988) 'I: A Retrospective: A Morning with Judah Waten', *Melbourne Chronicle*, 57, March–April: 5–6.

Fein, Y. (1993) 'Parents and Children in Australian Jewish Literature', *Melbourne Chronicle*, 63: 13–18.

Feinstein, E. (1984) 'Elaine Feinstein', *Contemporary Authors Autobiography Series*, 1: 215–23.

Feinstein, E. (1987) 'Writers in Conversation: Dannie Abse', London: ICA Video.

Feinstein, E. (1994) *Selected Poems*, Manchester: Carcanet.

Feinstein, E. (1994; 1996) *Dreamers*, Basingstoke: Pan.

Felman, J.L. (1995) 'Lost Jewish (Male) Souls: A Midrash on *Angels in America*', *Tikkun*, 10: 27–30.

Ferguson, I. (1998) 'Foreword', in D. Gow, *Cherry Docs*, Winnipeg: Scirocco, 11.

Ferris, K.R. (1989) 'James Joyce, Wandering Jew', unpublished PhD thesis, Emory University, Ann Arbor.

Finkelstein, N. (1992) *The Ritual of New Creation: Jewish Tradition and Contemporary Literature*, New York: State University of New York Press.

Fishman, C. (2002) 'Memory and Identity', *American Book Review*, 23: 8.

Fishman, J.A. (1991) *Yiddish: Turning to Life*, Amsterdam: Benjamins.

Fludernik, M. (2003) 'The Diasporic Imaginary. Postcolonial Reconfigurations in the Context of Multiculturalism', in M. Fludernik (ed.) *Diaspora and Multiculturalism: Common Traditions and New Developments*, Amsterdam, New York: Rodopi, xi–xxxviii.

Forché, C. (1993) *Against Forgetting*, New York: W.W. Norton.

Fränkel, S.I. and Bresslau, I.M. (eds) (1819) *Ordnung der öffentlichen Andacht für die Sabbath- und Festtage des ganzen Jahres nach dem Gebrauche des Neuen Tempel-Vereins*, Hamburg.

Frantzen, A.J. (1998) *Before the Closet: Same-Sex Love from* Beowulf *to* Angels in America, Chicago: University of Chicago Press.

Freadman, R. (2000) 'Jewish literature between Judaism and secularism: focus on Serge Liberman', unpublished address to a seminar in Melbourne (29 September 2000): 1–7.

Fredman, L.E. (1956) 'Introduction', in *Selected Short Stories of Nathan Spielvogel*, Melbourne: The Hawthorn Press, i–iv.

Freedman, J. (2000) *The Temple of Culture: Assimilation and Anti-Semitism in Literary Anglo-America*, New York, Oxford: Oxford University Press.

Freifeld, E.L. (22 March 2005) ' "BOOOP"/socio/politico/ecosystemic poems', *Ariga*. Online. Available HTTP: <http://www.ariga.com/visions/poetry/larry001.shtml#about>

Freiman, M. (1995) 'A triumph over loss', *Australian Jewish News* (Melbourne edition), 25 November: 38.

Fremd, A. (1984) 'Interview with Maria Lewitt', *Outrider*, 1: 2–9.

Freud, S. (1908; 1985) 'Creative Writers and Day-Dreaming', *Freud Penguin Library*. Vol. 14: *Arts and Literature*, trans. J. Strachey, London: Penguin, 131–41.

Fried, L. (ed.) (1988) *Handbook of American-Jewish Literature. An Analytical Guide to Topics, Themes, and Sources*, New York: Greenwood.

Friedländer, S. (1991). ' "The Final Solution": On the Unease in Historical Interpretation', in P. Hayes (ed.) *Lessons and Legacies: The Meaning of the Holocaust in a Changing World*, Bloomington: Indiana University Press, 23–35.

Friedman, L.S. (1991) *Understanding Cynthia Ozick*, Columbia: University of South Carolina Press.

Friesem, R. (2004) 'History', *Ariga*, January–March. Online. Available HTTP: <http://www.ariga.com/visions/poetry/rickyfriesem001.shtml> (accessed 22 March 2005).

Furman, A. (2000) *Contemporary Jewish American Writers and the Multicultural Dilemma: The Return of the Exiled*, New York: Syracuse University Press.

Fussell, P. (1975) *The Great War and Modern Memory*, New York: Oxford University Press.

Galchinsky, M. (1998) 'Scattered Seeds. A Dialogue of Diasporas', in D. Biale, M. Galchinsky and S. Heschel (eds), *Insider/Outsider. American Jews and Multiculturalism*, Berkeley: University of California Press, 185–211.

Galgut, D. (1991) *The Good Doctor*, London: Viking.

Gargani, A.G. (2001) 'Die religiöse Erfahrung: Ereignis und Interpretation', in J. Derrida and G. Vattimo (eds), *Die Religion*, Frankfurt/Main: Suhrkamp, 144–70.

Gavron, J. (2002; 2003) *The Book of Israel*, London: Scribner.

Geiger, A. (ed.) (1854; 2nd edn 1891) *Israelitisches Gebetbuch für den öffentlichen Gottesdienst im ganzen Jahre*, Frankfurt/Main: Brönner.

Geiger, L. (1905) 'Die deutsche Literatur und der Zionismus', *Kölnische Zeitung*, 22 January: 1.

Geis, D.R. and Kruger, S.F. (eds) (1997) *Approaching the Millennium: Essays on* Angels in America, Ann Arbor: University of Michigan Press.

George, R.M. (1996) *The Politics of Home. Postcolonial Relocations and Twentieth-Century Fiction*, Cambridge: Cambridge University Press.

Gerson, C. (1982) 'Some Patterns of Exile in Jewish Writing of the Commonwealth', *ARIEL. A Review of International English Literature*, 13: 103–14.

Gilboa, A. (1979) *The light of lost suns: selected poems of Amir Gilboa*, sel. and trans. from the Hebrew by S. Kaufman with S. Rimmon, New York: Persea Books.

Gilman, S.L. (2003) ' "We're not Jews" – Imagining Jewish History and Jewish Bodies in Contemporary Multicultural Literature', in *Jewish Frontiers. Essays on Bodies, Histories, and Identities*, New York: Palgrave, 169–206.

Glezer, L. (1973) 'The Personal Experiences and Views of Young Jewish Intellectuals (II)', in P.Y. Medding (ed.) *Jews in Australian Society*, Melbourne: Macmillan/Monash University, 229–33.

Gluzman, M. (2003) *The Politics of Canonicity*, Stanford, CA: Stanford University Press.

Golan, A. (2001) 'European Imperialism and the Development of Modern Palestine: Was Zionism a Form of Colonialism?', *Space and Polity*, 5: 127–43.

Goldberg, M. (1995) *Why Should Jews Survive? Looking Past the Holocaust toward a Jewish Future*, New York: Oxford University Press.

Goldhar, P. (1946) 'Café in Carlton', in *Southern Stories, Poems and Paintings*, Melbourne: Dolphin Publications, 29–47.

Goldsmith, E.S. (1997) *Modern Yiddish Culture: The Story of the Yiddish Language Movement*, New York: Fordham University Press.

Goldstein, M. (1912) 'Deutsch-jüdischer Parnaß', *Der Kunstwart*, 25: 281–94.

Goodman, A. (1996) *The Family Markowitz*, New York: Farrar, Straus & Giroux.

Goodman, A. (1997; 2005) 'Writing with a Return Address', in D. Rubin (ed.) *Who We Are: On Being (and Not Being) a Jewish American Writer*, New York: Schocken, 267–76.

Goodman, A. (1998) *Kaaterskill Falls*, New York: Dial.

Gordimer, N. (1953; 1978) *The Lying Days*, London: Jonathan Cape.

Gordimer, N. (1958; 1983) *A World of Strangers*, Harmondsworth: Penguin.

Gordimer, N. (1966; 1986) *The Late Bourgeois World*, Harmondsworth: Penguin.

Gordimer, N. (1979; 1980) *Burger's Daughter*, Harmondsworth: Penguin.

Gordimer, N. (1987) *A Sport of Nature*, Cape Town: David Philip.

Gordimer, N. (1988) *The Essential Gesture*, Emmarentia, Claremont: Taurus and David Philip.

Gordimer, N. (1994) *None to Accompany Me*, Cape Town: David Philip.

Gordimer, N. (1995) *Writing and Being*, Cambridge, MA, London: Harvard University Press.

Gordimer, N. (1998) *The House Gun*, Cape Town: David Philip.

Gordimer, N. (2001) *The Pickup*, New York: Farrar, Straus & Giroux.

Gordon, L. (1992) *Shared Lives*, Cape Town: David Philip.

Gow, D. (1998) *Cherry Docs*, Winnipeg: Scirocco Drama.

Grant, L. (1998) *Remind Me Who I Am, Again*, London: Granta.

Grant, L. (2000) *When I Lived in Modern Times*, London: Granta.

Green, J.M. (2001) *Thinking Through Translation*, Athens: University of Georgia Press.

Greenberg, R. (2003) *Take Me Out: A Play*. New York: Faber & Faber.

Greenstein, M. (ed.) (2004) *Contemporary Jewish Writing in Canada: An Anthology*, Lincoln: University of Nebraska Press.

Gronow, J. (2000) 'Awards shortlist excites Caulfield writer', *Port Phillip/Caulfield Leader*, 8 May.

Gruen, E.S. (2002) *Diaspora: Jews amidst Greeks and Romans*, Cambridge, MA: Harvard University Press.

Gur, B. (1992) 'Eimat ha'imahut shel orly kastel-bloom' [Orly Castel-Bloom's Dread of Motherhood], *Ha'aretz*, 8 May.

Gur, B. (1995) 'Sod hakesem shel realizem mugaz' [The Secret Magic of Dissipated Realism], *Ha'aretz*, 'Tarbut vesifrut' [Culture and Literature], 16 June: 8b.

Gurevitch, D. (1990) 'Be'eizo safa nedaber mahar' [What Language Will We Speak Tomorrow], *Yediot aharonot*, 20 February.

Gurevitch, D. (1996) 'Halomot memuhzarim' [Recycled Dreams], *Iton 77*, March.

Haley, A. (1976) *Roots*, Garden City, NY: Doubleday.

HaLevy, S. (2003) 'Let Not Suddenly Boom', *Shevo*, 10: 36–7.

Halkin, Hillel (2005) 'What is Cynthia Ozick About?', *Commentary*, January: 49–55.

Halkin, Talya (2005) 'Israelis, Palestinians to talk – on-line', *Jerusalem Post*, 20 January. Online. Available HTTP: <http://www.jpoStcom/servlet/Satellite?pagename=JPost/JPArticle/ShowFull&cid=1106104802000&p=1078027574097> (accessed 22 March 2005).

Hammer, G. (comp.) (1988) *Pomegranates: A Century of Jewish Australian Writing*, Newtown, NSW: Millenium Books.

Hammer-Schenk, H. (1981) *Synagogen in Deutschland: Geschichte einer Baugattung im 19. und 20. Jahrhundert (1780–1933)*, 2 parts, Hamburg: Hans Christians Verlag.

Harshav, B. (1990) *The Meaning of Yiddish*, Berkeley, Los Angeles, Oxford: University of California Press.

Hartman, G.H. (1980) *Criticism in the Wilderness: The Study of Literature Today*, New Haven, CT: Yale University Press.

Hartman, G.H. (1995) 'Cultural Relativism and the Literary Critic', in H. Wirth-Nesher (ed.) *The Sheila Carmel Lectures: 1988–1993*, Tel Aviv: Tel Aviv University Press, 59–79.

Hasan-Rokem, G. and Dundes, A. (eds) (1986) *The Wandering Jew: Essays in the Interpretation of a Christian Legend*, Bloomington: Indiana University Press.

Heidegger, M. (1956) *Sein und Zeit*, Tübingen: Niemeyer.

Herman, A. (1988) '*Rachel's Chance* by Peter Kohn', *Australia-Israel Review*, 29 March–14 April.

Heuer, R. (ed.) (2000) *Lexikon deutsch-jüdischer Autoren*, vol. 8, Munich: Saur.

Hever, H. (2003) 'Israeli Fiction and the Occupation', *Tikkun*, January–February. Online. Available HTTP: <http://www.tikkun.org/magazine/index.cfm/action/tikkun/issue/tik0301/article/030151.html> (accessed 22 March 2005).

Hezser, C. (2005) '"Are You Protestant Jews or Roman Catholic Jews" – Literary Representations of Being Jewish in Ireland', *Modern Judaism*, 25: 159–88.

Hillquit, M. (1934) *Loose Leaves from a Busy Life*, New York: Macmillan.

Hirschfeld, A. (1992) 'Tehomot me'ahorei etz hashesek' [Abysses Behind the Loquat Tree], *Ha'aretz*, 29 May.

Hoffmann, Y. (1991) *Kristus shel dagim* [Christ of Fish], Jerusalem: Keter.

Hollander, J. (1988; 1994) 'The Question of American Jewish Poetry', in H. Wirth-Nesher (ed.) *What is Jewish Literature?*, Philadelphia: The Jewish Publication Society, 36–52.

Hollinger, D. (1995) *Postethnic Identity: Beyond Multiculturalism*, New York: Basic Books.

Holm, N.G. (1990) *Einführung in die Religionspsychologie*, München: Reinhardt.

Hornshoj-Moller, S. (1995) *"Der ewige Jude". Quellenkritische Analyse eines antisemitischen Propagandafilms*, Göttingen: Institut für den Wissenschaftlichen Film.

Houpt, S. (2002) 'Who Owns the Holocaust?', *Globe and Mail*, 20 March.
Howe, S. (2000) 'The Politics of Historical "Revisionism": Comparing Ireland and Israel/Palestine', *Past and Present*, 168: 227–53.
Hyman, L. (1972) *The Jews of Ireland: From Earliest Times to the Year 1910*, Shannon: The Jewish Historical Society of England.
IAWE (22 March 2005), Israel Association of Writers in English. Online. Available HTTP: <http://www.geocities.com/iawe_mailbox/>
Indyk, I. (2001) 'A moment in wonderland', *Sydney Morning Herald*, 24 February.
Itwaru, A. (1989) "Exile and Commemoration", in F. Birbalsingh (ed.) *Indenture and Exile: The Indo-Caribbean Experience*, Toronto: TSAR, 202–6.
Jacobson, D. (1985) *Time and Time Again*, London: André Deutsch.
Jacobson, D. (1994; 1995) *The Electronic Elephant*, Harmondsworth: Penguin.
Jacobson, D. (1998) *Heshel's Kingdom*, London: Hamish Hamilton.
Jaffé, R. (1898) 'Unsere Dichtung', *Die Welt*, 8 July, 13–15.
James, C.L.R. (1963) *Beyond a Boundary*, London: Stanley, Paul & Co.
Jewish Australia (2006) *Database of Australian Jewish Writers*. Online. Available HTTP: <http://www.jewishaustralia.com/?Page = writers-jewishaustralia-database> (accessed 13 December 2006).
Johnston, B.H. (1988) *Indian School Days*, Toronto: Key Porter Books.
Joseph, J.E. (2004) *Language and Identity: National, Ethnic, Religious*, Basingstoke: Palgrave Macmillan.
Joyce, J. (1922; 1984) *Ulysses: A Critical and Synoptic Edition*, 3 vols, eds H.W. Gabler, W. Steppe and C. Melchior, New York: Garland Publications.
Kafka, F. (1915; 2000) 'Metamorphosis', in *Metamorphosis and Other Stories*, trans. M. Pasley, London: Penguin.
Kafka, F. (1977) *Letters to Friends, Family, and Editors*, trans. R. and C. Winston, New York: Schocken.
Kalechofsky, R. and R. (eds) (1984) *Jewish Writing Down Under. Australia and New Zealand*, Marblehead, MA: Micah.
Kasrils, R. (1993; upd. edn 2004) *Armed and Dangerous: From Undercover Struggle to Freedom*, Johannesburg: Jonathan Ball.
Katz, L. (2002) ' "A Hyphenated Poet": An Interview with Shirley Kaufman', *Primtemps Sources*, 15: 106–22. Online. Available HTTP: <http://www.paradigme.com/sources/SOURCES-PDF/Pages%20de%20SOURCE12-1-6.pdf> (accessed 22 March 2005).
Kaufman, M. (1999; 2001) *The Laramie Project*, New York: Dramatists Play Service.
Kaufman, S. (1991) *Rivers of Salt*, Port Townsend, WA: Copper Canyon Press.
Kaufman, S. (2003) *Threshold*, Port Townsend, WA: Copper Canyon Press.
Kaufman, S., Hasan-Rokem, G. and Hess, T.S. (eds) (1999) *The Defiant Muse: Hebrew Feminist Poems from Antiquity. A Bilingual Anthology*, New York: Feminist Press at the City University of New York.
Kauvar, E.M. (1993) *Cynthia Ozick's Fiction: Tradition and Invention*, Bloomington: Indiana University Press.
Keesing, N. (ed.) (1978; rev. edn 1988) *Shalom: A Collection of Australian Jewish Short Stories*, Melbourne: Penguin.
Kelman, H.C. (1998) 'Israel in Transition from Zionism to Post-Zionism', *Annals of the American Academy of Political and Social Science*, 555: 46–61.
Keneally, T. (1982) *Schindler's List*, New York: Simon and Schuster.
Keogh, D. (1998) *Jews in Twentieth-Century Ireland. Refugees, Anti-Semitism and the Holocaust*, Cork: Cork University Press.

Keown, D. (2001) *Der Buddhismus: Eine kurze Einführung*, Stuttgart: Reclam.

Kerbel, S. (ed.) (2003) *Jewish Writers of the Twentieth Century*, New York, London: Fitzroy Dearborn.

Klein, A.M. (1953; 1982) 'In Praise of the Diaspora (An Undelivered Memorial Address)', in *Beyond Sambation. Selected Essays and Editorials, 1928–1955*, ed. M.W. Steinberg, Toronto: University of Toronto Press, 463–77.

Klein, M. (1957) *Envy and Gratitude: A Study of Unconscious Sources*, New York: Basic Books.

Klingenstein, S. (1991) *Jews in the American Academy, 1900–1940: The Dynamics of Intellectual Assimilation*, New Haven, CT: Yale University Press.

Kohn, P. (1987) *Rachel's Chance*, Hawthorn, Vic.: Hudson Publishing.

Kohn, P. (1996) unpublished conversation with Elisa Morera de la Vall (Melbourne, 1 August 1996).

Kohn, P. (1998) *View from a Sandcastle*, Kew, Vic.: Hudson Publishing.

Körte, M. (2000) *Die Uneinholbarkeit des Verfolgten: Der ewige Jude in der literarischen Phantastik*, Frankfurt/Main, New York: Campus.

Kosinski, J. (1965) *The Painted Bird*, Cambridge, MA: Riverside Press.

Kovner, A. (1973) *A Canopy in the Desert: Selected Poems by Abba Kovner*, trans. S. Kaufman, with R. Adler and N. Orchan, Pittsburgh, PA: University of Pittsburgh Press.

Kramer, L. (1985) *The Normal Heart*, New York: New American Library.

Kramer, M.P. (2003) 'Beginnings and Ends: The Origins of Jewish American Literary History', in M.P. Kramer and H. Wirth-Nesher (eds) *The Cambridge Companion to Jewish American Literature*, Cambridge: Cambridge University Press, 12–30.

Kramer, M.P. and Wirth-Nesher, H. (eds) (2003) *The Cambridge Companion to Jewish American Literature*, Cambridge: Cambridge University Press.

Krämer, S. (2001) *Sprache, Sprechakt, Kommunikation: Sprachtheoretische Positionen des 20. Jahrhunderts*, Frankfurt/Main: Suhrkamp.

Kraus, K. (1898) *Eine Krone für Zion*, Vienna: Moriz Frisch.

Kremer, S.L. (1999) *Women's Holocaust Writing: Memory and Imagination*, Lincoln: University of Nebraska Press.

Krieger, K. (ed.) (2003) *Der Berliner Antisemitismusstreit 1879–1881. Eine Kontroverse um die Zugehörigkeit der deutschen Juden zur Nation*, 2 vols, Munich: Saur.

Kruger, S.F. (1997) 'Identity and Conversion in *Angels in America*', in D.R. Geis and S.F. Kruger (eds) *Approaching the Millennium: Essays on* Angels in America, Ann Arbor: University of Michigan Press, 151–69.

Kruglanski, O. (22 March 2005) Online. Available HTTP: <http://www.voyd.com/ia/pdaorit.htm>

Krupnick, M. (1986) *Lionel Trilling and the Fate of Cultural Criticism*, Evanston, IL: Northwestern University Press.

Kushner, T. (1993) *Angels in America: A Gay Fantasia on National Themes. Part One: Millennium Approaches*, New York: Theatre Communications Group.

Kushner, T. (1996) *Angels in America: A Gay Fantasia on National Themes. Part Two: Perestroika* [revised version], New York: Theatre Communications Group.

Kushner, T. (1998) 'Remembering to Forget: Racism and Anti-Racism in Postwar Britain', in B. Cheyette and L. Marcus (eds) *Modernity, Culture and 'the Jew'*, Cambridge: Polity Press, 226–41.

Kushner, T. (screenplay) and Nichols, M. (dir.) (2003) *Angels in America*. HBO Films.

Kushner, T. and Solomon, A. (2003) *Wrestling with Zion: Progressive Jewish American Responses to the Israeli-Palestinian Conflict*, New York: Grove Press.

Langbehn, J. (1890) *Rembrandt als Erzieher. Von einem Deutschen*, N.p.: N.p.

Lanzmann, C. (1985) *Shoah*, Paris: Editions Fayard.

Laor, Y. (1998) 'Sefer haval al hazman' [An Awesome Book], *Ha'aretz*, 18 December.

Laor, Y. (2001) 'Schizolingua: Or, How Many Years Can Modern Hebrew Remain Modern? On the Ideological Dictates of the Hebrew Language', in E.M. Budick (ed.) *Ideology and Jewish Identity in Israeli and American Literature*. Albany: State University of New York Press, 213–34.

Lappin, E. (2001; 2002) *The Nose*, London: Picador.

Laufer, P. (2003) *Exodus to Berlin: The Return of the Jews to Germany*, Chicago, IL: Ivan R. Dee.

Lawson, P. (2001) 'Way Out In the Centre: In Conversation with Elaine Feinstein', *The Jewish Quarterly*, 48: 65–9.

Lefevere, A. (ed.) (1992) *Translation/History/Culture*, London, New York: Routledge.

Lehmann, S. (1998) 'In Search of a Mother Tongue: Locating Home in Diaspora', *MELUS. The Journal of the Society for the Study of the Multi-Ethnic Literatures of the United States*, 23: 101–19.

Lenta, M. (2001) 'Choosing Difference: South African Jewish Writers', *Judaism*, 50: 92–103.

Lentin, R. (1996) *Songs on the Death of Children*, Dublin: Poolbeg.

Lev-Ari, S. (2003) 'Diverse voices', *Ha'aretz*, 10 October.

Leveson, M. (1996) *People of the Book: Images of the Jew in South African Fiction*, Johannesburg: Witwatersrand University Press.

Levi, P. (1947; 1961) *Survival in Auschwitz: The Nazi Assault on Humanity*, trans. S. Woolf, New York: Collins.

Levi, P. (1984) *The Periodic Table*, trans. R. Rosenthal, New York: Schocken.

Lévinas, E. (1992) *Schwierige Freiheit: Versuch über das Judentum*, Frankfurt/Main: Jüdischer Verlag.

Lévinas, E. (1999) *Otherwise Than Being or Beyond Essence*, trans. A. Lingis, Pittsburgh, PA: Duquesne University Press.

LeVine, M. (1996) 'Is Post-Zionism Postmodern?', *Response*, 66: 14–27.

Lewisohn, L. (1928; 1997) *The Island Within*, Syracuse, NY: Syracuse University Press.

Lewitt, M. (1976) *Just Call Me Bob*, Melbourne: Macmillan Australia, Orbit Series.

Lewitt, M. (1980) *Come Spring: An Autobiographical Novel*, Melbourne: Scribe Publications.

Lewitt, M. (1985) *No Snow in December: An Autobiographical Novel*, Melbourne: Heinemann Australia.

Liberman, S. (1981) *On Firmer Shores*, Melbourne: Globe Press.

Liberman, S. (1983) *A Universe of Clowns*, Brisbane: Phoenix Publications.

Liberman, S. (1986) *The Life That I Have Led*, Melbourne: Fine-Lit.

Liberman, S. (1987) 'A Jewish Writer Today', unpublished ms address to the 'Tuesday Club at the Kadimah', 28 July: 1–5.

Liberman, S. (comp.) (1987; 2nd edn 1991) *A Bibliography of Australian Judaica*, Sydney: Mandelbaum Trust.

Liberman, S. (1990) *The Battered and the Redeemed*, Melbourne: Fine-Lit.

Liberman, S. (1998) 'Is there a Jewish Literature?', *Australian Jewish News*, 6 November: 6–7.

Liberman, S. (1999) *Voices From The Corner*, Melbourne: Fine-Lit.

Library of Congress (1949) *Press Release No. 542*, 20 February.

Liebman, C.S. (1965) 'Orthodoxy in American Jewish life', *American Jewish Year Book*, 66: 21–98.

Lipski, S. (2005) [Review of: Zable, A. (2004) *Scraps of Heaven*] *Australian Jewish News*, 11 February.

Lloyd, D. (1993) *Anomalous States: Irish Writing and the Post-Colonial Moment*, Dublin: Lilliput.

Loeffler, J. (2002) ' "Neither the King's English nor the Rebbetzin's Yiddish": Yinglish Literature in the United States', in M. Shell (ed.) *American Babel: Literatures of the United States from Abnaki to Zuni*, Cambridge, MA: Harvard University Press, 133–62.

Lowin, J. (1988) *Cynthia Ozick*, Swansea: University of Wales.

Lustick, I.S. (1993) *Unsettled States, Disputed Lands: Britain and Ireland, France and Algeria, Israel and the West Bank-Gaza*, Ithaca, NY: Cornell University Press.

Lyons, B. (1988) 'American-Jewish Fiction Since 1945', in L. Fried (ed.) *Handbook of American-Jewish Literature*, New York: Greenwood, 61–89.

M. b. M. (1921–2) 'Die Lehren von Irland' [The Lessons of Ireland], *Der Jude*, 5: 265–7.

Maccoby, D. (1999) *God Made Blind: Isaac Rosenberg, His Life and Poetry*, London: Symposium.

Maclean, P. (1987) 'The convergence of cultural worlds – Pinchas Goldhar: *A Yiddish Writer in Australia*', in W.D. Rubinstein (ed.) *Jews in the Sixth Continent*, Sydney: Allen & Unwin, 127–50.

Maclean, P. (1995) 'The Australian-Yiddish Writer, Pinchas Goldhar (1901–1947)', *Southerly*, 55: 29–34.

Maggid: A Journal of Jewish Literature (22 March 2005). Online. Available HTTP: <http://www.tobypress.com/books/maggid.htm>

Malamud, B. (1957; 1963) *The Assistant*, New York: Farrar, Straus and Company.

Malamud, B. (1966) *The Fixer*, New York: Farrar, Straus and Company.

Malouf, D. (1993) *Remembering Babylon*, New York: Pantheon.

Marcus, D. (1954) *To Next Year in Jerusalem. A Novel*, London, New York: Macmillan.

Marcus, D. (1986) *A Land Not Theirs*, London: Bantam.

Marcus, D. (2001) *Oughtobiography. Leaves from the Diary of a Hyphenated Jew*, Dublin: Gill and Macmillan.

Marcus, S. (2003) 'Staging Change: The Revolutionary Rigor of Tony Kushner' [Interview], *Heeb*, 4: 57–60.

Marks, M.A. (ed.) (1996) *Nice Jewish Girls: Growing Up in America*, New York: Plume.

Marovitz, S.E. (1996) *Abraham Cahan*, New York: Twayne.

Mass, R. (22 March 2005) 'Hands on a Gun'. Online. Available HTTP: <http://www.ariga.com/visions/poetry/mass005.shtml>

Massarwa, O. (2003) *Quest for Peace of Heart*, Taibe: Al-Taybah.

Matta, N. (2003) 'Postcolonial Theory, Multiculturalism and the Israeli Left. A Critique of Post-Zionism', *Holy Land Studies*, 2: 85–107.

Maxwell, W. (1948) *Time Will Darken It*, New York: Harper.

McCabe, T. (2003) ' "Angels" in Our Midst', *Chronicle of Higher Education*, 5 December.

McDonald, F. (1998) 'No Longer an Indian: My Story', in J. Weaver (ed.) *Native American Religious Identity: Unforgotten Gods*, Maryknoll, NY: Orbis Books, 69–73.

McGinn, B. (1996) 'The Meanings of the Millennium', address presented at the Inter-American Development Bank, Washington, DC, 17 January.

McGreal, C. (2004) 'Madonna in Mystical Mode Dismays Orthodox Jews', *Guardian*, 20 September. Online. Available HTTP: <http://www.guardian.co.uk/religion/Story/0,2763,1308199,00.html> (accessed 2 February 2005).

McLeod, J. (2000) *Beginning Postcolonialism*, Manchester: Manchester University Press.

Melamed, A. (1995) 'Hazayot mima'amakei hadikuy' [Hallucinations from the Depths of Oppression], *Ha'ir*, 'Sfarim' [Books], 9 June.

Meltzer, Y. (1998) 'Mevutseret me'ahorei hamikledet' [Fortified Behind the Keyboard], *Ma'ariv*, 27 November.

Mendelsohn, D. (2004) 'Winged Messages', *The New York Review of Books*, 12 February.

Mendelson-Maoz, A. (1996) 'Olamot efshariyim bitsiratam shel orli kastel-bloom ve'etgar keret' [Possible Worlds in the Works of Orly Castel-Bloom and Etgar Keret], *Aley si'ah*, 38: 39–64.

Meredith, G. (1970) *The Collected Letters of George Meredith*, 3 vols, ed. C.L. Cline, Oxford: Oxford University Press.

Miller, K.A. (1985) *Emigrants and Exiles: Ireland and the Irish Exodus to North America*, New York: Oxford University Press.

Mills, S. (2002) *The Danish Play. A True Tale of Resistance*. Toronto: Playwrights Canada Press.

Miron, D. (1989) 'Mashehu al orly kastel-bloom' [Something on Orly Castel-Bloom], *Al hamishmar*, 3 June.

Mirzoeff, N. (ed.) (2000) *Diaspora and Visual Culture: Representing Africans and Jews*, New York: Routledge.

Mishra, V. (1996) 'The Diasporic Imaginary: Theorizing the Indian Diaspora', *Textual Practice*, 10: 421–47.

Mitchell, D. (1985) 'Elaine Feinstein', in *Dictionary of Literary Biography 40: Poets of Great Britain and Ireland Since 1960*, Part 1: *A–L*, Detroit: Gale, 116–21.

Mitchell, T.G. (2000) *Native vs. Settler: Ethnic Conflict in Israel/Palestine, Northern Ireland, and South Africa*, Westport, CT: Greenwood Press.

Monde, D. (2004) 'A Soul On Fire', *The Jerusalem Report*, 3 May: 34–9.

Moon, M. (2004) 'Turning from the National to the Multilingual', *American Literature*, 76: 677–85.

Morphet, T. (1991) 'After Solidarity', *Current Writing: Text and Reception in Southern Africa*, 3: 166–70.

Morrison, B. (1980) *The Movement: English Poetry and Fiction of the 1950s*, Oxford: Oxford University Press.

Mulhern, F. (1990) 'English Reading', in H.K. Bhabha (ed.) *Nation and Narration*, London: Routledge, 250–64.

Mullan, J. (2002) 'After Post-Colonialism', *Guardian*, 12 October. Online. Available HTTP: <http://www.guardian.co.uk/reviewbookclub/story/0,810146,00.html> (accessed 14 February 2003).

Myhill, J. (2004) *Language in Jewish Society: Towards a New Understanding*, Clevedon: Multilingual Matters.

Nadel, I.B. (1989) *Joyce and the Jews: Culture and Texts*, Basingstoke: Macmillan.

Naipaul, V.S. (1962; 1969) *The Middle Passage. Impressions of Five Societies – British, French and Dutch – in the West Indies and South America*, Harmondsworth: Penguin.

Ngugi wa Thiong'o (1965) *The River Between*, London: Heinemann.

Ngugi wa Thiong'o (1981) *Writers in Politics*, London: Heinemann.

Nicholas A. and Torok, M. (1994) *The Shell and the Kernel*, ed. and trans. N.T. Rand, Chicago, IL: University of Chicago Press.

Niger, S. (1941) *Bilingualism in the History of Jewish Literature*, trans. J.A. Fogel, New York: University Press of America.

Nimni, E. (ed.) (2003) *The Challenge of Post-Zionism. Alternatives to Israeli Fundamentalist Politics*, London: Zed Books.

Nissim, K. (1992) 'Begova einayim' [At Eye Level], *Al hamishmar*, 5 June.

Nyburg, S.L. (1917; 1986) *The Chosen People*, New York: Markus Wiener.

O'Neill, E. (1956) *Long Day's Journey Into Night*, New Haven, CT: Yale University Press.

OED (1989; 2001) *The Oxford English Dictionary*, ed. J.A.H. Murray et al., Oxford: Clarendon.

Oppenheimer, Y. (2003) *Lo hazchut hagdola lomar: shira politit beyisrael* [No Big Right to Say: Political Poetry in Israel], Jerusalem: Magnes.

Ormsby, R. (2002) '*The Danish Play*'s Disturbing Resonance', www.drama.ca (accessed 26 November 2002).

Ornitz, S. (1923; 1986) *Allrightniks Row: "Haunch Paunch and Jowl". The Making of a Professional Jew*, New York: Markus Wiener.

Ozick, C. (1969; 1971) 'Envy; or Yiddish in America', in *The Pagan Rabbi and Other Stories*, New York: Alfred A. Knopf, 41–99.

Ozick, C. (1970) 'America: Toward Yavneh', *Judaism*, 19: 264–82.

Ozick, C. (1970; 1983) 'Toward a New Yiddish', in *Art & Ardor: Essays*, New York: Alfred A. Knopf, 151–77.

Ozick, C. (1970; 1994) 'America: Toward Yavneh', in H. Wirth-Nesher (ed.), *What is Jewish Literature?*, Philadelphia: The Jewish Publication Society, 20–35.

Ozick, C. (1972; 1983) 'Literary Blacks and Jews', in *Art & Ardor: Essays*, New York: Alfred A. Knopf, 90–112.

Ozick, C. (1976) 'Preface', in *Bloodshed and Other Novellas*, New York: Alfred A. Knopf, 9.

Ozick, C. (1976; 1984) 'Usurpation (Other People's Stories)', *Bloodshed and Three Novellas*, Syracuse, NY: Syracuse University Press, 129–78.

Ozick, C. (1982; 1983) 'I.B. Singer's Book of Creation', in *Art & Ardor: Essays*, New York: Alfred A. Knopf, 217–23.

Ozick, C. (1983; 1991) 'Bialik's Hint', in *Metaphor & Memory: Essays*, New York: Alfred A. Knopf, 223–39.

Ozick, C. (1984; 1989) 'What Drives Saul Bellow', in *Metaphor & Memory*: *Eassys*, New York: Alfred A. Knopf, 49–57.

Ozick, C. (1989; 1990) *The Shawl*, New York: Vintage.

Ozick, C. (1996) 'Saul Bellow's Broadway', in *Fame & Folly: Essays*, New York: Alfred A. Knopf, 171–84.

Ozick, C. (1997) *The Puttermesser Papers*, New York: Alfred A. Knopf.

Paolini, A.J. (1999) *Navigating Modernity: Postcolonial Identity and International Relations*, London: Lynee Rienner.

Patraka, V.M. (1997) 'Situating History and Difference: The Performance of the Term *Holocaust* in Public Discourse', in J. Boyarin and D. Boyarin (eds) *Jews and Other Differences: The New Jewish Cultural Studies*, Minneapolis: University of Minnesota Press, 54–78.

Penslar, D.J. (2001) 'Zionism, Colonialism and Postcolonialism', *Journal of Israeli History*, 20: 84–98.

Phillips, A. (1994a) *On Flirtation*, Cambridge, MA: Harvard University Press.

Phillips, A. (1994b) 'Isaac Rosenberg's English', in *On Flirtation*, Cambridge, MA: Harvard University Press, 175–95.

Phillips, A. (2001) 'Poetry and Psychoanalysis', in *Promises, Promises: Essays on Literature and Psychoanalysis*, New York: Basic Books, 1–34.

Phillips, A. (2002) *Equals*, New York: Basic Books.

Press, K. (1998) *Echo Location: A Guide to Sea Point for Residents and Visitors*, Durban: Gecko.

Press, K. (2000) *Home*, Manchester: Carcanet Press.

Press, K. (2004) *The Little Museum of Working Life*, Pietermaritzburg: University of KwaZulu-Natal Press.

Raz, H. (ed.) (1998) *The Prairie Schooner Anthology of Contemporary Jewish American Writing*, Lincoln: University of Nebraska Press.

Redkay, E.S. (1969) *Black Exodus: Black Nationalist and Back-to-Africa Movements, 1890–1910*, New Haven, CT: Yale University Press.

Reizbaum, M. (1999) *James Joyce's Judaic Other*, Stanford, CA: Stanford University Press.

Reuveny, R. (2003) 'Fundamentalist Colonialism: The Geopolitics of Israeli–Palestinian Conflict', *Political Geography*, 22: 347–80.

Rex, J. (2002) 'Communities, Diasporas and Multiculturalism', *Migration – A European Journal of International Migration and Ethnic Relations*, 33/34/35: 51–67.

Rhodes, R.W. (1995) *The Lion and the Cross: Early Christianity in Victorian Novels*, Columbus: Ohio State University Press.

Ricks, C. (1988) *T.S. Eliot and Prejudice*, Boston, MA: Faber.

Rivers, P. (2001) [Review of: Gow, D. (1998) *Cherry Docs*], *Canadian Theatre Review*, 106.

Rivlin, R. (2003) *Shalom Ireland. A Social History of Jews in Modern Ireland*, Dublin: Gill and Macmillan.

Rolston, B. (1991) *Politics and Painting: Murals and Conflict in Norther Ireland*, Rutherford, NJ: Fairleigh Dickinson University Press.

Rose, J. (1996) *States of Fantasy*, Oxford: Clarendon Press.

Rosenberg, A. (1987; 2000) ' "Was the Holocaust Unique" A Peculiar Question?', in I. Walliman and M.N. Dobkowski (eds) *Genocide and the Modern Age: Etiology and Case Studies of Mass Death*, Syracuse, NY: Syracuse University Press, 145–61.

Rosenberg, I. (1979; 1984) *The Collected Works of Isaac Rosenberg*, ed. I. Parsons, London: Chatto & Windus.

Rosenberg, R. (22 March 2005) www.ariga.com

Roskies, D. (2003) 'Coney Island, USA: America in the Yiddish Literary Imagination', in M.P. Kramer and H. Wirth-Nesher (eds) *The Cambridge Companion to Jewish American Literature*, Cambridge: Cambridge University Press, 70–91.

Roskies, D.G. (1985; 1994) 'The Story is the Thing', in H. Wirth-Nesher (ed.) *What is Jewish Literature?*, Philadelphia: The Jewish Publication Society, 119–28.

Ross, L.Q. [i.e. L. Rosten] (1937) *The Education of Hyman Kaplan*, New York: Harcourt, Brace & Company.

Rosten, L. (1972) *Leo Rosten's Treasury of Jewish Quotations*, New York: McGraw Hill.

Roth, H. (1934; 1970) *Call it Sleep*, New York: Cooper Square Press.

Roth, P. (1959) 'Eli, The Fanatic', in *Goodbye, Columbus and Five Short* Stories, Boston: Houghton Mifflin, 247–98.

Roth, P. (1969) *Portnoy's Complaint*, New York: Random House.

Roth, P. (1975) *Reading Myself and Others*, New York: Farrar, Straus and Giroux.

Roth, P. (1987) *The Counterlife*, New York: Vintage.

Rouart, M.-F. (1988) *Le mythe du Juif Errant dans l'Europe du XIXe siècle*, Paris: Corti.

Rubens, B. (1999; 2000) *I, Dreyfus*, London: Abacus.

Rubens, B. (2003) *The Sergeants' Tale*, London: Little, Brown.

Rubin, D. (ed.) (2005) *Who We Are: On Being (and Not Being) a Jewish American Writer*, New York: Schocken.

Rubin, R. (2006) 'Wall', in V. Eden, 'At One Remove', *Ha'aretz*, 9 November 2006. Online. Available HTTP: <http://www.haaretz.com/hasen/spages/783362.html> (accessed 10 January 2007).

Rubinstein, H.L. (1991) *The Jews in Australia: A Thematic History.* Vol. 1: *1788–1945*, Melbourne: Heinemann Australia.

Rubinstein, W.D. (1991) *The Jews in Australia: A Thematic History.* Vol. 2: *1945 to the Present*, Melbourne: Heinemann Australia.

Rubinstein, W.D. (1995) *Judaism in Australia*, Canberra: Australia Government Publishing Service.

Rubinstein, W.D. (1996) *A History of the Jews in the English-Speaking World. Great Britain*, London: Routledge.

Rüsen, J. (2001) 'Einleitung. Geschichtsbewußtsein thematisieren – Problemlagen und Analysestrategien', in J. Rüsen (ed.) *Geschichtsbewußtsein. Psychologische Grundlagen, Entwicklungskonzepte, empirische Befunde*, Cologne: Böhlau, 1–13.

Rushdie, S. (1995) *The Moor's Last Sigh*, London: Jonathan Cape.

Russell, G.W.E. (1904) *Matthew Arnold*, New York: C. Scribner's Sons.

Sachs, A. (1966; 1990) *The Jail Diary of Albie Sachs*, Claremont: David Philips.

Sachs, A. (1990; 2000) *The Soft Vengeance of a Freedom Fighter*, Claremont: David Philips.

Sachs, A. (2004) *The Free Diary of Albie Sachs*, Johannesburg: Random House.

Safran, W. (1991) 'Diasporas in Modern Societies: Myths of Homeland and Return', *Diaspora. A Journal of Transnational Studies*, 1: 83–99.

Said, E.W. (1978) *Orientalism*, New York: Pantheon Books.

Said, E.W. (1978; 1995) *Orientalism.* With a new afterword, London: Penguin.

Said, E.W. (1983) *The World, the Text and the Critic*, Cambridge, MA: Harvard University Press.

Said, E.W. (1984) 'Reflections on Exile', *Granta*, 13: 159–72.

Said, E.W. (1986) 'Michael Walzer's *Exodus and Revolution*: A Canaanite Reading', *Arab Studies Quarterly*, 8: 289–303.

Samuel, M. (1945) *The World of Sholem Aleichem*, New York: Alfred A. Knopf.

Samuels, D. (1996) *Kindertransport*, London: Nick Hern Books.

Sarna, J.D. (ed.) (1986) *The American Jewish Experience*, New York: Holmes & Meier.

Sarna, N.N. (1986) *Exploring Exodus: The Heritage of Biblical Israel*, New York: Schocken Books.

Sartre, J.-P. (1943; 1961) *Réflexions sur la question juive*, [Paris:] Gallimard.

Sassoon, S. (1942) *The Weald of Youth*, London: Faber & Faber.

Sassoon, S. (1983) *The War Poems*, ed. R. Hart-Davis, London: Faber & Faber.

Schoeps, J.H. et al. (eds) (2002) *Deutsch-jüdischer Parnaß. Rekonstruktion einer Debatte*, Berlin: Philo.

Scholem, G. (1973) *Zur Kabbala und ihrer Symbolik*, Frankfurt/Main: Suhrkamp.

Schreiber, M. (1998) 'The End of Exile: Jewish Identity and Its Diasporic Poetics', *PMLA*, 113: 273–87.

Schwartzstein, T. (2002) 'Habayit hu beit kvarot gadol' [Home is a Big Cemetery], *Iton 77*, 267, May 2002.

Schwarz, D.R. (1999) *Imagining the Holocaust*, New York: St Martin's.

Schwarz-Bart, A. (1959; 1960) *The Last of the Just*, trans. S. Becker, New York: Atheneum.

Seidman, N. (1997) *A Marriage Made in Heaven: The Sexual Politics of Hebrew and Yiddish*, Berkeley, Los Angeles, London: University of California Press.

Seltzer, R. (1980) *Jewish People, Jewish Thought*, New York: Macmillan.

Sergeant, H. and Abse, D. (eds) *Mavericks: An Anthology*, London: Poetry and Poverty.

Shafir, G. (1996) 'Zionism and Colonialism: A Comparative Approach', in M.N. Barnett (ed.) *Israel in Comparative Perspective. Challenging the Conventional Wisdom*, Albany: State University of New York Press, 227–42.

Shaked, G. (2000) *Modern Hebrew Fiction*, trans. Y. Lotan, E.M. Budick (ed.), Bloomington: Indiana University Press.

Shandler, J. (2003) 'Imagining Yiddishland. Language, Place and Memory', *History and Memory*, 15: 123–48.

Shapiro, S. (1984) 'Hearing the Testimony of Radical Negation', in E. Schüssler Fiorenza and D. Tracy (eds) *The Holocaust as Interruption. Concilium*, 175: 3–10.

Sharan, S. (ed.) (2003) *Israel and the Post-Zionists. A Nation at Risk*, Brighton: Sussex Academic Press.

Sharlin, S. (1990) ' "Childhood Landscapes": Ronit Lentin in Conversation with Shifra Sharlin', *The Jewish Quarterly*, 138: 48–51.

Shatzky, J. and Taub, M. (eds) (1997) *Contemporary Jewish-American Novelists. A Biocritical Sourcebook*, Westport, CT, London: Greenwood Press.

Shawcross, W. (1999) 'Montenegro, the Next Holocaust?', *The Sunday Age*, 30 May.

Shechner, M. (1990) *The Conversion of the Jews and Other Essays*, New York: St Martin's Press.

Sheffer, G. (2003) *Diaspora Politics – At Home Abroad*, Cambridge: Cambridge University Press.

Shell, M. (2002) 'Babel in America', in M. Shell (ed.) *American Babel: Literatures of the United States from Abnaki to Zuni*, Cambridge, MA: Harvard University Press, 3–33.

Sher, E. (1998) 'Past Imperfect', in *Making Waves. Three Radio Plays*, Toronto: Simon & Pierre.

Shifman, S. (2002) 'Realizem mugaz' [Dissipated Realism], *Ha'aretz*, 'Sfarim' [Books], 24 April.

Shohat, E. (1989) *Israeli Cinema: East/West and the Politics of Representation*, Austin: University of Texas Press.

Siegel, B. (1997) 'Introduction: Erasing and Embracing the Past: America and Its Jewish Writers – Men and Women', in J.L. Halio and B. Siegel (eds) *Daughters of Valor. Contemporary Jewish American Women Writers*, Newark: University of Delaware Press, 17–47.

Silberstein, L.J. (1999) *The Post-Zionism Debates: Knowledge and Power in Israeli Culture*, New York: Routledge.

Silkin, J. (1959) 'The Poetry of Isaac Rosenberg', in *Isaac Rosenberg 1890–1918: A catalogue of an exhibition held at Leeds University May–June 1959, together with the text of unpublished material*, Leeds: Partridge, 1–3.

Silkin, J. (1967) 'Anglo-Jewish Poetry', *The Jewish Quarterly*, 15: 22–4.

Silkin, J. (1972; 1978) *Out of Battle: The Poetry of the Great War*, Oxford: Oxford University Press.

Silkin, J. (1986) *The Ship's Pasture*, London: Routledge & Kegan Paul.

Silkin, J. (1987) 'The First Twenty-Four Years', in *Contemporary Authors Autobiography Series*, 5, Detroit: Gale, 243–65.

Silkin, J. (1989/1990) 'Seven Poems', *The Tel Aviv Review*, 2: 166–76.

Silkin, J. (1997) *The Life of Metrical and Free Verse in Twentieth-Century Poetry*, Basingstoke: Macmillian.

Silkin, J. (2000) 'Four Poems', *The Jerusalem Review*, 4: 174–7.

Silkin, J. (ed.) (1979) *The Penguin Book of First World War Poetry*, Harmondsworth: Penguin.

Silkin, J. and Thwaite, A. (1963) 'No Politics, No Poetry?', *Stand*, 6: 7–23.

Singer, I.B. (1985) 'Nobel Lecture', *Yiddish*, 6: 169–72.

Slovo, J. (1995) *Slovo: The Unfinished Autobiography*, Johannesburg: Ravan and London: Hodder and Stoughton.

Smith, Z. (2002) *The Autograph Man*, New York: Vintage.

Snider, E.D. (2000) '*Goodbye Marianne*, at BYU', *The Daily Herald*, 20 February.

Sollors, W. (1996) ' "A world somewhere, somewhere else." Language, Nostalgic Mournfulness, and Urban Immigrant Family Romance in *Call It Sleep*', in H. Wirth-Nesher (ed.) *New Essays on Call It Sleep*, Cambridge: Cambridge University Press, 127–87.

Sollors, W. (1997) 'For a Multilingual Turn in American Studies', *American Studies Association Newsletter*, 20: 13–15.

Sollors, W. (1998) 'Introduction', in W. Sollors (ed.) *Multilingual America: Transnationalism, Ethnicity, and the Languages of American Literature*, New York: New York University Press, 1–13.

Solomon, A. (1997) 'Wrestling with *Angels*: A Jewish Fantasia', in D.R. Geis and S.F. Kruger (eds) *Approaching the Millennium: Essays on* Angels in America, Ann Arbor: University of Michigan Press, 118–33.

Spielberg, S. (1993; 2004) *Schindler's List* [motion picture], Universal City, CA: Universal.

Spielvogel, N.F. (1956) *Selected Short Stories of Nathan Spielvogel*, Melbourne: The Hawthorn Press.

Spivak, Gayatri Chakravorty (1990) 'The Making of America, the Teaching of English, and the Future of Culture Studies', *New Literary History*, 21: 781–98.

Stähler, A. (2003) 'The Black Forest, the Unspeakable Nefas, and the Mountains of Galilee: Germany and Zionism in the Works of A.M. Klein', in H. Antor et al. (eds) *Refractions of Germany in Canadian Culture and Literature*, New York, Berlin: De Gruyter, 171–93.

Starr, D.A. (2000) 'Reterritorializing the Dream: Orly Castel-Bloom's Remapping of Israeli Identity', in L.J. Silberstein (ed.) *Mapping Jewish Identities*, New York: New York University Press, 220–49.

Steiner, G. (1967; 1979) *Language and Silence: Essays 1958–1966*, Harmondsworth: Penguin.

Steiner, G. (1975; 1981) *After Babel: Aspects of Language and Translation*, London, Oxford, New York: Oxford University Press.

Steiner, G. (1985; 1996) 'Our Homeland, The Text', in *No Passion Spent. Essays 1978–1996*, London: Faber & Faber, 304–27.

Steinmetz, S. (1986) *Yiddish and English. A Century of Yiddish in America*, Alabama: University of Alabama Press.

Sternberg, M. (1981) 'Polylingualism as Reality and Translation as Mimesis', *Poetics Today*, 2: 221–39.

Stockwell, A. (2004) 'About Amy Bloom: A Profile', *Ploughshares*, 30: 205–9.

Strandberg, V. (1994) *Greek Mind/Jewish Soul*, Madison: University of Wisconsin Press.

Styron, W. (1976) *Sophie's Choice*, New York: Random House.

Szirtes, G. (2000) *The Budapest File*, Newcastle: Bloodaxe.

Taubenfeld, A. (1998) 'Only an "L": Linguistic Borders and the Immigrant Author in Abraham Cahan's *Yekl* and *Yankel der Yankee*', in W. Sollors (ed.) *Multilingual America: Transnationalism, Ethnicity, and the Languages of American Literature*, New York: New York University Press, 144–65.

Taureck, B.H.F. (2002) *Emmanuel Lévinas zur Einführung*, Hamburg: Junius.

Taylor, K. (2002) 'Heroes of the hard route', *The Globe and Mail*, 25 November.

Tepper, E. (ed.) (1980) *Southeast Asian Exodus: From Tradition to Resettlement: Understanding Refugees from Laos, Kampuchea, and Vietnam in China*, Ottawa: Canadian Asian Studies Association.

The Tal Brody Legacy (15 January 2005). Online. Available HTTP: <http://www.talbrody.co.il/high.html>

Tikkun (2004) 'Writing Jerusalem'. Online. Available HTTP: <http://triangletikkun.tikkun.org/index.cfm/action/article/id/112.html> (accessed 22 March 2005).

Tobenkin, E. (1916; 1968) *Witte Arrives*, New York: The Gregg Press.

Treitel, J. (1998) 'Selflessness; or Alexander and His Electric Wok', in B. Cheyette (ed.) *Contemporary Jewish Writing in Britain and Ireland: An Anthology*, London: Halban, 321–8.

Trilling, D. (ed.) (1980a) *Lionel Trilling: Speaking of Literature and Society*, New York: Harcourt Brace Jovanovich.

Trilling, D. (1980b) 'Editor's Foreword', in D. Trilling (ed.) *Lionel Trilling: Speaking of Literature and Society*, New York: Harcourt Brace Jovanovich.

Trilling, L. (1939) *Matthew Arnold*, New York: W.W. Norton and Co.

Trilling, L. (1950) *The Liberal Imagination: Essays on Literature and Society*, New York: The Viking Press.

Tuerk, R. (1983) 'Jewish-American Literature', in R.J. di Pietro and E. Ifkovic (eds) *Ethnic Perspectives in American Literature*, New York: MLA, 133–62.

Unger, L.M. (unpublished) 'Suicide bomb at the Carmel Shuk'.

Urofsky, M.I. (1974; 1986) 'Zionism: An American Experience', in J.D. Sarna (ed.) *The American Jewish Experience*, New York: Holmes & Meier, 211–21,

Utterback, C. (2004) 'Unusual Positions', *Electronic Book Review*, 28 November. Online. Available HTTP: <http://www.electronicbookreview.com/v3/servlet/ebr?command=view_essay&essay_id = utterback> (accessed 22 March 2005).

Varga, S. (2002) [Review of: Zable, A. (2002) *The Fig Tree*], *Australian Book Review*, June–July.

Venuti, L. (1988) *The Scandals of Translation: Towards an Ethics of Difference*, London, New York: Routledge.

Voices (22 March 2005), Voices Israel Group of Poets in English. Online. Available HTTP: <http://www.poetry-voices.8m.com>

Wachtel, E. (1992) 'George Steiner Interviewed by Eleanor Wachtel', *Queen's Quarterly*, 99: 837–48.

Wain, J. (1962; 1965) *Sprightly Running: Part of an Autobiography*, London: Macmillan.

Waldenfels, B. (1999) *Topographie des Fremden: Studien zur Phänomenologie des Fremden 1*, Frankfurt/Main: Suhrkamp.

Walzer, M. (1985) *Exodus and Revolution*, New York: Basic Books.

Wasserstein, B. (1996) *Vanishing Diaspora. The Jews in Europe since 1945*, London: Hamish Hamilton.

Waten, J. (1949) 'Contemporary Jewish Literature in Australia', *Australian Jewish Historical Society Journal*, 3, December, 92–6.

Waten, J. (1952) *Alien Son*, Sydney: Angus & Robertson.

Waten, J. (1954) *The Unbending*, Melbourne: Australasian Book Society.

Waten, J. (1964; 1978) *Distant Land*, Sydney: Angus & Robertson.

Waten, J. (1971a) 'My Two Literary Careers', *Southerly*, 31: 83–92.

Waten, J. (1971b) *So Far No Further*, Mt Eliza, Vic.: Wren.

Waten, J. (1981) 'Seventy Years' (Extracts from Judah Waten's speech on the occasion of the tribute paid to him in Melbourne, on 29 July 1981, to celebrate his seventieth birthday), *Overland*, 86: 16.

Waten, J. (1984) 'A Writer's Youth – A Memoir', *Outrider*, 1: 114–21.

Watts, I. (1994; 2001) *Goodbye Marianne*, Winnipeg: Scirocco Drama.

Watts, I. (n.d.) 'Background to the play', in R. Epp, *Kristallnacht*, Toronto: Playwrights Guild of Canada (typescript), n.p.

Watts, I. (n.d.) *Remember Me*. Typescript, kindly provided by the playwright.

Weinberg, W. (1981) 'Die Bezeichnung Jüdischdeutsch', *Zeitschrift für deutsche Philologie – Sonderheft Jiddisch*, 100: 253–90.

Weinfeld, M. (2001) *Like Everyone Else…But Different. The Paradoxical Success of Canadian Jews*, Toronto: McClelland & Steward.

Weinreich, M. (1959) 'History of the Yiddish Language: The Problems and Their Implications', *Proceedings of the American Philosophical Society*, 103: 563–70.

Weinreich, M. (1980) *History of the Yiddish Language*, trans. S. Noble, Chicago, London: University of Chicago Press.

Weinstein, B. (1924) *Fertsig yor in der yidisher arbeter bavegung: mit a forvort fun Ab. Cahan*, New York: Wecker.

Welsch, W. (1999) 'Transculturality: the Puzzling Form of Cultures Today', in M. Featherstone and S. Lash (eds) *Spaces of Culture: City, Nation, World*, London: Sage, 194–213.

Whitaker, T.R. (1999) *Mirrors of Our Playing: Paradigms and Presences in Modern Drama*, Ann Arbor: University of Michigan Press.

White, P. (1995) 'Geography, Literature and Migration', in R. King et al. (eds) *Writing Across Worlds. Literature and Migration*, London, New York: Routledge, 1–19.

Whitfield, S. (1999) *In Search of American Jewish Culture*, Hanover, NE: Brandeis University Press.

Wiesel, E. (1958; 1960) *Night*, foreword by F. Mauriac, trans. S. Rodway, New York: Hill and Wang.

Wieseltier, M. (2003) *The Flower of Anarchy: Selected Poems*, trans. S. Kaufman, with the author, Berkeley: University of California Press.

Williams, P.J. (1991) *The Alchemy of Race and Rights*, Cambridge: Harvard University Press.

Willis, J. (1974) *Geniesh: An Indian Girlhood*, Toronto: New Press.

Wilson, J. (1995) *The Hiding Room*, New York: Viking.

Wilson, J. (2003) *A Palestine Affair*, New York: Anchor Books.

Wilson, J. (2005) 'How I Became a Jewish Writer in America', in D. Rubin (ed.) *Who We Are: On Being (and Not Being) a Jewish American Writer*, New York: Schocken, 151–8.

Wilson, J.M. (1998; 1999) *Siegfried Sassoon. The Making of a War Poet*, London: Duckworth.

Wirth-Nesher, H. (ed.) (1994a) *What is Jewish Literature?*, Philadelphia: The Jewish Publication Society.

Wirth-Nesher, H. (1994b) 'Defining the Indefinable: What is Jewish Literature?', in H. Wirth-Nesher (ed.), *What is Jewish Literature?*, Philadelphia: The Jewish Publication Society, 3–12.

Wirth-Nesher, H. (1998) 'Language as Homeland in Jewish-American Literature', in D. Biale, M. Galchinsky and S. Heschel (eds) *Insider/Outsider. American Jews and Multiculturalism*, Berkeley: University of California Press, 212–30.

Wirth-Nesher, H. (2001) 'Magnified and Sanctified: Liturgy in Contemporary Jewish American Literature', in E.M. Budick (ed.) *Ideology and Jewish Identity in Israeli and American Literature*, Albany: State University of New York Press, 115–30.

Wirth-Nesher, H. (2006) *Call It English: The Language of Jewish American Literature*, Princeton, NJ: Princeton University Press.

Wisse, R.R. (1976) 'American Jewish Writing, Act II', *Commentary*, 61: 40–5.

Wisse, R.R. (2000) *The Modern Jewish Canon: A Journey Through Language and Culture*, New York, London: The Free Press.
Yerushalmi, Y.H. (1982) *Zakhor: Jewish History and Jewish Memory*, Seattle: University of Washington Press.
Yezierska, A. (1925; 1999) *Bread Givers*, New York: Persea Books.
Young, R.J.C. (1995) *Colonial Desire. Hybridity in Theory, Culture and Race*, London, New York: Routledge.
Yudkin, L. (1982) *Jewish Writing and Identity in the Twentieth Century*, London, Canberra: Croom Helm.
Zable, A. (1991) *Jewels and Ashes*, Melbourne: Scribe Publications.
Zable, A. (1998) *Wanderers and Dreamers: Tales of the David Herman Theatre*, Melbourne: Hyland House.
Zable, A. (2001a) *Cafe Scheherazade*, Melbourne: Text Publishing.
Zable, A. (2001b) unpublished conversation with E. Morera de la Vall (Melbourne, 27 July 2001).
Zable, A. (2002) *The Fig Tree*, Melbourne: Text Publishing.
Zable, A. (2004) *Scraps of Heaven*, Melbourne: Text Publishing.
Zach, N. (1967) *Against Parting*, trans. N. Zach and J. Silkin, Newcastle: Northern House.
Zangwill, I. (1898; 1925) *The Dreamers of the Ghetto*, London: Globe.
Zeller, U. (2003) 'Between *goldene medine* and Promised Land. Legitimizing the American Jewish Diaspora', in M. Fludernik (ed.) *Diaspora and Multiculturalism: Common Traditions and New Developments*, Amsterdam, New York: Rodopi, 1–43.
Zisquit, L. (2004a) 'Line of Defense', *Bridges*, 10.1: 45.
Zisquit, L. (2004b) 'The Secret Life', *Tikkun*, July–August. Online. Available HTTP: <http://www.tikkun.org/magazine/index.cfm/action/tikkun/issue/tik0407/article/040726.html> (accessed 22 March 2005).
Žižek, S. (1989) *The Sublime Object of Ideology*, London: Verso.
Žižek, S. (1991) 'The Truth Arises from Misrecognition', in E. Ragland-Sullivan and M. Bracher (eds) *Lacan and the Subject of Language*, New York: Routledge, 188–212.
Zuckermann, G. (2003) *Language Contact and Lexical Enrichment in Israeli Hebrew*, New York: Palgrave Macmillan.
Zurawik, D. (2003) *The Jews of Prime Time*, Hanover, NE: Brandeis University Press.
Zwi, R. (1980) *Another Year in Africa*, Johannesburg: Bateleur Press.
Zwi, R. (1984) *Exiles*, Craighall: Ad. Donker.

Index

For Product Safety Concerns and Information please contact our EU representative GPSR@taylorandfrancis.com
Taylor & Francis Verlag GmbH, Kaufingerstraße 24, 80331 München, Germany

www.ingramcontent.com/pod-product-compliance
Lightning Source LLC
Chambersburg PA
CBHW060242100726
47907CB00003B/736

* 9 7 8 1 1 3 8 0 1 0 5 5 0 *